Law, Women Judges and the Gender Order

This book seeks to understand how women judges are situated as legal knowers on the High Court of Australia by asking whether a near-equal gender balance on the High Court has disrupted the Court's historically masculinist gender regime.

This book examines how the High Court's gender regime operates once there is more than one woman on the bench. It explores the following questions: How have the Court's gender relations accommodated the presence women on the bench? How have the women themselves accommodated those pre-existing gender relations? How might legal judgments and reasoning change as a result of changing gender dynamics on the bench? To develop answers to these (and other) questions the book pursues a methodology that conceptualises the High Court as an institution with a particular gender regime shaped historically by the dominant gender order of the wider society. The intersection between the (gendered) individuals and the (gendered) institution in which they operate produces and reproduces that institution's gender regime. Hence, the enquiry is not so much asking 'have women judges made a difference?' but rather is asking how should we understand women judges' relationship with the law, a relationship that is shaped as much by the individual judge as by the institutional context in which they operate.

Scholars, legal practitioners and researchers interested in judicial reasoning, gender diversity and the legal profession, gender and politics will be interested in this book because it breaks new ground as a case study of a Court's gender regime at a particular time.

Kcasey McLoughlin is a Senior Lecturer at Newcastle Law School, Australia.

Law, Women Judges and the Gender Order

Lessons from the High Court of Australia

Kcasey McLoughlin

Routledge
Taylor & Francis Group
a GlassHouse book

First published 2022
by Routledge
2 Park Square, Milton Park, Abingdon, Oxon OX14 4RN

and by Routledge
605 Third Avenue, New York, NY 10158

a GlassHouse book

Routledge is an imprint of the Taylor & Francis Group, an informa business

British Library Cataloguing-in-Publication Data
A catalogue record for this book is available from the British Library

Library of Congress Cataloging-in-Publication Data
A catalog record has been requested for this book

ISBN: 978-0-367-23035-7 (hbk)
ISBN: 978-1-032-13240-2 (pbk)
ISBN: 978-0-429-28853-1 (ebk)

DOI: 10.4324/9780429288531

Typeset in Bembo
by Taylor & Francis Books

Contents

Acknowledgments

This book has taken some time to come to fruition and it has only been made possible with the support of many people. It began its life as my doctoral thesis and, as such, I remain indebted to my principal supervisor, Jim Jose, for his unswerving patience, belief in challenging disciplinary boundaries, and for the care and respect he has shown for my ideas. He generously read drafts of this book and I am immensely grateful for his sharp insights and sage advice. I am honoured to have been in receipt of his friendship and owe him an enormous debt of gratitude for his unstinting support. I am also grateful to my co-supervisor, Katherine Lindsay, for generously sharing her expertise in Constitutional Law and for fostering my interest in the High Court of Australia and the judges who sit on it. My sincere thanks goes to thesis examiners, Clare McGlynn and Katharine Gelber, not only for their insightful and generous feedback, but also, for their ongoing encouragement and guidance. I further acknowledge the judging panel for the Australian Political Studies PhD Prize, in particular AJ Brown and Linda Hancock for their very supportive encouragement in pursuing this book project.

I gratefully acknowledge the support I have received from the University of Newcastle to support the research underpinning this book including funding from the Women in Research Fellowship scheme and the Gender Research Network's Program in Gender Based Violence. I acknowledge the support of the Gender Research Network, a wonderfully supportive group of inter-disciplinary feminist scholars and activists led by Trisha Pender. Newcastle Law School has provided a supportive space to pursue my research and I thank my Head of School, Tania Sourdin, for cultivating such an environment. I acknowledge my colleagues at Newcastle Law School, many of whom have become firm friends. In particular, I am grateful to John Anderson, Ann Apps, Rachel Brien, Sher Campbell, Tim Connor and Amy Maguire for their collegial support and good humour over many years. I have been privileged to have worked with some very talented research assistants during the writing of this book. I thank Hannah Stenstrom for her sharp analytical insights, exceptional skills in editing and for keeping me on track. I am also grateful to Rhanee Rego for her careful attention to detail in following up additional sources.

I have been fortunate to have received mentoring, encouragement and feedback from many wonderful feminist scholars, working in both Law and Political Science. I am very grateful to have had the opportunity to visit Queen Mary University of London, University of Kent and the Human Rights Institute at the University of New South Wales. I thank Rosemary Hunter for her exceedingly generous mentorship—in acting as host during my visits to Queen Mary and Kent, and for providing very helpful feedback on earlier iterations of some of the ideas explored in this book. I also acknowledge Louise Chappell's generous mentorship and kindness—I am grateful to her for hosting me at the Human Rights Institute, for including me in her larger research project about gender and judging at the International Criminal Court and for modelling care and collaboration in all that she does. I would also like to acknowledge feedback, support and encouragement from Margaret Thornton, Ann Genovese, Erika Rackley, Hilary Sommerlad, Kate Malleson, Lizzie Barmes, Renee Knake Jefferson and Kim Rubenstein.

I thank Colin Perrin at Routledge for his advice when drafting the proposal for this book (and patience as deadlines passed us by). Thanks also to Ajanta Bhattarcharjee for guiding the manuscript through the publication process so smoothly.

Heartfelt thanks are due to all of my family and friends for their patience, interest and efforts to ensure I retained a sense of humour during the research and writing process. Thank you to Alexander Winn, Kerrin Houghton, Elicia Kristenthal, Danielle Ingle and Mark Gauntlett for their friendship, moral support and many acts of kindness, both big and small. Thanks also to my brother, Jake McLoughlin, and sister in law, Francesca Hague-Blundy, for their support and encouragement. Special thanks are due to my parents, Caroline and Aug McLoughlin for offering a lifetime of love and support. As doting grandparents, they have gone above and beyond providing extensive childcare which has given me the time and space to write. My in-laws, Anne and Denis Forrest, have likewise provided practical support and encouragement and I thank them for their generosity.

And finally, I do not have the words to adequately express my gratitude to my husband, Dave Forrest for his commitment to me and to our family. He has demonstrated enormous patience and unwavering support and I am grateful for his insistence not only that I was capable of finishing, but that the book was worth finishing. I am grateful to our son Arthur for his joyful sense of fun and for reminding me what truly matters. Our daughter, Imogen, arrived shortly before this book went to print but it feels as though she has been here all along. Dave, Arthur and Imogen have provided me with more happiness, adventure and love than I could have ever imagined. I am so very fortunate to have them in my life and their love and support means the world to me.

This book contains substantially revised versions of my earlier work including: 'Judicial fictions and the fictive feminists: Re-imagination as feminist critique in PGA v The Queen' (2016) *Griffith Law Review* 24: 592–615; '"Collegiality is not compromise": Farewell Justice Crennan, the consensus woman' (2016) *The*

Australian Feminist Law Journal 42: 241–271; 'A particular disappointment? Judging women on the High Court of Australia' (2015) *Feminist Legal Studies* 23: 273–294; 'The politics of gender diversity on the High Court of Australia' (2015) *Alternative Law Journal* 40: 166–170 and (with Jim Jose) 'The politics of the public and private spheres: The High Court's decision in Monis and the gendered privileging of free speech' (2017) *Australian Journal of Political Science* 52(4): 565–579.

Introduction

'Men in skirts' and other dilemmas and disappointments[1]

In 1987 Mary Genevieve Gaudron, a trailblazing woman lawyer, took her place on the High Court of Australia, the first woman to serve on the Court since its establishment in 1903. She retired in 2003 well before the constitutionally prescribed retirement age of 70. In her farewell speech to Australian Women Lawyers, Justice Gaudron, perhaps understanding better than most the complex gender politics at play in disrupting masculinist gender regimes, remarked that leaving the Court was the best way of ensuring that another woman was appointed (Gaudron cited in Batrouney 2004: 343). Unfortunately it proved to be otherwise. Her vacancy was not filled by another legal woman of standing, but by a man, Dyson Heydon, described by the then Justice Kirby as 'a most accomplished and civilised judge and man' (Kirby 2003). Outside the High Court building while his swearing-in ceremony was in progress, 2-year-old Vivien Clarke and her mother staged a protest—not so much about the new judge in particular, but rather, that his appointment meant that the Court would be restored to its traditional composition of all men. The daughter held aloft a sign which read: 'Mum, Can Women Be High Court Judges?' On the reverse side were the words, 'Yes, darling—there was a good one when I was a girl'.[2] The then Prime Minister John Howard had justified the appointment on the basis of merit and suggested that it would be 'quite unrealistic' to 'choose people according to some strict gender or geographical basis, when you're dealing with the highest court in the country' (Howard cited in Donald 2002). In any case, two years would pass before Vivien Clarke's question received an affirmative answer. In 2005 the Liberal–National Coalition government appointed Susan Crennan, and then followed

1 Parts of this chapter draw on material and arguments previously published in McLoughlin. K. 2015. 'A particular disappointment? Judging women and the High Court of Australia'. *Feminist Legal Studies*. 23 (3): 273–294. Reprinted by permission from Springer, *Feminist Legal Studies* 'A particular disappointment? Judging women and the High Court of Australia', Kcasey McLoughlin [COPYRIGHT] (2015).

2 This account is taken from Crabb's (2003) article on Justice Heydon's swearing-in as a Justice of the High Court.

DOI: 10.4324/9780429288531-1

in 2007 with the appointment of Susan Kiefel. In 2009 the Labor government appointed Virginia Bell.

In what might then be construed as a triumph for the politics of diversity and gender inclusion these appointments meant that between 2009 and very early in 2015 three women judges sat concurrently on a court which had up until that point been the almost exclusive preserve of men judges (with the exception of Gaudron, the lone woman who had served). The High Court of Australia, the highest court in Australia's judicial hierarchy, is comprised of seven judges meaning that three women judges constituted a near majority. For a brief period in 2015 it looked as if near-equal representation of men and women was to be short-lived with Susan Crennan's retirement and the appointment of Geoffrey Nettle to replace her. But the appointment of Michelle Gordon in 2015 (perhaps made more interesting given she was replacing her husband Kenneth Hayne on the bench) meant that the condition of a near-equal gender balance returned. It had taken 84 years for the first woman to be appointed, another two decades for the second, and then the third, fourth, and indeed fifth woman arrived within the one decade. Susan Kiefel's elevation to Chief Justice of the High Court in 2017 marked yet another important milestone in women's access to legal authority in Australia.

Affording a particular prescience to the protest scene staged almost two decades earlier, by mid-2020 Chief Justice Kiefel presided over a High Court that commissioned an independent investigation following allegations that former Justice Dyson Heydon had sexually harassed six staff members (five of whom were judges' associates)[3] during his time on the Court (2003–2013). These revelations were explosive. Although Heydon was by this stage retired, his eminence and standing meant that he still loomed large as a prominent and powerful figure in the Australian legal profession. That the events in question were so intimately connected to his judicial role exacerbated the extent to which they reflected poorly on the High Court, both in terms of its inability to provide a safe place of work, but also as a broader reflection of the legal system's failure to appropriately respond to sexual harassment and bullying.

Whatever failings had permitted sexual harassment to go unchecked on the High Court, the Chief Justice's response (both in setting the inquiry in motion and her statement about it) made it clear that sexual harassment would not be tolerated. She offered an apology to the victims and in so doing acknowledged

3 In Australia judges' associates work closely with judges and provide legal research, in-court duties and other support as required. Much like their North American equivalent, Law Clerks, associate positions are highly coveted (especially for more senior appellate courts) and usually go to the most academically brilliant law students. They serve as an important entrée to professional success. These kinds of opportunities can shape careers (and potentially reproduce privilege). For example, two of the justices currently sitting on the High Court, Justices Gageler and Edelman, both served as High Court associates.

the difficulties in coming forward and emphasised that they had been believed. For his part, Heydon denied any allegations of predatory behaviour or breaches of the law. In response to the inquiry commissioned by the High Court, Heydon's lawyers emphasised that this process was an internal administrative inquiry conducted by a public servant and not by a lawyer, judge or a tribunal member. It remains to be seen how these events will shape Kiefel's legacy on the Court,[4] but it is noteworthy that her leadership on this issue has been widely praised. As for Heydon's legacy, his conduct has been widely condemned by those who have been willing to be drawn on it, but it remains to be seen how this reputational damage will inform his jurisprudential legacy. One especially high-profile exception to the widespread condemnation was former Prime Minister John Howard's comments in the aftermath (cited in Maley and McClymont 2020), noting that he stood by his judicial appointments, describing Heydon as an 'excellent' judge.

What (or who) makes an excellent judge is doubtless in the eye of the beholder, but Howard's comments give weight to the ongoing concerns about the lack of accountability and transparency when it comes to appointing High Court judges. More broadly, these revelations prompt questions about how the legal system sees and treats women—reflecting a concern that despite women's visible ascension to the very peak of the legal profession, they remain marginalised within it. In this important respect, this moment of reckoning reignited questions about who our judges are, why that matters and about the significance of, and conditional nature of, women's access to authority in Australia's constitutional framework.

The historic first period of an almost equal gender balance on the High Court (and indeed, at least some of Heydon's time on the Court) coincided with a time in which women also held peak positions within various branches of government in Australia. For example, at the Commonwealth level, Julia Gillard became Australia's first woman Prime Minister holding office between 2010 and 2013, Nicola Roxon[5] became the nation's first woman Attorney-General from 2011 to 2013, and Quentin Bryce served as Australia's first woman Governor-General between 2008 and 2014. These achievements may well have demonstrated women's equal capacity to occupy the most senior positions of political power and authority within Australia's constitutional framework, but this must be tempered by acknowledging the (gendered) backlash that coincided with this state of affairs. Granted, much of the backlash was directed towards the first woman Prime Minister and at least some of that can be explained by ordinary partisan politics. However, the gendered criticisms of

4 I will return to this question in the final chapter of the book.

5 Perhaps demonstrating the ways in which working as a High Court Associate might serve as an important entrée to professional success, it is noteworthy that Nicola Roxon served as Justice Mary Gaudron's Associate during her time on the High Court of Australia.

the Prime Minister and the sexism she encountered were 'visceral and often grotesque' as journalist Julia Baird described in an article in the *New York Times*:

> There were placards crying "Ditch the Witch," toys designed for dogs that encouraged them to chew on the fleshier parts of her anatomy, and, most recently, a menu offering "Julia Gillard Kentucky Fried Quail—small breasts, huge thighs and a big red box".
>
> (Baird 2013)

The particularly vicious responses which arose when she highlighted the sexism she confronted in her role demonstrate the precarious and problematised issues which arise when women exercise political power (Johnson 2015; Summers 2013).

In Prime Minister Gillard's experiences and, indeed, the revelations about Heydon's conduct, we are reminded just how deeply ingrained assumptions about gender relations and the regimes of practice built around them are within Australia's political and legal institutions. We are reminded, if such a reminder were needed, of just how easily past forms of gender entitlement could be reactivated and pressed into service. In terms of its gender dynamics the High Court is no exception, though it is fair to say that in the period in question these dynamics were (publicly, at least) far less sensational than those in the parliamentary arena. Reflecting on the implications of Gaudron's retirement, Kirby (2003) observed, '[i]nevitably, since her retirement, the High Court is a more "blokey" place.' That the gender ratio, or gender balance, of the High Court is noteworthy is of course itself reflective of the historical composition of courts as being exclusively the domain of men—it has always been a "blokey" place. Perhaps recognising this, Gaudron attempted to play down the historical significance of her own appointment by commenting at her swearing-in that she wanted to be seen as 'simply one of seven' (Gaudron 1987 cited in Roberts 2012a). Given the circumstances this was unlikely to happen. But her comment is significant because it points to the problem that sits at the centre of this book; namely, what difference it makes to the High Court when a woman enters the domain that was up until that time the exclusive preserve of men. And if Justice Gaudron aimed to be 'one of seven', how should we understand how being 'three of seven' might affect the gender regime of the High Court?

The politics of gender and judging has long occupied feminist legal scholars as they have pondered the dilemmas and contradictions of difference. Feminist legal theorists of various hues have been motivated to examine how the law is gendered, why we want a more diverse judiciary and whether a diverse judiciary will (or can) change decision-making. While this book is likewise concerned (but only partially so) with the politics of difference as it might be applied to women judges, its principal focus is developing insights into how their presence impacts on the gender relations or gender order of a particular court. Prompted by the arrival of an 'almost-equal' gender balance on the High

Court of Australia this book is a case study of the (gendered) composition of the High Court of Australia at a particular time.

This book asks what the arrival of an 'almost-equal' gender balance or the 'three of seven' means for the masculinist gender regime that has long shaped the operations of the Court. Its analysis has much wider implications in theorising the relationship between gender and judging and in demonstrating how a particular gender regime can survive the appointment of a significant number of women judges. The idea of a 'gender regime' means the enduring patterns of gender relations within an institution which provide 'the context for particular events, relationships, and individual practices' (Connell 2006: 839). Importantly these patterns might reproduce or depart from the wider societal pattern of gender relations (Connell 2006: 839). In this way, the gender regime that shapes the High Court of Australia will bear important similarities to equivalent constitutional courts around the world (reflecting wider societal patterns of gender relations), but will also be specific to the High Court as an institution.

Perhaps in recognition of the far-reaching consequences of women's exclusion from the legal profession, the stakes wagered on their inclusion have been particularly high. It was hypothesised, at least by *some* feminist legal theorists, that women judges would be the panacea to law's gender-blindness (Menkel-Meadow 1985; Sherry 1986a, 1986b). To be clear this is not to say that this ever represented *the* feminist orthodoxy—there has always been resistance to the notion that woman alone would be able to transform the masculine bias of law (see e.g. Smart 1989). These tensions aside, it has not been uncommon for women's difference to be used as a central pillar in the arguments justifying their inclusion. These threads of argument have meant that the very reasons for denying women admission to positions of legal authority (namely, their assumed 'difference', 'femininity' or 'otherness') were subsequently deployed by some feminist theorists as justifications for the appointment of women judges. In the context of a speech arguing for greater gender diversity in the judiciary, former Justice of the High Court of Australia Michael Kirby (2002: 154) offered that women 'have a different life's experience' and they 'sometimes have a different way of looking at problems'. For Kirby 'women [were] not just men who wear skirts'. And perhaps here was also a gentle allusion to the idea that being one (or three) of seven did not mean becoming like the mythical 'man of law'. Kirby's comments—especially delivered in the context of agitating for the appointment of women judges—capture some of the expectations around women judges.

Women's exclusion from judicial power and authority has meant that their inclusion has required justification. These justificatory arguments have tended to be based on two broad strands of argument, difference and equality. The first strand, difference, posits that the quality of justice available will be improved because women offer something different, perhaps by 'speaking in a different voice' or by bringing an 'ethic of care' to the judicial role (Gilligan 1982; Menkel-Meadow 1985; Sherry 1986a). The second strand, equality, contends that the 'principle of equity requires that women have an equal opportunity to participate in public decision-making institutions and that their absence undermines the democratic legitimacy of those bodies' (Malleson 2003: 14). Similar arguments have also been made about the need for women judges so that the judiciary 'reflect[s] the make-up of the society from which its members are drawn' (Davis and Williams 2003: 844; see also Kirby 2002: 154; Cooney 1993). However, arguments based on principles of equality are often eager to distinguish between the need for a *diverse*[6] judiciary and the need for a *representative* judiciary, arguing that while diversity is desirable, the notion that any judicial officer should represent the interests of their gender (or class or race) is objectionable because it misconstrues the very nature and function of the judiciary as an institution which is unresponsive to political pressure (Davis and Williams 2003: 844; see also O'Sullivan 1996). These arguments about the capacity for women judges to make a difference (in terms of their judicial approach), although appealing, are also difficult to sustain in practice.

Yet, the notion that women judges have not been as different, or different in the ways that were originally hypothesised by some feminist legal theorists (Menkel-Meadow 1985; Sherry 1986a), is a recurring and important theme in the literature about gender and judging (e.g. Hunter 2008, 2013, 2015; Douglas et al. 2014a; Kenney 2008, 2013; Rackley 2002, 2006, 2009, 2013; Sommerlad 2013; Neave 1995; Dixon 2010). The alacrity with which some feminist "theorists have been willing to defend certain notions of difference has therefore waned considerably. But the arrival of women judges nonetheless 'puts us on notice; it encourages us to both look for—and more importantly—find difference' (Rackley 2009: 16). The point here is that the idea of 'difference' is not that women are different from men or that men are different from women. Rather it is to ask the question of what, if anything, might have changed with respect to judicial reasoning and practices on the High Court as a result of a change in the gender composition of the court.

Some insight into the ways in which gender puts us on notice was provided by the journalistic commentary which arose during the tenure of Justices Crennan, Kiefel and Bell. The potential implications of the elusive nature of difference were aptly captured by journalist Jack Waterford in reference to the

6 This book is limited to an examination of gender and the judiciary prompted by the changing composition of the High Court, but this is not to discount the importance of claims based on race, ethnicity or sexuality, nor the fact that such claims are not mutually exclusive. Although the High Court is currently more representative on the basis of gender than in any other time in the Court's history, its composition nonetheless remains homogenous on the basis of race. As Hunter (2015: 4) acknowledges many of the arguments for gender diversity in the judiciary also apply to claims based on race, ethnicity or sexuality. I acknowledge that as much as (some) of the arguments and justifications for a more diverse judiciary apply on the basis of these attributes, such an acknowledgment is not to discount the additional barriers faced by other marginalised groups in seeking advancement within the legal profession.

composition of the High Court of Australia when he remarked that 'the women [judges] have seemed *a particular disappointment*, especially for those who have hoped for different or wider perspectives than from those steeped in old styles of the law' (2012: 16, my emphasis). In the same article, Waterford (2012: 16) made reference to the authorship practices of the High Court noting that 'three hands' appeared to be responsible for authoring most of the judgments, so much so he concluded that '[i]t would be cruel, but fair, for the outsider to wonder what the other four judges do, apart from sign on to drafts written by Gummow or French'.

These expectations, and the claim that women have been disappointing in these roles, raise significant questions about the dichotomy between the theoretical justifications for appointing women judges and the reality of their contributions. The very notion that the women judges have been disappointing is disconcerting even though it is qualified by reference to the fact that at least some of the disappointment might be felt by those who hoped that the women judges would bring 'different or wider perspectives than from those steeped in old styles of the law' (Waterford 2012: 16). Or put more baldly, what Waterford was really articulating, albeit from a journalistic perspective and maybe even unconsciously, is the awkward paradox at the heart of feminist engagement with gender, difference and judging, namely, the uncomfortable suggestion that Australia's women judges might be a disappointment to the feminists who agitated for them to be appointed. There is also a thinly veiled and gendered assumption about the internal operations of the High Court, that women judges (and indeed some of the men judges) are not up to it, not showing leadership and not pulling their weight. And in this respect, his perspective, while seemingly couched in the language of women's advancement, also played a 'gender card' for those attuned to that particular "dog whistle".[7]

And what about the women judges themselves? Some women judges in other jurisdictions have been disinclined to embrace the notion that they speak in a different voice (e.g. Wilson 1990; Day O'Connor 1991) although others have embraced a version of difference or even feminist judging (e.g. L'Heureux-Dubé 1997; Hale 2008). While it is certainly arguable that individual judges are correct in their insistence that there is nothing about their gender that has any necessary bearing on their approach to judicial reasoning, it may also be the case that their perspective is evidence of what Thornton (1996: 203) termed the 'exceptional women syndrome'. This syndrome allows women judges (and women in other positions of power) 'to be distinguished from other women, so that the masculinist character of the office is not diminished'.

7 The Australianism 'dog whistle' refers to a coded political message which is meant to be heard a particular way by supporters but is framed in a way so as to avoid alienating others. See Goodin (2008: 7) where he explained 'the fundamental perversity of dog-whistle politics, whereby political parties send coded messages that will be heard one way by their core supporters and another way altogether by others'.

In extra-curial remarks, Mary Gaudron (1997) spoke to the existence of such a syndrome, positing that women did not dare to be different:

> To be different, to challenge the codes of conduct derived, as often as not, from rules developed on the playing fields of Eton for the male members of the British aristocracy, would have been to invite ostracism, perhaps, even, the attention of the Ethics committee; to assert that women were different with different needs would have been construed as an acknowledgment of incompetence; to question the bias of the law would have been to invite judgment as to one's fitness to be a member of the profession. And, thus, very many of us became honorary men. We thought that was equality and, on that account, we rightly deserved the comment of the graffitist who wrote "Women who want equality lack ambition."

Certainly, the notion that simply adding women would transform the law has been largely abandoned. For example, Smart (1989: 66) pointed to the shift in (some) feminist approaches 'away from a concentration on law reform and "adding women"' to concerns about legal consideration of 'fundamental issues like legal logic, legal values, justice, neutrality, and objectivity'. The problematic (Harris 1990; Rhode 1988) and elusive (e.g. Davis 1993; O'Sullivan 1996; Mack and Roach Anleu 2010) nature of some versions of difference has led to its reconceptualisation. This has involved recasting not only how we *understand* difference itself, but also recasting expectations around *who* might make that difference. One more recent focus has been on reconfiguring expectations around the notion that *feminist* judges, rather than *women* judges, might make a difference (e.g. Hunter 2008; Kenney 2008). This is not a mere shift in semantics, but rather an acknowledgment of some of the difficulties and limitations associated with more wide-reaching expectations about difference.

There now exists a very large volume of empirical studies (many of which emanate from the United States) that have attempted to find or ascribe certain characteristics, sometimes understood as a 'different voice,' to women judges sitting on various courts (e.g. Cook 1981; Martin 1982; Songer, Davis and Haire 1994). Two problems or issues might be said to arise from these studies. First, the results were often inconclusive in terms of finding difference. Second, was the way in which the very notion of 'difference' was cast. For instance, Kenney (2008: 105), a particularly forceful critic of empirical studies of this kind, saw as problematic the way in which researchers used 'sex as a proxy for feminist' which construed women as more likely to be concerned with:

> children and better at juvenile justice, pro-defendant in sex discrimination cases, pro-choice, pro-woman in divorce, employing communitarian reasoning, inclined to seek mediate solutions, likely to raise women's issues in speeches, and likely to inflict harsh or lenient sentences.

Methodological issues notwithstanding, these kinds of studies have not had the same appeal in Australia—at least in part because the structure of Australia's legal system limits the scope for large-scale empirical studies, and perhaps because of the disciplinary norms and preferences when it comes to studying courts. Although no such 'cottage industry' in studies seeking to examine the relationship between judging and various attributes has developed in Australia, there has nonetheless been interest in interviewing judges (particularly lower in the judicial hierarchy) to glean their views and trajectories.[8] Laster and Douglas' (1995) study regarding Australian magistrates did not disclose any apparent differences in approach on gender lines. While they found that women were somewhat more likely to refer to parenting or 'an intuition', for the most part they found that 'the attitudes of male and female magistrates were marked more by congruence than divergence' (Laster and Douglas 1995: 200). Similarly, Mack and Roach Anleu's (2010: 385) survey of the Australian judiciary found marked similarities between men and women in backgrounds, experiences and attitudes, a result they argue may well explain the 'lack of empirical evidence showing differences in men's and women's judging processes'.

As a consequence of the lack of empirical support for certain conceptualisations of difference, there have been 'calls for a change in strategy on the part of feminists to focus more directly on the demonstrated jurisprudential commitments, rather than on the gender, of future judicial nominees' when it comes to agitating for judicial appointments (Dixon 2010: 298). It is important to note that feminist judging, understood in either a theoretical[9] sense or on real life benches, is not about deciding *for* women but rather an approach to judging which is simultaneously consistent with the judicial oath and feminist principles (broadly construed). To this end, there has been focused examination of the jurisprudential contributions of self-described feminist judges, or judges whose approach might nonetheless align with feminist sensibilities (see Baines 2013). For example, the jurisprudential contributions of Baroness Hale (Rackley

8 A large interdisciplinary research project, the 'Trailblazing Women and The Law Project', sought to examine the stories and experiences of trailblazing Australian women in law. The project employed a range of methods to analyse the experiences of seven decades of Australia's pioneer, 'trailblazing' women lawyers so as to fill the 'well-noted absence of leading women lawyers' lives from national history and Australian scholarly analysis'. For further details see http://www.tbwl.esrc.unimelb.edu.au.

9 'Feminist Judgment Projects' have involved re-writing well known judgments and infusing them with feminist reasoning in order to demonstrate the plausibility and possibility of feminist reasoning across a wide range of substantive areas of law. Although such projects have now emerged in various jurisdictions, the idea came from the Women's Court of Canada where feminist scholars and litigators wrote shadow judgments of major judgments of the Canadian Supreme Court in respect of the equality clause in the Canadian Charter of Rights and Freedoms. For further background to the Canadian project see Majury (2006).

2006), Justice Gaudron[10] (Hunter 2008: 24) and Justice Neave (Hunter 2013) have been examined with a view to assessing whether a feminist difference could be discerned in their judicial voices. The opportunity to bring feminist perspectives to the fore, 'even for judges who are willing to be feminist activists, … might be few and far between' (Hunter 2015: 16). The limited potential for feminist interventions in the law to challenge legal approaches in traditionally gendered legal constructions is perhaps not especially surprising. However, one of the significant contributions of various feminist judgment writing projects has been in demonstrating the potential for gender sensitive (feminist) decisions in areas of law not hitherto conceived as gendered or obviously concerning women (Hunter 2015: 18).

Very significant questions remain about what space is left to consider and examine the contributions and appointment of women judges where those women eschew feminist identities. To be clear, I do not assume women judges will or should be feminists. Nor do I assume that men cannot be feminists. Leaving aside questions about the precise definition of a feminist judge (see e.g. Hunter 2008), and by extension questions about self-identification as a feminist judge (see e.g. Baines 2013), women's relationship with the law must remain a site of interrogation for feminist theorists. Of the women appointed to the High Court, only the first, Justice Mary Gaudron, could be said to have evidenced a willingness to reflect on the possible relationship between gender and judging. Justices Crennan, Kiefel and Bell (and later, Gordon) have each—to varying degrees—eschewed feminist identities or at least eschewed the notion that there might be any relationship between their gender and judging. This is not to discount the possibility that men might reflect on this relationship—in fact, the idea that women judges will judge in a particular way that reflects their experiences as women (as contested as these ideas might now be) invariably fails to counter that men's judgments similarly reflect their own experiences. However, the point here is about how these notions have shaped our understandings of the role of the judge and how this in turn shapes arguments about why we need women judges.

Although there will be space to unpack this further in later parts of the book, their extra-curial remarks, particularly in institutional settings (see Roberts

10 There has been considerable interest in Justice Gaudron's jurisprudential legacy, and no doubt much of this interest arises from her status as the first woman appointed to the High Court of Australia. Recognising the 'distinctive contribution of the first and only woman High Court Justice of Australia' was referenced in Rubenstein's (2004a: 281) introduction to the *Public Law Review*'s 'Collection Honouring Justice Mary Gaudron'. Although not all of the papers in the collection engaged in an explicitly gendered analysis, this aspect of her legacy was specifically interrogated in Batrouney's (2004) examination of the contribution Gaudron made to women in the law, Justice Susan Kenny's (2004) analysis of 'Concepts of Judicial Responsibility: The Contribution of "One of Seven"' and Rubenstein's (2004b) analysis of Gaudron's contribution to citizenship jurisprudence.

2012b), have seen the women appointed to the High Court attempt to neutralise their gendered state of being women and being judges. Kiefel has typically been restrained. Her publicly recorded comments by and large avoided (at least until her ascension to Chief Justice) any reference to questions of gender and judging whatsoever. The one exception was some commentary which attended her earlier judicial appointments which suggested that Kiefel did not like 'lipstick feminists'. This comment was not directly attributed to Kiefel herself but from an unnamed woman barrister and was used to caption a photograph appearing alongside an editorial in the *Sydney Morning Herald* (Editorial, *SMH*, 30 November 2016). The same quote also appeared in the text of a later newspaper article commenting on her perceived judicial leanings to the effect that 'lawyers familiar with her work regard her as broadly conservative' (Patrick 2017). Bell has been more willing to describe herself as a feminist but has been critical of attempts to ascribe this as having any bearing on her judging (Bell 2017: 9), whereas this has not been a matter on which Gordon has been very willing to be drawn. In contrast, Crennan's attempt to distance herself from feminism was especially overt. In fact, the way in which she distanced herself from feminism appears to have been associated with her suitability for the role. Throughout the 1990s Crennan made public comments which distanced her from feminist concerns or perspectives. In her view,

> They (feminists) want to be compensated for the fact that women have come to the profession late by having an accelerated rite of passage to the top echelons. I think that's wrong.[11]

In fact, Crennan's 'not a feminist' stance even informed some of the public commentary in ways which depicted her appointment as a blow to feminists who had agitated for diversity in judicial appointments. For example, one conservative commentator (who also referenced Crennan's comments above) suggested that 'the nation's foremost feminists have been caught out and left uncharacteristically speechless by the appointment of Susan Crennan to the High Court because she was not "a strident member of the bra-burning brigade", "an equal opportunity appointee" or "an affirmative action quota queen"' (Akerman 2005). The complex interrelationship between gender, judging and feminist perspectives is made out in this very commentary. Akerman's pejorative comments notwithstanding, the way in which a woman's suitability for judicial office might be underscored by her distance from feminist thought not only serves as a compelling reminder not to conflate 'woman' and

11 These comments were made in the context of a 1992 interview and were widely cited and reproduced in articles published at the time of her appointment to the High Court. Her comments further suggested that women's careers had been limited by matters of biology (subsequently remedied by the pill) rather than other forms of exclusion (see e.g. Pelly 2005; Akerman 2005; Shiel 2005).

'feminist'. That distance also might suggest that the closer a woman is to the 'bench-mark man of law,' the easier it is to accept her status as legal knower (Thornton 1996).

In light of perspectives such as this, how might feminist theorists examine women's relationship with the law as judges? Specifically, in circumstances where women judges do not embrace feminist identities, what space remains for examining their contributions through a feminist lens? Are they, contrary to Justice Kirby's hopes, merely 'men in skirts'? Is it possible for feminists to interrogate women's relationship with the law as judges without reproducing essentialist arguments about difference? These questions and the dilemmas they pose are things that this book seeks to address. The notion of 'men in skirts' conjures the imagery of drag—and as such at once subverts and reinforces constructions of gender. Given the performative aspects of both gender (Butler 1990) and judging (see e.g. Hunter et al. 2010; Davies 2012), the notion that women are not *just men in skirts* implies that women, dressed up in judicial robes and gowns, will offer something different (to men judges). Some women judges *may* bring different life experiences and perspectives to the judicial role. In turn these differences *might* also manifest in challenging the gender blindness of the law. But the contingencies and uncertainties of difference have left many questions either unanswered or unanswerable. What is this difference of which we speak? A difference to what and to whom? Do women judges make a difference? Rather than take an approach focused around and limited by the questions of 'what's the difference?' and 'what do feminists mean by difference?', this book opts for a different approach.

My concern in this book is in understanding how women judges are situated as legal knowers on the High Court of Australia. My aim is to examine whether a near-equal gender balance on the High Court has changed the Court's historically evolved gender regime, or indeed, has the capacity to disrupt or change it. In answering that question, the aim is to provide the wherewithal to determine whether women remain as 'fringe-dwellers of the jurisprudential community' (Thornton 1996: 3–4) such that their membership is in fact conditional on being 'men in skirts'. There are a number of subsidiary questions which further frame the book's attempts to situate women judges on the High Court of Australia. How might the presence of women judges change or disrupt the dynamics of the gender regime, and in what directions might it change? Does having one or more women on the bench make a difference? Does a woman Chief Justice make a difference? And if so what might that difference (or those differences) be? How might the legal judgments and reasoning change as a result of their appointment to the bench? What space is there for disrupting the gender regime given the prevailing models of collegiality on the High Court? What accommodations might women appointees have to make to survive within the dynamics of that regime? And, finally, how is judicial authority constructed, legitimated and understood?

To develop answers to these questions I pursue a methodology that conceptualises the High Court as an institution with a particular (masculinist) gender regime shaped historically by the dominant gender order of the wider society. Hence, the enquiry is not so much asking 'have women judges made a difference?', but rather is asking how we should understand women judges' relationship with the law, a relationship that is shaped as much by the individual judge as by the institutional context in which they operate.

Conceptualising the High Court as a masculinist gender regime

The High Court is an institution but above all it is also a political institution having been created through the enactment of the Australian Constitution. As such it has its own historically embedded patterns of gender relations which are best described as its particular gender regime (Connell 1987, 2006). This regime is embedded within society's wider gender order (Matthews 1984). A gender order 'establishes the definition or the meaning of "women" and "men" in any particular society by sanctioning the patterns of relations between women and men' such that they find the means to 'measur[e] themselves and others against their understanding of the ideal standard' posited by that regime (Matthews 1984: 23). This means is provided by a gender regime.

What does it mean to say that an institution is gendered? And what does that in turn say about the individuals within that institution? Pointing out that it is individuals who 'do' gender (West and Zimmerman 1987: 126) necessarily underscores the variable and socially constructed nature of gender— this 'doing' is nonetheless situated in and shaped by the institution in which it takes place:

> To say that an institution is gendered, then, is to recognise that constructions of masculinity and femininity are intertwined in the daily life or logic of political institutions rather than existing out in society or fixed within individuals which they then bring whole to the institution.
>
> (Kenney 1996: 456)

Although Connell (2006: 839) saw individuals as being implicated in gender arrangements, the gender order or gender regime is about 'a set of relationships—ways that people, groups and organizations are connected and divided.' She reconceptualised gender as 'a linking concept', as a verb that signified a (social) process 'rather than a thing' (Connell 1987: 140). In this way Connell challenged and moved beyond the dominant view that 'gender is a property of individual people' and argued that it should be understood *also* as 'a property of collectivities, institutions and historical processes' (Connell 1987: 139).

There are four dimensions to a gender regime that operate with varying levels of intensity and effect, and hence in their operation can serve to distinguish between particular gender regimes. These four dimensions are: the gendered division of labour, gender relations of power, emotion and human relations, and finally, gender culture and symbolism (Connell 2002, 2006, 1987). The gendered division of labour refers to 'the way in which production and consumption are arranged along gender lines, including the gendering of occupations and the division between paid work and domestic labor' (Connell 2006: 839). Given the law's historical exclusion of women, it is not surprising that the highest court in the land in most countries is marked by a gendered division of labour in which men occupy (at least until quite recently) the most prestigious positions. Similarly, the idea of 'gender relations of power' captures the various practices and means by 'which control, authority, and force are exercised along gender lines'. In Connell's formulation gender relations of power include 'organizational hierarchy, legal power, and collective and individual violence' (Connell 2006: 839). Emotion and human relations are contributing features which refer to the various ways 'in which attachment and antagonism among people and groups are organized along gender lines, including feelings of solidarity, prejudice and disdain, and sexual attraction and repulsion' (Connell 2006: 839). To these we might also add feelings of collegiality. Finally gender culture and symbolism refers to 'the way in which gender identities are defined in culture, the language and symbols of gender difference, and the prevailing beliefs and attitudes about gender' (Connell 2006: 839). While Connell (2006) developed this approach to better understand the gender regime in various public sector organisations, its theoretical precepts can be applied to any institutional context (Chappell and Waylen 2013). As will be demonstrated later in the book these four dimensions are all present within the workings of the Court's gender regime, shaping in multiple ways the hegemonic idealisation of the 'man of law', and hence contributing to establishing what it means to be a High Court judge.

The ways in which the dynamics of these four dimensions play out also contribute to the creation of what Connell (1987) has termed 'hegemonic masculinity', the form of masculinity that dominates within the gender regime and which provides the lodestar for the formation and reproduction of gender identities. Crucially, hegemony does not necessarily 'mean total cultural dominance', but rather 'ascendancy achieved within a balance of forces' (Connell 1987: 184). There is an ordering of both masculinity and femininity—demonstrated by what Connell (1987) terms 'hegemonic masculinity' and 'emphasized femininity'. Emphasised femininity is 'oriented to accommodating the interests and desires of men', but there is no hegemonic form of femininity 'in the sense that the dominant form of masculinity is hegemonic among men' (Connell 1987: 183). The cultural construction of emphasised femininity, like that of hegemonic masculinity, is 'very public' but 'its content is specifically linked with the private realm of the home and the bedroom' and thus 'organized around themes of sexual receptivity in relation to younger women and motherhood in relation to older women' (Connell 1987: 187). The focus on sex and receptivity means that hegemonic masculinity and emphasised femininity are therefore premised on a heteronormative ideal insofar as 'a key form of subordinated masculinity is homosexual[ity]' and conventional constructions of femininity similarly obscure the experience of 'spinsters, lesbians, unionists' (Connell 1987: 186, 188).

Noting Connell's conception of the ordering of masculinity and femininity, Naffine (1990: 118) emphasised that the peculiar masculinity of the man of law 'is not the masculinity of all men' but rather 'a masculinity considered desirable by a dominant, middle-class type of male who is able to earn a living through his intellect rather than with his hands'. Hence the man of law is 'a myth of masculinity, not male reality' because '[p]ure reason, pure detachment, pure objectivity, pure self-interest, absence of emotions' describes 'a middle-class ideal, but few actual men' (Naffine 1990: 119). The ordering and interplay between these cultural constructions of what it is to be a man or a woman further underscore the fact that experiences of femininity or masculinity are neither similarly experienced within a particular gender regime, nor of course are they confined or congruent with the bodies of women or men. For instance, Justice Kirby's vocal support for judicial diversity[12] might well be informed by his own experiences as a gay man navigating and negotiating the gender regime on the Court. Moreover, the differences amongst women judges *as women* will also have a bearing on the ways in which they encounter the prevailing gender regime. For example, Justice Bell's sexuality[13] and Justice Crennan's status as a mother and grandmother have featured in public constructions of their respective judicial personae.

As a concept, 'gender' has, of course, been employed in a myriad of ways by feminist theorists in exposing the socially constructed nature of women and men. Its meaning has been highly contested. The implications and processes associated with this construction have sometimes been especially fraught. For instance, Butler's (1990) theorisation of the performative aspects of gender explored the potentially punitive aspects of that performance. Hawkesworth (1997: 668) argued that Butler's view of gender is problematic because it is confined to the private and hence 'leaves gender too much a matter of the self'. However, the punitive aspects of that performance (for those who fail to get their gender right) underscore the important processes in which gender is a matter of both private and public production. Importantly then, a gender

12 This is not to suggest that support for judicial diversity is contingent upon such experiences. For example, the Hon Michael McHugh argued publicly that a woman should succeed him on the High Court. On one occasion, speaking at a Women Lawyers' Association of NSW event in Newcastle, he remarked (2005) 'women lawyers will bring a different approach to legal problems' and this is important because 'at the margins of the law … the approach of individuals is frequently decisive.'

13 See for example Biegel (2010: 201) who described Justice Bell as 'openly lesbian' in his book titled *The Right to Be Out*. Justice Bell has not made an official statement, but her sexuality has been remarked upon in a number of academic sources (see e.g. Moran 2011; Roberts 2012b). Of course, the notion of publicly speaking about sexuality or 'coming out' is itself demonstrative of heteronormative assumptions but the point is made simply to note that the experience of femininity is not universal.

analysis does not mean only considering women. Gender is not a synonym for woman/women, nor is it possible to view the world through a gender-free lens:

> Many people do not recognize how obvious gender is because they think it means women: if women are not there it is not gendered. In this view, we need to add a gender perspective to explain where women are, notice their hidden activities, and denounce the injustice of their exclusion. On the contrary, I propose that it is ontologically impossible not to have a gender perspective: It is implicit in all domains of academic inquiry. The more interesting question then becomes: what research agendas and hypotheses will lead us towards a better understanding of gender?
>
> (Htun 2005: 162)

Certainly, conceptually and theoretically, there might be some problematic distinctions between sex and gender, and in particular the conceptual adequacy of its binary formulation has been questioned by a number of feminist theorists (e.g. Gatens 1991; Butler 1987, 1990, 2004). Moreover, some feminist legal theorists argue that it is more appropriate to say the 'law is sexed' rather than 'gendered' on the grounds that the slippage between sex and gender means that distinctions between the two are not particularly meaningful (Davies 1997; Thornton 1996; Conaghan 2013). Some theorists such as Cornell (1991: 139), Harris (1990: 604) and Strossen (1995: 117) have argued that a MacKinnon-esque approach to gender ends up as a preoccupation with women premised on the assumption that womanhood is experienced similarly, and further fetishises women's oppression. However, MacKinnon's approach recognised that gender is 'the congealed form of the sexualization of inequality between men and women' and hence is 'an inequality of power'; in short, 'gender inequality is sexualized as dominance and subordination' (MacKinnon 1989: 6, 8, and 241). The issue was not women as such but that of the social and political power mediated by, if not made possible by, sexualised gender relations. But even if one discounts MacKinnon's approach, the historical exclusion of women is at least sufficient justification for examining women in a specific sense.

Feminist legal theorists have undertaken this kind of analysis to address one or more of these questions, but in different temporal spaces and by employing different methodologies. For example, in Australia both Thornton (1996) and Hunter (2003) have considered women's entry into discrete masculine domains. Thornton (1996: 131) pointed to the slippage between sex and gender, and preferred to conceptualise a sex regime, not just a gender regime. In any case, she argued that although women had been 'let in' (as legal knowers), their status as 'other' in relation to the benchmark man of law meant that women had remained 'fringe-dwellers of the jurisprudential community' (Thornton 1996: 3–4). Hunter (2003) interviewed men and women barristers in Victoria as part of an examination of the 'culture of the Bar' where such a culture 'involves the production and performance of particular forms of masculinity'. She drew on Anderson's (1991) notion of an 'imagined community' and treated the Bar 'as an imagined community sustained by acculturation processes, a hierarchal power structure and invented traditions of behaviour that reproduce and reinforce hegemonic masculinity' (Hunter 2003: 119).

The disruption of gender regimes may well encompass some aspects of difference as conceptualised by feminist legal theorists. However, the very arrival of women in spaces once the exclusive domain of men is disruptive by definition. Drawing on the work of Gherardi and Poggio (2001), Connell (2006: 838) observed that 'women's entry into masculine domains triggers complex adjustments in which symbolic gender dichotomy may be preserved while other changes are conceded'. Yet 'gender norms have proven to be very "sticky"':

> Challengers of existing gender logics of appropriateness have often been treated as 'deviants' and punished through acts of censure, ridicule, or harassment. With the weight of history on their side, defenders of the gender status quo—those advantaged by existing power arrangements—have often defeated attempts to subvert the existing regime. The intersection between the gender regime and other structures of power further compound the challenge for those seeking change and improved outcomes.
>
> (Chappell and Waylen 2013: 603)

The question is not so much why this happens, but why it continues to happen. What makes it possible for the gender regime to reproduce its 'stickiness' such that it is much more difficult for women to be recognised as legal knowers of substance? This book seeks to answer this by examining how women judges (and their men colleagues) negotiate the dynamics of the High Court's institutionalised gender regime.

As a matter of history the way in which law was invented, interpreted and enforced has produced and reproduced a masculinist legal system. Thinking about the High Court as an institution shaped by a gender regime means that the inquiry undertaken in this book encompasses an examination of the individual and the institution and the dynamic interplay between them. Understanding or identifying 'the gender foundations of taken-for-granted rules and practices' is part of the process of disrupting or challenging their taken-for-granted-ness (or point-of-viewlessness) 'within legislative, bureaucratic, and legal arenas' (Chappell and Waylen 2013: 603). The prevailing rules will 'constrain and empower actors along gendered lines, specifying mechanisms of regulation, obligation and persuasion' while at the same time these actors will also 'reproduce and consolidate gendered institutions through enacting', and occasionally adapting or resisting, these rules (Lowndes 2020: 545).

How might we unearth these rules? In political science (and feminist institutionalism more specifically) there is a certain methodological pluralism in the range of approaches that have been deployed including comparative approaches across case studies, interviews, ethnography, and more quantitative data to ascertain the characteristics and gendered effects of both formal and informal institutions (Chappell and Mackay 2017). Yet for the most part feminist legal theory has been 'clearer in its understanding of *rules* than in its understanding of institutions,' despite the fact that law has a 'privileged role in defining institutions' (O'Rourke 2014: 691 emphasis mine). Importantly, 'rules' are not only those formal rules that in law we understand as expressed through juridical text, or statute. There are also other contexts where the rules might be codes of conduct or formal policy, and those informal rules such as norms, practices or narratives (Lowndes and Roberts 2013). The relationship between the formal and the informal has been of particular interest to scholars seeking to uncover the gender dynamics of institutions, but the 'informal' has oftentimes been especially challenging to uncover. This is because 'informal rules are often undocumented, tacit, taken for granted, and not written down, although they can sometimes be better known and understood than formal rules' (Galea et al. 2020: 3). In order to translate this approach to law, I have sought to examine both the formal and informal through an analysis of juridical texts (which are afforded particular authority) on the one hand, and on the other hand through an analysis of various rituals and practices where the more informal aspects of the gender dynamics on the High Court might be discerned.

It might be hypothesised that in law, given the weight of history in upholding certain power arrangements, gender norms might be especially sticky. Yet when an institution once occupied only by men admits women into its space, the existing gender relations and gender norms cannot remain unaffected. How they might change, in what directions they might change and their degree of resilience, remain open questions. At the same time, new members of an institution like the High Court have to negotiate and accommodate themselves to the already prevailing gender regime.

Attempting to answer these questions then involves taking seriously the notion that the High Court has been shaped by and continues to be shaped by a masculinist gender regime. These questions will be addressed through an exploration of various rituals, authorship practices and judicial reasoning that serve to contribute to the shaping of the identity of a High Court Justice. The stories produced by members of organisations, what Gherardi and Poggio (2001: 248–249) term 'discursive artifacts', are therefore a means of revealing how 'gender culture is constructed and legitimated'. For the most part, the stories examined in this book are stories situated within the institutional context under examination. In legal and political spaces certain narratives are imbued with authority. Legal judgment (expressed in the judge's reasons for judgment) is perhaps the most obvious example of the judge's authority, but whenever a judge speaks, or a judge is spoken about in legal contexts (e.g. in the physicality of the courtroom) or political contexts, 'discursive artefacts' are produced with gendered and gendering consequences. I acknowledge that I do not engage in this exploration as an entirely neutral observer or interpreter, that my understanding of these artefacts is shaped by my view of the world (and experience of it) as a white, able-bodied, woman-identifying feminist. Tracing these 'discursive artefacts' through various rituals and practices from the politics of judicial appointment, to swearing-in speeches, first (or 'maiden') judgments, to key judgments where gender was especially pronounced, the ritual of the judicial farewell, and finally, the implications of Susan's Kiefel's elevation to Chief Justice, the book follows a broad chronological trajectory.

Outline of the book

The book is about women judges—specifically about the arrival of near gender-parity on the High Court of Australia. This is not to valorise or over-emphasise the significance of these numbers in any empirical sense, nor to gloss over the continued barriers (formal and informal) to women's participation in the legal profession. In fact, that is precisely my point. Parity or near-parity at the highest echelons of the legal profession must be qualified and understood in the context of a history that has shaped (and continues to shape) women's relationship with the law as judges. The focus then is principally the 'three of seven' after the landmark appointment of Justices Crennan, Kiefel and Bell but the book also considers the changing dynamics presented by the second iteration of the near-parity involving Justices Kiefel, Bell and Gordon.

Because gender is not a synonym for women, the book is also necessarily about the men justices, and how those who appointed them negotiated the shifting gender dynamics of the High Court and the gender order of the wider society in which the High Court is embedded. The men who served as judges concurrently with Crennan, Kiefel and Bell (at least in the latter part of their joint tenure) were Justice William Gummow (appointed in 1995), Justice Kenneth Hayne (appointed in 1997), Justice Dyson Heydon (appointed in 2003), Chief Justice Robert French (appointed in 2008), Justice Stephen Gageler (appointed in 2012), and Justice Patrick Keane (appointed in 2013). These (gendered) dynamics are indeed literally shifting because, of course, the composition of the High Court itself is always shifting. Where relevant, I note what has happened since the first iteration of near parity (2009–2015), especially given Kiefel's subsequent elevation to Chief Justice in 2017. This means that I also consider the appointments of Geoffrey Nettle in 2015, Michelle Gordon in 2015, and James Edelman in 2017.[14] The book's analysis of the

14 At the time of writing two new High Court appointments were announced: the appointment of Justice Simon Steward (to replace Geoffrey Nettle) and the appointment of Justice Jacqueline Gleeson (to replace Virginia Bell). Their appointments (and the ongoing implications for the changing gender dynamics of

High Court's evolving gender regime spans an almost two-decade period, but it does not purport to be a comprehensive account in the tradition of analyses of a particular Court (e.g. The Barwick Court, The Mason Court, The French Court etc). Rather, it aims to provide a way of *seeing* how the identity of High Court judges is crafted and a way of *understanding* how gender dynamics play out, and how those within the institution (and those outside of it) respond to those dynamics.

It might be useful here to justify or give context to my use of language insofar as it reflects my approach. First, I am conscious that by writing about women judges I might reinforce the notion that judging is a masculine activity (e.g. reproducing, even unintentionally, the language of the past and its paternalistic references to 'lady lawyers'). Graycar (1998: 4) cautioned against this kind of terminology, arguing that '[e]very time we use an adjective to describe a woman judge, or a judgment written by a woman, we are implicitly distinguishing her from the norm and reinforcing the underlying assumption that judges are men and judging is a male activity.'[15] While this argument is certainly persuasive, we are nonetheless restricted by the linguistic marker 'woman judge' if we intend to discuss women judges as a collective. On this point, I note that I shall be speaking of women and men judges, not male and female judges. The former acknowledges their human commonality and social construction, whereas the latter risks grounding the judges within a biologising frame of reference. While using the nouns 'woman' and 'man' as adjectives occasionally jars our long-gendered sensibilities, it is preferable to reproducing and perpetuating the commonplace practice of treating 'male' and 'female' as interchangeable nouns and adjectives when referring to human constructs such as judges or lawyers or any other occupation.

Second, I prefer to use 'masculinist' to describe the High Court's (and indeed, the wider societal) gender regime. Feminist political discourses have recognised bias at the level of content, structure and social organisation, variously describing it as 'malestream bias' (e.g. O'Brien 1981), 'masculinist bias' (e.g. Di Stefano 1983, 1991; Brown 1988), 'masculinism' (Duerst-Lahti 2008), or 'patriarchal bias' (e.g. Pateman 1986, 1988). Most feminist writers subscribe to one or more of these ways of describing the biases within political theory. Each has its virtues in providing us with analytical leverage to understand these

the Court) are beyond the scope of this book. See McLoughlin (2020) where I note that the appointment of Justice Gleeson to replace Justice Bell represents the first time a woman has been appointed to replace another woman.

15 On this issue I would push Graycar's point further to note that we should also remove the biologising markers of 'female' and 'male'. Where she notes that 'judging is a male activity', the activity comes to be naturalised in ways that it would not if the description were 'judging is a man's activity'—that is, it is what men judges do. Graycar is quite correct to point to the problem of 'reinforcing the underlying assumptions'; it is just that she too continues to do just that by continuing to use 'male' (and by extension 'female') as adjectives.

processes. Similarly, feminist legal theorists have exposed the ways in which law is gendered (e.g. Graycar and Morgan 1990), or indeed, sexed (see e.g. Davies 1997; Conaghan 2013), variously describing the process as reflecting the law's masculine or patriarchal biases and/or foundations. I prefer 'masculinist' and 'masculinism' to that of 'patriarchy' as the latter falls short as a descriptor both linguistically and ideologically (Duerst-Lahti 2008: 170). Linguistically, 'patriarchy' has numerous meanings including its focus of the rule of the father and in more recent interpretations as the rule of the brothers (Pateman 1988). In ideological terms, and unlike masculinism, 'patriarchy is not readily recognizable as an ideology despite clearly functioning as the guiding thought that advocates rule by men' (Duerst-Lahti 2008: 170). I acknowledge that there is considerable potential for slippage between terms like 'masculinism'/'masculinist' and 'patriarchy' insofar as they describe a social ordering which preferences men. It is the *ordering* that is the crucial point—and it is understanding how women are situated as legal knowers within a particular institutional (and wider societal) framework that has excluded them that is of central interest for what follows.

Chapter 1 provides a brief history of Australia's constitutional framework. This chapter sets out the masculinist ethos which underpinned the creation of the High Court as an institution, and indeed, the wider legal system which has reflected the same ethos. In this way, this chapter sets the scene for, and gives substance to, the book's examination of the gender regime which has shaped the Court.

Chapter 2 considers the political discourse around the appointment of women and men judges to the High Court. In order to give context to the politics of gender diversity and the judiciary, and the conditional and contested nature of women's access to judicial authority, I examine the gendered deployment of the idea of 'merit' and the recurring practice of decision makers' failure to frame diversity in positive ways. It is argued that the focus on merit is really one of the many ways of emphasising women's difference, or status as other, so as to reinforce and reproduce the gendered regime, or at least to render the appointment safe for that regime.

The political processes which result in the appointment of judges leave little space for the newly appointed judge to speak to their new role. Yet, the way in which judges conceive of their own judicial identities can be significant—particularly outside the rigid confines of legal judgment. Hence Chapter 3 examines the narratives presented in the swearing-in speeches of High Court justices. This is the formal process and ritual whereby an individual is transformed into a Justice of the High Court. It presents an opportunity for the new judge to reflect publicly on how they conceive their newly acquired judicial authority. It also offers an opportunity for key stakeholders to reflect on the appointee's suitability for their new position. These speeches are rare glimpses into the 'private' judge, or at least the private judge packaged for public consumption. In many instances much of what we might know about judges' life narratives is sourced from these speeches. By recognising that a traditional measure of judicial authority has been framed from a masculinist perspective, Chapter 3 provides an insight into how these notions continue to inform understandings of judicial authority.

In different ways, then, Chapters 2 and 3 examine the stories told by and about judges as part of their appointment to the High Court. These stories are imbued with claims about the qualities associated with and sought in judges and about the nature, purpose and scope of judicial authority. The speeches made at this time therefore inform our understanding of various dimensions of the gender regime, from the symbolic imagery of the judge through to conceptions of power. In both of these chapters, the narratives record aspects of both women's and men's experiences as they undergo the very public rituals associated with their new status. Examining discourses around men and women judges enables a wider consideration of the peculiar way in which the arrival of women has been framed.

Chapter 4 examines the first or 'maiden' judgments handed down by women judges who comprised the first iteration of near parity. The focus here is on the relationship between practices of authorship—understood in other institutional contexts as the division of labour—and prevailing notions of judicial collegiality. Since 1995 the High Court has adopted an interesting informal practice of welcoming new judges by allowing the newest member to author the lead judgment of a case. Her judicial colleagues offer a one-line concurrence. In this chapter I argue that a judge's first judgment is a useful way of situating a discussion about women judges' contributions vis-à-vis difference by querying the extent to which the woman judge can ever shake-off her status as the 'maiden' bound to conform for the sake of comity. Chapter 4 is the beginning of the examination of what the gendered division of labour might reveal about the gender regime on the High Court. The first judgments, understood as an informal welcoming ritual, are revealing as markers of building a culture of consensus and collaboration rather than as the particularities of legal reasoning adopted in any of the specific cases. This division of labour might thus serve to reinforce and even valorise collegiality on the Court. In some respects, like the appointment and swearing-in processes, the first judgment ritual is about fitting into the accepted and dominant way of doing things. When it comes to actual cases beyond the first judgment, things look a little different.

Chapters 5 and 6 examine two High Court decisions in which the gender dynamics were especially significant for understanding the shifting dynamics of the Court's gender regime. The rationale for selecting the two decisions to subject to close scrutiny was not because they might be representative of the particular approaches of specific judges. Rather, they were selected precisely because the gender dynamics at play meant that the decisions stood out in the sense of being 'illustrative and indicative' (Rackley 2007: 76) in terms of how they might illuminate an understanding of the operation of the gender regime. In fact, the juxtaposition of the two decisions serves as a reminder that gender is not a reliable indicator of how cases will be decided. In *PGA v The Queen* (2012) 245 CLR 355 ('*PGA*') the gender dynamics stood out in terms of subject matter as the High Court was tasked with determining when the spousal immunity for rape ceased to exist at common law. It was also of some benefit that *PGA* was the only decision involving Crennan, Kiefel and Bell JJ to be reimagined by the *Australian Feminist Judgments Project*. Whereas in *Monis v The Queen; Droudis v The Queen* (2013) 249 CLR 92 ('*Monis*') the fact that a six-member Court was split along gender lines made gender especially visible. In the context of the analysis of the Court's gender regime and the gender balance, this decision is especially noteworthy because of the visibility of the gender balance. The decision saw Crennan, Kiefel and Bell JJ write together in a single joint judgment, which came to an entirely different conclusion from the three men who also sat on the case.

The notion of the women judges writing together is not especially momentous (in fact, they did so regularly). I do not wish to overstate the extent of their joint judgment writing so as to conflate their contributions as women judges. *Monis* stands out in part because the three women judges wrote a joint judgment in direct opposition to the men judges' reasons. As will be examined in more detail in Chapters 4 and 7, the extent of joint judgment writing was particularly high during their time on the Court, but this is not to suggest that the women judges always wrote as a bloc. In many instances the men judges participated in joint judgments with the women judges, as reflected by the high levels of joint authorship across the Court. However, it was sometimes the case that the women exhibited a preference for writing together. For example, in 2013 'Justices Crennan, Kiefel and Bell were all more regular co-authors for each and other members of the Court than anyone else' and 'the most regular co-authoring relationship was between Crennan and Kiefel JJ which reached the same level—around 70 per cent of the opinions authored by each—attained by Gummow and Hayne JJ in earlier studies in this series' (Lynch and Williams 2014: 558).

In both *PGA* and *Monis*, gender was present in other less obvious but nonetheless significant ways. *PGA* and *Monis* raise (albeit in distinct ways) issues about the very substance of law which point to the ongoing implications of women's exclusion from law and legal authority. In this respect, both decisions reveal the continued public/private dichotomy in how the law responds to and regulates what happens in the public sphere and in the private sphere. Hence, in these decisions we see judges negotiating (and grappling with) the very baggage of the masculinist gendering of the law. In the substance of the decisions, in the reasoning employed, and even in the rhetorical framing of the arguments, the dynamics of the gender regime are clearly at work.

The almost-equal gender balance, or at least the first iteration of it, came to a close with the retirement of Justice Crennan—announced in late 2014 and effective in early 2015. Hence Chapter 7 takes up the examination of a different ritual, the farewell speech. This has not been an area to which scholars have paid much attention. However, it provides a unique opportunity to examine critically the legacy Crennan and others sought to craft in the speeches delivered on that occasion. Justice Crennan's judicial farewell speech is the centrepiece of the chapter but the imagery cast by the speech, and the way in which ideas about humanity and collegiality were valorised, perhaps underscoring then Justice Kirby's comments about the need for the profession to become 'humanis[ed]' (Kirby 2002: 148), give some insight into the shifting dynamics of the Court's gender regime. The valorisation of the ideas of humanity and collegiality points to their wider significance for the book in terms of the impact of women on the workings of the Court.

Chapter 8 looks at the High Court in 2020 and how Kiefel has navigated the still novel state of being a woman and Chief Justice. Examining Kiefel's elevation to Chief Justice, I consider how gender was framed by those making this historic appointment and by the new Chief Justice herself, including her increased willingness to reflect on matters of gender and judging and women's place in the legal profession. The Chief Justice takes on a unique symbolic role (beyond the more obvious intellectual leadership) as the leader of the judiciary and by extension, the legal profession. Kiefel's handling of revelations that Dyson Heydon had sexually harassed judicial associates during his time on the Court represented a particularly significant moment, both in terms of her judicial leadership, and what it revealed about the gender dynamics on the High Court. What then does it tell us about the High Court as an institution and the extent to which women's entry into the legal profession has made actual inroads into the culture and values of the dominant regime?

Finally, in the concluding chapter, I draw together the various threads examined throughout the book, both in setting out conclusions about the evolving gender order on the High Court of Australia, but also in situating the Court within the wider societal gender order. I argue that the gender balance has made a difference because the visibility of women on the bench, literally and figuratively, cast by the almost equal gender balance, has made an important symbolic statement about women's admission to legal authority in Australia. But I also consider whether that difference is only one of symbolism and access to authority. There were instances which showed the difference gender diversity can bring to bear not only in judicial decision-making, but also in those matters which sit outside the Court's formal Constitutional remit. Although the arrival of the gender balance has not seen marked levels of dissent or even staunch individuality on the part of the women judges, this is not to say that their collective and individual presence did nothing to (re)shape the Court's gender regime. Rejecting the idea that the legal profession or indeed the Court has been 'feminised', I conclude that women judges were not necessarily 'just men in skirts,' though the dynamics within which they performed their tasks encouraged them to be just that.

Chapter 1

The masculinist foundations of Australia's legal and constitutional framework

As a matter of history, the way in which law in Australia was invented, interpreted and enforced produced and reproduced a masculinist legal system. The High Court of Australia is readily identifiable as an institution shaped by a masculinist gender regime. This regime has its genesis in the Court's historical origins within a masculinised federation and its accompanying Constitution—which was created without the input of women as drafters or as interpreters. In this chapter I set out a brief history of the masculinist foundations of Australia's Constitutional framework to give substance to my argument that these terms are both applicable and appropriate for developing an analysis about what sort of difference (if any) a near-equal gender balance on the High Court judicial bench has made. Setting out this history, albeit briefly, provides important context for the analysis that follows. This chapter shows that women were excluded from building these foundational legal institutions and this necessarily sets the scene for examining the conditions of their later entry or 'letting in'.

The Australian Constitution, an act of the British Imperial Parliament, was drafted at a series of conventions during the 1890s, and in crafting a federal system of government the framers' intentions in many respects were reflective of the colonial interests of the time. Importantly, these interests did not align with the traditional inhabitants of the land, Indigenous Australians, who had inhabited what would become known as Australia for at least 65 000 years prior to the arrival of English colonists in 1788.[1] The federal compact emerged

1 As Moreton-Robinson (2009: 64) explains, the origins of sovereignty in Australia rest on the legal fiction of *Terra Nullius* (land belonging to no-one) 'which functioned as a truth within a race war of coercion, murder and appropriation carried out by white men in the service of the British Crown.' As the then Aboriginal and Torres Strait Islander Social Justice Commissioner, Mick Gooda (2011: 4) explained, this fiction, and the explicit exclusion of Aboriginal and Torres Strait Islander peoples from nation building processes has had devastating ongoing implications 'the Constitution did not—and still does not—make adequate provision for us. It has completely failed to protect our inherent rights as the first peoples of this country'. There has been growing acceptance that this history needs to be redressed through Constitutional reform but to date no such structural reforms have been adopted. See *Uluru Statement from the Heart* (2017) which calls for 'Voice, Treaty and

DOI: 10.4324/9780429288531-2

as a matter of political expediency, reflecting the anticipated trade and defence benefits that would come from federating British colonies rather than a 'Damascus Road Miracle' slouching towards democracy (Crisp 1983 quoted in Blackshield and Williams 2010: 122). The Constitution could not be said to be preoccupied with individual rights but rather it reflects the primary aim in uniting separate British colonies into one federal compact. The democratic impulse notwithstanding, the political foundations of the Constitution were exclusionary with respect not only to race and class but also gender. The masculinist political ethos meant that women were formally excluded from almost every aspect of the emergence of modern Australia.

Women's exclusion from the drafting of the Constitution shaped the document that emerged in important ways. One result was that the Constitution is silent on the topic of women. Reflecting on these silences, Priest and Williams (2010: 417) note 'the problem is not what Australia's Constitution says about women, but what it fails to say'. This silence has ongoing implications for the way in which women are situated within Australia's constitutional framework. Four principles or concepts underpin Australia's Constitutional framework, namely federalism, responsible government, representative democracy and the separation of powers. In different but nonetheless significant ways, each of these concepts reflects the masculinist foundations of Australia's Constitutional framework. That is, in terms of the very concepts underpinning the Constitution (e.g. what it values and thus seeks to protect), women's concerns and perspectives have been largely elided. It was certainly not envisaged that women would exercise legal or political authority within the new federation—in fact they were formally excluded from doing so. On one view it might be easy to dismiss these features as a matter of history, particularly given more recent events which have seen women exercising authority at the peak of Australia's Constitutional framework. But, as I will examine in this chapter, the very text and structure of the Constitution, particularly with respect to the system of government it creates, continues to bear the masculinist hallmarks of its creation.

The events leading to the formation of the Australian federation are oftentimes referred to as the 'birth of a nation' and the men responsible have since been commemorated as the 'founding fathers'. Yet that is not to say that the federation was entirely 'motherless', as has been noted by a number of scholars of history, law and politics in their efforts to reveal women's contribution to nation-building (see e.g. Irving 1996, 1997, 2007; Cass and Rubenstein 1995; Grimshaw et al. 1994). As Irving (1996: 1) has noted:

> The voices of those women who were involved in Federation cry out to be heard. How is it possible that there were 'fathers' without mothers?

Truth' to establish a 'new relationship between First Nations and the Australian nation based on justice and self determination where Indigenous cultures and people can flourish' (available at https://ulurustatement.org).

> How could a nation be born without a female presence? Where were the thinking, organizing, active women, those we know of as tireless in the suffrage campaigns of their time?… And what of the 'ordinary' women, caught up in the daily contribution of bringing babies into the world, nurturing and educating them, and doing the bulk of the charitable work as well? Is this not part of the 'nation-building' process? The story of women as 'founding mothers' is one in which this contribution to 'nation-building' must be understood.

Indeed, despite being formally excluded (save in South Australia), women's groups sent petitions to the series of Constitutional Conventions which were held during the 1890s to allow men delegates to debate and draft the Constitution. These constitutional debates are illuminating as to what issues seemed significant and what did not, what the framers hoped to craft, and who did and did not warrant particular attention. It was 'within such political debates that bids for a say in defining the national character, and of promoting images of what Australia might become, were made' (Grimshaw et al. 1994: 181). Not the least of these arguments concerned the issue of gender. Writing about the Federation movement's concern for preserving white society, Grimshaw et al. argued that the 'racial exclusionist appeal' in debates around federation 'was conducted in masculinist terms,' the aim of which was to enhance a sense of common destiny for Australian men. As one politician proposed:

> As a true federationist, I believe that the only federation that can be effective is a federation of the manhood of Australia—a truly representative federation. It is not a question of federating acres and wealth; it is a question of federating the spirit of the manhood of Australia and that is what we should seek to do.
>
> (quoted in Grimshaw et al. 1994: 192)

Thus it came about that because two states (South Australia and Western Australia) had already given women the vote, 'within this masculine federation women would have to be citizens',[2] though the rationale was less about women's rights as such and more about 'white women's common links with

2 There is some slippage here between notions of 'citizenship' and the 'franchise'. Although the ability to vote is an important formal indicator of citizenship, it is perhaps important to note that the Constitution itself did not define citizenship or formally provide for it. See Davidson's (1997) *From Subject to Citizen* for an analysis of the evolving notion of citizenship in Australia during the twentieth century. Moreover, these points have also been made from an explicitly feminist perspective. For example, Thornton (2000: 112) has argued that citizenship was not important to the drafters of the Constitution because their concern was fundamentally about delineating powers in the new Federation, not with individual rights. Some of these themes around the meaning of citizenship are revisited in Chapter 5.

their menfolk' (Grimshaw et al. 1994: 192–193). For at least some of the male politicians who welcomed (white) women's political participation, 'women's main contribution was not forecast as active citizenship, but prolific child-bearing' (Grimshaw et al. 1994: 193).

Citizenship itself is a fraught concept within Australia's legal framework and constructing the substance of citizenship specifically for women[3] has been an ongoing dilemma in Australia (Cox 2000: 57). Citizenship itself is not defined in Australia's Constitutional framework (and only mentioned with respect to foreign aliens), hence Australians remained subjects until the passage of specific citizenship laws (Thornton 2000). Yet citizenship is also understood as making a civic contribution and to this end Irving (1997: 158) pointed out that prior to Federation 'women argued for the vote, not in order to become citizens but because they were already citizens'. Thornton (1995b: 200) notes that citizenship 'is the status determining membership of a legally cognisable community, although it involves more than a passive belonging' and it therefore encompasses rights and a degree of participation on behalf of the citizens. Enfranchisement is an obvious manifestation of participation, and in this respect liberal legalism implies 'that enfranchisement bestowed upon women the entire complement of formal rights enjoyed by men' (Thornton 1995b: 201). Yet this implication does not necessarily bear fruit, at least in part because citizenship itself has been defined in masculinist terms.

Another example of women's less formal but nonetheless significant contributions to the Constitutional drafting process was that made by Catherine Helen Spence (an unsuccessful candidate for election as a South Australian delegate to the Conventions) and the Christian temperance groups in articulating women's concerns at the time. Irving (1996: 15–16) highlights these contributions, reasoning that their input can be seen in the Constitution's preamble and s 113, but arguing that 'the presence of women is most clearly identified in section 41'. The inclusion of this section effectively provided the groundwork for (white) universal suffrage, as it meant that no person who had the right to vote in State elections could be deprived of the right to vote in Federal Elections. Although proponents of women's suffrage were ultimately unsuccessful in having women's suffrage included in the actual text of the Constitution, the inclusion of s 41 was nonetheless an important component in

3 Rubenstein's (2004b) examination of Justice Gaudron's jurisprudential contributions to Australian citizenship is apposite here. Rubenstein (2004b: 313) argued that although Gaudron J had explicitly stated in *Re Minister for Immigration and Multicultural Affairs; Ex parte Meng Kok Te* (2002) 212 CLR 162 'citizenship is a statutory, not a constitutional concept', her approach 'underlines citizenship as a fundamental criterion for determining membership of the body politic'. Rubenstein's (2004b: 305) emphasis on the distinction between citizenship as a legal and normative concept is important here. Although citizenship has a specific legal meaning, understandings about citizenship and the demands of representative government are infused with normative ideas about what membership of the polity entails.

securing the political will and power to enact the *Commonwealth Franchise Act 1902* (Cth) (Oldfield 1992: 64).[4] Moreover, as Irving (1996: 16) discovered, the substance of the Convention debates around the wording of s 41 were particularly illuminating in 'forcing the delegates to touch upon matters they normally avoided':

> as they grappled to find the right words for this section, so that South Australian women would not be disenfranchised but that the other States would not be forced to grant their women the vote (and at the same time to ensure that neither 'Chinamen' nor 'infants of sixteen' could be enfranchised) they argued about the nature of rights, the experimental character of Federation, the identity of the new Australian citizen, and the nature of representation.

The High Court subsequently conceived of s 41 in narrow terms as merely a transitional guarantee, rather than a right to vote. For example, in *R v Pearson; Ex parte Sipka* (1983) 152 CLR 254, the Court (Murphy J dissented) held that s 41 did not afford any protection of the right to vote as it was merely a transitional provision which served to secure the federal franchise[5] and, therefore, the fact that s 41 does not warrant attention as a component entrenching a system of representative government is hardly surprising. Cass and Rubenstein (1995: 12) observed that the High Court's approach to the interpretation of s 41 in more contemporary times 'did not bode well for women or their representation' and thus emphasised 'the difficulty in discerning the Court's view of the scope or content of the principle of representative democracy'.

Also, it is necessary to note here the limited provision of express rights in the Constitution, despite the agitations of at least one delegate, Andrew Inglis Clarke. For most delegates the dominant viewpoint, informed by the works of A.V. Dicey and Bryce, was that civilized nations did not need to provide expressly for individual rights (see e.g. Patapan 1997: 218). The inclusion of

4 See Oldfield (1992) for a comprehensive overview of various suffrage campaigns in Australia. Oldfield's (1992: 65) account of the relationship between Commonwealth and State voting rights for white women noted that 'the proud boast that Australia was the second nation in the world to federally enfranchise its women ignores the fact that black women and their men in two states had to wait until 1962 to gain access to the ballot-box'.

5 See Cass and Rubenstein (1995: 11–12) for an analysis of how the High Court's interpretation of s 41 has obscured women's contribution to public political life at the time of federation and as a consequence, the (potential) role of s 41 in enhancing the reach of representative democracy in Australia's Constitutional framework. See also Rubenstein's (2014b: 61) alternative feminist judgment drafted in response to *Sipka* considered the 'objectives of those women who were instrumental to the insertion of s 41' beyond what is recorded in Convention Debates and therefore adopted a broader interpretation [of the] provision as one that has an ongoing role in protecting voting rights.

express rights would have arguably benefited women. Yet, who knows what might have happened if women had been (formally) involved in the drafting?[6] Of course, even if women had been formally involved in drafting the Constitution, this is not to say that it would have enshrined express rights or equality in any case:

> the Australian Constitution was never intended to describe or protect the kinds of equality rights that we expect for women today. Fixed in a racist and sexist ideology, anything it might have had to say about women's rights would not have been something that we would have wanted entrenched for all time.
>
> (Karpin and O'Connell 2005: 46)

Karpin and O'Connell's argument touches on an important point. There was much about the politics of the time that was best left unentrenched.[7] The question, however, is what has become entrenched, or perhaps more pointedly, what is now interpreted as entrenched? For practically the whole of the twentieth century it was relatively uncontroversial to suggest that 'the failure of the constitution-making process to conform to the principle of representative democracy boded poorly for the type of constitutional system which followed,' in particular the way women were represented *in* and *by* the Constitution (Cass and Rubenstein 1995: 30). Moreover, the nature of Australian federalism itself is imbued with certain masculinist characteristics insofar as those matters identified as national were associated with the sphere of masculine activities (Irving 2007: 169). The federal compact delineated the activities that would be the

6 See Irving (1994: 191) for specific examination of how women *might* have shaped the Australian Constitution noting that 'if women had gained the suffrage prior to the Conventions of 1897 and 1898, some sections at least of the Constitution would necessarily have been written differently.' As Irving notes (191), s 41 would not have been necessary and there is some evidence to suggest that women delegates to the Convention (had they been permitted and thus elected) 'might have gone as far as pressing for the inclusion of a general right to vote' given 'their petitions to the Convention suggest they supported such a position.' Irving reasoned that it is less clear whether women delegates would have demanded an express right to stand for Parliament, arguing that the most clear example where women might have diverged from that of men is in the powers set out in s 51 (e.g. the 'heads of power'). For more general feminist critiques about the extent to which Constitutions can ever properly reflect the concerns of women see for example: Vicki C. Jackson (2016) 'Feminisms and constitutions' in *The Public Law of Gender: From the Local to the Global* edited by Kim Rubenstein and Katherine G. Young. Cambridge University Press. 43–72

7 The forgoing arguments about the masculinist foundations of Australia's Constitutional framework were previously published in McLoughlin. K. and Jose, J. 2017. 'The politics of the public and private spheres: the High Court's decision in Monis and the gendered privileging of free speech.' *Australian Journal of Political Science* 52.4: 565–579.

proper domain of the Commonwealth and circumscribed its legislative power within s 51 and s 52 (i.e. the 'heads' of powers). The areas for which the Commonwealth gained specific responsibility, namely defence, treaties (i.e. international affairs), immigration, and trade, are '[t]he belligerent powers, the outward-looking, border-crossing, "big-picture" powers' (Irving 2007: 169). All other activities remained within the purview of the States. Over time the reach of Commonwealth powers has expanded, and areas that were 'once associated with the local or "domestic"' (e.g. matters that had been traditionally understood to concern women) such as a raft of social welfare activities are now within the ambit of the Commonwealth. The successful referendum in 1946, which expanded the Commonwealth's legislative power in social welfare, is a case in point (Irving 2007: 169).

The so-called 'social welfare' power was inserted into the Constitution in 1946 by referendum. Prior to the referendum, the Commonwealth had legislative power under s 51(xxiii) to legislate for pensions but this was extended to include: 'The provision of maternity allowances, widows' pensions, child endowment, unemployment, pharmaceutical, sickness and hospital benefits, medical and dental services (but not so as to authorise any form of civil conscription), benefits to students and family allowances'. The impetus for the referendum was the '*Pharmaceutical Benefits Case*' (*Attorney-General (Vic); Ex rel Dale v Commonwealth* (1945) 71 CLR 237) which held that the scheme designed to fund reduced prices for prescription medicine was beyond the scope of s 81 of the Constitution. As a number of other government welfare schemes such as child endowment and widows' pensions had also been enacted without the support of a constitutional head of power, the need to incorporate a social welfare power, rather than erroneously relying on s 81, became apparent.

Ultimately, then, federalism as embodied in Australia's constitutional framework elided women's perspectives and concerns, which in turn has had very real impacts on women's lives.[8] Where the Commonwealth has shared legislative competence with the states over an area there have also been impacts, such as in relation to the marriage power provided in s 51(xxi) of the Constitution and the divorce and matrimonial power provided in s 51(xxii). In these cases, the Commonwealth was given power over some—but not all—aspects of family relationships, 'ma[king] women's lives more complicated, difficult and

8 Although these concerns have been examined in more recent times (see e.g. Chappell, Brennan and Rubenstein 2012; Cass and Rubenstein 1995, Irving 2007; Rubenstein 2006), these concerns were also ventilated at the time of federation. As Chappell, Brennan and Rubenstein (2012: 229) note, anti-Billite Rose Scott opposed federation not only because suffrage had been excluded from the draft constitution, but also because was she sceptical about the capacity of federal institutions to achieve gender equality in a nation-state 'concerned primarily with armies and government buildings, seen as expressions of male power and authority, at the expense of matters of higher priority to women.'

time consuming' (Rubenstein 2006: 9). Addressing the particularly complex issue of violence against women, which involves many policy arenas, is a salient example (see Chappell, Brennan and Rubenstein 2012). Rubenstein (2006: 4) notes that in the welfare arena, for example, women's reliance on state governments for support caused problems given that matters of particular concern to women such as child welfare and family health care were (and are) not territorially derived.

Although the Constitution could be said to be expansive in terms of assigning legislative power (even if its focus reflects a particularly gendered hierarchy) as well as demarcating the separation of powers and the judiciary's role within the Constitutional framework, it offered comparatively scant detail about how judges might come to be appointed.[9] It can scarcely be imagined that it was envisaged that women would one day come to exercise legal authority as judges of the High Court (or indeed exercise legislative or executive power).[10] The selection of the High Court's first bench was itself a political affair. While 'the original judicial triumvirate of Griffith, Barton and O'Connor was indeed impressive', the political connections were fairly explicit as all had been involved in the drafting of the Constitution, and Barton had been the first Prime Minister (Galligan 1987: 77).[11] The identities of those first judges, and their public connection to the drafting of the federal compact, meant that they carried a level of authority that overshadowed concerns about 'logical consistency or a literal reading of the constitution's text' (Galligan 1987: 80). Indeed, as legal knowers the early Justices of the High Court were accorded an

9 See *Australian Constitution* s 72. See also the *High Court of Australia Act 1979* (Cth) which was subsequently enacted and nonetheless provides scant additional detail in requiring that an Attorney-General is required to 'consult' in making appointments and provides that in order to be eligible for appointment a person must be enrolled as a legal practitioner for at least 5 years. I will take up the issue of judicial appointments (and the implications of unfettered executive discretion in making these appointments) in the next chapter.

10 The focus of this book is women judges on the High Court of Australia but it is worth noting key milestones in terms of women's ascension within the political sphere, particularly at the Commonwealth level. As noted in the introduction, the historic first period of an almost 'gender' balance on the High Court coincided with a time in which women also held peak positions within various branches of government in Australia. For example, at the Commonwealth level, Julia Gillard became Australia's first woman Prime Minister holding office between 2010 and 2013, Nicola Roxon became the nation's first woman Attorney-General from 2011 and 2013, and Quentin Bryce served as Australia's first woman Governor-General between 2008 and 2014. Notably, although *The Commonwealth Franchise Act 1902* (Cth) meant that (white) women were formally permitted to stand for election in 1903 (and indeed a number of women did stand), it would be another 40 years before Dame Enid Lyons was elected to the House of Representatives and Dorothy Tagney was elected to the Senate.

11 Although the Court was originally comprised of three judges, the Court's workload was such that its membership expanded to accommodate the demands being placed upon it.

authority that went beyond their strictly legal expertise. That they were members of the group known as the 'founding fathers' of the Australian Constitution enhanced the authority of their judicial voices, rather than diminishing it.

The separation of powers between the legislature, executive and judiciary entrenched by the text and structure of the Constitution has had important consequences, especially in safeguarding judicial power and in envisaging the High Court's role as encompassing judicial review. Yet, the separation of power between the branches of government has never been absolute—the judiciary for instance is appointed, formally by the executive, but by convention, by the government of the day. That men have historically held power within each of these branches demonstrates how this in turn reproduced a masculine regime. The High Court's role in adjudicating contentious political disputes, especially those about the delineation between state and federal powers, and later, for example, in finding implied rights in the Constitution, means that its exercise of power has had important political consequences. Despite the early High Court's approach to constitutional interpretation—obviously informed by the political experiences of the 'original judicial triumvirate' as drafters of the very document their Honours were tasked with interpreting—in the years which followed, many of the Court's members subsequently secured its legitimacy by a persistent commitment to legalism (Galligan 1987: 252). In the middle of last century, Sir Owen Dixon made one of most famous pronouncements about the High Court's purported approach to Constitutional interpretation at his swearing-in when he said, '[t]here is no other safe guide to judicial decisions in great conflicts than a strict and complete legalism'.[12]

This cloak of legalism acted like a shield, enabling the Court 'to perform a high profile but delicate political function without becoming embroiled in political controversy' (Galligan 1987: 252). That shield, or indeed, the wider arsenal provided by traditional theories of jurisprudence, came under particularly heavy scrutiny in the latter half of the twentieth century, 'Traditional'[13]

12 See '*Swearing In of Sir Owen Dixon as Chief Justice*' (1952) 85 CLR xi at xvi. It has sometimes been pointed out that Dixon CJ's comments with respect to legalism have been widely misunderstood as his Honour was referring to the role of the High Court in Federal conflicts (see Ayres 2003: 233). But Dixon CJ's actual commitment to legalism, or indeed, his preferred judicial methodology is not the point here. In fact, the widespread (mis)understanding about his Honour's judicial methodology further underscores Galligan's point—the notion that the High Court embraced legalism has served an important political and rhetorical function in justifying the Court's work. Much the same point was made by former Chief Justice of the High Court, Sir Anthony Mason (1986: 5) in the context of explaining the impossibility of 'interpreting any instrument, let alone a constitution, divorced from values'; he posited that the 'ever present danger is that "strict and complete legalism" will be a cloak for undisclosed and unidentified policy values'.

13 There is not the space here to do justice to the history of legal theory beyond situating 'traditional' theories as the counter to feminist legal theory. There are, of course, important distinctions between classical common law theory, natural law

jurisprudential theories rested on two core assumptions. The first was that judges are impartial, and as a corollary did not make laws, but merely 'interpreted' what was already there. The second, perhaps more significant although tellingly unconscious factor, was that the role of judge has been, at least historically, decidedly masculinist, as reflected by women's exclusion from the legal profession. That only men were admitted as legal knowers or interpreters of law became deeply problematic once the role of judge was understood and appreciated from a feminist perspective.

Barriers to women's entry into the legal profession

Underscoring the exclusionary origins of the High Court were related barriers to women's entry into the legal profession itself. This is a much longer history that is neither unique to Australia nor the legal profession. Over the course of the twentieth century (and in some cases, earlier) women agitated for reforms which would see them accepted (at least in principle) on equal footing to men in parliaments, courts and other public and private institutions. Women's entry into the legal profession hinged on 'the crucial significance of women acquiring the legal status of "persons" before becoming eligible for legal office, as maleness was equated with humanness and accordingly with "persons" in the legal sense' (Schultz 2003: xxxiii). Thus, in many countries (notably those countries connected to the British Empire) special enabling legislation was required to pave the way for women's formal entry into the profession. Typically, enacting legislation followed "persons" cases, where women literally petitioned that they should be permitted to practise law on the basis that they were persons within the meaning of the relevant statutory provisions. These cases provide important insights into not only the extent to which women's admission to the legal profession was vigorously denied by those who already had power within it, but also, the myth of neutrality informing legal method itself (see Thornton 1996; Thornton 2018; Mossman 2009; Auchmuty 2011). In Australia, reflecting its status as a federation, these cases occurred state by state (and by extension the date for women's entry into the profession varies by state).[14]

Victoria was the first of the Australian states to enact enabling legislation in 1903. As a result, Flos Greig became the first woman in Australia to practise law. Tasmania and Queensland followed soon after, but New South Wales and Western Australia were amongst the more recalcitrant states in permitting women entry to the profession. In 1904 Edith Haynes applied to the Western

and positivism. Although feminist legal theory was not the first to challenge the demarcation between the judge and the law, the key point of departure between feminist legal theory and other non-positivist theories is that it aims to 'show that the supposed gender-blind approach to legal scholarship is problematic, since the claim of neutrality is often a cover-story for male orientated and discriminatory legal knowledge and policy' (Davies 2008: 213).

14 See Thornton (1996) for a comprehensive examination of this history.

Australian Supreme Court seeking a mandamus that she be admitted as an articled clerk, but was unsuccessful—the three judges presiding declined to accept that a woman was a person within the meaning of the *Legal Practitioners Act 1893* (WA). In separate but concurring judgments the three men judges Parker, McMillan and Burnside JJ pointed to the lack of precedent 'in the civilized world' (the judges each referenced the United States, Canada and of course, England) for admitting women lawyers. They reasoned that 'persons' could not have been intended to mean 'women' (notwithstanding the *Acts Interpretation Act's* 1898 statement to the contrary explicitly setting out that 'person' includes 'woman'). Importantly, Thornton noted the judges' (purported) disinclination to engage in lawmaking—using the law and legal method as a cloak or shield for their own partiality. In her view, this decision upheld 'the prevailing gender order' where 'male judges acted as the supposedly neutral arbiters of women's fitness for the public realm' (Thornton 1996: 59)

The prevailing sentiment about women's place within the legal profession (and indeed, the judicial role itself) is aptly summarised by Burnside J in his judgment:

> It is a privilege which has been conferred by the Courts originally, and then been regulated subsequently by Statute from almost time immemorial, and which has been confined to the male sex. I agree with my learned brothers, and I'm not prepared to start making law. When the legislature in its wisdom confers the right on women, then we shall be pleased to admit them. But we must leave it to the legislature to decide on the desirability or otherwise of such legislation.[15]

Women's admission to the legal profession thus was secured in the legislative arena, in many instances following an individual woman's legal challenge to the purported status quo.[16] It is not entirely clear who the 'we' was but we can assume Burnside J was speaking for his brother judges, and indeed, perhaps the wider legal fraternity. Thornton (2018: 15) wonders if a different conclusion would have been reached had Haynes appealed to the High Court, asking, '[w] ould the three neonate High Court judges have taken judicial notice of the recent enfranchisement of women and the flurry of activity it engendered to achieve a radically different outcome in the interpretation of "any person"?' It is true that two of the three judges of the Griffith Court of the day were former politicians in the new federal parliament—Edmund Barton as Prime

15 *In re Edith Haynes* (1904) 6 WAR 209, 214

16 As noted, owing to Australia's status as a Federation (after 1901), legislation which enabled women to be admitted to legal practise was enacted in each state. See for e. g. *Practitioners* Act 1904 (Tas), *Legal Practitioners Act 1905* (Qld), *Female Law Practitioners Act 1911* (SA), *The Women's Legal Status Act 1918* (NSW) and *The Women's Legal Status Act 1923* (WA). In the United Kingdom women's admission was enabled by the Sex Disqualification (Removal) Act 1919 (UK).

Minister and Richard O'Connor as leader of the Senate. Both had voted for the *Commonwealth Franchise Act* in 1902, with O'Connor having been a particular advocate for women's greater civic engagement. And early decisions of the Court reflect a regard for the changing status of women (Thornton 2019: 17). But surely the ideologically burdened decision of the WA Supreme Court would not have been overturned in such an act of daring? In imagining a likely successful outcome, Thornton perhaps gives the early High Court more credit than many would be able to muster. As it turned out, of course, Burnside J's assurance that 'we shall be pleased to admit them' was something of a misnomer—even when the formal rules were specifically amended to let women in, what followed was reluctance and resistance (see Mossman 2006: 156).

Leaving to one side what decisions *might* have been made within the bounds of the common law, the reality is that women's entry into the legal profession was secured in the legislative arena. On what basis were these rights secured? As Campbell (1961: 204) observed despite the fact that political rights for Australian women had been secured 'earlier and with less resistance than was the case in Britain', 'the idea of a general sex disqualifications removal statute was clearly not thought necessary until the English courts had revealed the extent of common law disabilities and the British Parliament provided a model statute.' Although the removal of these disabilities or disqualifications (e.g. being a woman) were not identical across jurisdictions, the history of these changes provides important insights not only into the contingent and conditional nature of women's eventual access to legal authority but also the extent to which changing the formal rules will not necessarily disrupt the gendered status quo.

Gwyneth Bebb's attempt to enter the profession is set out in *Bebb v Law Society* [1914] 1 CH 286—a case which largely mirrored the 'persons' cases that had come before it (e.g. a woman is not a person within the meaning of the *Solicitors Act* 1848 and Bebb therefore was properly refused admission to the preliminary examination held by the Law Society). Importantly, Gwyneth Bebb's unsuccessful attempt to enter the legal profession demonstrated the necessity of enabling legislation in the United Kingdom.[17] There is not space here to adequately recount the history of the *Sex Disqualification Act 1919* (UK)[18] (and its limitations) beyond acknowledging that it was a political compromise achieved after many years of feminist agitation, of which the Bebb case is one chapter. It is noteworthy that Bebb's story has been particularly significant in the United

17 This meant that Bebb had to wait for legislative action and this delay effectively denied her the opportunity to enter the legal profession as, sadly, Bebb died in childbirth. See (Auchmuty 2011: 227).

18 For a comprehensive analysis of the history of the Sex Disqualification (Removal) Act 1919 (UK) see Takayanagi (2020: 575). Explaining that the Act was a government replacement for a more radical private members bill, and therefore represented a compromise, Takayanagi (2020: 575) notes that 'the two radical clauses on the franchise and woman peers were lost' and 'it removed barriers rather than actively giving women rights.'

Kingdom taking on an important symbolic role in accounts of women and the law. Writing about how the Bebb case (and its aftermath) has been depicted in traditional historical accounts 'as a reform handed down by a benevolent legislature to an unresisting profession at the due time', Auchmuty (2011: 229) emphasised the ways in which this interpretation of the past diminishes the reality of women's experiences:

> Such interpretations paint institutions in the best possible light, as responsive to social change and capable of reforming themselves from within; they excuse the grudging and belated nature of the response and, crucially, they minimise—if possible, deny—any feminist agency in bringing about reform.

In New South Wales (one of the more recalcitrant Australian states) the passage of *Women's Legal Status Act 1918* (NSW) removed sex as a disqualification for admission as a barrister, solicitor, appointment as a judge, election as a Member of the Legislative Assembly or Lord Mayor (or councillor). Some 16 years earlier Ada Evans was the first woman law graduate in Australia—she graduated from Sydney University in 1902 but admission to the legal profession was denied to her. Evans continued to agitate for admission but had been advised that no precedent existed for women's admission not least because 'that was not what happened in London' (cited in Beazley 2018a).[19] Certainly, at first glance the passage of enabling legislation in New South Wales potentially paints the legislature in a more positive light than the legal profession itself. The tenor of the parliamentary debate indicates support for the bill-partially in acknowledgment of the fact that it was justified by suffrage, and partially because there was a sense that the bill was harmless (in the sense that it would not disrupt the existing gender regime). Yet there remained a strong sentiment that women's proper place was in the private rather than public sphere. As Dr Nash put it 'the atmosphere of the courts *would not be very congenial to those who are to be the mothers of the nation*, and who ought to be the best women in the State'.[20] Specifically addressing concerns that the bill did not simply allow women to enter the legal profession, but also permitted women to enter parliament and serve as judges, one speaker sought to downplay its practical significance,

19 At every turn Evans was not welcome—the Dean of Law at Sydney University made no secret of the fact that he thought she did not belong and it was said that 'every judge in Sydney was opposed to her admission'. Evans, then, had to wait for legislative action by which time she had decided not to pursue a career in the law owing to the lengthy delay since the conferral of her degree. The dogged resistance to women's admission to the legal profession has been examined elsewhere, both generally and specifically in relation to Evans' attempts to enter the profession (see Thornton 1996; Bell 2018, Beazley 2018a).

20 New South Wales, Legislative Assembly, Parliamentary Debates (Hansard), 5 December 1918 at 3464 (the Hon Dr Nash). Emphasis my own.

arguing, 'I think the bill is a perfectly harmless one. I believe that because it emanated in a spirit of spurious chivalry it over- reached itself.'[21] It was harmless then, in the sense that it was not thought that it would disrupt men's monopoly in the legal and political spheres because 'the social and economic pressures which largely kept women in the home were not about to give way in the face of a change to their status at law' (Bell 2018: 19–20).

The recent centenary of these enabling acts (specifically in NSW in 2018 and in the UK in 2019) has sparked renewed interest in this chapter of history, generating inevitable introspection about the trials and triumphs of the past 100 years. The alleged incongruity between femininity and the practise of law was noted by Justice Virginia Bell (2018: 29) in a speech reflecting on the centenary of the *Women's Legal Status Act 1918* (NSW), where she noted that 'the notion that as a woman lawyer you were at risk of losing your femininity—if you did not take steps to keep a pretty steady grip on it' still had currency when she commenced her law studies in 1969. If the notion of the woman lawyer was disruptive to the masculine norm early last century, then the notion of the woman judge was simply preposterous. As Bell (2018: 27) explained, the fact that the enabling legislation did not prohibit women from being appointed as judges, but expressly prohibited women from serving as jurors, speaks[22] to a mindset that simply could not conceptualise women as legally authoritative:

> The prospect of women jurors was threatening on two fronts: it would take women away from their household responsibilities; and, perhaps more troubling, it would empower them to sit in judgment on men. While the Women's Legal Status Act permitted women to be appointed as judges, it can hardly be thought that anyone who supported it entertained the least notion that a woman would be appointed as a judge. And they were right. No woman was appointed as a judge in New South Wales until the appointment of Jane Mathews to the District Court in 1980.

Certainly, the removal of formal barriers to women's legal admission (itself, of course, a necessary precondition to women's access to legal power and authority within Australia's legal system), did not dislodge the idea that the law (and indeed the public sphere) was "a man's game." As Margaret Beazley (2018b: 107) (first woman President of the New South Wales Court of Appeal)

21 New South Wales, Legislative Assembly, Parliamentary Debates (Hansard), 5 December 1918, at 3470 (The Hon J Lane Mullins)

22 Although Bell notes that this was a deliberate omission in NSW, in other jurisdictions enabling legislation also saw women permitted to serve as jurors see e.g. *The Sex Disqualification Removal Act 1919* (UK). The present point however is that despite the removal of the formal exclusion to women's entry into the legal profession, there was generally a very considerable lag between the removal of these formal barriers and women's access to authority at the peak of the profession.

reflected in her speech marking the centenary of *Women's Legal Status Act 1918* (NSW):

> although women had been granted the right to practise, their acceptance into the profession was painfully slow. Up to half a century later, the prevailing attitude throughout the 1960s and 1970s remained that law was not "a woman's game".

In a speech on the same topic, Beazley noted that concerns about the ways in which women's entry into this masculine domain would diminish their femininity have been longstanding. As evidence of this concern she referenced an article published in the *Sydney Morning Herald* in 1921 which suggested that women's appointment as justices of the peace represented a 'further stage in the insidious process of "unsexing"' (cited in Beazley 2018a: 14). To 'unsex' in this context reflects a concern that women would lose their femininity – that the practise of law was antipathetic to the feminine, or put another way, that the law was properly a masculine pursuit. Giving some insight into what Backhouse (2003) termed the 'chilly climate' faced by women in the legal profession Beazley (2018a: 16) recounted an example which spoke to the resilience of this kind of thinking:

> In 2002, Justice Roderick Meagher of the Court of Appeal drew the ire of Mary Gaudron, and others, when he told Good Weekend Magazine that the current crop of female barristers were "hopeless". He also referred in that article to "hairy-legged lesbians", and lamented that court corridors were now "thronged with unmarried mothers and abused children, people who are stoned, or were hatched in bottles, or have been raped or cloned".

In this story, we see that the ascension of *some* women within the profession has not necessarily negated the perception that the legal profession is the proper domain of men – indeed, it has sometimes amplified these sentiments generating a particularly pernicious backlash.

To the extent that triumph means succeeding on equal terms with men as measured by access to legal and political authority, the last century has seen slow but nonetheless noteworthy gains for women. As tends to be customary at these kind of events, in her speech, Beazley noted the various 'firsts'[23] both at the state level (including her own historic role in comprising the first all-

23 There is not space here to note all of the women 'firsts', I note that Dame Roma Mitchell was the first woman to be appointed as a judge of an Australian Court. She was appointed to the Supreme Court of South Australia in 1965. For a more comprehensive account of trailblazing women lawyers in Australia see the First Hundred Years, Timeline, at https://first100years.com.au/about-us/timeline.

woman bench in Australia)[24] and at the Commonwealth level including Mary Gaudron's appointment as first woman on High Court and Susan Kiefel's appointment as the first woman Chief Justice. Women's elevation to the highest levels of judicial authority (perhaps the most visible 'letting in'), reinforces a narrative of progress. Reflecting this sentiment, Beazley (2018b: 108) observed:

> We have come a long way since 1973, when an article was published in the *Sydney Morning Herald* which referred to the following remark made by an unidentified "distinguished law lord" in the United Kingdom: "[s]ome day a woman will be appointed to the Bench. By that time, thank God, I will be dead".

The unidentified Law Lord's commentary was prescient on at least one front. Women judges now sit at the peak of the judiciaries in Australia, Canada, New Zealand, the United States and United Kingdom.[25] More pointedly, *multiple* women judges sit on each of those Courts, and in some instances serve (or have recently served) as Chief Justice or President. As Beazley concluded in her speech, on one hand, women have certainly come along way, at least measured against the history of formal exclusion.

Yet, there is a certain danger in how these stories are told insofar as individual success has the potential to obscure the wider institutional picture. Underscored by a liberal progressive ethos, there is temptation to leave this foundational exclusion of women as something confined to the far off and distant past. But how we understand that past, and how we tell those stories, has important implications for understanding the present. As Rackley and Auchmuty (2019: 9) explained in their book celebrating *Women's Legal Landmarks in the UK and Ireland*, focusing on Gwyneth Bebb's case, for example, reflects and reproduces a particular hierarchy of legal knowledge by fixating on a legal source given that 'legal scholars are infamous for relying on legal sources and ignoring or dismissing extra-legal ones'. In so doing, the story is potentially made too much about Bebb as an individual and heroine, thus taking away

24 As Beazley (2018b: 108) noted in a piece published in Judicial Officer's Bulletin which largely drew on her 100 Years of Women in the Law Speech, '1999 marked the first time an all-female bench sat in an Australian court and, it is understood, in the common law world, when Justices Virginia Bell, Carolyn Simpson and myself sat in the NSW Court of Criminal Appeal'.

25 This list is illustrative rather than exhaustive—the examples share commonalties of history as outlined above. However, see Schultz and Shaw (2003) for an analysis of not only the common law world, but also the civic law world (including Germany, Netherlands, Poland, Finland, France, Italy, Brazil, South Korea and Japan). While their edited collection predates a number of key milestones for women in the legal profession, its breadth provides important insights into how women are situated in civil and common law legal systems across the world. For more recent analysis of the politics of gender parity (specifically in Africa) see Dawuni and Bauer (2015).

from the *real* story. The real story is about the troubling persistence of a particular attitude underpinning masculinist legal systems: that women are not really legal persons and not really 'up to it'.

This thinking persisted long after the formal barriers to women's exclusion were removed. Indeed, it continues to exist in the present day and this book seeks to contribute to our understanding of this thinking. As we know, women's entry into masculine domains does not necessarily disrupt or dislodge the existing gender regime. The purpose of this chapter was to set out a brief history of Australia's constitutional framework and to demonstrate how women have been situated within in it (and indeed, its wider legal system). Women were excluded from building these foundational legal and political institutions and this in turn meant that their concerns and perspectives were not reflected or represented. Subsequently, this meant that women were not envisaged as exercising authority within these legal and political institutions. Women's exclusion was literally woven into the fabric of Australia's legal and political institutions. As I will examine in the chapters that follow, this is not to be dismissed as some artefact of history, but rather continues to shape the wider constitutional framework from (gendered) conceptualisations of who the judge is to the very understanding of the substance of law. This is evident in the politics of judicial appointment in Australia, as I will examine in the next chapter. The formal rules are gender neutral (insofar as they are silent on gender) and yet informal rules have continued to reinforce a masculine regime.

Chapter 2

Jobs for the girls

Judicial appointments to the High Court of Australia and the politics of merit[1]

For more than 80 years the High Court of Australia remained the exclusive preserve of men. Although women were only formally excluded from the practise of law for a comparatively short period, the barriers to their advancement persevered. As the previous chapter demonstrated, women were never intended to exercise authority at the peak of Australia's legal and political institutions, and this is reflected in the troubling persistence of a particular attitude underpinning masculinist legal systems: that women are not really up to exercising legal authority. In this chapter I examine the politics of gender inclusion when it comes to the High Court of Australia, arguing that the conditions of joining the institution have upheld the masculine regime. Though the conditions of entry are arguably gender neutral on their face (particularly when it comes to the 'formal' rules for admission), the 'informal' rules (specifically the framing and of notions of both merit and diversity) paint a decidedly different picture.

The value of diversity in judicial appointments has been acknowledged in various contexts[2] but has been absent from the political rhetoric which has attended the appointment of women judges. Despite the fact that women judges have been appointed to the High Court in more recent years with what could almost be described as a degree of regularity, their appointments have largely been framed as happy coincidences rather than as part of any commitment to securing a more diverse judiciary. These appointments have not been couched in terms of the difference women judges might make, or even less controversially, in terms of increasing the diversity of the membership of the

1 This chapter draws on material and arguments presented in a much shorter piece published as McLoughlin, K. 2015a. 'The politics of gender diversity on the High Court of Australia'. *Alternative Law Journal*.40 (3): 165–170, copyright © 2015 by Sage UK

Reprinted by Permission of SAGE Publications, Ltd.

2 See 'Introduction' to this book for a summary of these arguments. My interest in this chapter is not in reasserting the various arguments in favour of judicial diversity, but rather in demonstrating how the reluctance to reform these processes and the manner in which notions of diversity and merit are cast by decision-makers serves to uphold a masculinist gender order.

DOI: 10.4324/9780429288531-3

High Court. The ad hoc appointment of women judges over almost three decades has sometimes involved an appeal to merit, but it has never involved any explicit statement from those making the appointment about the importance of gender diversity (or indeed diversity more broadly) in judicial appointments. Even implicitly, this unfortunately suggests that gender considerations are somehow illegitimate and consequently continues to reinforce the gender regime.

In Australia announcements of the appointments of women judges to the High Court generate a discourse that centres on merit either on behalf of those making the appointment or in the wider commentary around it. This is in contrast to the appointment of eminent men, whose suitability is similarly acknowledged, but usually without an appeal, or even an allusion, to the terminology of merit, though their gender is often a taken for granted norm. Where women appointees are concerned, at least from the perspective of those making the announcement, merit discourse steers carefully away from linking their gender to the job. This differential commentary suggests that different standards are at play, even on the part of those making the appointment. If gender equity has really arrived then why is it necessary to couch women's appointments in terms of merit whereas the appointment of men rarely occasions a consideration of it?

Although this chapter invokes examples of women's appointments to demonstrate a gendered merit discourse— the issue is gendered beyond the notion that questions of merit are more likely to arise when women are appointed. Of course, it is not the case that men's merit never enters discourses of judicial appointment—it is that *men* have historically been the standard bearers of merit, making decisions about what it entails, and crucially, for most of our history, deciding who our judges should be. The conditions of entry have historically disadvantaged women (and by implication advantaged men), and the reluctance to reform these conditions of entry needs to be understood against this backdrop. Indeed, as I will demonstrate in this chapter, the reluctance to reform the existing approaches to High Court judicial appointment practices (which might enhance transparency and give substance to what is meant by 'merit' through the publication of a clear selection criteria) demonstrates a particularly dogged degree of commitment to upholding the gendered status quo. It is not only the notion that what counts are meritorious is determined by those already in power, it is that women are more likely to have to contend with questions about their lack of merit or 'token' status.

For instance, the appointment of the first woman to the High Court, Mary Gaudron, occurred at a time when two vacancies arose more or less at the same time. This made it possible for the Prime Minister, Bob Hawke, to appoint a woman without making it appear as if he was pandering to special interests, which in Australia meant the so-called 'femocrat lobby' (Eisenstein 1996; Sawer 1990). It might be argued that the appointment had more to do with political expediency than with an active pursuit of gender equity. Appointed at the same time as Justice Toohey, Justice Gaudron's appointment was said to be the more controversial of the two (see P. Burton 2010: 255). Anonymous commentary published in the legal periodical, *Justinian*, criticised Justice Gaudron's appointment, noting that 'academic distinction alone cannot make a practitioner strong in merit' (cited in P. Burton 2010: 258). The columnist reasoned that her 'melancholy of sins of omission and commission as well as better claims of other candidates' were all matters which should have counted against her appointment. Although the Labor affiliations of both appointees were criticised at the time, Prime Minister Hawke was called upon to deny that Gaudron's was a 'tokenistic' appointment. Hawke responded to these calls arguing, 'Mary Gaudron is not a token appointment to the High Court. She won the University Medal [in law] and that is a very considerable achievement' (Hawke cited in Steketee 1986: 3).

One does not need to look too far to find more recent examples of negative ways of framing a (woman) judicial appointee's gender, and hence to place in question her suitability for the job. A similar sentiment was expressed when the appointment of Justice Virginia Bell shifted the gender balance on the High Court to almost equal. One conservative commentator was moved to suggest that 'when the imagery of jobs for the girls starts flying around, and merit appears to be a secondary consideration, the consequences are unedifying for all' (Albrechtsen 2008). Such comments illustrate how political and ideological adversaries denigrate an opponent's judicial appointment by suggesting that their appointment must have been motivated by some illegitimate reason rather than that they are appropriately qualified to take up the appointment. These examples, albeit isolated and very specific, show how the rhetoric of merit is deployed, implicitly or otherwise, to intimate that women judges have been appointed without the requisite level of merit.[3] This thereby serves to not only undermine the legitimacy and authority of women appointed to the judiciary but it also reinforces a masculine gender regime about who counts as a legal knower. Perhaps more insidiously—precisely because it seems so innocuous—is the refusal to engage with diversity as a public good.

The chapter begins by examining briefly the basic legal framework that guides the appointment process. This is undertaken in the context of a discussion of the various arguments calling for amendments to the appointment process with a view to improving diversity on the bench. Within these arguments there is a continued insistence that appointments be made on the basis of merit. It is the taken for granted discourse that informs the judicial appointment

3 It needs to be stressed that for the purposes of this chapter the focus is not upon interrogating the concept of 'merit' as such (i.e. *what* constitutes merit) but rather with examining *how* it is deployed within the various views announcing, denouncing, or commenting on the qualities and qualifications of the judicial appointments. Nor is this chapter concerned with assessing whether women, or for that matter, men, judges were sufficiently meritorious to warrant their appointment.

process. This is a necessary backdrop for understanding how the rhetoric of merit envelopes judicial appointments in Australia. The next section examines the announcements of the Australian Attorney-General of the day (or where relevant, the Prime Minister) concerning the appointment of the Justices serving on the Court in 2014 and those beyond. The lack of transparency around appointment processes means that the political rhetoric surrounding the announcements of judicial appointments is especially significant for those of us seeking to understand how diversity is enacted and represented. There is nothing which legally compels the government to consider notions of diversity in making these historic appointments. Nor is there anything which compels the government to explain publicly their motivations for making the appointment. The announcement of an appointment to judicial office nonetheless serves as a useful site of analysis as it is at this point that the decision maker assumedly (especially in a democratic context) makes some attempt to justify his or her decision, and the substance and tone of that conversation literally speaks volumes. Although this chapter is primarily concerned with the politics of merit in these announcements, it also considers the commentary offered by those seeking to shape public perceptions of the appropriateness of the appointment. The purpose of considering this material is not to review every statement made at the time, but rather to identify the merit-related discourse around appointments where it existed.

The 'selling' of the judicial appointee on gendered lines delivers the unsurprising news that judicial diversity is not yet a norm that passes without comment. The core argument to emerge in part three of this chapter is that the deployment of merit as either a criterion or explanatory adjective (or both) in the public and political discourse surrounding the judicial appointments of women is a gendered process that serves to reinforce the gender regime on the Court. The way that notions of gender, difference and merit interact in these important political announcements is indicative of the way that messages about difference, gender and diversity are being received and transmitted by the politically powerful.

The (gendered) politics of judicial appointments

In Australia, the government of the day faces few statutory constraints when it comes to making appointments to the High Court. In fact, the Australian Constitution provides little direction regarding appointment processes beyond specifying that Justices of the High Court '(i) shall be appointed by the Governor General in Council.'[4] Slightly more guidance is found in the *High Court of Australia Act 1979* (Cth), which provides (see sections 6 and 7) that an appointee must be a judge or enrolled as a legal practitioner for more than 5 years and that the Attorney-General shall consult with state Attorneys-

4 *Commonwealth Constitution* s 72.

General.[5] In practice, the appointment is generally made by the government of the day with the Attorney-General directing the process in most cases and presenting a nominee to Cabinet. Should Cabinet accept the nominee, the person is then formally recommended for appointment to the Governor-General.[6]

Calls to reform High Court appointment practices, in order to improve not only diversity but also transparency and accountability, are certainly not new (see e.g. Williams 2008; Winterton 1987). As Hobbs (2015: 13) argued, the discretionary powers afforded to Australian Attorneys-General in making these appointments 'is becoming increasingly difficult to maintain,' particularly in light of measures to enhance transparency elsewhere in the world. Attempts to reform these processes have had limited measure of success. Measures implemented by Attorney-General McClelland[7] in 2008 to improve transparency in Federal Court appointments were abandoned by the Coalition government upon their election in 2013. McClelland's reforms included the requirement that vacancies be advertised, the introduction of publicly available selection criteria for appointments and the use of advisory panels to make recommendations. As Handsley and Lynch (2015: 199) point out, promoting diversity was not embedded in these reforms in any case, noting that 'McClelland was candid about his interest in promoting diversity but refrained from its direct inclusion in the design of the appointments model.' Importantly, the High Court was insulated from these reforms, a decision that was justified on the basis of questionable justifications (that appointees would be drawn from inferior Courts and that the High Court 'enjoys a different status to other Federal Courts') (see Handsley and Lynch 2015: 198).[8] The fact that these reforms were never intended to extend to the High Court (and the subsequent abandonment of reforms in any case) demonstrates a dogged commitment to the status quo in determining the conditions for entry into the peak of Australia's judiciary.

Some scholars have called for more significant reforms to judicial appointment practices to specifically address the current situation and disrupt the status quo. For instance, Rubenstein (2014a) has suggested that at any given time, the High Court should be comprised of at least 40 per cent of either gender.[9] Of course, quotas are not the only means of achieving diversity. As Lynch (cited in

5 *High Court of Australia Act 1979* (Cth) ss 6–7.

6 For a discussion of the process see Campbell and Lee (2001: 76).

7 See Robert McClelland's (2008d) Speech at the Bar Association Conference, titled, 'Judicial Appointments Forum'.

8 Querying the High Court's exceptionalism in this respect Handsley and Lynch (2015: 198) argued that in 'the absence of any clearer explanation, the particular exclusions from the McClelland reforms suggest an attitude that there is something slightly undignified about nominating oneself for high office or the prospect of transparent processes being applied to highly visible courts with few members.'

9 Noting that this suggestion casts gender as a binary, it would be possible of course to reframe this kind of quota to stipulate that the Court should not be comprised of more than 40 per cent of a particular gender at a given time.

Nelson 2015) has argued, 'one way to create a more representative judiciary is to develop clear and articulated processes of judicial appointment that express diversity as "an aspiration underpinning those processes"'. In demonstrating that Australian High Court appointment practices[10] have failed to keep in step with developments elsewhere, Hobbs cited criteria in other jurisdictions such as the United Kingdom, Canada and New Zealand which make explicit that certain matters (e.g., gender, race, ethnicity, linguistic background and so on) might be considered as part of the appointment process.

Calls to reform judicial appointment practices were again renewed in 2020 in response to allegations that Dyson Heydon had sexually harassed legal associates during his time as a Justice on the High Court of Australia. In an open letter to Attorney-General Christian Porter more than 500 legal women[11] called for reforms to how Australia appoints and disciplines its judges (Appleby et al. 2020). The letter set out proposed reforms to the process of judicial appointments to 'increase transparency and promote the independence, quality and diversity of the judiciary.' It argued that 'reforms must be targeted to select candidates that will bring not just excellent legal skills to the office, but also the highest personal integrity, and contribute to greater diversity in the senior ranks of the profession'. Amongst the key principles proposed in this letter were the appointment of an independent body[12] to advise the government in its role in judicial appointments (the body's function would be to advertise widely for judicial vacancies, and to shortlist candidates who are suitable for appointment, from whom among the government may select). Importantly, shortlisting would occur against publicly available criteria and must include legal knowledge, skill and expertise in addition to essential personal qualities (e.g. integrity and good character). It was further proposed that the value of diversity in judicial appointments should also be respected in formulating criteria. Through

10 Australian Courts lower in the judicial hierarchy have adopted reforms to appointment practices which have seen the adoption of more transparent practices—although they vary between jurisdictions; examples include published selection criteria, provision to express interest, and interviews with candidates. For further discussion of reforms to judicial appointment practices, see Sackville (2005).

11 I note that I was a signatory to this letter.

12 In some key respects the model proposed in this letter modelled the Judicial Appointments Commission (JAC) in the United Kingdom. I acknowledge that the JAC has not been without its detractors in terms of its effectiveness in securing a more diverse judiciary (see Gee and Rackley 2018). An examination of the strengths and limitations of the JAC model is beyond the scope of this chapter although I note that I have elsewhere engaged with this issue (see McLoughlin and Williams 2019), arguing that when it comes to reforming appointment practices in Australia, the fundamental issue isn't necessarily the executive having the power to make these decisions, the issue is the unfettered executive discretion and lack of accountability. In any case, the point I wish to press for present circumstances is the lack of engagement from the Government with this proposal or about reforms designed to enhanced diversity, transparency and accountability in judicial appointment processes.

his media office Attorney-General Porter expressed open-mindedness about a federal judicial commission to handle complaints in relation to the federal judiciary but did not comment on the proposed reforms to judicial appointment processes.[13]

It is clear that political expediency has meant that there has been some political currency in adopting more inclusive appointment practices even in the face of ongoing reluctance to implement formal reforms. Taking into account the powerful political imperatives at play in making High Court appointments, it is perhaps unsurprising that those appointments deemed to be overtly political are arguably most likely to attract criticism. Curiously, given the breadth of discretionary power afforded to the Government of the day, High Court appointments have remained relatively uncontroversial for the most part. The controversies surrounding the appointments of Justice Murphy and Chief Justice Barwick, to cite just two examples, have been well documented[14] and point to the inherent dangers of allowing political imperatives to direct the appointment process. Naturally, where appointments are made along seemingly political lines this will often draw out political adversaries to criticise the appointment on these grounds.

The appointment of the now retired Justice Heydon by the then Howard Government led then Shadow Minister for Population and Immigration, Julia Gillard (2003) to claim that the appointment of Dyson Heydon and, before him, Ian Callinan, evidenced 'a ruthless stacking of public bodies'. Heydon's appointment also raised the issue of gender because he was replacing the first and, at that time, only woman member of the High Court, Justice Mary Gaudron. Thus commentators Ackland (2002), Rubenstein (2002) and Crabb (2003) all pointed to the homogeneous composition of the Court: 'same city, same gender, same club, now the same Court' (Ackland 2002: 15), and 'the

13 Email from Professor Gabrielle Appleby on file with the author.

14 Lionel Murphy was serving as the Commonwealth Attorney-General when he was appointed as a justice of the High Court of Australia in 1975 by the then Prime Minister, Gough Whitlam. Justice Murphy's appointment was seen as a controversial not least because it was the first time a serving Labor politician had been appointed directly to the Court since the appointment of H.V Evatt in 1931. The circumstances of Justice Murphy's appointment and the controversy surrounding his conviction (and subsequent acquittal) of charges relating to an attempt pervert the course of justice are examined in detail in Hocking (1997). Similarly, Chief Justice Garfield Barwick served as the Commonwealth Attorney-General before his appointment to the High Court in 1964. Chief Justice Barwick's affiliations with the Liberal Party of Australia came under close scrutiny when, in 1975, while still serving as Chief Justice of the High Court of Australia he advised the Governor-General, Sir John Kerr, about the constitutionality of dismissing Prime Minister Gough Whitlam on the basis that he declined to call an election when he was unable to obtain supply (e.g. pass the necessary appropriation bills to finance government expenditure). A comprehensive account of these events is provided in Galligan (1987).

Court's traditional constitution was restored—blokes on bench, women taking notes' (Crabb 2003: 8).

Hence 'merit' entered into the discourses surrounding Justice Heydon's appointment but more as a secondary issue. In relation to Justice Heydon's appointment, Rubenstein's (2002) comments shifted the focus to include merit, though not as a criticism:

> [W]hen male politicians gaze at the available gene pool of potential High Court appointees, they only see reflections of themselves, and what they understand as depictions of merit.

The contested nature of merit was also seized upon in two letters written to *The Age* in response to Heydon's appointment. Melbourne Barrister, Michael Gronow (2002) described him as someone who has the 'intellectual and personal qualities required to be a first-class High Court judge' but nonetheless questioned the extent to which such appointments could be said to be made on merit alone:

> Believing that appointments are made on merit alone would mean accepting that five-sevenths of Australia's legal merits live in NSW, and all are to be found in one sex and race.

Legal academic Beth Gaze's (2002) letter published the same day noted that it 'appears that merit is hard to see when it comes in a female body' and that using this term (merit) to validate a choice 'should not be obscured by mystical use of language'. The point here is that none of the responses to Justice Heydon's or any of the other appointments suggested that unmeritorious appointments had been made, but rather, that the concept of merit was not self-evident, especially as it seemed to be synonymous with either being a man or a resident of the state of New South Wales.

In recent times, allegations of 'gender politics' have been levelled at decision-makers who have appointed women to judicial roles in lower court jurisdictions. What is significant about invoking claims of 'gender politics' is it goes further than suggesting that the government has appointed an ideological crony and is an even greater criticism which suggests that appointments have been made without the requisite level of merit. For example, barrister, Ian Spry (2004: 59) asserted that in recent judicial appointments 'there have been departures from the merit principle' because of the 'tendency of Labor governments to appoint unsuitable female judges, often at the insistence of feminists.'

According to Spry these departures from the merit principle mean that 'many of the female judges—there are some few exceptions—who sit in various Australian courts are there by reason of gender and lack the necessary abilities'. Yet he nowhere defines 'merit' or 'merit principle', leaving it to his readers to fill the discursive space with their own content. With astounding clarity Spry's commentary encourages the reader to conclude that many apparently unmeritorious women judges have been appointed. This kind of commentary denigrates the appropriateness of the appointment of a whole group of individuals (women), and in so doing asserts that the characteristics associated with 'real' merit are irreconcilable with being a woman. Spry's comments are illuminating even in their extremity because of the way in which he joins together the notion that women have been appointed 'at the insistence of feminists' and the notion that this has resulted in unmeritorious appointments. While it is certainly true that getting gender on the agenda was a key feminist agitation (see e.g. Eisenstein 1996; Sawer 1990), the idea that this has been at the expense of making meritorious or appropriate appointments completely disregards the conditions that the politically powerful appear to have attached to their sparse commitment to appoint women judges.

Indeed, a commitment to 'merit' based appointments has repeatedly been invoked in a response to concerns about existing approaches to judicial appointments. For example, shortly after the adoption of the McClelland reforms, the Senate Standing Committee on Legal and Constitutional Affairs completed its inquiry into *Australia's Judicial System and the Role of Judges* (2009). The terms of reference for this inquiry were relatively wide and considered 'procedures for appointment and method of termination of judges; terms of appointment, including the desirability of a compulsory retirement age, and the merit of full-time, part-time or other arrangements; the judicial complaints handling system; and jurisdictional issues' (2009: 6). For present purposes, the report's recommendation regarding High Court appointment processes is most relevant:

> The committee recommends that the process for appointments to the High Court should be principled and transparent. The committee recommends that the Attorney-General should adopt a process that includes advertising vacancies widely and should confirm that selection is based on merit and should detail the selection criteria that constitute merit for appointment to the High Court.
>
> (SSCL&CA 2009)

This report also concerned other federal courts and acknowledged the purported tension between merit and diversity. It was noted that the committee received 'extensive evidence about the importance of appointment based on merit and strongly supports this approach'. The Committee acknowledged that it received considerable evidence 'that appropriately encouraging diversity in judicial appointments is not inconsistent with the principle of merit selection.' Yet, the Committee's report framed its recommendations squarely around merit, declining the opportunity to include strategies for enhancing diversity.

The commitment to merit-based judicial appointments was also emphasised in an earlier report prepared in 1994 by the Australian Senate, titled, *Gender Bias and the Judiciary*. That report was commissioned to determine whether the negative publicity surrounding judicial comments in sexual assault cases was 'a proper reflection of a failure to understand gender issues by the judiciary' and to determine 'the appropriate response to any such failure'. For present purposes, the most pertinent of the Committee's (SSCL&CA 1994: 77) findings and recommendations were those directed towards improving the judicial appointment process in order to redress issues regarding gender bias. The inquiry found that part of the problem with the process was its lack of transparency. As a result, the Committee favoured establishing both a clear set of criteria and a judicial commission to assist in making the appointments. However, the Committee neglected to consider how the dominant narrative of merit might actually be working in ways that disadvantaged women. Given that this narrative had informed judicial appointments to the High Court for almost 100 years, the Committee did not see a need to question it. Indeed, it invoked the narrative's alter-ego and stated that 'non-meritorious appointments, or any semblance of tokenism' should be avoided (SSCL&CA 1994: 106). It endorsed existing practice concerning assumptions of merit and suggested that appointments based on merit should continue to occur, notwithstanding that it had found evidence to suggest that current appointment processes failed to measure up to reasonable standards of gender equality. The Committee's (SSCL&CA 1994: 105–106) own statistics indicated 'that the proportion of women appointed to the judiciary is nowhere near the proportion of women in the legal profession'.

In these Committee reports we see at least some acknowledgment of the need to give context and content to what it meant by 'merit' through the publication of selection criteria. Despite recommendations to provide clarity about what constitutes merit, these Committee reports have mostly eschewed engaging with the subjective and problematic nature of merit insofar as it potentially disadvantages women. Granted, by specifying the need to publish specific selection criteria these reports provide some level of critique of existing practices where there is no transparency. Importantly, others have sought to expose the limitations of 'merit' as a clarion call to address concerns about existing appointment practices. To this end, feminist legal scholars have explored the different treatment given to women judges in the judicial appointment process and in the general public discourse surrounding their appointments. Much of this work has involved an examination of the deployment of the unassailable concept of 'merit' in ways which act to exclude rather than include women (Thornton 2007; Hamilton 1995). Thornton in particular has pointed to the gendered nature of merit, arguing that what counts as meritorious is determined by those already in positions of power and privilege and that '[i]ts claim to produce an objective "best person" is a rhetorical claim designed to maintain the judiciary as a gendered regime' (Thornton 2007: 391). Thornton (2007: 391) argued that merit is essentially a masculinised concept and that a special appeal to merit is more often deployed in justifying the appointment of women judges. She further noted that concerns regarding a judge's capacity to engage in 'impartial' adjudication more commonly arise if the judge was a woman, or black or gay because such attributes are implicitly regarded as 'necessarily taint[ing] the adjudicative role and render the delivery of justice problematic' (Thornton 2007: 392). Nearly two decades earlier, the same point was being argued by Burton in the context of employment practices, which remains apposite for the practices surrounding judicial appointments. Burton (1988: 1, emphasis added) noted that 'merit is rarely defined' and argued that 'more often than *not*[,] attempts to define it emphasize what it is not, such as appointments based on patronage or favouritism or on a person's sex, race, marital status, or other criteria unrelated to job performance'. Prefiguring Thornton's point about power relations, Burton (1988: 1) argued that 'merit refers to a relationship between a person's qualities and those required for performance in particular positions'. She noted that the need to discuss and redefine merit stems from the way in which sex stereotypes have influenced decisions. In her view this meant that 'we [would] likely [...] be saddled with narrow and traditionally defined notions of merit' resulting in gendered regimes in the workplace, the judiciary no less than any other.

Certainly, elsewhere in the world, merit has taken on a particular significance in debates about reforms to judicial appointment practices. In a chapter length discussion about the strategic partnerships required between feminists and the administration in getting more women on the federal bench in the United States, Kenney (2013: 82) stressed that President Jimmy Carter's commitment to appoint more women to the judiciary was based on a firm commitment to merit based appointments. This, according to Kenney (2013: 82–83), was a radical shift in the language around appointments. Although President Carter did not appoint the first woman to the Supreme Court, his support for such an appointment, and his success in appointing women elsewhere in the judicial hierarchy was instrumental in getting women on the agenda. Carter emphasised merit as the guiding light in his introduction to the *Omnibus Judgeship Act* where he said that the Act 'will provide a test for the concept of merit selection' (Kenney 2013: 83).

Similarly, in response to debates about the importance of and benefits of judicial diversity, 'merit' has remained the absolute 'bedrock' of judicial appointments in the United Kingdom. As Malleson (2006: 140) argued, reflecting on the consistent rejection of affirmative action policies in order to enhance the diversity in judicial appointments in England and Wales, 'affirmative action is a radical development not because it threatens the merit principle but because it seeks to counter the weight traditionally given to power, similarity, and familiarity in determining what constitutes merit.' Rackley (2013: 192), acknowledging the (gendered) ways in which merit becomes distorted, has argued that the problem is not so much merit itself but 'how we have gone about interpreting, identifying and assessing merit'.

Former Australian High Court Justices Michael Kirby and Mary Gaudron have also commented on the subjective nature of merit in public speeches about women and the law. Kirby (2003) explained that when people insist that High Court appointments should only be made on merit 'they use that word in a different ways' and when some people speak of merit 'it simply means "merit" of the kind that produces persons just like themselves'. Gaudron (2000) similarly argued that merit is often invoked in ways which exclude rather than include women because 'the way in which debate turns to "merit" when but only when a woman is considered for a particular position' is really a manifestation of a 'belief that women are inferior and ought to be treated as such'.

Theoretical engagement with the conceptual and definitional limitations of merit in fields outside of the law is also useful in understanding how the rhetoric of merit can be used in exclusionary ways. Such rhetoric has been revealed as problematic in relation to employment in law schools and academia generally (Krefting 2003). There are large scale debates about merit (Posner 1990; cf Kennedy 1990) which began (in part at least) in the context of affirmative action in law school faculty hiring, but went on to traverse much larger philosophical ground in terms of our understandings of the limits of knowledge and objectivity (Farbert and Sherry 1995). Although radical constructivism sees no merit in the very concept of merit, it is of course possible to raise questions about the limitations of the term without pushing the argument that far.

In the context of discussions around the intersection between cultural capital and social mobility, Jewel (2012: 251) contends that the rhetoric of merit actually 'obscures how cultural disadvantage works'. In an attempt to underline the limitations of merit in improving social mobility, Jewel explained how Bourdieu's (1972) cultural theory neatly counters the American theory of the economic individualism, 'which posits that social outcomes are a result of individual hard work, innate talent and merit' (Jewel 2012: 251). Bourdieu's approach counters the theory of economic individualism by theorising that an individual's outcomes 'are bounded by the collective expectations internalized in her habitus and the amount of cultural capital she possesses' (Jewel 2012: 254). Further, Bourdieu's approach understands that misrecognition is rife in the merit narrative because people who do well in the given culture cannot see their own privilege or the role that it, rather than individual skills and education, have in attainment. Given the 'smoke and mirrors' capacity for the discourse of merit to conceal and explain away disadvantage or lack of success, it is not difficult to see that merit does heavy political and rhetorical lifting. It is clear that consciously or unconsciously, the discourse of merit can be invoked to produce and reproduce the gender regime.

It is telling that when the conversation turned to the need to appoint women judges, the answer offered by those in positions of power, at least initially, was that appointments should be made on merit. Leaving aside the fact that the insistence that appointments would be made on merit raises questions about patronage and cronyism that might have previously informed the process, it is revealing that merit is seen as a solution. We see here that merit is really a shorthand way of invoking a notion of difference. Granted, it is done in a context that is trying to advance women—but only insofar as women, or other minorities can fit into an existing paradigm of what it means to be qualified or meritorious. Pointing to merit is a useful way of making the problem about finding appropriate individuals rather than addressing the collective and structural disadvantage which may prevent women (and other minorities) from attaining the necessary cultural capital to be deemed meritorious. It could even be said that pointing to merit is really about applying the same old standards in an effort to get the same kind of people. The duality of difference is clearly made out in the rhetoric surrounding getting gender on the agenda. On the one hand, political decision-makers frame their (albeit very limited) discussions about gender and judicial appointments around representative diversity rather than *difference* because that kind of difference is too dangerous and destabilising. But, on the other hand, women's difference, manifested by the fact that they are *other* (i.e. not men) is highlighted by the merit discourse, as they are treated *as different* and *differently from* men.

While we are frequently reminded that merit must be the guiding principle in making all judicial appointments, discussions (and sometimes, doubts) about an appointee's merit are more likely to come to the fore when that appointee is a woman. It is also clear that placing gender on the appointment agenda has been a political process involving many tensions. This is likely the case as although successive governments seem to agree that appointing women to the bench is an appropriate goal, there is no consensus about *why* this is so and *how* this should be effected. These complexities are played out in the announcements of new judicial appointees. It is now time to turn to the discursive circuits of merit in the individual announcements of Australian High Court appointments.

Discourses of merit in High Court appointments

In what follows, I examine the public statements accompanying the appointments of the seven judges making up the High Court bench in late 2014. This bench is significant as it was the first to involve an almost-equal gender balance among the judges: Justices Susan Crennan, Susan Kiefel and Virginia Bell sat with Justices Kenneth Hayne, Stephen Gageler, Patrick Keane, and Chief Justice Robert French. What is interesting is that the appointments of the women to this landmark bench occasioned discourses about merit in a way that was absent for the men. Further, subsequent appointments (of Justices Gordon, Justice Nettle, the elevation of Chief Justice Kiefel and the appointment of Justice Edelman) confirm only too clearly a pattern of gendered discourse centring on 'merit' in relation to women appointees. Not all of these appointments led to controversy, but the appointments of the women resulted in some degree of controversy in that they occasioned a discourse about merit. This was the salient feature. When women were the subject of an appointment merit became an issue.

In terms of the appointment announcements made by the governments of the day, only two directly appealed to merit—those in relation to Justices Crennan and Kiefel. It is therefore not surprising that the term featured in wider discussions at the time. Since Justice Bell's appointment in 2009 meant that three women would be serving concurrently on the High Court, there had been public commentary about gender and merit. The idea of merit also arose in 2008 during speculation about who might be elevated to the position of Chief Justice (see Pelly 2008: 31–32). Prior to the announcement, journalist Michael Pelly (2008: 32) likened the search to a beauty pageant as he assessed the chances of the frontrunners: Robert French, James Spigelman, and Patrick Keane. Here he pointed to the highly subjective nature of merit:

> When the announcement is made on Gleeson's successor, it will be said that merit was the only consideration. Yet merit is a bit like beauty. It's in the eye of the beholder.

But merit was not really at issue. Even if difficult to pin down, its reality was simply assumed. However, things were different when gender, or more accurately, the status of being a new woman judge, featured in the process.

When the appointments of Justices Gageler, Hayne, and Bell, and Justice French to the position of Chief Justice, were announced, the relevant Attorney-General did not mention merit. Each was hailed for their experience and achievements during their careers. The announcement of Justice Hayne's appointment in 1997 emphasised his distinguished career as barrister and time as a Judge of the Victorian Supreme Court (Williams 1997). Chief Justice French was described on his elevation as 'well regarded across the legal profession' and 'respected for the clarity of his reasons and his ability to express the law in clear and concise terms' (McClelland 2008a). Justice Bell's appointment was accompanied by no mention of merit, but there was acknowledgment that she was a woman, and like that of most of the other announcements, emphasis was placed on her career and achievements (McClelland 2008b).

Two appointments to the Australian High Court were announced in 2012 by Attorney-General Nicola Roxon, the first woman to serve in that role. Neither announcement mentioned the word merit although both of the announcements reflected briefly on the stellar careers of the new appointees. In announcing the appointment of Justice Gageler, who was at the time the Commonwealth Solicitor-General, the Attorney-General described Gageler as 'a highly distinguished barrister' and predicted that he would fill his new role as a Justice of the High Court 'with distinction' (Roxon 2012a). Similarly, in announcing the appointment of Justice Keane only a few months later, the Attorney-General noted that 'Chief Justice Keane has served as Chief Justice of the Federal Court since March 2010. Prior to that he served as a Judge on the Court of Appeal, Supreme Court of Queensland, and was Solicitor-General for

Queensland for 13 years' (Roxon 2012b). Neither appointment was particularly controversial[15] and this is reflected in the brevity of the announcements and the simplicity of the messages therein. When eminent and obviously appropriate men judges are appointed in Australia little needs to be said about the matter and of course, it is taken for granted that they were appointed on the basis of merit rather than for some other, less legitimate, reason.

Conversely, the appointment of women has generated a merit discourse. When Justice Susan Crennan was appointed to the High Court the then Attorney-General, Philip Ruddock (2005a), was at pains from the outset to establish that the Howard Government's appointment was 'based upon one criteria (sic) and one criteria alone, and that is merit'. He even sought to define what merit meant, stating that it 'of course means legal excellence; a capacity for industry; a temperament suited to performance of the judicial function'. Even more curiously, Ruddock (2005a) appeared reluctant to acknowledge in any explicit way the gender of the appointee as he simply referred to Justice Crennan as 'the new judge' until almost the end of the announcement. While it is quite plausible that Ruddock (2005a) was simply trying to add to the suspense of such an announcement, this does not explain why the fact that Crennan was a woman was concealed for the bulk of the speech in ways that rendered his oral expression somewhat awkward. For example, rather than explaining that 'at the bar, *her* practise included,' he said:

> At the bar *the* practise included constitutional law; administrative law; criminal law; migration; intellectual property; trade practises; general commercial law and tax. And I think you can see that that's a very wide pedigree.
>
> (my emphasis)

15 In fact, in Roxon's relatively short tenure as Attorney-General, her judicial appointments were regarded by some commentators as one of her best achievements as Attorney-General. See for example: Chris Merritt (2013) where he describes her judicial appointments as her 'saving grace', perhaps a politically motivated comment but one that also could be revealing of a masculinist bias. But compare Handsley and Lynch's (2015: 213) argument that Roxon 'sent confusing signals about Labor's priorities in judicial appointments by repeatedly stressing her desire to draw on a much wider pool of candidates in order to diversify the senior judiciary and then, after making two squarely traditional appointments High Court in the form of Justices Keane and Gageler, falling back on unsatisfyingly generic claims about "merit". Significantly, Handsley and Lynch certainly do not suggest that Roxon's appointees lacked merit, or that these appointments might not have enhanced the diversity of High Court by some other reference (legal expertise or background for example), but rather, point out the issue is one of transparency. As they argued, the pertinent issue is that 'the public should be given a clear explanation as to how the Attorney-General has determined the identity of his or her "preferred" candidate.'

Interestingly, Ruddock made mention of the fact that the new appointment would mean that there would be 'two Victorian judges serving on the High Court of Australia'. It was not until the very end of his statement that Ruddock disclosed the identity of the new appointee, stating that he was delighted to announce that he would be recommending 'to His Excellency the Governor-General that Justice Susan Crennan be the 45th person appointed to the High Court since Federation' (Ruddock 2005a).

Responses were generally supportive. The Shadow Attorney-General at the time, Nicola Roxon (2005), issued a media release explicitly commending the appointment of a woman as cause for some celebration. She pointed to Justice Crennan's 'outstanding reputation as a barrister' and her 'long record of public service and a commitment to the legal profession'. Perhaps unsurprisingly, Roxon did not let slip the opportunity to score a political point at the expense of her counterpart. She noted that the 'absence of any women on the Court has been a longstanding embarrassment and an insult to the many female judges and lawyers who are clearly up to the job', and that she was pleased that the government had finally taken steps towards 'rectifying this omission'. Indeed, if Ruddock was conscious of 'rectifying this omission' he certainly did not say so. In response to a question from a journalist asking if he was 'pleased to be able to appoint a woman?', Ruddock (2005a) said 'I simply make the point I'm pleased to be able to appoint the best person for the job'. In response to a journalist asking him if he was annoyed that he would have to in some ways justify or explain or address the fact that Justice Crennan was a woman, Ruddock replied he was an advocate 'for non-gender based appointments' and that he did not think there should be any doubt that 'people are appointed on the basis of their ability'.

In 2007 the Howard Government appointed another woman to the High Court, Justice Susan Kiefel. At the press conference announcing this appointment, a journalist noted that this was 'an historic occasion' because this was the first time two women would be sitting on the bench and asked the Attorney-General, 'was her gender taken into consideration?' Ruddock (2007) denied that gender was a relevant consideration, stating that 'any suggestion that this appointment was to secure two female appointments would be quite wrong'. After pointing to her Honour's eminence and the fact that 'she is a woman of extraordinary attainment', Ruddock reassured the journalists that this appointment, like the appointment made two years prior, was made on the basis of merit alone:

> It is a factual matter that there are five male Judges and now there'll be two female Judges. But they are both people who were appointed on their merits, worthy of the appointment and a great credit to the profession.

In response to another question relating to 'her being a Queenslander replacing another Queenslander?' Ruddock did concede that he did 'look at these matters', but was quick to play down the relevance of her state of origin by again pointing to the fact that the decision 'was a merits based decision'. Given that the Howard Government had appointed two women to the High Court in such a short space of time, its approach to announcing these appointments appeared cognisant of the possibility that it may face similar castigation to that which was leveled at Labor Governments for their alleged tendency 'to appoint unsuitable female judges, often at the instance of feminists' (Spry 2004: 92). Ruddock's zealous appeal to the concept of merit in announcing these appointments suggests that this was the Government's strategy in signaling to their supporters that although they were appointing a woman, there was no tokenism or 'progressive' or 'gender' politics at play and that they could be relied upon to appoint suitable candidates.

Others were less convinced that gender had been an irrelevant factor in Justice Kiefel's appointment. Columnist Michael Pelly (2007: 11) was explicit that her Honour had two things in her favour: 'she is female and a Queenslander.' Somewhat ironically, given Ruddock's disinclination to accept that gender played any role in his decision to appoint either of the women, Pelly (2007: 11) reasoned that 'Philip Ruddock has long been a promoter of women in senior judicial roles and it is significant that his only two appointments to the High Court as Attorney-General have been women'. Similarly, for columnist Janet Albrechtsen (2007: 14) gender was an issue and her commentary suggests that she did not accept the Howard Government's siren call to their supporters or that they had simply appointed on the basis of merit rather than actively pursuing gender equity. She damned the appointment with faint praise when she noted that Kiefel's elevation occasioned 'many reasons to celebrate' in a context in which she also outlined examples where women had been inappropriately appointed to judicial offices in ways that meant 'you face an extra hurdle these days if you are a middle-class, white, Anglo-Saxon man'.

In stark contrast to the announcements of the appointments of Crennan and Kiefel, the announcement of Justice Virginia Bell's appointment in late 2008 did not involve merit, nor did it shy away from the fact that she was a woman. Attorney-General McClelland (2008b, emphasis added) stated explicitly that 'Justice Bell will be the 48th person*, and the fourth woman*, appointed to the High Court since Federation' (my emphasis). McClelland pointed to Justice Bell's distinguished career history and noted her achievements: her position as a Judge of Appeal of the NSW Supreme Court, her time in practise as a Public Defender, as Counsel Assisting the Royal Commission into the NSW Police Service, and as a part-time Commissioner of the NSW Law Reform Commission. Consistent with the stance he had taken in announcing the appointment of Chief Justice French, McClelland made note of the 'Government's public commitment to extensive consultation' and referred to the many individuals he had consulted in making this appointment. Certainly, the Government's approach in announcing Justice Bell's appointment without appeal to the terminology of merit suggests that Rudd's Labor Government was not overly concerned about the political ramifications of such an appointment and nor was it deterred by earlier criticism such as that voiced by Spry in 2004.

However, for some the appointment of Justice Bell and the prospect of three women sitting on the High Court was clear evidence of 'gender politics' at play. Albrechtsen (2008) returned to the theme she had adopted in 2007 and reasoned that there 'are plenty of male members of the legal profession—on the bench and at the bar—of equal if not greater ability who are entitled to mumble that this is a deliberate gender-based appointment'. Indeed, Albrechtsen's comments in response to a Labor Government's appointment of a woman took on a vehemence that went beyond the veiled criticisms she had mounted at Justice Kiefel's appointment. She had no qualms in suggesting that Bell's appointment had not been made on the basis of merit, but rather stated that 'when the imagery of jobs for the girls start flying around, and merit appears to be a secondary consideration, the consequences are unedifying for all' (Albrechtsen 2008).

Since the Attorney-General saw no need to mention merit, it was then necessary for critics to insert it into the discourse about Bell's appointment. Not content merely to suggest that Justice Bell lacked the requisite level of merit, Albrechtsen also took issue with the fact that three women would now sit on the High Court. She asserted that this situation 'raises doubts about whether this was truly an appointment on merit' because this proportion was 'vastly in excess of the proportion women represent of the pool of judges and barristers from which High Court judges must be drawn'. It is not clear here whether Albrechtsen was mainly taking issue with what she regarded as Justice Bell's individual lack of merit, or whether she was inferring that finding three women of appropriate merit to sit on the High Court concurrently would be in the realms of the impossible. Either way, the inference was that women are appointed without possessing the appropriate levels of merit. Her views here echoed those of Spry's (2004) polemic of four years earlier concerning his belief that politicians playing 'gender politics' had diminished judicial appointments.

The gendered deployment of merit has continued in subsequent appointments after Justice Crennan's retirement brought an end to the near gender-balanced bench in 2014. Attorney-General George Brandis made only brief remarks to announce Justice Geoffrey Nettle's appointment, noting his 'brilliant' legal career but not answering questions or invoking the concept of merit. While other commentators (see e.g. Gans 2014) observed that Nettle's appointment would shift the gender dynamics of the High Court, Brandis instead emphasised the consensus on Nettle's suitability for the role:

> I can tell you that in consulting widely in relation to this appointment, Justice Nettle's name came up time and time again as a particularly eminent candidate for appointment to the High Court.
>
> (ABC online 2014)

Other commentators affirmed the absence of politics at play in the Abbott Government's appointment, with Lee (SMH 2014) reporting that 'it was a credit to the Attorney-General and the Coalition that they had chosen Justice Nettle purely on merit, rather than along political lines.'

In 2015 Attorney General George Brandis announced another appointment, this time of Justice Michelle Gordon to replace the retiring Justice Hayne. No obvious merit discourse attended the announcement but in a now familiar pattern, any explicit statement about diversity was avoided. The announcement was brief and focused on Gordon's 'distinguished' and 'widely recognised' career particularly in the area of commercial law (Brandis 2015a). The spousal connection (Michelle Gordon is married to Kenneth Hayne) was a useful rhetorical device for Brandis (2015a), who was able to join together notions of merit and gender without saying as much. He remarked, 'It would, of course, in this day and age, be outrageous for a person who was otherwise well-qualified for an appointment as Justice Gordon certainly is, to be disqualified on account of who they were married to'. This dispelled possible criticism (none which was forthcoming).

With Susan Kiefel's elevation to Chief Justice in 2017 there was nothing implicit about the recourse to merit. Echoing the framing of her appointment as a Justice of the High Court a decade earlier, Attorney General George Brandis (2016) pointed to Kiefel's suitability for the role on account that each step she had taken in her career was 'a step that she took on merit'. While this is discussed in further detail in Chapter 8, it is useful here to simply acknowledge the appeal to merit made in her elevation and the contrast with the appointment of Justice James Edelman made at the same time, which featured no such commentary. In announcing Edelman's appointment, Prime Minister Malcolm Turnbull (2016) deferred only to merit in response to questioning about the continuing lack of South Australian representation on the High Court, perhaps highlighting how 'merit' serves as a useful rhetorical tool that stands in for a meaningful explanation.

The gendered deployment of merit in judicial appointments and particularly the kind of commentary that surrounded the advent of the historic near-to-equal gender balance on the High Court bench goes further than simply admonishing politicised appointments. It denigrates the appropriateness of the appointment of a whole group of individuals (women), and in so doing asserts that the characteristics associated with 'real' merit are irreconcilable with being a woman. It is not the qualities, the professional merits, of any individual woman appointee that are at issue, but rather the merits of women as a group. In the hands of critics like Albrechtsen and Spry, merit is not really the issue; it is the means to discredit the perception that women occupying judicial positions is a norm that should warrant no particular comment. This kind of deployment of a merit discourse reproduces and reinforces the notion that women are not really up to, that legal authority is the proper preserve of men.

A masculinist meritocracy?

The arrival of women judges further reveals the difficulties in dislodging the long-ingrained imagery of the judge as a man (Rackley 2002). The conceptual difficulty in changing what we understand to be the gender of 'the judge' can, according to Thornton (1996: 201), be explained by the fact that the 'judicial enterprise is regarded as the quintessential locus of legal authority, a perception that is antipathetic to the feminine'. Similarly, Berns (1999: 202) has suggested that judgment remains explicitly 'male' and 'white' because the accoutrements associated with the judicial role, the very judicial robes and gown, 'superimpose something very close to a raceless and genderless persona upon the judge'. No doubt these issues are compounded when women judges are subject to assertions such as Albrechtsen's that Justice Bell's gender may have 'allow[ed] her to leap-frog a few chaps'.

It seems that de Beauvoir's (1997: 29) claims about the way that women are compelled to assume the status of 'other' still ring true. Given the gendered, disproportionate and disparate way in which an appeal to the terminology of merit is only deemed necessary when women are appointed to the High Court of Australia, combined with a tendency to raise questions about an appointee's merit only where the appointee happens to be a woman, it seems that women have thus far been unable to shift their categorisation as 'other' as far as legal authority is concerned. Diversionary tactics questioning the suitability of a whole group of appointees (women) serve to denigrate the public perception of the judiciary on dubious and unfounded grounds. Consciously or unconsciously, this focus on merit is really one of myriad ways that women's difference is emphasised to mark their otherness and reproduce traditional gender hierarchies as to who should possess the highest judicial authority.

The examples above are instructive insofar as they reveal a tendency for merit to take centre stage when women are appointed and to warrant barely a mention when men are appointed. The issue here is not that any of the appointees were unmeritorious. Rather, it is that 'merit,' given its central position in the rhetoric regarding the guiding principles for judicial appointment, is generally absent from the press releases concerning the appointment of men, and far more likely to feature when women are appointed. Save for the appointment of Chief Justice French, where some attempt was made to explain the reasons for appointment and the decision-making process, it is quite clear that the relevant Attorneys-General did not feel compelled to justify the government's ultimate decision or decision-making process in a thorough or extensive manner. In this sense, the lack of appeal to the terminology of merit in instances where men have been appointed reinforces Thornton's (2007: 402) argument that announcing that a 'Man "of merit" joins High Court' amounts to a tautology 'because masculinity is already a tacit criterion of judicial merit'. There may be a case for suggesting that the government was merely eager to avoid any suggestion that 'tokenism' was at play in a genuine attempt to emphasise the objective suitability of these appointments. Nonetheless, even if this was the rationale for the extensive appeal to the rhetoric of merit, it remains concerning and problematic that the government deems these kinds of justifications necessary (for whatever reason) when no such language or explanation was required in justifying the appointment of eminent men. Furthermore, it is also of note that media commentary (granted, primarily from a couple of particularly loud, critical voices) regarding the three women sitting on the bench in 2014 (the first almost equal gender balance) appointed to the High Court demonstrates a certain fixation on querying the motivations underpinning the decision to appoint women.

Granted, some commentary around judicial appointment processes, both in the replacement of Justice Gaudron with Justice Heydon, and in subsequent appointments outlined above, was driven by party-political point-scoring as in the case of Gillard (2003) or commenting on it (Ackland 2002; Crabb 2003). However, these criticisms were not concerned with undermining the appointee's personal characteristics or suggesting that the individual did not possess the requisite level of merit. In contrast, the criticisms of women appointments (albeit made by conservative commentators) not only suggested that these appointments were to placate the feminist left (Spry 2004; Albrechtsen 2008; 2007), they also either said or implied that the upshot of these appointments was that women were being appointed without the requisite levels of merit, and implied that such women exercised illegitimate judicial authority.

The political rhetoric of the announcements of judicial appointments is a significant site of analysis for those of us seeking to understand how diversity is enacted and peddled in democratic contexts. It is important to emphasise, notwithstanding the precarious nature of the term, that there is nothing wrong with purporting to make judicial appointments on merit. The difficulty is when merit is used in gendered ways. The reasons decision-makers frame their decisions in this language are not entirely clear but the implications which stem from this kind of political rhetoric are much easier to make out. The rhetoric of merit reinforces women's status as 'other' and as such, it can be (and has been) deployed in ways which serve to question and potentially erode women's legal authority. In examples discussed above, a discernible pattern can be detected regarding the gendered use of merit in the public discourse pervading judicial appointments. This is not to say that the appointment of men has come without criticism. However, it seems more likely that these criticisms are levelled at the government for making *a political* (or at least self-serving) appointment. Conversely, in situations where the appointment was not just deemed to be political, but apparently based on *gender politics*, we are far more likely to hear suggestions that the appointment was made on terms other than merit. This undue focus on merit unfortunately invites the (erroneous) inference that to be meritorious and a woman simultaneously either requires extensive explanation and justification, or is something of a contradiction in terms. Certainly, the Australian focus on merit may well be about appeasing critics who make it their business to deride what they regard as 'tokenistic' appointments.

Judicial announcements do heavy political lifting in terms of creating a narrative which serves the interests of both the party and the individual making the appointment. It is perhaps important here to acknowledge, and give context to, the broad ideological differences between the Liberal–National Coalition and the Labor Party regarding the appropriateness of measures to advance women's political participation. Although the gender politics (in terms of their policies concerning women and the prospects for women parliamentarians) of both major parties have oftentimes been problematic, it is noteworthy that the Labor Party formally supports affirmative action[16] in pre-selection for women, whereas the Liberal Party[17] does not (see McCann 2013: 12–13). Of course, there are important differences between political and judicial power and I do not suggest that any appointments to the High Court have been the result of such a policy. But the politics around the legitimacy of such measures in the legislative branch is salutary in that it illuminates the precarious and contested *value* of gender diversity within a wider masculinist gender order. The contested politics of gender diversity might then explain Attorney-General Ruddock's zealous appeal to the terminology of merit in announcing the appointments of Crennan and Kiefel as contrasted to Attorney-General McClelland's approach in announcing Bell's appointment.

In the current political space, notwithstanding the different views about the appropriateness of explicit measures to secure women's advancement in the legislative branch, when it comes to judicial appointments at the peak of Australia's judiciary, there seems to be little appetite for reform and limited space for a discussion about the importance or desirability of diversity in judicial appointments. This may well be a reflection of the anxiety about allegations of 'tokenism', which is not an unfounded fear given this exact allegation arose on the appointment of the Court's first woman judge and has routinely arisen in

16 The Australian Labor Party has adopted quotas since 1981, the most recent of which is a 40:40:20 quota system. Parliamentary Research Paper on quotas for women in Australia noted that '[t]his means that 40 per cent of seats held by Labor will be filled by women, and not less than 40 per cent by men. The remaining 20 per cent may be filled by candidates of either gender' (McCann 2013: 13). The views about quotas within the party ranged 'from concern about tokenism and preserving the concept of merit, to those who point to the results in the number of Labor women in parliament' (McCann 2013: 13).

17 Although 'the merit principle' is commonly invoked as an argument against measures to enhance women's representation within the Liberal Party, that is not to say that there is consensus regarding this issue. Liberal Senator, the Hon Judith Troeth (cited in McCann 2013: 13) argued '[i]f it's demeaning for women to have quotas, it's equally demeaning to sit in a Parliamentary party room for 20 years without seeing a progressive increase in the number of women members. As if those handful of women members who are there were the only "women of merit" who put themselves forward for preselection!'

similar iterations since. Rather, the focus seems to be on ensuring that the message conveyed by decision-makers is that gender has had nothing to do with its judicial appointments and all decisions were made within the neat and convenient little frame of reference we call merit. In this respect, the announcements are actually manifestations of the difficulties decision-makers have in dealing with difference at individual and collective institutional levels. The announcements reflect individual notions of being worthy or meritorious appointees and there is little space for discussions about the collective good that gender diversity may bring.

Granted, criticism about the way in which political rhetoric is complicit in re-producing gendered hierarchies and subversive notions of difference needs to be tempered with the reality of what have been clear gains for women. Space quite literally had to be made for women on the highest judicial benches simply because getting women into positions of judicial authority was a departure from the overtly gendered regimes of the past. In making this discursive space, the politically powerful have invoked notions of difference in ways that have been politically self-serving but have not always been particularly helpful insofar as diversity is concerned.

There is something of a chicken and egg scenario at play when it comes to diversity and appointment practices. It is not clear whether decision-makers steer clear of placing any emphasis on diversity because it is not currently a criterion for appointment, or because of an actual underlying view that diversity is an illegitimate consideration. In either case, it is clear that the relationship between diversity and merit needs to be recast. In part, this means beginning from the position that diversity is a public good which will improve rather than diminish the judiciary. Once we accept that a more diverse judiciary might result in a better judiciary 'we are able to say that diversity is an important factor in making judicial appointments while *at the same time* accepting the orthodoxy that appointments must be made on merit' (Rackley 2013: 194). This involves rejecting the false dichotomy between merit and diversity and seeking both, explicitly and unashamedly, in judicial appointments. Certainly, this false dichotomy is reflected in the formal institutional responses to calls to reform judicial appointment practices. It is significant that the relatively modest proposals for reform recommended by Parliamentary Committees (that did not seek to entrench enhancing diversity as goal underpinning appointments but instead simply advocated for published selection criteria) have not been adopted by either major political party in making appointments to the High Court. The conditions of entry (the 'rules') were crafted by men and for men and the ongoing commitment to an unarticulated notion of merit as the sole guiding principle in making these appointments reflects a persistent commitment to the (gendered) status quo. Similarly, the refusal to embed enhanced diversity as a goal underscoring judicial appointment processes likewise reflects a commitment to the prevailing gender regime.

As a matter of strategy one might argue that recent appointment practices on the High Court are working as women are now being appointed to it. But, in the just over 30 years since Mary Gaudron was appointed there have been eighteen appointments to the High Court and only six of them women. Recent appointment practices in the High Court show significant improvements in gender diversity, but experiences in the legislative and executive branches indicate that achieving diversity is by no means guaranteed.[18] Moreover, recent improvements to the gender balance of the High Court are something of an anomaly when gender diversity remains a real challenge in the Federal and State Courts.[19] Reforms at the peak of Australia's judiciary—especially given its visibility—might therefore be salutary in reforming judicial appointment practices elsewhere in Australia's judicial hierarchy. The slow and sometimes meandering gains in judicial diversity should not act as a disincentive for adopting formal reforms. Rather, formalising a commitment to judicial diversity across Australia's judiciary (as a matter to be taken into consideration rather than a quota) would safeguard any gains so that they are not at the whim of the politics of the day and further enhance the capacity to improve upon them.

Appointments which undermine the homogeneity of the Court are steps in the right direction in disrupting the masculinist gender regime on the Court. But with no formal recognition of the importance of diversity in appointments, these steps remain at the whim of the government of the day. Diversity and merit are not mutually exclusive. Diversity can and should have a legitimate and meaningful role in appointment practices. However, if the utterances of

18 In 2015 the OECD recently acknowledged Australia's gender balance in its Senate (38.2% women) as one of the best in the world while the number of women in the Lower House remained relatively stagnant (26.7% women). Conversely, the number of Commonwealth women ministers (17.2%) revealed a lack of progress in gender diversity and that Australia was lagging behind other OECD countries on this indicator. These figures were compiled when Tony Abbott was Prime Minister and had only appointed one woman to cabinet and rather incongruously, appointed himself as 'Minister for Women'. See *Government at a Glance 2015* (OECD Publishing, 2015); http://dx.doi.org/10.1787/gov_glance-2015-en. In the most recently published figures (published in 2019 but reflecting the situation in 2017), women represented less than one-third of the seats in the House of Representatives of Australia similar to the OECD average of 30%. Furthermore, in 2019, women held 21% of the ministerial positions in Australia, which was lower than the OECD average of 31%. See *Government at a Glance 2019* (OECD Publishing, 2019); https://www.oecd.org/gov/gov-at-a-glance-2019-australia.pdf.

19 See Australian Institute of Judicial Administration's (AIJA) gender statistics, compiled in June 2020. These are illustrative of the continuing struggle to improve gender diversity in Australia's judiciary. Despite the 'almost equal' composition of the High Court, women make up 37% of Commonwealth judges. In no state or territory do women make up half or more than half of the judiciary (although at the time of the first near-equal gender balance on the High Court in 2014, women made up more than half of the judiciary in the ACT, with 55% of judges). Currently, in SA women make up 35% of the state's judges, Tasmania 29%, NSW 36%, Victoria 45%, NT 40%, WA 39% and 43% in ACT; https://aija.org.au/wp-content/uploads/2020/07/2020-JUDICIAL-GENDER-STATISTICS-v3.pdf.

the politically powerful are to be taken at face value, diversity does not inform their decision-making processes. This is disappointing. Although diversity may sometimes be understood as 'merit's servant or foot-soldier' (Rackley 2013: 194), it is entirely possible to implement measures to secure a more diverse judiciary without sacrificing 'merit'. In fact, once we accept a more diverse judiciary is a better judiciary, we are able to have important conversations about the scope and content of reforms which might then secure a truly diverse judiciary. Reforms to the judicial appointment process—especially those designed to enhance judicial diversity by explicitly including it as a matter to be considered among others in the appointment process—will only be plausible if the relationship between merit and diversity is recast.

Chapter 3

Sworn to be

Gender, difference and judicial swearing-in speeches

The public virtues sought in the judiciary are made apparent in the political discourse around judicial appointments. Even without being required to justify their appointments, the politically powerful nonetheless make important statements about those attributes which are compatible with judicial office in what is said and what is left unsaid. Unlike other jurisdictions[1] where the judge is required to participate in this justificatory process, and in so doing, participates publicly in the fashioning of judicial virtues, no such requirement exists in Australia. With the announcement made by the government of the day, the new judge takes on the persona of the High Court Judge, removed from the vagaries of public discourse and is therefore, by extension, removed from the public debate as her appointment is digested and evaluated in the political sphere. Yet taking on the persona of a High Court judge does not happen simply as a result of the announcement of their appointment, even if they are being elevated from an already existing judicial position. There are a number of rituals and performances shaping the persona of the judge, rituals that transform the ordinary judicial person into one of seven, the elite of the legal knowers. These rituals allow some space for judges to reflect on how they conceive the judicial role, in particular that of the swearing-in speech.

1 For example, in the United States, the Constitution confers the power of judicial appointment in generally vague terms in that it states that the President 'shall nominate, and by and with the Advice and Consent of the Senate, shall appoint … Judges of the Supreme Court', but the words 'advice and consent' have caused untold grief for Presidents and nominees alike as this partisan process has acted as a limit on Presidential power in this context. This is the case because it is not just a matter of nominating a preferred candidate, but nominating a candidate who will survive the Senate's confirmation process whereby nominees are required to speak to their qualification for judicial office. On the gendered implications of this process see Brenner and Knake (2012). Brenner and Knake (2012: 381) conducted an empirical study using both qualitative and quantitative analysis to examine media coverage of Supreme Court nominees in the week following the President's announcement. Their findings revealed 'an ongoing struggle for equal access to and ascension in the power pipeline for women in the legal profession that is linked to motherhood, appearance and competence'.

DOI: 10.4324/9780429288531-4

High Court judicial swearing-in speeches are time-honoured, traditional ceremonies. The formality is marked by the traditional trappings of the judicial role; the wigs, the imposing courtroom space, the sombre seriousness that underlines the constitutional and cultural significance of judicial power. Juxtaposed against these formal dimensions are speeches of welcome and acceptance that mostly reference, with the occasional lighthearted joke or two, the newcomer's school days, family, career trajectories, and sporting achievements. Such speeches serve as reminders that judges are indeed human. However, the formality of the occasion is never far from the surface because with the closing of the ceremony the newcomer is a High Court Justice. In this way the swearing-in ceremonies might well be regarded as 'the jubilees of the legal profession, marking its continuity and change' (Kirby 1996). Beyond the celebratory glimpses into the lives and times of judicial officers these ceremonies mark the formal temporal shift from 'ordinary citizen' (or judge of a lower Court) to Justice of Australia's highest Court. And second, this transformation and the ceremony that celebrates it illuminate for a brief moment the intersection of the personal and the professional and bring into question what it means to be a judge of the High Court.

The formal transformation occurs with the taking of the official oath as set out in the *High Court of Australia Act 1979* (Cth) and the Schedule of that Act which dictates the content of these scripts. Section 11 of the Act states that '[a] person who is appointed as a Justice after the commencement of this Act shall, before proceeding to discharge the duties of his or her office, take an oath or make an affirmation in accordance with the form in the Schedule'. The set script is as follows:

> I, __, do swear that I will bear true allegiance to Her Majesty Queen Elizabeth the Second, Her Heirs and Successors according to law, that I will well and truly serve Her in the Office of Chief Justice [or Justice] of the High Court of Australia and that I will do right to all manner of people according to law without fear or favour, affection or ill-will. So Help me God.

The only aspect of the script which might be altered is the phrase 'So Help me God!' which can be omitted if the person makes an affirmation. All judicial officers are required to swear allegiance to the monarch. The judicial oath specifically can be traced to a statute enacted by King Edward III in 1346 and, no doubt, the judicial oath retains much practical and ritualistic importance ensuring the independence of the judiciary (Toohey 1999: 2). Little has changed since then. The form and content of oaths were, and remain, a means of 'identifying individual commitment and defining group solidarity' and the oaths were especially important markers of men's level of power within the democratic sphere (Guettel Cole 1996: 227). What is important to note here is that the oath is a pre-written script from which a new judicial appointee cannot deviate and therefore tells us little about a new judge beyond a mere glimpse into their levels of religiosity. Juxtaposed against the rigidities of the oaths are the social scripts constructed anew with each swearing-in ceremony and seemingly spontaneously tailored to the person being admitted to the bench.

The language and content of the swearing-in speeches are forms of storytelling, creative social scripts that give us insight into those qualities which are apparently compatible with the highest judicial office and, in so doing, the institutional values of the High Court. For most of the twentieth century these scripts gave us the measure of judicial man. But since 1987, with the appointment of a woman to the bench, the measure of a High Court judge has become far more complicated. The gendered strands of these social narratives can no longer be taken for granted. Examining these social scripts reveal complex and contradictory ways in which gender is woven into the identities of those at the peak of the legal profession. This is not to say that gender only becomes an issue once women are appointed to the High Court. Gender was always present, if not entirely visible. The appointment of women to the High Court only makes the fact of gender more obvious. What is less obvious, and far more interesting, is the shift in content and style of the swearing-in speeches.[2] As the gendered homogeneity of judicial appointments has begun to wane, the ways in which gender and notions of difference intersect in these speeches have become all the more significant. Given the duality at play in these ceremonies, whereby statements as to the suitability of the judge for the new role are joined with the judge's own musings about their life and the law, the judicial swearing-in ceremony offers an opportunity to explore what differences might emerge when the appointees are women.

Examining the ways in which gender weaves itself through these speeches is problematised, in part, because gender itself is problematised. The very concept of gender as both 'historical' and 'performative' stands in stark contrast to 'some versions of sexual difference' (Butler 2004: 10). Leaving aside, for the moment at least, some of the broader theoretical debates about the social construction of gender, for present purposes it is sufficient to proceed on the basis that there are normative views about masculinity and femininity and as such gender is 'the apparatus by which the production and normalization of masculine and feminine take place' (Butler 2004: 42). My intention in examining the construction of masculinity and femininity in these speeches is not to impose normative standards on how gender is or should be constructed, but rather to understand how these scripts produce and reproduce the gender order. This chapter therefore examines how women and men judges, and those who welcome

2 The full transcripts of High Court swearing-in ceremonies have been made available online since 1996. The transcripts of the swearing-in ceremony for each of the justices currently sitting on the High Court are available online at *High Court of Australia Transcripts* on AustLii: http://www.austlii.edu.au/au/other/HCATrans . In this chapter the transcripts are cited in footnotes rather than in-text as this makes it much easier to distinguish the speechmaker and the judicial subject.

them to the bench, emphasise or de-emphasise the gendered state of being a judge in the narratives they present at their swearing-in ceremonies. Those matters which are either emphasised or de-emphasised in any given story are mostly a matter of choice on the behalf of the narrator. It therefore provides a unique opportunity to see how the judges interact with, and contribute to, the gender regime on the Court.

Storytelling, and the importance of telling women's stories, has been an important component of the work that feminists have done in exposing the limits of law's claim to impartiality (Smart 1990; Naffine 1990). The incredulity with which the law has treated women's stories as witnesses and litigants has been one feature of the legal system exposed as problematic by feminist legal theorists (Scutt 1997). In this respect and others, women's stories have been counter-narratives in their various interactions with the law. As judges too, women's stories have been counter in that they have stood in stark contrast to the stock narrative which held sway for most of human history—namely that judicial authority rested only with men, i.e. the judicial man. Some of these stories have been characterised by grim tales of exclusion, and these stories have (rightly) been the focus of much feminist academic attention (Rackley 2007). Why then should we tell, or retell rather, the stories which emanate from swearing-in speeches when by design they 'have a strong hagiographic quality?' (Moran 2011: 274).

Despite the approbatory dimensions of these speeches, they also contribute to the narratives of 'formulating and fashioning the subject not only as an exemplary individual life but also as a subject that embodies the virtues of the judicial institution' (Moran 2011: 273). Indeed, the value of these stories is in what might otherwise be cast as their weakness. The kind of bias arising from the narrator having a stake in the appointment (either politically or as the appointee) might be methodologically challenging for the historian seeking to establish an (albeit contested) truth. But for present purposes the way in which judges and those who seek to welcome them fashion these narratives is all the more revealing because of the intersection between subject and narrator. Of particular interest is the possible disparity and tension between the stories told by the judicial subject and those told about them. Stories do heavy lifting, both in reinforcing the hegemony of stock narratives, and in revealing counter narratives (Delgado 1989: 2441). Though it is not simply the case that all men's stories are stock and all women's are counter narratives, it is true that the status of women as outsiders has formed a huge part of their stories—especially in the stories told by others. Examining the stories about and by men and women judges in Australia's highest Court allows 'us to climb into and walk around in the skin of others' and perhaps even more significantly when we tell stories and listen to them too, we not only 'begin to understand their world differently, but ours too' (West 1993: 419 cited in Rackley 2007: 78).

Hence, I examine the way in which gender weaves its way into the speeches of both men and women judges. The analysis is not restricted just to the new women appointees as it is instructive to compare the respective speeches of the women and men as a means to identify the workings of the gendering process. This comparative approach is adopted, at least in part, because much of our understanding of women and difference has been premised on the basis that women are different *from* men. Or put another way, their otherness, has simply been referenced to the fact that they are not men. This is not to ignore the fact that feminist theorists and philosophers of various persuasions have rightly problematised the methodology of analysing woman's difference with reference to the 'benchmark man' (see e.g. Thornton 1996; see also Irigaray 1985). Certainly, the conflation of 'gender' and 'women' has problematic implications in that, as was noted in the introduction to this book, it obscures the full gamut of the gendered meanings and processes (see e.g. Htun 2005).

This chapter contends that the swearing-in ceremony is riddled with numerous cultural representations some of which give substance to gendered understandings of judicial power. One of these is the notion of the 'judicial man' who has been historically understood as 'antipathetic to the feminine' (Thornton 1996: 141), and with which the new 'judicial woman' must contend. The point here is to recognise that a traditional measure of judicial authority has been framed from a masculinist perspective and to determine to what extent these notions continue to inform understandings of judicial authority (Thornton 1996). Although anchoring women's difference *from men* remains problematic, the fact remains that it must still be taken into account when considering how gender intersects with the construction of judicial identities. The chapter begins with a brief overview of the formal context of the rituals that constituted these ceremonies. Though subject to ever so subtle changes over time, these rituals form a constant within which specific speeches are performed for both professional and public consumption. They are also gendered in various ways and hence they already set up a gendering frame that those participating in the ceremonies will be obliged to negotiate.

Recent scholarly engagement with these speeches, although thus far limited, further reveals that there is much richness in these speeches, especially for those of us wanting to better understand the portrayal of judicial otherness in these legal and cultural narratives. With the formal context established, the chapter then turns to the examination of the swearing-in ceremonies of the seven justices currently sitting on the Australian High Court. As with the previous chapter, in what follows, I then examine the swearing-in speeches of the seven judges making up the High Court bench in late 2014. This bench is significant as it was the first to involve an almost-equal gender balance among the judges: Justices Susan Crennan, Susan Kiefel and Virginia Bell sat with Justices Kenneth Hayne, Stephen Gageler, Patrick Keane, and Chief Justice Robert French. Further, subsequent swearings-in (of Justices Nettle, Gordon and Edelman)[3] are also (briefly) noted where matters of gender were especially pronounced. In

3 I address Kiefel's swearing-in as Chief Justice in the final chapter.

addition to the speeches of the Justices are the welcoming commentaries of the relevant Attorneys-General and others invited to participate in these rituals. The politically (and legally) powerful are comfortable in emphasising the feminine (and masculine) so long as the overarching narrative remains that a deserving and meritorious person has been appointed. What is perhaps unsurprising is that women appear to be at pains to quell the influence or significance of their gender when producing their narratives of becoming judges. Slightly more surprising is the revelation that the men and women judges alike are keen to tell a story of belonging and diminish any apparent otherness, although for men there is often less work to be done in conforming to stock narratives. The gaze of the judicial subject and storyteller alike reveals much about the gendered values which are associated with judicial being. The potential intersectional and oppositional nature of these stories is at the crux of this chapter. Even though these speeches have been traditionally understood as entirely removed from the legal contest between competing narratives, typical of adversarial processes, the swearing-in speeches actually reveal acutely (gendered) tensions between judicial subject and storyteller.

Rites of passage and praise: judicial swearing-in speeches

Swearing-in speeches abound in narratives which explicitly and implicitly signify how judicial 'others' fare. Philosophical conceptualisations of the 'Other' cut across time and disciplines—from Hegel (1977) to de Beauvoir (1997) to Butler (1987) we see the invocation of 'Other' as a way of explaining internal and externalized social order and structures. One of de Beauvoir's most well-known and important contributions is her conceptualisation of woman as 'other.' De Beauvoir challenged the Hegelian narrative to explain the relationship between men and women and the notion is well encapsulated by her statement that women found themselves 'living in a world where men compel her to assume the status of "other"' (de Beauvoir 1997: 29). This conceptualisation of women as 'other' has been adopted in feminist legal theory as a way of accounting for and giving meaning to what Thornton (2007: 392) explains as the way in which otherness 'taints the adjudicative role and renders the delivery of justice problematic'. Otherness is therefore manifest in cases where 'the subjectivity of the embodied persona of the judge cannot be sloughed off'—and that persona most frequently causes quibbles where the judge is a woman, or gay, or of colour (Thornton 2007: 392).

Recent examinations of swearing-in speeches have evidenced a distinct focus on judicial 'others' in scrutinising these social scripts through the lens of gender and sexuality. Moran's (2006; 2011) work has focused on the way in which sexuality and notions of heteronormativity infuse swearing-in speeches. Moran's (2011: 285) recent analysis of swearing-in for those appointed to Supreme Court of New South Wales in Australia argued that not only is sexuality 'a very public dimension of the judicial institution' but also that 'the institution of the judiciary has long been fashioned (and in many instances continues to be fashioned) as exclusively heterosexual'. Similarly, Roberts' (2012a) examinations of the swearing-in of Australia's first woman High Court judge, Mary Gaudron, and her (2012b) comparative paper analysing the swearing-in speeches of all of the women judges appointed to the High Court pursued a line of enquiry which focused on the novelty of the feminine in these narratives. She found that the speeches 'tell the story of a continuing perception of the "otherness"' of women judges (Roberts 2012b: 131). More recently Roberts' (2014: 161–162) examination of women judges' swearing-in speeches on the High Court, Federal Court and Family Court between 1993 and 2013 found that a 'feminizing discourse' dominated earlier stories but a 'feminist consciousness' emerged towards the end of the period.

A common thread can be seen in the work of Moran and Roberts in that these speeches allow us to probe levels of acceptance and modes of representing the almost dogged markers of otherness. There are nonetheless differences in Moran and Roberts' approaches beyond the fact that they focus on different levels in the judicial hierarchy. Whereas Moran's work is more comparative, drawing on stock narratives to punctuate his analysis of the silent and explicit performance of sexuality, Roberts sets up no such foil for her analysis. Although Roberts draws on some examples from the swearing-in speeches of men to shore up her argument, her analysis is resolutely about women and the framing of their gender. I point to this not as a matter of reproach, but rather in justifying the opportunities available for the analysis undertaken in this chapter, which juxtaposes constructions of masculinity and femininity in order to account for the (evolving) gender regime on the Court. Scrutinizing the scripts about men and women judges therefore demonstrates that sexuality and gender are *also* deeply embedded in the speeches of the man of law, but, because of the prevailing masculinist gender regime, so taken for granted and normalised that their gender is almost rendered invisible.

That recent scholarly interest in swearing-in speeches coincides with increased diversity in judicial appointments is no mere happenstance. The High Court is an institution marked by 'remarkable homogeneity' as Dominello and Neuman (2001: 49) have explained, not just in terms of gender but also race and for the most part, background and geography. While it is also the case that there have been exceptions, the general 'sameness' of those appointed does not leave much space for new plotlines in the stories presented. Predictably, our interest piques as difference stories begin to be told. Even judicial officers confess to finding the swearing-in words somewhat innocuous. Justice Kirby (1996) said on the occasion of his swearing-in, '[p]ortentous words of the newly sworn judge, or a departing judicial tyro, hang in the air and then evaporate and are gone. So it will be with my words today' (Kirby 1996). This observation might once have been well justified, because these ceremonies have been largely overlooked, with 'legal historians and biographers instead favouring Courts' official pronouncements, and, more recently, to Justices' non-ceremonial extra-curial writings and speeches' (Roberts 2012a: 495). Yet shifts in scholarly focus as the judiciary transforms into a more heterogeneous institution mean that even if it ever were the case that swearing-in speeches were simply to be forgotten, now more than ever they represent a 'valuable narrative history of the High Court of Australia and the community it serves' (Roberts 2012a: 496).

Before turning to the speeches themselves, it is necessary to comment briefly upon the gendered hierarchies which are purportedly diminishing in the legal profession, but clearly still exist. Where masculinist qualities are seen as more compatible with judicial office we will still see 'the valiant attempts of some women judges to present themselves as "neutral" and to stave off criticism by denying the feminine' (Thornton 1996: 209). What Thornton (1996: 203) termed the 'exceptional women syndrome' also manifests in these scenarios as it allows women judges (and women in other positions of power) 'to be distinguished from other women, so that the masculinist character of the office is not diminished'. In this way the gender regime accommodates difference in almost imperceptible ways and yet at the same time is protected by the very women whose presence poses challenges to how it has operated in the past. Historically, neutralising their gendered state of being has been one of the ways in which women judges have been able to succeed in arenas typically reserved for men. It is here we can see the way in which all judges negotiate the gender regime upon their appointment. The very masculinism of the institution means that masculinity is equated with neutrality in this space. These narratives of neutrality are revelatory in giving meaning to and understanding the gendered values embedded in the scripts that follow. As will be shown, the point of noting this is neither to essentialise difference nor to demand that women or men adopt certain gendered modes of behaviour. Rather the point is to examine the meanings behind the practices adopted.

In another's eyes: speeches welcoming the new judge

The speeches which attend the formal swearing-in of judges are political scripts made by political actors. This is obviously so in the case of the Attorney-General, who has a clear political stake in justifying the government's choice, but also for the other speakers who are leaders in the field such as presidents of State Bar Associations and Law Societies. Given the lack of transparency around judicial appointments these speeches are particularly significant for the government of the day (through the Attorney-General) in justifying its appointment. The speeches follow a fairly familiar theme. They begin with the narrative of the judge's enormously successful career. Many of these speeches are punctuated with "in" jokes and lighthearted stories. There are references to sporting fraternities, families, and other matters which might be of interest in affirming why this person has been elevated to the highest Court in the land. In the speeches made in honour of the new judge, rather than by the new judge themselves, there are various ways in which the judge's gender, or notions of masculinity or femininity, is either emphasised or de-emphasised.

There are, of course, clear examples where an individual's gender assumes centre stage in overt and obvious ways in these social scripts. At the swearing-in of Justice Hayne in 1997 the then Attorney-General, Mr Williams (1997), thought it apt to commence the speeches with a cricket joke. In playing the numbers game, Williams (1997) emphasised that Hayne was not only the '41st person to be a member of the High Court' but also 'the 12th man from Victoria to have held the office'.[4] Note here how 'person' quickly transforms to 'man'. This linguistic shift reinforces the masculinist underpinnings of the institution, in drawing on the sporting metaphor but also in inadvertently pointing out that the gendered state of judicial appointments mean that the number would have almost been correct in substituting man and person in the first part of the sentence. Playing on the cricket joke, he said 'unlike the other 12th man you will be expected to do more than carry the drinks'.[5]

Of course, for most of Australia's history pointing out that a judge was a man would be pointing out the obvious but this turn of phrase is more than just the mere use of a sporting metaphor; it is about the inclusivity, the insider status, that comes from being a member of the Court, or part of a fraternity which has privileged certain traditionally masculinist sporting cultural norms. Although sport is not only the domain of men, it has historically been associated with masculine qualities. For example, Chief Justice French's 'passion for health and fitness'[6] and 'parochial' approach to football were mentioned. Keane J's 'obsession with cricket and the fervent support' for Queensland sporting teams was noted,[7] as was Crennan J's proficiency as a schoolgirl in netball.[8] Sporting prowess and the asymmetrical competitive features of Kiefel J's introduction to rowing while in Cambridge were also noted in her welcome. Fraser pointed out that Kiefel J married her rowing coach although '[r]owing is generally not regarded as a contact sport, but I am told that the Bumps on the River Cam brought out your Honour's competitive spirit.'[9] These references are examples of how sporting backgrounds serve to 'connect members of the legal profession' and come to operate like fraternal bonds that in turn become 'part of a

4 Transcript of proceedings, *Swearing in Ceremony, Hayne J* [1997] HCATrans 294 Court (Williams, Commonwealth Attorney General).

5 Ibid.

6 Transcript of proceedings, *Swearing-In of Chief Justice, the Hon R.S. French* [2008], HCATrans 318, (McClelland, Commonwealth Attorney General).

7 Transcript of proceedings, *Swearing-in of Keane J* [2013] HCATrans 40, (Catanzariti, President of the Law Council of Australia).

8 Transcript of proceedings, *Crennan J—Swearing-in* [2005] HCATrans 895 (8 November 2005) (Ruddock, Commonwealth Attorney-General).

9 Transcript of proceedings, *Swearing-in of Kiefel J* [2007] HCATrans 493, (Fraser, President of the Bar Association of Queensland).

complex web of relationships linking business, professional and political life' (Thornton 1996: 170).

Crennan J's status as the second woman was noted by the then Attorney-General, Phillip Ruddock, describing her as 'the 45th person to be appointed to this Court, the 13th Victorian and the second woman'.[10] Conversely, Kiefel, Bell and Gordon JJ's status as the third, fourth and fifth women appointed to the High Court passed without specific mention in the Attorney-General's introductory remarks.[11] This is not to say that their status as women did not inform the tenor of the welcome speeches, but it did so in more nuanced ways. As each speaker brought to bear their recollections of one or more aspects of each appointee's career trajectories, family responsibilities and other professional affiliations, perceptions of gender were present, shaping the dominant understanding of the way that gender differences punctuate public conceptions of judicial power.

Swearing-in speeches confirm our suspicions (and desires) that only those with the most impressive curriculum vitae make their way to the highest Court in Australia's judicial hierarchy. Of the judges considered here, all but Justice Kiefel completed their undergraduate education at one of Australia's 'sandstone' universities, usually after a stint in private school. However, Kiefel J is not the first Justice of the High Court of Australia with a 'non-traditional' legal education. McHugh J was admitted also after taking the Barristers Admission Board Examinations. Some Justices, such as Hayne, Kiefel, Gageler, Nettle and Edelman JJ, had also pursued postgraduate study. Aside from Stephen Gageler who, at time of his appointment was the Solicitor-General for the Commonwealth, all judges in this sample came to the High Court from a lower court, hence all had proven their judicial mettle in one way or another. The descriptions brim with adjectival embellishment such that they are marked by similarity that almost renders the narratives meaningless. The relevant Attorney-General as the first speechmaker and as the official representative from the Executive Branch sets the standard for what is to follow and the comments are similar in substance and tone. Thus in welcoming Hayne J, Attorney-General Williams suggested the appointment was an acknowledgment that his Honour had 'attained excellence in [his] chosen career.'[12] Attorney-General Ruddock, having had the opportunity to welcome both Crennan and Kiefel JJ, described the latter as 'brilliant'[13] and the appointment of the former as a recognition of her 'intellect, skill, determination and commitment to justice.'[14]

10 *Swearing-in Ceremony, Crennan J*, (Ruddock).

11 See *Swearing-in of Justice Bell*, Canberra [2009] HCATrans 4, (McClelland, Commonwealth Attorney General). See also *Swearing-in Ceremony Kiefel J*; Ceremonial—Swearing in of Gordon J—Canberra [2015] HCATrans (Brandis, Commonwealth Attorney General).

12 *Swearing-in Ceremony, Hayne J* (Williams).

13 *Swearing-in Ceremony, Kiefel J* (Ruddock).

14 *Swearing-in Ceremony, Crennan J* (Ruddock).

In welcoming French CJ and Bell J, Attorney-General McClelland similarly emphasised their skills and attributes. In the case of the Chief Justice he said that his 'background', 'fine personal characteristics,' and 'wealth of experience in careful analysis and exposition of the law would serve him well.'[15] In welcoming Bell J the Attorney-General described her career as 'distinguished' and noted her reputation 'as a strong advocate with a sharp legal mind and an engaging sense of humour.'[16] Attorney-General Roxon (notably the first woman to appear in such a ceremony as Attorney-General) made reference to Gageler J's 'prodigious work ethic, a quiet but purposeful demeanour' and 'steely resolve.'[17] Similarly Attorney-General Dreyfus referenced Keane J's 'prodigious intellect' and other personal characteristics 'such as integrity, generosity and an ability to inspire others' in underscoring his suitability.[18]

Crucially, wherever a judge deviated from what has generally been regarded as a clear path to judicial appointment or the 'stock narrative' (education at an elite institution, time in commercial practice, time at the bar and appointment as a judge to a court elsewhere in the court hierarchy), the speechmakers emphasised those aspects of the judge's trajectory that distinguished their experiences from what has been constructed as the stock narrative of the judicial appointee. This emphasis has usually been gendered in that the different aspects of the women's careers paths have been at the forefront and, indeed, this emphasis will be dealt with more fully below.

Difference was not only found in the women members. The socio-economic backgrounds of Gageler and Keane JJ, for example, received some special attention. Gageler J's journey to the High Court was described as 'remarkable'. The 'remarkable' features noted by the Attorney-General were listed as follows: 'Country boy, public schooling, no lawyers in the family.'[19] The notion of remarkable stories was again invoked in reference to Keane's appointment. In reflecting on the sacrifices Keane's mother had made as a war widow raising her son, Mr Catanzariti, President of the Law Council of Australia, made an attempt to cast the Court as a more egalitarian institution for Keane's appointment. Mr Catanzariti invoked the notion of 'remarkable' stories explicitly in saying the Court's 'members are not drawn from a ruling class and those who are appointed invariably have a remarkable story to tell. Today is no different.'[20] Although it is actually true that High Court judges have not been drawn from the 'ruling classes', insofar as most come from what we might commonly describe as middle-class backgrounds (Dominello and Neuman 2001: 49), the comments made in celebration of the appointment of individuals from less

15 *Swearing-in Ceremony, French CJ* (McClelland).
16 *Swearing-in Ceremony, Bell J* (McClelland).
17 Transcript of proceedings, *Swearing-in of Gageler J* [2012] HCATrans 258, (Roxon, Commonwealth Attorney-General).
18 *Swearing-in Ceremony, Keane J* (Dreyfus, Commonwealth Attorney-General).
19 *Swearing-in Ceremony, Gageler J* (Roxon).
20 *Swearing-in Ceremony, Keane J* (Catanzariti, President, the Law Council of Australia).

privileged backgrounds is evidence of the apparent political importance of reinforcing the egalitarian nature of the High Court as an institution.

It is perhaps unsurprising that the judges whose career trajectory was painted as most different were the women judges. The speechmakers at Crennan, Kiefel and Bell JJ's ceremonies were especially keen to emphasise the non-traditional elements of their career trajectories. This was less pronounced at Gordon J's swearing-in that took place some years later. At Justice Crennan's swearing-in, her Honour's status as a mother and grandmother featured prominently in those stories elected to punctuate her career achievements. For example, family responsibilities were given as a reason for her non-linear career path with Attorney-General Ruddock explaining:

> When you became a teacher in order to work part time while your children were small—meanwhile you also began studying law part time, first at the University of Melbourne and then completing your degree at the University of Sydney.[21]

Crennan J's family responsibilities were further emphasised by Ruddock in praising her Honour's capacity to raise her children 'despite the demands of your legal career.'[22] The Attorney also noted that she raised her children with her husband Michael, 'also a distinguished Victorian Silk'.[23] The only other woman to speak at Crennan's swearing-in, Ms McMillan, President of the Victorian Bar, continued with the theme, drawing on a description of Crennan J as a 'renaissance woman' and her status as a 'Nanna judge.' In so doing she referenced grand-daughter Hannah's query "If Nanna's going to be working in Canberra, what is happening about our Sundays?"[24] Having already referenced her Honour's status as a grandmother, Ms McMillan continued with the maternal motif saying, 'if further proof of your quality as a grandmother were needed, one would merely refer one's audience to your most recent visit to your neighbour's adoring 2-year old, little Jimmy O'Mara.' The story, as recounted by Ms McMillan further served to highlight those 'grandmotherly' qualities:

> In order to attract your attention whilst you were telling his parents a story, Jimmy was climbing all over you and finally in desperation he gave you a toddler's whack on the face. With your Honour's well-earned reputation for patience, you dealt with the issue fittingly by continuing on with your story, remaining unruffled and unperturbed.[25]

21 *Swearing-in Ceremony, Kiefel J* (Ruddock).
22 Ibid.
23 Ibid.
24 *Swearing-in Ceremony, Crennan J* (McMillan, Chairman, The Victorian Bar).
25 Ibid.

Although Crennan J's status as the first grandmother to sit on the High Court is not disputed, she is certainly not the first grandparent to sit on the Court. Hence we see the gendered emphasis on these aspects of her identity.

Kiefel J's elevation was depicted as all the more extraordinary given her more humble beginnings as someone who began her career 'working in an administrative capacity.'[26] Kiefel J's early brilliance was given as an explanation for her 'rapid transformation from legal secretary to barrister'.[27] This transformation which saw Kiefel J 'qualified for admission through the Barrister's Board examinations, with honours and in the minimum possible time' was described as 'an early manifestation' of Kiefel J's 'innate academic ability and energy'.[28] Mr Fraser, President of the Bar Association of Queensland, pointed out 'when it was you that typed up the first draft of an opinion, it seemed unnecessary for the barrister to spend any more time on it'.[29] There was an unspoken and gendered dimension to the story of Kiefel J's elevation within the profession. It is no accident that we would struggle to find examples of men judges' elevation from the typist pool to the powerful echelons of the profession, although the gendered nature of administrative work is now arguably less pronounced than it was in the 1970s.

That Virginia Bell was a *different* kind of judge was a strong theme at her swearing-in ceremony. In welcoming Bell to the bench Attorney-General McClelland described her career as 'a little less ordinary.'[30] Some of those aspects which might be said to have made Bell less ordinary (namely her gender and her sexuality) were in some respects hidden in plain sight as the speech makers sought to emphasise Bell J's difference couched in terms of her 'long experience in life, law and ordinary people'.[31] Bell's humanity and focus on social justice work were noted as special or different features of her career and hence this was a kind of difference worthy of emphasis. The Attorney-General linked Bell's humanity and her gender in noting that some had given her the moniker "Mrs Judge". He continued with this theme in noting that 'pleasingly [she] has not been able to mask [her] humanity'.[32] Ms Katzmann, President of the New South Wales Bar Association, further sought to emphasise Bell J's humane qualities and similarities with her predecessor Kirby J, in suggesting that her Honour had 'an empathy for people and a passion for securing justice and protecting the rights of the underprivileged'.[33]

Bell J's individual identity as a woman judge and the more collective implications of her appointment in terms of gender equity featured prominently in

26 Ibid (Ruddock).
27 Ibid (Fraser).
28 Ibid.
29 Ibid.
30 *Swearing-in Ceremony, Bell J* (McClelland).
31 Ibid.
32 Ibid.
33 Ibid (Katzmann).

the speeches welcoming her. Katzmann's welcome speech was the most celebratory with reference to Bell's status as a woman judge. There were numerous references to the significance of the number of women sitting on the bench that were notably absent in respect to the appointments of Crennan and Kiefel JJ. For example, Katzmann opened her address with a clear statement about what the appointment meant for gender equity on the bench because 'until recently there was only one woman on the High Court bench. Now there are three. The surge appears to be working'.[34] Mr Corcoran, President of the Law Council of Australia, similarly stressed the significance of the appointment in terms of gender equity, suggesting that '[a] welcome aspect of our own nation's development has been the recognition that gender is not a fit ground upon which to limit opportunity and advancement'.[35] He further pointed out Bell J's status as the fourth women to join the High Court hinting at future possibilities in saying 'it is now quite possible during your time here that the majority of members of this Court will be women'.[36] Attorney-General McClelland's comments about gender exhibited a curious balance in underscoring the government's achievement in appointing another woman, yet he still tempered that with the suggestion that gender does not really matter too much at all:

> Your Honour, we are proud and grateful to live in a country *ruled by law and not by men*, but we are grateful too that you will be adding to the ranks of the very talented women who are interpreting and applying that law at the highest level.[37]

The appointment of the next woman justice, Michelle Gordon, did not attract comment about the fact that her appointment was returning the Court to an almost equal gender balance after Justice Nettle had replaced Justice Crennan on the Court. Indeed, the speeches scarcely[38] commented on the novel fact that Gordon was replacing her husband, Kenneth Hayne, on the Court, beyond veiled references which would only be understood by a legal 'insider.' Of course, legal 'insiders' are the assumed audience for such speeches—these ceremonies are attended by senior members of the profession. In any case Attorney-General Brandis described her appointment as 'a well-deserved recognition of [her] exceptional skills as a lawyer'.[39] Ms McCleod (President of the Australian Bar Association) noted that one former Federal Court associate had written 'pithily in the online bulletin Women's Agenda: "she's cool—really cool"'. Mr Peters

34 Ibid.
35 Ibid (Corcoran).
36 Ibid.
37 Ibid (McClelland). My emphasis.
38 Note that the marital connection had been acknowledged in Attorney-General Brandis' announcement of her Honour's appointment. See Chapter 2.
39 Ceremonial—Swearing in of Gordon J—Canberra [2015] HCATrans (Brandis, Commonwealth Attorney General).

(President of the Victorian Bar) noted her kindness and empathy, offering as evidence her support and mentoring of women in the profession:

> Little is known of your Honour's role in Victoria in a private workshop which focuses on increasing the representation of women barristers in commercial litigation. Your Honour, together with Susan Crennan QC, and others, chose to promote this issue vigorously without seeking publicity or credit, as is your Honour's style.[40]

He cited this work as 'an example of your Honour inspiring others through your judicial role but working quietly behind the scenes to support women and change the attitudes that affect their careers'.[41] Although this kind of behind the scenes work without expectation for personal praise or advancement is something which might be lauded, there is also perhaps the inference that this is the kind of work which should be done quietly.

At Justice Nettle's swearing-in (which had taken place a few months earlier than Justice Gordon's) Attorney-General Brandis described his Honour's appointment to the High Court as 'a fitting pinnacle to a glittering career' and that he was regarded by 'Bench and Bar alike as one of Australia's finest jurists'.[42] His many achievements over a long and successful career were noted although his age (specifically that at 65 years of age at the time of his appointment, his time on the Court would be limited) was not specifically referenced—this came in his Honour's own speech. Conversely, at Justice Edelman's 2017 swearing-in the precocious nature of his achievement appointed 'at the young age of only 43' was described as 'yet another significant moment in what has been, by any measure, already a remarkable career.'[43]

The familial was interwoven into these more recent speeches in ways that both reflected and disrupted more traditional divisions of labour in the private or domestic sphere. Attorney-General Brandis described Nettle J as 'a dedicated family man with three grown-up children' and suggested that he must be proud that his daughters had followed him into a career in the law (and that his son had pursued a career in medicine).[44] Although fatherhood is presented as a virtue here, it is perhaps difficult to imagine a woman being described as a 'dedicated family woman' (because, of the course, the inference is that women will take on this role). In the case of Edelman J (whose children were much younger at the time of his appointment), his status as a 'devoted son, husband

40 *Swearing-in Ceremony, Gordon J* (Peters, President, The Victorian Bar).
41 Ibid.
42 Ceremonial—Swearing in of Nettle J—Canberra [2015] HCATrans (Brandis, Commonwealth Attorney General).
43 Ceremonial Sitting on the Occasion of the Swearing in of Edelman J [2017] HCATrans (30 January)(Brandis, Commonwealth Attorney General).
44 *Swearing-in Ceremony, Nettle J* (Brandis, Attorney-General).

and father' was framed in a positive manner and linked by one speaker to specific examples of his fathering responsibilities intervening with his judicial responsibilities:

> An urgent application for an injunction was made and it fell to your Honour. Your Honour formed the view that the matter could wait until the Monday. Counsel, unwisely, insisted that the matter needed to be heard immediately that afternoon. Court was convened, and counsel, perhaps even more unwisely, did not then seek to make good the urgency of the application. After a short hearing, your Honour then conveyed two children dressed in swimming gear from the public gallery to swim class.[45]

Moreover, Justice Edelman's family life was not only cast in terms of his caring responsibilities for his children. The Attorney-General described Edelman's family as 'very accomplished', pointing out that his 'marriage to Sarah was itself an Oxford romance' and that his wife, Sarah Percy 'is an Associate Professor in International Relations at the University of Queensland.'[46]

Responding as a judge

The ways in which the judges responded to the laudatory remarks at their swearing-in offers an interesting insight into the kind of story that the judge wants told about their life and career trajectory. In this regard the judge has the opportunity to respond to specific matters mentioned by the speechmakers as well as to reference matters which they might regard as personally significant. It also gives the new judge a space in which to reflect on their own judicial authority and how they see the role of judges in the judicial hierarchy more generally. What becomes remarkably clear in these texts is an attempt to quash the effect of any markers of otherness in order instead to tell a story of belonging. For the women judges this sometimes involved overt attempts to diminish the significance of their gender in their life and career narratives. For the men judges this was often less necessary as their stories more closely resembled the stock narratives. That being said, it seems that over the past two decades there has been a shift in the way that judges approach their chance to respond in that in nearly all of their narratives they have all become increasingly willing to reflect on matters more personal in their speeches. This might suggest a softening of the dominant institutional gender regime of the Court as a result of there being more women participating on the bench.

Most significantly, however, is the tension which plays out in the portrayal of the judge. Former Chief Justice, Murray Gleeson remarked on the occasion

45 *Swearing-in Ceremony, Edelman J* (Howard, President of the Western Australian Bar Association).

46 *Swearing-in Ceremony, Edelman J* (Brandis, Attorney-General).

of his own swearing-in that '[a]lthough they have some of the external form of Court proceedings, they do not represent the adversary system in its full rigour' because the 'procedure on occasions such as this makes no provision for a contradictor.'[47] Technically, this is correct in the rigid space which dictates comity and courtesy. But even so, the women judges still presented oppositional narratives, at least insofar as their 'otherness' was concerned since they were women, not men judges. This may well be one of the differences gender makes and is therefore revelatory as to how judges negotiate the gender regime.

Justice Hayne's speech in reply is noteworthy for its brevity and the extent to which he distanced himself from any reflection on those matters which might be considered personal. He emphasised his gratitude for his opportunities in the law and for the privileges that had been bestowed upon him. For example, he spoke of his 'privilege in being taught at the University of Melbourne' and later that he had been privileged to sit on the Court of Appeal 'with a group of fine lawyers who not only were my colleagues, they were, and are, my friends'.[48] On a personal level Hayne J was similarly reserved, he simply thanked 'many who have offered [him] love and support', remarking that there had been 'circumstances where [he had] not been deserving of that gift'. The only reference to family was that he regretted that his father 'did not live to see this day.'[49]

Chief Justice French's speech stands in stark contrast to that of Justice Hayne. Like Hayne J, French CJ's career and life certainly fitted the stock narrative of what we might expect from a judge of the High Court of Australia, despite the fact that his state of origin, Western Australia, made him an outlier. French CJ was especially willing to reveal much of himself in his response. The Chief Justice presented himself as an insider within the legal fraternity. He pointed out that he was connected to former High Court judges in mentioning that he had known former High Court Justice John Toohey since he was a schoolboy because the Tooheys were neighbours and friends of his parents in the 1950s. Chief Justice French remarked that it was a 'matter of sadness that [his] parents were not alive to share this occasion' but suggested that along 'with my brothers and my sister, Rebecca, who are here today, John Toohey provides a link to that past'.[50]

Although it is customary for judges to thank their family for their support and to give special thanks to spouses[51] (if they have one), French CJ gave

47 Transcript of proceedings, *Swearing-In of the Chief Justice, The Honourable Anthony Murray Gleeson*, AC C00/1998 [1998] HCATrans 192 (22 May 1998) (Gleeson CJ).
48 *Swearing-in Ceremony, Hayne J* (Hayne J).
49 *Swearing-in Ceremony, Crennan J* (Williams).
50 *Swearing-in Ceremony, French CJ* (French CJ).
51 See Moran (2011: 278) for a discussion of the way in which marriage and more specifically, women's roles have traditionally been framed in judicial swearing-in speeches. As Moran explains 'when women do appear in the texts of male appointees, and they always do, their role is overwhelmingly formally outside the professional family, confined to that other realm: domestic/biological reproduction.

particular recognition to his wife, Valerie, and this was the most fulsome mention of any of the judicial partners in the judges examined. He began by framing something of confession to his former Jesuit masters for his current agnostic beliefs and also his 'diverse personal relationships over the years':

> They have included the first woman at the Independent Bar in Western Australia, a stipendiary magistrate, a District Court judge, a president of the Children's Court of Western Australia and, most recently, the Chairman of the Prisoners' Review Board.[52]

He tempered his 'confession', pointing out that its entertainment value was 'significantly qualified by the fact that they are all one person—Valerie, my wife and partner for the past 32 years and mother to the three fine young men who are our sons.'[53] It is not entirely clear whether Chief Justice French's glowing appraisal of his partner's career achievements was personally distinctive to him, or evidence of generational shifts for judges where they and their partners were equally career focused. Certainly, Edelman's comments eight years later (see below) reflect something of a generational shift[54] in this respect.

The speeches delivered by Gageler[55] and Keane[56] JJ both displayed a distinct level of comfort in telling personal narratives but neither speech evidenced any attempt to discount the stories told by those who had delivered the speeches of welcome. Although both men have had fairly stock career narratives, neither came from a legal background. Gageler J had humble beginnings as the 'boy from Sandy Hollow' and the son of saw-millers, a feature of his life that had been relatively prominent in the speeches which preceded his own. Therefore, some of Gageler J's speech in reply was in recounting that story and also in re-asserting his status as an insider in the law. As such Gageler J juxtaposed his familiarity with the High Court as an advocate with his inexperience as a judge:

And when women do appear in the professional context they tend to occupy "reproductive" and "domestic" roles, valued as marginal to the real business of the profession (as secretaries), performing menial tasks supporting the male legal professional/judicial office holder'. We can therefore see that the manner in which French CJ describes the contribution of his spouse, Valerie, is in stark contrast to more historical constructions which have usually confined the description and acknowledgement of the spouse to more domestic roles.

52 *Swearing-in Ceremony, French CJ* (French CJ).

53 Ibid.

54 I acknowledge that as much as this shift might reflect wider institutional generational changes in terms of expectations about gender roles, I also acknowledge that such sentiments might simply also reflect the experiences and perspectives of particular individual judges. Indeed, as we know, thinking about the High Court as an institution shaped by a gender regime encompasses an examination of the individual and the institution and the dynamic interplay between them.

55 *Swearing-in Ceremony, Gageler J* (Gageler J).

56 *Swearing-in Ceremony, Keane J* (Keane J).

> I find myself dressed in unfamiliar robes, seated in an unfamiliar position, in a setting that has otherwise long been familiar to me, if never entirely comfortable. There is no institution with which I have had a longer continuous association than the High Court of Australia. There is no building, indeed no room, in which I have experienced the highs and the lows of legal practice more intensely than the one in which we now sit. There have been few significant events in the last quarter of the history of the High Court and few significant events in the entire history of this building in which I have not, in some way, shared.

Although Gageler J acknowledged that 'much has been said today of the journey that has brought me to this point from a small country town in New South Wales'[57] he did not seek to challenge the veracity of that story as part of his attempt to belong. He acknowledged his parents and said that 'their sacrifice and encouragement gave [him] opportunities denied to themselves by social and economic circumstances'. He further acknowledged his teachers, all the way from his one teacher primary school at Giants Creek Public School to Muswellbrook State High School to Law School at the Australian National University. Although Gageler J pointed to his ample experience as an advocate in the High Court to underscore his suitability for his new role, he also demonstrated his otherness from the law as someone who did not come from a legal family and explained that his interest in the law was engendered by a group of barristers buying the farm across the road. He sought advice and was told: '"Finish high school, get a law degree with honours, get some legal experience and preferably get a Master's degree." Ten years or so later I called him up. I said, "I've done all that."'[58] In telling this story as an outsider who made his way to become an insider in the law, Gageler J does not disrupt the narrative set up by those who welcomed his appointment, but rather reinforces it.

Similarly, in recounting his own life stories, Keane J's recollections served to reinforce, rather than undermine those narratives told by others in welcoming his appointment. He reinforced what had been said about his own background and the sacrifices of his parents and went even further in exploring the purported egalitarian values of the Court.[59] Justice Keane's speech in reply at his swearing-in was fascinating in its unprompted and unparalleled focus on gender and the Australian judiciary as a reflection of an egalitarian democracy. He remarked that 'as a matter of social history,' the Australian judiciary is 'a truer reflection of our people and their values and aspirations than has been the case with judges in previous times and in other places'.[60]It is unspoken in any

57 *Swearing-in Ceremony, Gageler J* (Gagler J).
58 Ibid.
59 *Swearing-in Ceremony, Keane J* (Keane J).
60 Ibid.

explicit way, but of course the most obvious conclusion is that Keane J was joining a Court in which almost half of the members were women. He was quick to point out that in saying this he was not advocating for 'some more expansive role for judges within the tripartite division of the powers of government' but rather 'to make the point that the suggestions that one occasionally sees in the media to the effect that our judges are some sort of remote elite are quite wrong.'[61]

In making the point about the perils of a remote judiciary, Keane J pointed to an article by Sir Stephen Sedley about the resistance of English judges to the extension of the franchise and political rights to women in the United Kingdom. He noted that 'this resistance took the form of a number of decisions to the effect that women were not comprehended by the description "persons" when Parliament first conferred political rights on persons'.[62] Keane J pointed out that of course normal rules of statutory construction meant that the expression "person" should encompass both male and female. But it did not, as his stories of both Lady Sandhurst and Miss Jane Cobden demonstrated. Both had stood for election to the London County Council in 1889 in the period after the UK Parliament appeared to have given women the right to stand for election, and both were elected. However, as Keane J pointed out, Lady Sandhurst was unseated following a challenge lodged by her defeated Conservative opponent 'who claimed that [by] not being a "person" because she was not a man, she could not be a fit person of full age qualified to be a candidate for office.' As for Miss Cobden, Keane told his listeners that she too had been elected but opted to wait

> until the time for challenge was passed before taking her seat, [wherein] she was promptly prosecuted for being a person sitting as a councillor when unqualified. She put up the seemingly iron-clad defence that if she was not a person for the purpose of being elected, she could not possibly be a person for the purpose of being prosecuted. Naturally, she was convicted.[63]

Keane J's decision to focus on this specific story about women and democracy in order to underscore his argument that 'the Australian judiciary is not the champion of elite privilege, but the reflection of the egalitarian democracy' was prescient. His comments were the most overt statement from a High Court judge in the swearing-in context about the need for judicial diversity. It speaks volumes that it would appear that a man judge might find it easier to reflect on matters of gender diversity than the women judges themselves who instead seem intent on neutralising the impact of their gender.

61 Ibid.
62 Ibid. Indeed see Chapter 1 for a brief examination of the persons cases in securing women's access to the legal profession.
63 Ibid.

As the second woman ever appointed to the High Court, Justice Crennan was not interested in reflecting on her particular historical achievement or, indeed, on her status as a woman judge more generally. Her first task in responding to the swearing-in speeches and acknowledging those in attendance was to thank her family. She named her brothers and sisters, her husband, her children (and their respective partners) and her granddaughter in this component of her speech. As was noted above, much was made of Crennan J's status as a grandmother and as a woman in the speeches welcoming her to the High Court. Interestingly, aside from the proportion of her speech where she noted her pleasure in having her family attend, Crennan J did not reflect on this component or any specific experiences as a woman. Rather, her Honour chose to reflect on lofty matters of law:

> This Court is an integral part of the life of the nation with the responsibility of maintaining the Constitution and interpreting it in accordance with what Alfred Deakin called "the needs of time". The Court is also the final Court of Appeal in criminal and civil matters, determines disputes between citizens and government and between governments within our federal system. Because judicial power must be exercised in accordance with judicial process, it is the final protector of the rights of citizens.[64]

While Crennan J was disinclined to reflect critically on her status as a woman judge, she did allude to the social and cultural changes which made her appointment possible:

> Those developments have occurred against a background of significant social change and major shifts in public and private values, but the images to which I have referred of a judiciary which transfuses fresh blood into our polity and of the law as a living instrument conjure up the human qualities needed for the impartial dispensation of justice according to law.[65]

Significantly, Justice Crennan also referenced the human qualities needed for the dispensation of justice. Although her Honour was not willing to make any reference to her gender, she was willing to conjure notions of humanity into her conceptualisation of the judicial role.

Justice Kiefel adopted a similar strategy to that of Justice Crennan in attempting to neutralise the gendered dimension to her story. Whereas the gendered focus on Crennan J's story was on the maternal, for Kiefel J, the focus was on her elevation from 'legal secretary to barrister'. After her obligatory thanks, she set about diluting the significance or difference of her career trajectory. She remarked that she had been 'somewhat surprised about the level of

64 *Swearing-in Ceremony, Crennan J* (Crennan J).
65 Ibid.

interest' in a story that she did not 'consider to be so very different from that of many others'.[66] As examples of the seeming uneventfulness of her life trajectory Kiefel J pointed to 'the histories of [her] husband and [her] friend, Helen Lynch.'[67] In making this point Kiefel J joined together notions of merit and equal opportunity stating '[i]n each case we have made our way but we have also been given opportunities'.[68] If there were any particular trials and tribulations for her Honour as a woman in the law, or peculiar challenges in the transformation from legal secretary to barrister to judge, we would not know of them from her speech.

Although Justice Kiefel was disinclined to touch on any of the gendered aspects of her career trajectory, she did acknowledge that she was someone with a 'non-traditional legal education'. She expressed her gratitude to Professor Sir David Williams as President of Wolfson College for 'having the faculty overlook, for the first time, the absence of a first degree'. Kiefel J credited her time at Cambridge as 'a turning point in [her] understanding and love of the law.' She also mentioned that her year in Cambridge introduced her to her husband 'Michael Albrecht, an exceptional man'. In describing her husband, she said that she was 'privileged to have enjoyed [their] partnership in life' and hints at the extent of personal sacrifices which often attend career success at this level, mentioning the 'support account of which I know I have overdrawn'.[69] Aside from thanking her spouse, Kiefel J also named and thanked her personal assistant for twenty years of service and various members of her family for their support. She lamented the fact that her mother did not live long enough to see her appointment, but expressed gratitude that her father did. Justice Kiefel acknowledged the support and presence of her siblings and thanked them for the 'experience of her nieces and nephews'.[70]

Perhaps the most significant aspect of Justice Bell's speech in reply was her explicit statement about what she was not. Bell J was keen to emphasise that she did not see herself as filling the role of the judge whose seat she was taking on the Court.[71] She said that she would not, despite suggestions from others, 'fill the shoes of the Honourable Michael Kirby' because '[n]o *one* person could do that.'[72] Her decision to distance herself from Kirby might quite plausibly have been an attempt to cast aside any further characteristics which might further render her a judicial 'other', such as for example, her sexuality.[73] As

66 *Swearing-in Ceremony, Kiefel J* (Kiefel J).
67 Ibid.
68 Ibid.
69 Ibid.
70 Ibid.
71 *Swearing-in Ceremony, Bell J* (Bell J).
72 Ibid.
73 See Moran (2011) and Roberts (2012b) for an analysis of the way that Bell J seemed to evince a desire to distance herself from a lesbian, outsider identity. For example, in her speech she thanked her parents and her brother, but not her partner.

Roberts (2012b: 129) pointed out, for 'Bell, a lesbian judge succeeding the court's controversial 'out' (sider) judge' she may have felt pressure to distance herself from his identity and legacy in any case, but this was arguably exacerbated by Kirby's public attempts to draw similarities between their respective judicial personas.[74] Hence Bell evidenced an intention to neutralise this aspect of her 'otherness', and instead focused on the significance of the Court and her appointment to it:

> I am deeply conscious of the honour of appointment to this Court. It is a great and distinguished Court. Its important functions include that it is the ultimate protector of the liberties of all Australians. In 1923 Sir Isaac Isaacs, speaking of the personal right of an accused person to a fair and impartial trial, described it as being so deeply rooted in our system of law and so elementary that it needed no authority to support it.

Certainly, one of the themes marking Justice Bell's ascension to the High Court was her apparent difference from her colleagues, particularly with respect to her longstanding commitment to social justice work as a central and defining feature of her career, rather than as an appendage to more commercial work. In this regard, Bell J seemed content to emphasise this element of her career recounting that she had received a warm letter in response to her appointment from a solicitor who aptly summed up her appointment saying '"it's a long way from Redfern", and so it is'.[75] Notwithstanding her comparative comfort in emphasising this element of her career, Bell J was keen to dispel any feeling that she was a radical appointment. As such she described her almost ten years on the bench of the Supreme Court of New South Wales as 'intellectually stimulating'. Justice Bell further attempted to diminish the impact of any purported difference:

> To those outside the law, and to some within it, judges may be labelled according to whether they are seen to be conservative or progressive or indeed dangerously radical—of course judges have a range of backgrounds and views on social issues—but analyses of this sort take no account of the discipline of judgment writing or, as I have experienced it, the conscientiousness of judges.

In pointing to the discipline of judgment writing and the way judicial power is exercised, Bell made a powerful statement about belonging by representing herself as an insider in the law.

74 See Roberts (2012b: 129–130) where she cited Kirby's public comments as examples of his attempts to draw similarities between Bell's values and his own. These comments did not explicitly reference sexuality but instead, he suggested that 'Bell's experience as public defender would ensure *his* legacy as a protector of the "little people" in Australia would continue' (Roberts 2012b: 130 emphasis in original).

75 *Swearing-in Ceremony, Bell J*. The reference here is to Redfern Legal Centre where Bell was an early volunteer.

More recent speeches in reply reflect a similar theme. Certainly, Justice Gordon did not reflect on gendered aspects of her career trajectory. She did not for example, reflect on her work mentoring women in the profession that had been mentioned by Mr Peters. Her speech largely eschewed the personal—instead preferring to focus on recognising the contributions of others. This she reasoned, was 'because the credit for most, if not all, of what I have achieved is due to others.'[76] Referencing her own networks in the law (and indeed, perhaps even inadvertently men's dominance in the judicial hierarchy given the fact that those referenced were predominately men) she noted that she was 'fortunate to read in the chambers of Geoffrey Nettle (now Justice Nettle of the High Court of Australia) and then with Nemeer Mukhtar, now Associate Justice of the Supreme Court of Victoria.'[77] We cannot know the reasons for her Honour's lack of comment about the judge she was replacing (as tends to be common place for the new judge to acknowledge the contribution of the judge they are replacing), but we might speculate that such reticence reflects the somewhat awkward intersection between the public and private spheres. Justice Gordon nonetheless acknowledged the two men in her life (her husband and son) but her emphasis was on the familial support offered:

> Upon my appointment to the Federal Court, I said that no other partner or child would have tolerated the demands I had placed and would continue to place on each of them. Today—all I can say is sforzando—the musical term for "the same with a forcingly sudden emphasis".[78]

In the case of Justices Nettle and Edelman both reflected on the novelty of their respective ages at the time of appointment to the High Court. Perhaps unsurprisingly, Edelman's age had been more of feature in his speeches of welcome as it was conveyed as means of underscoring the particularly brilliant nature of his achievement. Nettle J nonetheless reflected 'the selectors may have backed a wild card, as the press put it, but, if one looks at the matter objectively, the selectors have also capped the risk.'[79] He wryly observed:

> Given the constitutionally entrenched statutory age of senility of 70 years, and that I am now three score years and four, any damage I might do in the time which remains available is bound to be relatively limited.[80]

76 *Swearing-in Ceremony, Gordon J.*
77 *Swearing-in Ceremony, Gordon J.* Her Honour also noted the (men) Chief Justices of the Federal Court during her time on that Court—Chief Justice Black, Chief Justice Keane and Chief Justice Allsop.
78 *Swearing-in Ceremony, Gordon J.*
79 *Swearing-in Ceremony, Nettle J.*
80 Ibid.

Whereas, Edelman J sought to downplay the significance of his age—acknowledging the potential length of service which might come with appointment at the age of 43 but countering 'Twenty-seven years as a Judge of this Court might seem to be a long time when measured against a single lifetime, but in the life of the law it will not be much more than a blink of the eye.'[81]

Both Edelman and Nettle JJ pointed to their insider status through their respective connections to the Court. Nettle recalled his first significant exposure to the High Court when he 'was sent to the old High Court in Melbourne to instruct the great Tom Hughes of Her Majesty's Counsel as he appeared before a Full High Court presided over by the then Chief Justice, Sir Garfield Barwick'.[82] He described a 'scintillating introduction to the level and pace of debate in this forum' where he marveled at Barwick's 'sagacity' and 'irascibility' and 'Hughes' ability to bend and shape the argument despite the constant verbal hammering to which he seemed to be subject'.[83] Although Nettle J lamented that he never had a chance to appear before Barwick, he noted that he did have the 'privilege of appearing before each of the subsequent Chief Justices, including even Chief Justice French when he was a member of the Federal Court.'[84] Edelman J referenced the anniversary of his time as a judicial associate, noting that it 'was exactly 20 years ago from today that I commenced work as an associate to Justice Toohey. He also acknowledged 'four of the six Judges who sat with Justice Toohey that year and who have shown kindness and offered guidance to me since were Chief Justice Brennan, Justices Gummow, Kirby and Hayne'.[85] Demonstrating the nature of these (fraternal) networks in the profession he observed that each 'of those Justices from that year is here today, together with four other associates and good friends.'[86]

Edelman J's speech in reply stood out for the extent to which it acknowledged the women in his life, offering 'almost all that I know of right was

81 *Swearing-in Ceremony, Edelman J.*
82 *Swearing-in Ceremony, Nettle J.*
83 Ibid.
84 Ibid.
85 *Swearing-in Ceremony, Edelman J.* Note also that Justice Edelman's reference to his time as an associate to Justice Toohey on the High Court emphasises the way in which the opportunity to work as an associate might serve as an important entrée to networks at the very peak of the legal profession. That these kinds of opportunities can shape careers (and potentially reproduce privilege) is readily apparent. And indeed, as we see in the wake of the Heydon sexual harassment revelations (examined in Chapter 8), the asymmetric nature of these power relations (and the fact that men dominate the upper the upper echelons) is especially problematic for women. It is especially problematic when power is abused because it not only potentially excludes the individuals affected but serves as a wider disincentive for women to enter a space that has been traditionally dominated by men.
86 Ibid.

learned from a loving family, and particularly from three women whose selflessness was far greater than the sometimes significant demands of social convention at the time'.[87] Here he was recognising his mother and grandmother who had raised him (and noting that his mother had been a single mother for at least some of his childhood).[88] Edelman J also explicitly recognised the contribution made by his wife, Sarah, and that her contribution to the private sphere had effectively enabled his focus on the public sphere:

> An irony of my appointment as a judge adjudicating in a country where a fundamental underlying legal value is equality of all under the law is that my passion for the law has often meant that Sarah has willingly assumed an unequal share of what should be an equal division of family labour.[89]

Indeed, the earlier remarks of Chief Justice French and those of Justice Edelman appear to evidence something of a shift from older constructions of judicial marriage relationships in swearing-in speeches, where wives were acknowledged for caring roles, or indeed, where the spouses of men judges were thanked but without reference to their contributions beyond the family unit.

The narratives recounted above are mere snippets of the lives, perspectives and times of the judicial officers sitting at the apex of Australia's legal system. The breadth of this chapter, in examining speeches by and about judges, means this is not a complete textual summary of the speeches. Rather, the chapter drew on key ideas and themes in order to examine the ways in which the gendered state of being a judge is represented in the narratives given at various swearing-in ceremonies. Certainly, the framing of the appointment of women was a manifestation of the awkwardness that continues to permeate the appointment of women judges. The tension exhibited by both the judicial subject and the storyteller alike resonated with the efforts of the politically powerful to celebrate increased gender diversity while simultaneously reinforcing that gender made no difference to the quality or nature of justice dispensed.

In those speeches welcoming new judges the politically powerful were comfortable with emphasising the feminine (and masculine) so long as the over-arching narrative clearly demonstrated that a deserving and meritorious person had been appointed. Given the relative similarity of those appointed, we actually see in many key respects how the speechmakers appeared to revel in the differences manifest in the life and career trajectory of the new judge. The further a judge departed from the stock narrative the more the speechmakers emphasised their purported difference. But what is the stock narrative and is it a

87 Ibid.
88 Ibid.
89 Ibid.

real or meaningful construct? It is perhaps worth acknowledging that although the very nature of a stock narrative might be contentious, what we imagine as the persona of the judge and the qualities associated with the judicial role are at least historically imbued with our collective recollection that women were literally excluded from exercising judicial authority. For reasons of history then, women's stories were more likely to be treated as counter stories in the law.

In the speeches examined here, we saw the focus on Crennan J's 'grandmotherly' qualities, Kiefel J's elevation from the typist pool to brilliant barrister and Bell J's elevation from community justice work to the highest echelons of judicial office. These were all matters which distinguished them from their judicial colleagues. Their gender remained the unspoken common denominator. There is nothing inherently negative about the level of interest women's appointments as judicial officers continues to generate. If anything, it is reflective of gender hierarchies which excluded women from accessing and exercising this kind of power. Moreover, nor is the kind of analysis undertaken in this chapter intended to be prescriptive about how gender should or could be framed in these cultural scripts. The point is to examine the values embedded in the scripts, in part to understand how gender currently interacts with judicial power, and in part to think about how new scripts might be written into the future.

What we see from the speeches then is that men and women judges alike are keen to tell a story of belonging. When the judicial subject takes on the role of the storyteller we see the devices used, and the lengths the judicial subject will go to in casting themselves as insiders. The men judges reinforce or reproduce the stories that are told in celebration of their career, whereas the women judges offer narratives that are in some key instances oppositional. For example, the speechmakers emphasised the 'remarkable' stories of Gageler and Keane JJ succeeding despite socio-economic barriers. These themes were reinforced and embraced by both Keane and Gageler JJ, suggesting, even if only implicitly, that this was a kind of difference to be proud of. The way in which the women judges responded to the differences emphasised by those who welcomed them could not be starker.

Swearing-in speeches are traditionally understood to eschew adversarialism, yet the women judge's responses leaned in that direction. Even when a number of political stakeholders sought to emphasise gender, the women pushed especially against this in crafting their own oppositional narratives. This was more than the usual humble response to temper the speakers' hyperbolic praise, intended or otherwise. Appearing humble in the face of seemingly extravagant praise is a convention upheld by all judicial appointees. Rather, the women judges' narratives revealed something of an *oppositional cast*, a contest between competing narratives, in which the women judges directly subverted the veracity of the stories told about them. This was manifest in Crennan J's refusal to engage with her status as a woman judge or her 'grandmotherly qualities', Kiefel J's insistence that she did not think her career trajectory that different from any other, and Bell J's overt attempt to distance herself from the notion that hers was a radical appointment. Likewise, Gordon J's decision not to engage with her contributions to mentoring women in the law suggests a similar inclination to distance herself from an identity as a woman judge.

These attempts to neutralise the 'otherness' embedded in their stories therefore implied that these are differences with which the judicial subject does not want to be associated. The narratives of neutrality expose some of the (contested) values associated with judicial office. Significantly, the gendered tensions between judicial subject and storyteller reveal a challenge for legitimacy, although who exactly is doing the challenging, and what implications this has for women's authority as legal knowers remains to be seen.

Women's exclusion from legal authority has meant that the persona of the judge has long been associated with the masculine. In fact, the legal persona of the judge has been so closely entangled with notions of masculine rationality that it has obscured the persona of the judge, presenting the judge as a neutral and disembodied feature of the legal system. While men judges' individual personae and partiality might have once been obscured by the trappings of their judicial role, this concealment has been more difficult to maintain with the arrival of women judges. Hence in the speeches we see judges and those who welcome them grappling with evolving notions of judicial identity. Because men as a group have not been excluded (granted, not all men benefit from hegemonic masculinity and hence men's access to legal authority has been restricted by race, class and sexuality) there is less at stake in celebrating their individual identity. For women, whose exclusion from legal authority exists in recent memory, there is far more at stake in denying their individuality and particularity and thus aligning so far as possible with the persona of the disembodied judge (even if this persona itself is merely a constructed identity designed to legitimise the judicial role).

The oppositional narratives presented by women judges, insofar as they attempted to neutralise the feminine, are indicative of the prevailing masculinist gender regime. The evolving nature of gender regime in light of the arrival of women can nonetheless be seen in the way in which French CJ and Keane J reflect upon women's status as legal knowers. For French CJ the reflections were more personal (in that he was commenting on the career of his wife), whereas for Keane J the reflections were more broadly concerned with canvassing the progress which has been made towards gender diversity. That these reflections were made by men rather than women points to the manner in which the presence of women might disrupt a traditionally masculinist gender regime but it also points to the difficulty in dislodging certain masculine constructions about what it means to be a judge. We now turn to an examination of women judges' first judgments (itself another institutional ritual instrumental in shaping the persona of the judge) which provides further scope to observe how women are situated as legal knowers.

Chapter 4

A judgment of one's own? Staking a claim to judicial authority[1]

In the legislative branch of the Australian political system a newly elected member has their first opportunity to set out their identity and agenda in a speech free of the noise of dissent or debate. That opportunity is labeled, almost without irony, the 'maiden speech'. In recent times the official nomenclature has shifted so that such speeches are officially titled 'first' or 'inaugural speeches.' Even so old habits die hard as they are often still referred to as 'maiden speeches', an indication of the deeply 'entrenched nature' of the knot 'of gender, language and power' (Young 2007: 242; see also Power and Berardone 1998). Convention dictates that the price the incumbent must pay for being 'heard without interjection' in the 'bear pit' (as parliamentary arenas are often described) is that 'the Member should not be unduly provocative' (Barlin 1997: 159). The High Court has adopted a similar welcoming tradition whereby new judges write the lead judgment in an early judgment and their judicial colleagues agree with their reasons.

In this chapter, I argue that a newly appointed judge's first lead judgment, the 'maiden judgment', serves more than a ritualistic welcoming purpose. It might nonetheless function in reinforcing the gender regime. A first or 'maiden' judgment can be distinguished from ordinary joint judgment practices in Australia (where authorship is not usually explicit) because it involves the new judge writing the lead judgment and their judicial colleagues signaling their concurrence in one line, writing, 'I agree'. Thus these judgments are a useful way of situating a discussion about women judges' contributions vis-à-vis difference. The leadership opportunity afforded by the first lead judgments isolates the woman judge's nascent judicial voice. This feature alone suggests that such judgments might be an interesting but thus far largely overlooked site for interrogating the judicial perspectives women judges bring to their role.

1 Parts of this chapter draw on material and arguments previously published in McLoughlin. K. 2015. 'A particular disappointment? Judging Women and the High Court of Australia'. *Feminist Legal Studies*. 23 (3): 273–294.

Reprinted by permission from Springer, *Feminist Legal Studies* 'A particular disappointment? Judging Women and the High Court of Australia', Kcasey McLoughlin, [COPYRIGHT] (2015b).

DOI: 10.4324/9780429288531-5

The first judgments are illuminating in another way. At first glance the first judgments are ostensibly acts of judicial leadership, the new judge out on their own, perhaps elevated by the esteem conveyed by the concurrence of their colleagues. However, this ritual, especially if understood by reference to the way in which the individual and institutional interact in any gender regime, offers a glimpse into authorship practices. These first judgments are also a welcome to collegial practices because, for the institutional practice to work, the new judge must write in such a way that her colleagues agree with her. In light of institutional practices around collegial authorship on the High Court, the authoring practices of first judgments are themselves a first step in that direction which at the same time also illuminates changing dynamics of the High Court's institutionalised gender regime.

'Maiden' is itself a gendered term and of course has many meanings, some of which are relevant in this context both consciously and unconsciously. The word literally evokes the imagery of the virgin or something or someone new or untouched. This etymology explains why the term is used unflinchingly in reference to a first voyage and it is commonly used to refer to a new parliamentarian's first speech. So pervasive is this masculinist terminology that even scholars writing from a gender-friendly perspective reproduce the term in ways that at least appear unconsciously to reproduce the gendered baggage inherent in the term. Notwithstanding the masculinist assumptions underlying the terminology, the problematised imagery of the maiden is actually quite prescient in terms of the analysis which follows. In the parliamentary arena such speeches are frequently a 'moment in the sun' where the newly elected member is given their opportunity to create a voice and a chance to be heard before they retreat to the backbench. There are clear political purposes and dimensions in the parliamentary 'maiden speech', which contribute to the politician's self-fashioning of a nascent parliamentary identity.

I want to draw on these notions of self-fashioning and use them as a means to explore 'first judgments.' Although the craft of judgment writing and the conventions associated with it do not leave the space for the kind of identity markers made explicit in a parliamentary speech, to imagine that the judge leaves nothing of herself and her newly forming judicial identity on the pages of her first lead judgment, is to fall into a dubious positivist trap. Like political 'maiden speeches', these judgments give the newly minted women judges the space to explore, and to some extent set out, their new found identity as a judge on the highest court in Australia. The questions posed by this chapter consider the gender regime the new judge is required to negotiate. Does the woman judge ever shake off the status as 'maiden,' bound to conform for the sake of comity?

The practice itself might not appear to be particularly significant, but it has been identified numerous times by Lynch and Williams (e.g. 2008: 243; 2010: 274) in their annual statistics of High Court decisions but not through the prism of gender. The ritual has also been deemed newsworthy enough to prompt newspaper columnist Michael Pelly (2009: 27) to comment, almost as a throwaway line, 'perhaps this courtesy applies to women only'. What was significant about Pelly's commentary was his observation that there was a gendered dimension to this new practice because he noted that no such courtesy was extended to Chief Justice Robert French in his first decision in 2009. Pelly was perhaps a little overzealous in finding chivalry in the institutional practices of the High Court as it has routinely been adopted as a welcoming practice since 1995 and it has therefore applied to men and women alike. Despite the fact that this courtesy has been extended to men judges, Pelly's enthusiasm for finding difference, or at least differential treatment, is demonstrative of the potential for the presence of women judges to prompt commentators to search for difference, or at least for evidence of what might be described as special treatment simply because they are women. This kind of comment or observation, journalistic as it might be, provides a glimpse into the ways in which gender puts us on notice and potentially shapes the way judicial authority is received.

As I noted in the book's introduction, journalist Jack Waterford's (2012: 16, my emphasis) remark that 'the women [judges] have seemed *a particular disappointment*, especially for those who have hoped for different or wider perspectives than from those steeped in old styles of the law' is yet another example of the ways in which women's legal authority might be received. In the same article, Waterford (2012: 16) made reference to the authorship practices of the High Court noting that 'three hands' appeared to be responsible for authoring most of the judgments, so much so he concluded that '[i]t would be cruel, but fair, for the outsider to wonder what the other four judges do, apart from sign on to drafts written by Gummow or French'. Although Waterford did not explicitly say that the women judges were not pulling their intellectual weight or not quite up to 'it'—the inference is certainly there. Notice how quickly the notion that women judges were a 'disappointment' (for failing to offer different or wider perspectives) becomes women judges are not pulling their weight and are simply signing on to joint judgments.

This sort of commentary—about the purported special treatment women might receive or doubting the extent of their contributions to a collegiate Court (where authorship is not always clear in any case)—provides some insight into how women are situated as legal knowers. Moreover, these questions of authority and authorship take on a particular significance in light of debates about judgment writing which were especially pronounced in 2013 and 2014. As I will examine in the latter part of this chapter, extra-curial remarks from Justices Heydon, Gageler, Kiefel and Keane provide some insights into the perceived tensions between the individual and the collective in terms of approaches to judgment writing. In what follows I provide a (brief) sketch of the first lead judgment handed down by each of the women judges who comprised the first almost equal gender balance on the High Court of Australia. The justification for confining my analysis in this way is simply that it was the application of this ritual to the women judges who comprised the first almost equal gender balance that attracted gendered commentary. Indeed, it speaks to changing dynamics associated with women's entry into this domain. It is therefore useful to situate the examination undertaken here within the contemporaneous debates about questions of authorship, authority and collaboration and what these might tell us about the Court's gender regime. Justice Susan Crennan's first lead judgment was handed down in *Harriton v Stephens* (2006) 226 CLR 52, for Susan Kiefel this was in *Queensland Premier Mines v French* (2007) 235 CLR 81, and in Virginia Bell's case this was in *Hickson v Goodman Fielder* (2009) 237 CLR 130. In many respects, bringing these judgments together is quite a strange undertaking. In fact only one, *Harriton*, is especially legally significant in that it generated considerable academic commentary (see e.g. Grey 2006; Stretton 2006). Legally and factually these decisions have almost nothing in common. However, the concern here is not with their similarity in terms of their content, but with the purpose they serve as the first judgments of High Court women judges.

The first judgment practice, as a 'conscious tradition of the Court' (Lynch and Williams 2008: 243), clearly serves as a rite of passage for the newly-elevated justices. But it also raises important questions about their significance for providing an insight into the differences women judges might present, and their potential for disrupting what has traditionally been seen as a masculinist gender regime. Yet it is also fair to say that this practice remains somewhat ad hoc and varied. For example, it mostly involves concurrence across the entire Court, but in some instances the full bench was less willing to comply. Perhaps the most interesting feature—especially in light of the gendered commentary which attended the practice—is that although it has been mostly equivocal for men judges, this has not always been the case for the women judges. The most notable example is Crennan J's lead judgment in *Harriton v Stephens* (2006) 226 CLR 52 where the practice was diminished somewhat by the inclusion of separate reasons, one of which was a dissenting judgment. Although Crennan J's judgment appears to be the only one subject specifically to a dissenting judgment, partial adherence was also seen in judgments welcoming Kiefel and Heydon JJ as additional (but concurring) published reasons were included.[2] More fulsome adherence to the practice was seen in welcoming Bell, Keane, Gageler, Callinan, Hayne, Gummow JJ and Gleeson CJ.[3]

2 For example, Kiefel, Heydon and Bell JJ's lead judgments each conformed with the ritual but the inclusion of additional concurring reasons diluted the practice somewhat. See Kiefel J's judgment in *Queensland Premier Mines v French* (2007) 235 CLR 81 and Heydon J's judgment in *Eastman v Director of Public Prosecutions (ACT)* (2003) 214 CLR 31.

3 The informal welcome to the bench appears to have been in practice for some time now. For example, see Keane J's first judgment in *SZOQQ v Minister for Immigration and Citizenship* [2013] HCA 12; Gageler J's first lead judgment in *Mills v Commissioner of Taxation* (2012) 293 ALR 43; Callinan J's first lead judgment in

Nettle[4] and Gordon JJ's arrival to the High Court was marked by full adherence to the welcoming ritual.[5] More recently, Edelman J's arrival was marked by more partial adherence to the welcoming ritual.[6]

The timing of the judgments has also varied—for example in the cases of Crennan, Kiefel and Bell JJ the opportunity to exercise judicial authority and leadership occurred within the first three judgments they handed down but certainly represented the first time they wrote alone. The exact timing of the welcoming ritual varies but it is nonetheless distinguishable because it comes very early after a new judge is sworn-in and the authorship practice is distinctive, as the incumbent is clearly identified as lead writer. Although it is sometimes the very first judgment handed down by a new judge, in some instances the welcome judgment represents an early, but not first judgment. For example, Crennan J's first lead judgment was the third involving her Honour, for Kiefel J her Honour's first lead judgment was the second judgment handed down and for Bell J, her Honour's first lead judgment was her second.

The welcome for Chief Justice French seems to have been something of an anomaly as his opportunity for a first lead judgment did not occur until some months into his tenure on the Court. Despite the time lag, his Honour's judgment in *Keramianakis v Regional Publishers Pty Ltd* (2009) 237 CLR 268 conforms in terms of concurrence across the Court with each judge writing 'I agree'. This might explain why Pelly mistakenly noted that Chief Justice French had not been welcomed as the relevant judgment was handed down after the publication of Pelly's opinion piece. Nonetheless, the differences identified above notwithstanding, the purpose of this institutional practice in affording new High Court judges the opportunity to write a lead judgment very early into their term clearly serves to signal a welcome to them by the Court's existing members. Although the practice is not gendered in the sense imagined by Pelly (i.e. only applying to women), these institutional practices still have gendered and gendering consequences.

As noted above, the first judgment serves as more than a 'rite of passage'. Since the new judge acts as the major opinion author with the other judges offering a one-line concurrence (the above exceptions notwithstanding), the

Penney v R (1998) 155 ALR 605; Hayne J's first judgment in *Wynbergen v Hoyts Corporation* (1997) 149 ALR 25; Gummow J's first judgment in *David Grant & Co Pty Ltd v Westpac Banking Corporation* (1995) 184 CLR 265 and Gleeson CJ's first judgment in *Commissioner of Taxation v ANZ Savings Bank* (1998)194 CLR 328.

4 See Nettle J's first judgment in *Queensland Nickel Pty Limited v Commonwealth of Australia* [2015] HCA 12 (8 April 2015).

5 See Gordon J's first judgment in *Smith v The Queen* [2015] HCA 27 (5 August 2015).

6 See Edelman J's first judgment in *Kendirjian v Lepore* [2017] HCA 13 (29 March 2017), noting that Nettle and Gordon JJ gave short separate concurring judgments whereas Kiefel CJ, Bell, Gageler and Keane JJ each noted "I agree with Edelman J."

first judgment gives an obvious space for the new judge's individual judicial voice to be heard. Indeed, writing practices on the High Court generally mean that individual authorship is not made explicit in joint judgments so the first lead judgments are a unique space for understanding the intersection of leadership and collegiality.

Groves and Smyth (2004) undertook a study of patterns in judgment writing practices on the High Court decisions handed down between 1903 and 2001. Although their empirical analysis does not include many of the judgments with which I am concerned, their classifications of the various authorship practices and subsequent findings are salutary for the discussion at hand in that they explain the specific authorship categories which are adopted on the High Court. For the purposes of their study they identified four possible judgment categories: (a) joint judgments; (b) concurring judgments; (c) short concurring judgments; and (d) dissenting judgments. They explained their approach as follows:

> We classified a judgment as a joint judgment if it was delivered by two or more Justices who were in the majority, based on the orders of the Court. We classified a separate judgment as a concurring judgment if the Justice agreed with the reasons of the majority expressed in the orders of the Court, but did not agree with the reasons for reaching that conclusion. A judgment was classified as dissenting if the Justice disagreed with the result proposed by the majority expressed in the orders of the Court.
>
> (Groves and Smyth 2004: 257)

What Groves and Smyth termed "short concurring judgments" (i.e. where judges signal concurrence by stating "I agree" rather than providing reasons) fluctuated from 5 to 15 per cent of judgments delivered but had declined markedly towards the end of the period they examined (which predates the arrival of the almost equal gender balance). First lead judgments are a particular manifestation of 'short concurring judgments', a form of authorship that is not especially prevalent on the High Court in any case. Far more common are joint judgments, which because they involve judges collectively producing a judgment, obscure individual contributions. Making note of the potential for joint judgments to obscure the contributions of individual judges need not fall into the kind of critique posited by Heydon (see below) or Waterford (2012), but it might sometimes pose challenges in assessing the jurisprudential contributions of individual judges. For instance, authorship is most obvious when judges write alone either in separate concurring judgments or in dissent, but some judges are less inclined to do so. First lead judgments provide judges with an opportunity to exercise leadership (insofar as the other members of the Court agree with their reasons). Hence, they are especially noteworthy because authorship is so visible.

In the rest of the chapter I examine these interconnected layers of difference within the first judgments and then situate those findings within a broader (but necessarily ongoing) discussion about the contributions women judges have made. These judgments are illuminating because they contribute to our understanding of the gender regime on the High Court. They do so on three levels: first, they reveal a moment of judicial authority for women judges by isolating their judicial voice; second, they prompt questions about the extent to which there is space for the provocative judge's voice in the prevailing gender regime; and, third, they prompt questions about the ways in which women's jurisprudential contributions are received. In particular, given the model of collegiality adopted on the High Court in recent times, it raises questions about the nature of that voice, and hence the interactions between gender, difference and judicial authority.

Although attributing a causal link between the arrival of women judges and 'difference' (however construed) will always be fraught, it is at least possible to assert that the arrival of a near-gender balance saw high levels of consensus emerge. In any case, questions of causation do not preclude discussions around whether more women judges are contributing to this 'comity' and collaborative practice. The chapter examines this more general trend towards consensus and collegiality but does so in the context of the welcoming judgments. It does not purport to provide a comprehensive account of authorship practices across the full court.

With this in mind, it is useful to make clear the boundaries of what this chapter seeks to do. The chapter examines the *significance* of the first judgments of the women judges as part of a broader discussion about difference and the gender regime. The chapter draws tentative conclusions about possible links between the growing tradition of collaboration on the Court and the gender identities of those on it.

Captains on their 'maiden' voyage

Politicians' 'maiden speeches' are a peculiar juxtaposition of personal and political narratives. They set out the incumbent's life story, their political allegiances and their philosophy. Clearly, none of these matters has any place in legal judgments as traditionally framed. But this does not mean that this space cannot serve a similar kind of identity-creating purpose. The most striking similarity, especially in view of the way that the judgments fell, is in the significance of these first lead judgments in allowing a voice for women judges; a moment of authority without the distractions of debate or, for the most part, dissent. In comparing political 'maiden speeches' to 'a ship's first voyage,' Horn, Leniston and Lewis (1983: 232) describe it as 'a traditional launching provided but once,' a rite of passage that might be viewed as 'an artificial calm before the storm of parliamentary debate commences'. This imagery is almost prophetic when we consider that, in the cases examined, the women judges' first judgments also take on a similar temporal space by facilitating a space for seemingly unencumbered judicial authority. In jurisprudential terms, having your reasons agreed to is the closest equivalent to the quiet of a parliamentary speech without interruptions.

In the case of first judgments the woman judge is centre stage, her judicial authority presumably is in full force. However, these judgments are written to comply with the institutional practice of the Court in encouraging conformity. Yet what can these first judgments tell us about the contributions of women judges, or indeed, gender difference more broadly? The theoretical justification for continued discussions about women judges, broadly framed around notions of difference, is that even if the results of such inquiries are equivocal, they are useful insofar as they permit a 'fresh look' at the judiciary (Rackley 2009: 22). First lead judgments therefore offer the opportunity to take this fresh look insofar as they bring the gendered notions of power within a given gender regime and the division of labour to the fore. In addition, through a consideration of judicial authority and authorship in the first judgments we can gain some insight into understandings of difference (or its absence). The division of labour and judicial authority present in these first judgments will have a bearing on the craft of judgment writing and consensus building. Certainly, the welcome ritual contributes to a form of collegial writing on the Court that encourages writing in a style and form amenable to one's colleagues. In this way the first judgments actually serve to illuminate the extent of the consensus which has emerged on the Court.

Harriton v Stephens *(2006) 226 CLR 52*

Justice Crennan's leading judgment in *Harriton v Stephens* (2006) 226 CLR 52 is the most logical starting point, in part because it came first chronologically, but also because of the three first judgments by the women justices it is the one which most clearly raises potentially 'feminist' issues. It is also the most provocative of the judgments and this might give some clues as to the relative lack of consensus as compared with the other first judgments. Gleeson CJ, Gummow and Heydon JJ agreed with her Honour's reasons.

Although the facts are relatively straightforward, the legal, moral and philosophical dilemmas raised by the case are decidedly complex. Alexia Harriton was born profoundly disabled and in need of lifelong care. Her mother had visited her general practitioner, Dr Max Stephens, concerned that she might be suffering from rubella while pregnant. Dr Stephens did a blood test and found no evidence that Mrs Harriton had rubella. However, as it transpired Mrs Harriton did suffer from rubella during her pregnancy and this fact led to Alexia being born with significant disabilities. Alexia, through her tutor (Mr Harriton, her father), commenced a 'wrongful life' claim for damages. It was common ground between the parties that had Mrs Harriton been properly diagnosed, she would have terminated the pregnancy. As such the key issue for determination was whether a child who is born disabled has a cause of action against a doctor who 'failed to advise the child's mother during her pregnancy of circumstances which would have led the child's mother to obtain a lawful termination of that pregnancy'.

In her lead judgment Justice Crennan contended that because damage is an essential component of an action in negligence, Alexia's claim must fail, as damages could not be properly made out in such a case. This was the case, according to Crennan J because a 'comparison between a life with disabilities and non-existence, for the purposes of proving actual damage and having a trier of fact apprehend the nature of the damage caused, is impossible'.[7] According to Justice Crennan (and the majority who agreed with her reasons), the impossibility of this kind of comparison is underscored by the fact that:

> Judges in a number of cases have recognised the impossibility of the comparison and in doing so references have been made to philosophers and theologians as persons better schooled than courts in apprehending the ideas of non-being, nothingness and the afterlife.[8]

Wrongful life cases raise difficult questions about morality and philosophy. Interestingly, Crennan J sought to deny the existence of a duty of care on the basis of the perceived conflict such cases may create regarding the rights of a child and the rights of a mother in relation to abortion. Her Honour thus pointed out that certain duties were not in doubt as 'a doctor has a duty to advise a mother of problems arising in her pregnancy, and that a doctor has a duty of care to a foetus which may be mediated through the mother.'[9] However, in the balancing of duties owed, Crennan J was especially cautious in not elevating any duties insofar as abortion was concerned:

> To superimpose a further duty of care on a doctor to a foetus (when born) to advise the mother so that she can terminate a pregnancy in the interest of the foetus in not being born, which may or may not be compatible with the same doctor's duty of care to the mother in respect of her interests, has the capacity to introduce conflict, even incoherence, into the body of relevant legal principle.[10]

Hence, what we see here, despite the justification being couched in the language of coherence of legal principle, is a clear disinclination by Crennan J to make any judicial statement as to a positive duty of care to give advice which might lead to termination.

Hayne and Callinan JJ agreed with Crennan J in substance but each nonetheless offered some additional (short) remarks. Hayne J accepted that 'the

7 *Harriton v Stephens* (2006) 226 CLR 52, 126 (Crennan J).
8 Ibid.
9 *Harriton v Stephens* (2006) 226 CLR 52, 125 (Crennan J).
10 Ibid, 125 (Crennan J).

appellant ha[d] not suffered what the law should recognize as damage' but reasoned that the existence of a duty of care should be left aside because the essential elements for an action in negligence could not be established. Similarly, Callinan J agreed with the reasons offered by Crennan J but added that the action must fail because it is 'not logically possible for any person to be heard to say that they should not have been born because if they had never been born they would not be able to say anything at all'.[11]

Kirby J delivered the sole dissenting judgment, finding that wrongful life actions could succeed on the basis of ordinary principles of negligence. Justice Kirby took a decidedly different view and thought the more relevant question was 'who should pay for the suffering, loss and damage that flow from the respondent's carelessness' and on the basis of that characterisation found that the 'ordinary principles of negligence law sustain a decision' in Alexia's favour. Notwithstanding Justice Kirby's dissent in *Harriton*, given the complicated moral and legal questions at hand, it was a significant first lead judgment for Justice Crennan and no doubt made more significant by the fact that the other judges (by and large) agreed with her reasons.

Queensland Premier Mines v French *(2007) 235 CLR 81*

Justice Kiefel handed down her first lead judgment as a Justice of the High Court of Australia in *Queensland Premier Mines v French* (2007) 235 CLR 81. Like Justice Crennan before her, Kiefel J's judicial colleagues afforded her the courtesy of writing the lead judgment and agreeing with her reasons. Indeed, even though Kirby J again delivered separate judgment in this case, unlike his clear disagreement with Justice Crennan's reasons in *Harriton*, he noted that he had come to the conclusion expressed by Kiefel J in her 'careful reasons'. *Queensland Premier Mines v French* involved a relatively complicated set of facts in which the High Court was required to determine whether vested rights include the right to recover moneys owed under a separate loan agreement secured by a mortgage. In this case the lender provided money secured by mortgages over land in the State of Queensland to Queensland Premier Mines. Although this loan was made in 1989, no money was repaid by 1992 and as such, the lender then assigned his rights and interests in the loan to Mr. French. By 1999 no repayments had been made and Mr. French agreed to sell the mortgages to the Beckinsales, who were at this point acting on behalf of Marminta. In 2004 Marminta enforced their buy-back agreement and then became registered proprietors of the mortgages, but not the loan agreement. The mortgages were released and the land was transferred to Unison properties. They contended that their status as registered proprietors of the mortgages meant that the right to recover under the loan agreements became theirs. Hence the High Court was required to consider whether the construction of

11 Ibid, 113 (Callinan J).

section 62 of the *Land Title Act 1994* (QLD) operated to vest in transferee of the mortgage the right to recover monies under the loan agreement (in circumstances where the obligations were not comprised in the mortgage document itself). Ordinary principles of statutory construction meant that the words of the section could not support Marminta's contentions.

In dismissing the appeal Justice Kiefel held that such a right does not automatically vest in the transferee, because although 'Section 62 effected an assignment of both the mortgagee's interest in the land and the mortgagee's right of action with respect to moneys which become due under the mortgage' this did not go so far as to 'extend to obligations arising otherwise than under the terms of the mortgage'.[12]

Hickson v Goodman Fielder *(2009) 237 CLR 130*

Hickson v Goodman Fielder (2009) 237 CLR 130 was Justice Bell's first decision handed down as a Justice of the High Court of Australia. The other Justices who heard the matter, Justices Kiefel, Gummow, Hayne and Heydon all agreed with Justice Bell. Of the three women Justices' first judgments, Bell's was the only one handed down with the other judges only contributing a statement indicating that they agreed with her Honour's reasons. The case involved an employee, Glen Hickson, who collided with a motor vehicle on his bicycle while riding home from work. Given that the incident was deemed to have occurred while at work, his employer, Goodman Fielder Ltd made compensation payments to Mr Hickson. Mr Hickson then commenced proceedings for damages against the driver of the vehicle. The driver of that vehicle alleged that any damages should be limited by Mr Hickson's own contributory negligence in causing the accident. However, the District Court found no contributory negligence on Mr Hickson's behalf and awarded him a large sum of damages.

Mr Hickson's employer then commenced proceedings for recovery of compensation payments it made on the basis of legislation which provided that 'if a worker recovered damages against a person other than the worker's employer, the worker was liable to repay the employer out of those damages the amount of compensation received from the employer'.[13] Moreover, additional legislation provided for the reduction of the liability of a worker to repay workers' compensation where the damages recoverable at common law were reduced on account of contributory negligence.[14] Hence the question raised by the High Court appeal was whether:

> the reduction in the liability provided by s 10(2) of the *Law Reform Act* operates only where the third party tortfeasor is sued to judgment and the

12 *Queensland Premier Mines v French* (2007) 235 CLR 81, [56] (Kiefel J).
13 *Workers Compensation Act 1987* (NSW) s 151Z(1)(b).
14 *Law Reform (Miscellaneous Provisions) Act 1965* (NSW) s 10(2).

> Court has made a finding of the extent to which it is just and reasonable that the damages recoverable are reduced having regard to the worker's share in responsibility for the damage.[15]

Justice Bell reasoned that when read with s 10 (2) of *Law Reform (Miscellaneous Provisions) Act 1965* (NSW), the workings of s151Z(1)(b) of the *Workers Compensation Act 1987* (NSW) applied in such circumstances would 'reduce an employee's liability to repay the workers' compensation' received from his employer to such extent as the Court thought just and equitable having regard to the employee's share in the responsibility for his damage. Her Honour reached this conclusion notwithstanding the fact that the third party tortfeasor had not been sued to judgment and in further consideration that 'neither a finding of contributory negligence nor a reduction of damages on that account had been made by a Court'.[16]

Situating the first judgments and judges

Even a cursory glance at the first judgments outlined above indicates that these were not judgments infused with the feminist reasoning techniques which might support findings of difference framed in that way. This should come as no surprise. Both Kiefel and Bell JJ's first judgments raised very technical points of law in relation to the meaning of specific statutory provisions. There was little scope for broad comments about morality or other clearly value-based issues. To be fair, the fact that gender permeates all areas of life means that we know that gender can affect any aspect of the human condition, so this observation is not to discount the capacity for feminist reasoning to recast areas of law which have hereto appeared gender neutral. These issues aside, the point here is that the only judgment to tackle issues overtly relevant to women's lived experience was Crennan J's judgment in *Harriton*, and in any case, her Honour's reasoning does not seem to have challenged traditional notions of legal reasoning or adopted what would easily be construed as feminist reasoning. In this sense, there was a clear distinction between their judgments and that of Justice Crennan who was required to grapple with the difficulties associated with reconciling legal, moral and philosophical issues. As such, while each case might be significant in terms of the leadership role displayed by the woman judge in drafting the lead judgment, these cases, aside from *Harriton*, do not raise the kind of issues which easily lend themselves to feminist findings.

In fact, rather than tell a story of difference, these first judgments tell a story of conformity. This accords with the conventions we understand from first speeches in the legislative sphere. The price for unanimity (at least in some of the cases) is a lack of provocation. In substance and form these are not

15 *Hickson v Goodman Fielder* (2009) 237 CLR 130, 134 (Bell J).
16 Ibid, 145 (Bell J).

provocative judgments. The judgments conform to judgment writing conventions and reveal no departure from the doctrine of precedent. It is perhaps possible to make inferences about the models of consensus adopted in the first judgments. For the men judges appointed around a similar time, as has already been noted, the practice of one-line agreement was actually more fully adhered to. However, for the women judges, Bell J's judgment was the only one which saw full adherence to this practice. Granted, there are many factors which might influence this state of affairs: the individual propensity of some judges to dissent, the legal dilemmas and complications posed by the case and so on. However, as welcoming judges the women judges conformed to the practice across the board by signaling their concurrence to their new judicial colleagues when the opportunity to do so arose. The fact that adherence to the practice has been less fulsome in welcoming women judges (e.g. by virtue of the inclusion of additional and even dissenting reasons) while women judges have themselves complied with the practice when welcoming their judicial colleagues (e.g. none of the women judges have 'disrupted' the ritual by offering separate reasons),[17] may well evidence the implicit pressures women judges face to conform to institutionalised rituals.

As noted in the Introduction, Waterford's comments about authorship suggested that the responsibility for judgment writing was not being shared across the Court. Taking Waterford's characterisation at face value for the moment, it could be noted that it might not be entirely fair. As Lynch and Williams (2011) point out it is exceptionally difficult to critique the contributions of individual judges in not writing lead judgments when we are unsure of the way in which they are directing these jurisprudential contributions through collaborative practices with their fellow judges. However, low levels of dissent and high levels of unanimity expressed in joint judgments do tempt the conclusion that 'norms of collegiality' (Elliott 2001) had a profound impact on both the men and women of the Court. On a collegial Court, the art and craft of judging is informed by authorship decisions and practices. Who writes and with whom matters because it gives us scope to assess the individual jurisprudential contributions of judges. It also provides an indication as to how these contributions are situated within the institutional context in which they occur.

17 I note that subsequently Gordon J 'disrupted' the ritual by writing her own short concurring reasons in *Kendirjian v Lepore* [2017] HCA 13 (29 March 2017) (Edelman J's welcome judgment). This may well be evidence of shifting dynamics whereby women might feel more able to disrupt institutional norms as the place of women on the Court becomes more secure or normalised. Alternatively, of course, it could also simply represent the individual inclinations of a particular judge (noting that Justice Gordon has generally been more inclined to write alone (and dissent) than her sister judges) (see Lynch and Williams 2017; 2018, 2019; Lynch 2020). Indeed, in more recent years it has generally be observed that Chief Justice Kiefel and Justices Bell and Keane (reflecting their publicly stated views) have been more likely to participate in unanimous judgments than their colleagues (Lynch and Williams 2019: 1452).

There are disparate views about what patterns in judgment writing might tell us about gender, difference and judging. Notwithstanding the fact that gender is but one of several variables which might influence patterns in judgment writing, these patterns are nonetheless an important part of situating and understanding a judge's contribution to a given Court. Dissent and adherence to doctrines of restraint have been posited as potential ways of measuring the difference gender might make. Feminist legal theory's critique of law suggests that dissenting judgments will be especially important in challenging the gendered bias of the law. Feminist judgment writing as a form of critique revealed that although dissenting judgments are one manifestation of the disruptive power of difference, not all of the rewritten decisions were framed as dissenting judgments. For example, although the majority of the rewritten judgments in the *Australian Feminist Judgments Project* were written as dissents, seven rewritten judgments agreed with the outcome of the original decisions but provided separate reasons. Hence, we see that even when difference is framed in this manner, challenging the gender bias of the law is contingent upon and relational to the Court and decision in question (Douglas et al. 2014b: 21).

One study of dissent as a potential site of difference has been provided by Belleau and Johnson (2008) and is especially useful in understanding how to understand instances of dissent. They explain that 'dissent, in and of itself, it is not necessarily "progressive" or "reactionary"' but rather that 'dissents can lean in the direction of change, as well as pull towards a status quo' (Belleau and Johnson 2008: 65). For Belleau and Johnson the meaning of a dissenting judgment can only be understood by situating the individual (or individuals) within a particular institutional context. Hence the issue is not simply whether an individual judge dissents but the institutional context in which they do so. In contrast, Elliott (2001: 47) hypothesised that if 'women are prone to "tend or befriend," rather than fight or flee, women may be drawn to the work required to come to consensus, thus ensuring continued collegiality'. In Elliott's (2001: 50) view, what has been understood as a 'different voice' may instead be 'women's response to their position on the bench and the need to forge relationships with their male colleagues'. These seemingly incongruous patterns in judgment writing actually highlight the importance of understanding writing patterns as being situated within a particular temporal space—neither dissent nor collegiality is meaningful without understanding and situating those practices within the institutional regime in which they occur. It is important here to emphasise that I am not seeking to make the point that either collaboration or dissent is the exclusive domain of women (or men). Rather, what I'm seeking to interrogate is the gendered ways in which these contributions are framed.

The symbolic leadership opportunity afforded to each of the women judges in their first judgments therefore needs to be considered in the context of the Court itself and each woman's broader contribution to it. On this level these women cannot be said to have taken on a significant leadership role on the basis of reliable indicators such as levels of dissent or in the authoring of lead judgments (see e.g. Lynch and Williams 2010, 2011, 2012, 2013, 2014). That being said, authorship remains fraught in this respect, as joint judgments do not conventionally give away the identity of the writer in the Australian practice. This makes it difficult to discern the contributions of individual judges. The high levels of unanimity in decisions during 2010 prompted Lynch and Williams (2011: 1044) to observe that the Court 'has been able to speak with one voice'. The figures for 2009, the first year of the almost 'gender balance' reflected a similar state of affairs in terms of a disinclination to dissent coupled with high levels of unanimity. So low were the levels of dissent in 2009 that Lynch and Williams (2010: 276) posited that 'dissent has probably not been rarer in living memory'. This is not to say that the women judges never dissented but, if difference were to be measured by rates of leadership or dissent, it would be difficult to ascribe this characteristic to the women judges on the High Court.

Certainly, observations of authorship and judicial authority painted a picture of consensus amongst the French Court (Lynch and Williams 2014). However, this was not without controversy and further underscored the fact that 'who individual judges are and who they sit alongside matters in our attempts to fully appreciate the High Court as a public institution' (Lynch and Williams 2014: 545). The institutional practices of the Court (especially regarding authorship and consensus) were the subject of a speech delivered by Dyson Heydon while he was a member of the High Court but published at the time of his retirement in 2013. In the view of Lynch and Williams, Heydon 'revealed a strong distaste for the use by some judges of judicial conferences as an occasion on which to forge consensus over disagreement, branding it polite or jovial invitations … to tell lies' (Lynch and Williams 2014: 545–546). Heydon made clear that his comments were not to be taken as being about the Court he had sat on but rather warned of the potential institutional harm, which might be caused by 'judicial herd behavior' and 'excessively dominant personalities' (Heydon 2013: 212). In his view, the Court's preference for consensus as exhibited in joint judicial authorship practices raised important questions about the capacity for judges to exercise judicial independence:

> Composite judgments raise questions. Who did the work? Did every judge understand the judgment? Did every judge closely examine it? Did a confident 'specialist' assume dominance over nervous 'generalists'? What, if any, compromises were made? … The same difficulty exists where a judge delivers a full judgment and the remaining judges say 'I agree'. No doubt the judges do sincerely agree on something, but on what?
>
> (Heydon 2013: 212)

It is perhaps unsurprising that Justice Heydon's views elicited some response from members of the High Court.

Writing extra-curially, Justice Gageler (2014: 203) acknowledged the risks identified by Justice Heydon in contemporary practices whereby it has become increasingly common for members of an appellate Court to join in delivering a single set of reasons or express individual concurrence with the reasons of another judge. Although Justice Gageler (2014: 203) did not construe the risks in quite the same way as Justice Heydon, he still emphasised the importance of writing judgments 'to maximise the probability that the Court as an institution will give the best of possible judgment'. Justice Keane (2014: 13) directly addressed Heydon's commentary in a speech to the Judicial Conference of Australia Colloquium:

> Many of you will have read Mr Heydon QC's essay "Threats to judicial independence: The enemy within" in which he attacks joint judgments, pre and post hearing conferences and other forms of judicial cooperation and collegiate behaviour generally.

Although Justice Keane (2014: 14) accepted 'the right of each appellate judge to write his or her own judgment' he countered that 'like all rights, [it] carries with it institutional responsibilities, one of which is to provide clear, practical guidance to the community and the legal profession'. Pointing to matters of timeliness and coherence and clarity, he argued 'we cannot pretend that we work in isolation: we have institutional responsibilities which those writing academic treatises do not' (Keane 2014: 14).

Conversely, in a speech delivered in 2014, Justice Kiefel spoke in support of judicial collegiality but did not address Justice Heydon's commentary directly. Arguing that 'collegiality is not compromise', Justice Kiefel (2014: 7) defended the notion that judges may seek to influence their judicial colleagues in reaching decisions. Reasoning that judges seeking to influence other members of the Court will most likely be 'found among judges who favour joint judgments', she went on to ask, 'What is the vice in seeking to persuade colleagues, one's equals, to one's point of view? It is hardly as if they are unused to efforts of persuasion' (Kiefel 2014: 4). Interestingly, Justice Kiefel identified a possible tension between individualism and collegiality on the bench:

> A greater difficulty presented by the practice of joint judgments may arise not from the pressure of colleagues to join in, but from a personal desire to stand out, to have one's own voice and develop one's own reputation.

The distinction between judicial independence and individualism provides an important insight into the institutional and individual tensions within the division of labour around judgment writing. Judgment writing has important implications for the quality of precedent from a collective institutional perspective, but there are also conceivably more individual considerations arising from the desire to craft one's own judicial voice. Undoubtedly, a court's approach to writing judgments will have implications for difference—in terms of how it is understood and articulated—but also the extent to which it is possible.

The discursive practices adopted in the welcoming judgments point to the practices engendered on the Court around authorship and authority more broadly. In attempting to situate these judgments and assess their significance, it is perhaps useful again to make mention of the limitations of this kind of analysis. These judgments cannot be demonstrative of the wider jurisprudence of the judges. They are merely an introduction to their jurisprudence and are therefore 'neither definitive nor representative but rather illustrative and indicative' (Rackley 2007: 76). Leaving aside the fact that judges will likely become more comfortable with the craft of judgment writing over time, but noting that Crennan, Kiefel and Bell JJ all had prior judicial experience before being elevated the High Court, one would assume that some elements of style and reasoning would remain consistent and, in that regard, the first judgment might reveal a judge's particular approach at least in some respects. Rather than representing an anomaly whereby women judges are afforded a moment of judicial authority, it might instead be regarded as related to institutional practices which have facilitated the consensus building on the Court. Even unconsciously, the welcoming ritual may well set into motion and normalise institutional collegial writing practices. The welcome ritual, although seemingly innocuous and sometimes only partially adhered to, means that the new woman judge's introduction to judicial authority in Australia's highest court involves drafting a judgment that her colleagues on the bench are comfortable agreeing with. This may well dull the siren call of difference—if difference is to be understood as disruptive. Yet it might also be a partial diminution of an historically masculinist institution.

The masculinist character of law and its institutions is of ongoing concern to feminist legal theorists. It has long been thought that legal method itself might preclude the kind of differences some feminist legal theorists posited that women judges would bring to bear (see Smart 1989). Even for feminist theorists who have sought to work within the constraints of legal formalism in challenging dominant legal narratives it remains the case that there is something about law which has stayed resistant to the transformative potential of difference. Thornton (1996: 28) has explained the way in which legal discourses 'comport with prevailing political exigencies' so that 'supposedly neutral adjudicative techniques, such as *stare decisis*, have legitimated recourse to past representations in order to maintain the status quo'. Similar conclusions might be drawn about consensus in legitimating and preserving the status quo. Unanimity in the Court's decisions and women's complicity in it—understood in the context of their entry into a traditionally masculine domain—are indicative of their role in the preservation of law and its institutions rather than dismantling it. But this is not to suggest that women judges have not made *a* contribution.

The women who sat on the bench of the High Court during the first period in which the gender balance was 'almost equal' sat on a Court marked by consensus and collegiality. It is important to stress here that consensus and collegiality are not the same thing. However, consensus or near consensus in the Court's decisions is a possible consequence of collegiality, particularly when it is understood in the manner invoked by Justice Kiefel when she argued that collegiality (understood in the context of her speech as concurrence reflected in joint judgments) was not compromise. The jurisprudential contributions of women judges have not always resulted in the kind of difference in reasoning imagined by some feminist legal scholars. Indeed, the methodological and philosophical dilemmas of difference have meant that the search for difference has sometimes been disappointingly elusive. Even so, as Rackley (2009) has observed, the presence of women puts us on notice, especially insofar as difference is concerned. The leadership role afforded to women judges in their first lead judgment might pass without mention if it were not for the fact that this obvious leadership role seemed to be at odds with their jurisprudential contributions at large, at least in terms of 'standing out' or making a voice of one's own discernible. However, as I have argued in this chapter, rather than representing an anomaly, these first judgments are illustrative of, and arguably complicit in, facilitating the prevailing model of collegiality.

There is an important postscript to be noted here, particularly in thinking about questions of leadership in light of Justice Kiefel's subsequent elevation to Chief Justice in 2017. Subsequent analysis of institutional trends on the High Court of Australia suggests that the high levels of collegiality on the French Court have continued to be a feature of the Kiefel Court, although this has receded somewhat in more recent times (Lynch 2020: 1228).[18] Interestingly, her Honour has continued to speak in support of judicial collegiality. Indeed, in one of her earliest speeches after being elevated to Chief Justice, Kiefel reinforced her earlier comments about collegiality—even providing details about the process of judgment writing adopted on the Court. Recounting the current approach to pre and post hearing conferences (and acknowledging that these conferences may not have been a feature of the past), Kiefel (2017b: 3) described these conferences as 'informal' and an 'opportunity for persuasion, for criticism, and for debate'. For Kiefel (2017b: 3), 'the benefits of the conference should be obvious':

> Each justice has the benefit of the views of six legal minds which should be amongst the best in Australia. Why would one not listen to them? Even if one does not agree with another point of view, discussion can only assist in refining one's own. The final product is bound to be better.

On the question of authorship, Kiefel explained that where there appears to be a clear majority, one justice is usually tasked with writing the draft judgment.

18 See Chapter 8 where Kiefel's leadership and potential jurisprudential legacy in terms of institutional collegiate approaches to judgement writing is noted in more detail.

Importantly, Kiefel was of course very clear in explaining that there is nothing compelling a judge to join a judgment with which he or she could not agree. However, her comments about authorship provide some insights about how the process of joining might shape judicial method, and indeed gives context to the kinds of approaches to judgment writing that are likely to produce fewer individual judgments:

> There is a method to writing first drafts. They need to be succinct. A long judgment which says more than is necessary is less likely to attract agreement. Neither will a judgment written in the idiosyncratic style of the author, or in florid language from the classics or 19th century literature. It is better to resist the temptation to quote extensively from literature unless the aim is to not have others join in.
>
> (Kiefel 2017b: 5)

Kiefel (2017b: 7) also touched on how authorship and judicial authority might intersect, acknowledging that 'the effect of the High Court's practice of "joining in" is to render the author largely anonymous' but countered that 'it is difficult to see what the benefit of that knowledge [of the author] could be.' In so doing, she effectively refused to engage with suggestions that women (or indeed any individual judges) were not contributors to judgment writing[19]—preferring instead to emphasise the institutional benefits to eschewing the individual.

Interestingly, her willingness to provide this level of detail about approaches to judgment writing might be contrasted with that of her predecessor Chief Justice French. As Hobbs, Lynch and Williams (2017: 56) observed 'while French CJ presided over a court whose members were unusually candid about the institution's decision-making practices and their personal approach to the same, this was not a topic ever broached by the Chief Justice.' What might we make of Kiefel's comparative openness about this topic? Clearly, the notion that fewer (unnecessary) individual judgments is an important institutional goal appears to be something she has prioritised ahead of 'standing out' or a more individual legacy. 'Standing out' might take the form of the great dissenter or even the intellectual giant (whose reputation in many ways rests on 'going alone' so authorship is discerned). However, although Kiefel has spoken out against a kind of individualism and a desire to stand out as reflected in 'vanity judgments', her extra-curial comments *stand out* in a different way—demonstrating the *different* forms that leadership can take. Whether consciously or unconsciously, her institutional leadership on this issue is certainly a rebuttal of the idea of women judges not pulling their weight.

Thinking about difference—what it might look like and who might make it—has evolved in important ways. The first judgments examined in this

19 But see Chapter 7 for an examination of Justice Crennan's explicit engagement with this issue upon her retirement.

chapter tell a story of conformity and collegiality rather than of difference. That conformity effectively begins with the first judgment, itself a welcoming ritual to a masculinist institution. Making a causal link between the gendered identities of those sitting on the bench and the emergence of collegiality is fraught with many of the same problems associated with ascribing causal connections between difference (however it might be framed) and gender. But it is at least possible to assert that the arrival of the gender balance on the High Court saw the emergence of high levels of consensus—a theme which will be revisited in Chapter 7 in the context of the valorisation of collegiality. It is also possible to hypothesise that the discursive authorship practices might be some of the myriad ways the gender regime operates to dull dissent and disruption.

The analogy between 'maiden' speeches and first lead judgments is not perfect. The exercise of judicial authority can be distinguished from the work and speeches of parliamentarians in important ways. But the notion that first judgments bear similarity to 'maiden' political speeches is useful in detailing difference as it prompts important discussions about the interaction between the individual and the institution in a specific gender regime. Juxtaposed with wider trends regarding judgment writing on the High Court, first lead judgments illuminate the extent of collegiality on the Court. The key insight from this chapter is that women judges may not be strictly bound to conform for the sake of comity, but their contributions need to be understood in the context of their entry into a traditionally masculinist domain. The valorisation of collegiality, and the consensus it has arguably engendered, means that in many instances, the Court has been able to speak with one voice. The extent to which that voice is imbued with the perspectives and authority of the women on the Court (or indeed their individual sacrifices and concessions) is not always clear, but it nonetheless points more to the resilience of the gender regime than to its dismantling. That the lack of clarity about the identity of judgment writers led to the assumption that women were not contributors (and were simply signing on to the judgments of Gummow and French), further underscores the resilience of a masculinist gender regime whereby legal authority is conceived as the preserve of men.

Yet it is often surprising how what has appeared unmovable for so long in the popular imagination, like the wall that once divided the city of Berlin, suddenly gives way and another vista becomes possible. In 2012 the High Court heard the case of *PGA v Queen* and developed a new interpretation of the place of rape in marriage within Australian law. The Court turned its gaze to Australian legal history to find that, contrary to what had previously been thought, rape in marriage had not only always been a crime under Australian law, it had also been named as such. As will be argued in the next chapter this was not an act of interpretation driven by precedent, statute and legal argument. Rather it was an act of judicial reimagination. How did this happen? Was this an instance demonstrating that the presence of women on the High Court made a difference? It is to the case of *PGA v Queen* that we now turn.

Chapter 5

PGA v The Queen and the judicial imagination[1]

Much of the work undertaken by feminist legal theorists has been provocatively and powerfully imaginative, especially with respect to developing innovative ways of redressing the law's gender blindness. The law abounds with what Fuller (1967: 1) has described as 'conceits of the legal imagination,' or legal fictions. This is especially the case with legal judgments which by definition rely on the power of the legal imaginations of those comprising the judging authority. By exposing the judges' complicity in legal decision-making, feminist legal theory effectively reveals possibilities for transformation and change. Similarly, the project of feminist judgment writing combines critique, imagination and judicial reasoning to create fictional feminist judgments of significant, but already decided, cases. In so doing, feminist judgment writing occupies a unique space in the legal imaginary in that it reveals the ways in which feminist approaches to legal reasoning might change legal outcomes or at least prevent masculinist narratives from masquerading as genderless legal narratives. Crucially, the premise of feminist judgment writing is to explore the possibilities and limitations of feminist jurisprudence within the constraints of legal formalism, therefore maintaining that the decisions must be legally plausible.

Given the central role of legal imagination for this feminist method as well as for the judgment itself, this chapter aims to provide a novel, yet critical, interrogation of imagination as a form of feminist critique. It does so by examining, on the one hand, the High Court's decision about spousal immunity for rape in *PGA v The Queen* (2012) 245 CLR 355 ('*PGA*') and, on the other, the alternative feminist decision written in response to it. In the context of the book's examination of the gender balance and the gender regime, the decision to juxtapose the High Court's decision with the fictional feminist judgment written to counter it is disruptive. In part this is because the women judges are

1 Parts of this chapter are based on material and arguments published in McLoughlin. K. 2016. 'Judicial Fictions and the Fictive Feminists: Re-imagination as Feminist Critique in PGA v The Queen' *Griffith Law Review* 24(4): 592–615 copyright ©Griffith University, reprinted by permission of Informa UK Limited.

DOI: 10.4324/9780429288531-6

differentially placed in the decision—Crennan and Kiefel JJ joined the majority whereas Bell J was in dissent. However, the fact that women judges negotiated the gender dynamic differently in this decision is no surprise. Contrasting the real and imagined decisions is disruptive because it reveals the strength of the gender regime and, by extension, the difficulties associated with disrupting it.

Feminist judgment writing[2] enacts the separation of 'judgment-writing (legal method) from judicial authority' and in so doing questions 'judicial hegemony over this practice' and attempts to 'demystify it' (Hunter 2012: 144). Judicial hegemony, itself part of the power arrangements embedded in the gender regime, makes challenging legal rationalities handed down from judge to judge as precedent especially difficult. But what about when the received wisdom of the law is an obvious affront to contemporary understandings of the relationship between (and status of) men and women? These issues come to the fore in *PGA*.

As will be seen, the juxtaposition between the real and imagined decisions is not so straightforward because the so-called real judgment is itself an act of legal imagination, a composition of legal fictions. This complicates matters but it also provides an ideal opportunity to explore how 'conceits of legal imagination' (Fuller 1967: 1) inform legal judgments. It further provides an opportunity to examine the way in which gendered understandings of the law continue to shape and inform the gender regime. The intersection between the actual judgment and the counterfactual judgment also provides an opportunity to assess the contingencies involved in subverting the gender regime.

The chapter begins with a discussion of feminist engagement with the law around rape. Given that *PGA* is about the status of the law's truths and fictions about marital rape, it is especially important to reflect, albeit briefly, on the interactions between law and the popular imagination when it has come to conceptualising rape. The history of the legal treatment of rape is a particularly powerful metaphor for the force and consequences of the law's masculinist regime. The chapter then turns to the decision in *PGA* and provides an account of the attention afforded to legal fictions in the majority and minority reasoning. Consideration is given to the scholarly responses to *PGA* (see e.g. Sletvold 2012; Naffine and Neoh 2013; Larcombe and Heath 2012; Lesses 2014), much of which centre on the way in which the Court grappled with

2 Although there is no one correct and linear way of doing feminist judging, the 'feminist judging' checklist devised by Hunter (2010: 35) offers something of a benchmark. Amongst some of the suggested approaches are 'asking the woman question', 'including women', the use of feminist legal scholarship to inform decisions and 'challenging gender bias in legal doctrine and judicial reasoning'. Feminist judging might further bridge theory and practice by reasoning 'from [the] context and the reality of women's lived experience' (Hunter 2010: 35). Finally, the purpose of feminist reasoning might be broadly understood as 'seeking to remedy injustices and to improve the conditions of women's lives' and in promoting equality (Hunter 2010: 35).

the status afforded to legal fictions, before examining the alternative feminist judgment authored by Heath and Larcombe.

The final part of the chapter explicitly examines the conversations between fictions in feminist theory and practice. I argue that by effecting a conversation between the published judgments ('real') and the feminist response ('imagined'), we can think about the role of fictions in legal method more generally, and can also generate new conversations about what counts as feminist judging. Whether the disruption of the gender regime is only possible by explicit feminist judging is further considered. My focus is therefore at once narrow and broad. By examining the interaction between the real and the imagined with respect to a decision in which grand fictions about rape (i.e. the oxymoronic relationship between rape and marriage) were at the fore, the chapter is well positioned to examine the gaps between fictive feminist ruminations of the imagination and those imaginations which are afforded the status of law. In so doing, the chapter explores the weight of history in propagating a masculinist gender regime.

Law's truths and fictions about rape

The law around rape has concerned feminist legal theorists for decades not least because it symbolises and reflects gender biases embedded within the structure, content and scope of laws (see e.g. Brownmiller 1975; Millett 1974; MacKinnon 1987).[3] For married women, matters were previously even more complicated by the common-place acceptance of a long-standing dictum attributed to jurist Matthew Hale (1736: 621) that 'the wife hath given up herself in this kind unto her husband which she cannot retract'. That is, marriage meant that a woman gave ongoing consent to a husband's conjugal demands. Until late in the twentieth century this view underpinned legal authority in Australia. In *PGA* the High Court was tasked with determining exactly when and how the common law shifted in this respect.

The majority, consisting of French CJ, Gummow, Hayne, Crennan and Kiefel JJ, held that marital exemption ceased to exist from at least 1935, thereby effectively rewriting, or re-imagining the narrative of rape law that actually existed in this country. The majority determined that various legislative changes reconfiguring the relationships between husbands and wives in terms of divorce and property ownership had also fundamentally shifted the law in other areas (e.g. consent and rape). However, the minority, consisting of Bell and Heydon[4]

3 I use the term 'rape' as opposed to 'sexual assault' deliberately in recognition of the historical conceptualisation of the crime as such.

4 The revelations which came to light in 2020 about Heydon's sexual conduct during his time on the High Court have subsequently raised questions about whether and how this will shape his jurisprudential legacy. Specifically, questions have been raised about what the allegations reveal about bias against women, and how this might be reflected in his judgments, specifically relating to sexual offences. See for

JJ, each of whom delivered separate dissenting judgments, found that the immunity was part of the law in Australia for most of the twentieth century. On the surface the majority's decision appears 'feminist friendly' since it configures sexual violence, whether in marriage or otherwise, as contrary to the laws of this country. Yet the process by which the Court arrived at that decision was not straightforward but rather a reinterpretation of the legal, political and social reality of the way in which marital rape had hitherto been conceptualised at common law and in the popular imagination. The 'legal imagination' exercised by the majority created a new judicial fiction that ignored the inconvenient truths about the laws governing marital rape in Australia.

Given the majority's reasoning in *PGA*, it is perhaps not surprising that it was selected as one of the decisions meriting a feminist re-write in *Australian Feminist Judgments: Righting and Rewriting Law*. Feminist judgments are disruptive. They present counterfactual arguments to demonstrate 'how judgments could have could have been written and how cases could have been decided differently' (Hunter et al. 2010: 3). But, these judgments also exist within the constraints of legal formalism and their feminist reasoning must be legally plausible. The feminist judges who authored the re-imagined judgment, Wendy Larcombe and Mary Heath, are academics with expertise in the area and have elsewhere made significant contributions about the paucity of legal responses to sexual violence (see e.g. Heath 1998; Heath and Naffine 1994; Larcombe 2005).

Prior to the publication of their alternative judgment, Larcombe and Heath published a traditional critique of the decision in *PGA* which contended that in rejecting Hale's fiction, the High Court majority created a new and deeply problematic fiction that discounted the realities of women's lives (Larcombe and Heath 2012). Although their alternative feminist judgment is cogently written and masterfully argued, in some respects their imaginations did not need to stretch too far in crafting the alternative decision. The issue here lies in the interaction and gap between imagination and reality. Technically their decision concurs with Bell and Heydon JJ in that they also found that spousal immunity for rape formed part of the common law in Australia for longer than the majority was prepared to accept. Also, some divergences notwithstanding, Larcombe and Heath's reasoning accords with the minority's approach in many important respects.

e.g. Margot Saville (2020) Questions of Probity: was 'Dirty' Dyson biased against women? *Crikey,* June 23: https://www.crikey.com.au/2020/06/23/was-high-court-justice-dyson-heydon-biased/. Certainly, the allegations add another layer to how we read his judgments particularly regarding what are already gendered questions of judicial voice, authority and legitimacy. However, in my view the masculinist ethos underpinning his Honour's judgment can be discerned in the text without recourse to the revelations that have subsequently come to light. Although, I do not doubt that this information gives context to how we might read his judgments, I do not seek to press that point here.

Of course, in what follows it is acknowledged that a feminist judgment written in response to a published decision does not discount the possibility that there might have been other feminist voices in the published reasons (see Hunter 2012: 138). However, the very act of reimagining cases gives pause to consider what counts as feminist reasoning. Moreover, in the event that reimagined feminist judgments find themselves in conversation with published judgments (which might themselves adopt feminist reasoning), we are left wondering whether real life (but perhaps diluted) feminist judgments are more significant or powerful than strident but imaginative ones. The analysis presented in this chapter raises this very question and seeks to pose some tentative answers.

Moran (2012: 289) provides a useful explanation of the performative aspects of fiction in feminist judgment writing, especially with respect to the way in which they might interact with that which is said to be real or actual:

> These fictions perform the role of mirrors reflecting back onto judicial practice and more specifically reflecting back upon the art and craft of judging and judgment writing that is to be found in the published judgments that they are in conversation with.

While the conversation between the actual and the imagined judgment is of principal concern to this chapter, tensions between legal accounts of rape (the 'imagined' versus the 'real') infuse the entire chapter. This reflects the broader tension between truth and fiction that has been problematised by feminist legal theorists in theorising rape.

For feminist legal theorists the law around rape has served as compelling evidence of the patriarchal biases of the law and therefore provided a platform from which to agitate for legislative reform. Feminist critical engagement with rape has focused on what Ward (1995: 20) described as the 'reinterpretation of familiar phenomena from a women's perspective'. This has involved uncovering the assumptions and biases embedded in the law's characterisation as an objective set of rules, aptly summarised by MacKinnon's (1983: 644) observation that 'law sees and treats women the way men see and treat women'.

Storytelling, and telling women's stories, are important components of feminists' efforts to expose the limits of law's claim to impartiality (e.g. Smart 1989; Naffine 1990). Consequently, the incredulity with which the law treats women's stories, especially in sexual assault cases, has been exposed as deeply problematic (Scutt 1997). The law's approach to sexual violence is both informed and undermined by 'masculinist mythologies,' in which men's point of view is privileged and women's stories are distorted until 'they are virtually unrecognisable' (Kaspiew 1995: 354). Legal narrative theorists have likewise 'exposed the way in which the law operates to privilege the stories of the powerful and silence those who are subordinate' (Kaspiew 1995: 354; Delgado 1989). By exposing the alternative accounts that exist behind dominant narratives these theorists are able to 'expose and validate the experience and perspectives of those who are silenced—or disbelieved by the system' (Kaspiew 1995: 354).

A central critique offered by feminist theorists in this context is the argument that legal discourse regarding rape was concerned with protecting male property rather than women's bodily integrity. This economic reading of rape reveals the paucity of historical legal constructions of rape as a crime (Brownmiller 1975). The crime of rape was defined as 'the carnal knowledge of a woman against her will,' and to prove the offence it was necessary to show both the perpetrator's violence and the victim's resistance (McSherry 1998: 376).[5] Even when there was a change of emphasis from 'the prosecution having to prove that penetration occurred "against the will" of the victim to "without the victim's consent" [this] did not in reality alter the assumption that unless a woman resisted or struggled in some way, the act of penetration could not amount to rape' (McSherry 1998: 376).

The notion of 'carnal knowledge' contributes to a construction of rape as 'a theft of male property in female sexuality, a construction which can be traced back to women's historical status as men's possessions at English law' (Heath 1998: 16). The rationale for prohibiting carnal knowledge of the daughter (the theft of her virginity) in essence protected the father from 'the embezzlement of his daughter's fair price on the market' (Brownmiller 1975: 18). Likewise, prohibiting 'carnal knowledge' of a man's wife rather than other non-procreative sexual acts ensured 'that any inheritance would be passed on only to blood descendants of a particular man' (Heath 1998: 16). Here Heath is alluding to the definitional shift from 'rape' to 'sexual assault' which would eventually push understandings of sexual violence beyond law's focus on penetration of the vagina. Thus it was that the law constructed rape in such a way that the 'crime committed against her body [became] a crime against the male estate', with the woman's status as chattel being bolstered by the price she must pay for men's protection: the imposition of monogamy and chastity (Brownmiller 1975: 17).

The substance of the law's treatment of women in this context has most frequently been understood in terms of Sir Matthew Hale's (1736: 629) dictum:

> But the husband cannot be guilty of a rape committed by himself upon his lawful wife, for by their mutual matrimonial consent and contract, the wife hath given up herself in this kind unto her husband, which she cannot retract.

5 This was made explicit in English law in *R v. Howard* [1965] when the English Court of Criminal Appeal stated: 'the prosecution in order to prove rape, must prove either that [the victim] physically resisted, or if she did not, that her understanding and knowledge was such that she was not in a position to decide whether to consent or resist'.

While Hale's statement offered 'no argument, case law, or legal basis to support his assertion, nor did he acknowledge the existence of contrary legal authority', it nevertheless gained traction as a statement of law (Augustine 1990–1991: 560). Clearly, the view that a husband could not be convicted of raping his wife reflects the way in which rape laws were designed to protect male property, as Medea and Thompson note with considerable scorn a man could not rape his wife because 'he would have robbed himself' (Medea and Thompson 1974: 13). In a similar vein, women who were not 'owned' by one man, such as 'known prostitutes' or 'women of abandoned character', could expect that such evidence would be used not only to diminish their credibility as witnesses, but also to infer that the sexual intercourse was consensual (Henning and Bronitt 1998: 78).

It was Susan Brownmiller who came to be widely regarded as having pioneered a feminist theory of rape.[6] For Brownmiller (1975: 15) rape was an expression of patriarchal power and control, perhaps best articulated by her famous declaration:

> From prehistoric times to the present, I believe, rape has played a critical function. It is nothing more or less than a conscious process of intimidation by which *all* men keep *all* women in a state of fear.

Rape represented both a deliberate and a conscious act of domination that is inherent to the patriarchal power system. The 'politicisation' of rape, perhaps best reflected by the feminist idea that 'the personal is political,' came about when feminist theorists argued that rape was central to women's oppression. Kate Millett's (1970: preface), now classic, *Sexual Politics*, argued that sex 'has a frequently ignored political aspect'. Millett's theoretical perspective constituted an important radical shift that articulated the crucial idea that sex (and rape) has something to do with both power and politics, and that therefore the personal was political. Since the early 1970s, there have been many and varied legislative reforms regarding rape. Proposals for law reform have attempted to provide a legitimate legal framework for articulating counter narratives by expanding the

6 Brownmiller's theorising has been subject to numerous and important critiques for its race blindness and false universalism. As Seresier (2007: 93) pointed out, 'Politically, Brownmiller's most cogent critics have been African-American writers who contest the racial biases and false universalism of her book'. See bell hooks, Ain't I a Woman: Black Women and Feminism (London & Winchester: Pluto Press, 1982), Angela Davis, 'Rape, Racism and the Myth of the Black Rapist', in *Women Race and Class* (New York: Vintage Books, 1983), and J. D. Hall, '"The Mind that Burns in Each Body": Women, Rape and Racial Violence', in *Powers of Desire: The Politics of Sexuality*, ed. A. Snitow, C. Stansell and S. Thompson (New York: Monthly Review Press, 1983). Seresier (2007: 92) further argued that Brownmiller's anti-rape feminism has also subsumed femininity into victimhood, but notwithstanding these critiques, important for our purposes here is the invocation of patriarchal power.

definition of what counts as rape and who counts as a legitimate complainant. The proposals for reform have not only addressed the offence of rape, but also 'public and judicial attitudes, court procedures, rules of evidence and the policies and practices of the police' (Heath 1998: 13).

As the judges in *PGA* stated, the law is to be found in the pages of the law reports and the statute books, rather than in textbooks and commentaries.[7] That being said, the intersection between feminist agitations for law reform and popular understandings of rape are not without some significance for the discussion at hand. The status in 1963 of the spousal immunity for rape at common law can be determined from the recommendations and results of 1976 Criminal and Penal Methods Reform Committee (The Mitchell Committee). This is said to have 'presented the first substantial review of rape law by a reform body in Australia' although it was conservative in the limited extent of reforms recommended (Rush 2010: 238). For the minority in *PGA* the existence of this Committee, its Report, and moves to amend the law in the 1970s acted as proof positive of the existence of the spousal immunity before that time. O'Connor (1977: 314) explained that the abortive attempt to abolish the immunity entirely in South Australia effectively disregarded 'the Commission's recommendation towards "caution" where the parties were living under the same roof'.

A number of commentators writing at that time argued that the reforms had not gone far enough and that there had not been any 'satisfactory written explanation of why they retained the immunity' (O'Connor 1977: 314). For example, the justification given in the South Australian Report (1976: 14) that 'it is only in exceptional circumstances that the criminal law should invade the bedroom'[8] was not seen as satisfactory by some commentators although they accepted that perhaps 'these reports were concerned to reflect community attitudes on this issue' (O'Connor 1977: 314). Nonetheless, despite these concerns, Hale's dictum of immunity still had some supporters in the corridors of legal power. For example, Professor Lanham defended Hale against accusations of misogyny, arguing that his 'rationalisation of the immunity was the most pro-female one which could have been conceived'. He wrote in support of retaining the immunity, arguing that 'the law of rape is too blunt an instrument for dealing with the relationship between husband and wife and that marital immunity should be retained at least where the parties are living together' (Lanham 1983: 159–160).

The Australian High Court did not decisively undermine the fiction of spousal immunity until 1991 in *R v L*.[9] In a joint judgment, Mason CJ and

7 *PGA v The Queen* (2012) 245 CLR 355, 370 [22] (Joint Judgment); 406 [137–138] (Heydon J); 437 [222] (Bell J).

8 This passage was cited by Bell J in *PGA* at 442 [239]. Criminal Law and Penal Methods Reform Committee of South Australia, *Special Report: Rape and Other Sexual Offences* (1976), p 14 [6.2].

9 *R v L* (1991) 174 CLR 379 considered any potential conflict between Commonwealth and State Laws and therefore the Court's determinations regarding the status of the spousal immunity for rape were by way of dicta.

Deane and Toohey JJ denied the existence of a spousal immunity, stating 'if it was ever the common law that by marriage a wife gave irrevocable consent to sexual intercourse by her husband, it is no longer the common law'.[10] Justice Brennan described this immunity as a 'common law fiction' which 'has always been offensive to human dignity and incompatible with the legal status of a spouse'.[11] Easteal (1998: 112) argued even if the marital immunity was deemed to have been a fiction 'without backing of case law or a legal foundation' it was nonetheless a significant fiction 'which had a potent impact on the attitudes and actions of the Courts and the community'.

The comments of Justice Bollen in the Supreme Court of South Australia in *R v Johns* heard shortly after the High Court had decreed the marital immunity for rape a mere fiction emphasised the intransigence of such fictions with regard to marital consent:

> There is, of course, nothing wrong with a husband faced with his wife's initial refusal to engage in intercourse, in attempting, in an acceptable way, to persuade her to change her mind, and that may involve a measure of rougher than usual handling. It may be, in the end, that handling and persuasion will persuade the wife to agree. Sometimes it is a fine line between not agreeing, then changing of the mind, and consenting.[12]

Bollen J's construction of the kind of 'consent' that can be expected in the marriage bed, in particular his choice of the words ('a measure of rougher than usual handling'), points to the persistence of attitudes about the sexual arrangements between husband and wife which, despite a range of legislative reforms which had taken place by then, did not necessarily shift the popular, or indeed judicial, imaginations about what counted as sexual violence and who counted as a legitimate complainant. This is not to say that Bollen J's remarks went unnoticed, in fact his comments were seized upon by the media and gave impetus for further public debate about gender bias in the judiciary, thus underscoring the need for the subsequent Senate Standing Committee (1994) on that very issue (Thornton 1996: 202).

It has been alleged that there is sometimes an apparent 'discrepancy between "law as legislation" and "law as practice" which is probably most explicit in judicial decision making' (Ehrlich 2001: 25). Writing over 25 years ago, Smart (1989: 164) presciently argued that 'any feminist engagement with the law' will require the acknowledgment that 'judicial decisions and trials often contravene the hard-won statutory reforms of feminists'. And so it would come to be in the most peculiar of ironies, that in *PGA*, the majority's reasoning about legal fictions did just that. It is to those fictions that we now turn.

10 *R v L* (1991) 174 CLR 379, 390 (Mason CJ, Deane and Toohey JJ).
11 *R v L* (1991) 174 CLR 379, 402 (Brennan J).
12 *R v Johns*, Supreme Court, SA No. SCCRM/91/452, 26 August 1992 (Bollen J).

Whither fictions? *PGA v The Queen*

PGA is a curious decision both in reasoning and circumstance. Although the High Court had earlier made clear in *R v L* that the marital immunity was no longer law, they were not called upon to determine the particular timing of this shift. How then did Mr PG find himself in the High Court for events alleged to have occurred well over 40 years ago in 1963? The complaint emerged from evidence given by GP at the Mullighan Inquiry into the sexual abuse of children, which was in turn referred to police (Larcombe and Heath 2012). For much of the latter part of last century it was statute barred. However, with the passage of the Criminal Law Consolidation (Abolition of Time Limit for Prosecution of Certain Sexual Offences) Amendment Act 2003 (SA), the time bar against bringing PG's prosecution for rape was lifted.

In 2009, PG was charged with six offences alleged to have been committed against the complainant, GP. The parties were married in 1962 and divorced in 1969. Although no complaints of rape had been made during this time, it is understood that the police were aware of the alleged violence perpetrated by the husband against the wife during this period (Larcombe and Heath 2012: 788) Two counts of carnal knowledge were alleged to have taken place prior in the parties' marriage (because GP was 15 or 16 years of age), and two separate charges of assault occasioning actual bodily harm were alleged to have taken place in 1964. A further two counts of rape were alleged to have taken place shortly before and after the birth of their first child in 1963. The status of the law surrounding those counts was the key question of law requiring determination by the High Court.

The rape offences were charged as contrary to s 48 of the *Criminal Law Consolidation Act 1935* (SA), which at the relevant time provided 'Any person convicted of rape shall be guilty of a felony, and liable to be imprisoned for life, and may be whipped'. Although there was no longer a time bar limiting prosecution, the procedural history of the case reveals tensions between the public interest in the charges being heard and the potential prejudice to the defence resulting from the delay in bringing the prosecution. The Full Court of the South Australian Supreme Court was therefore required to determine, as a question of law, whether the offence of rape 'by one lawful spouse of another [was] an offence known to the law of South Australia as at 1963?'[13] Doyle CJ, with whom White J agreed, found that the immunity did not exist in 1963, whereas Gray J, in dissent, found that it did. Mr PG appealed from the judgment of the Supreme Court to the High Court of Australia. It was accepted that the elements of the offence of rape were supplied by the common law.[14]

The High Court determined that the issue before the Court was:

13 *R v P, GA* (2010) 109 SASR 1, 4 [6] (Doyle CJ). See also Toole (2011) for an analysis of the Supreme Court's decision and the emphasis on retrospectivity and human rights in the Court's reasoning.

14 *PGA v The Queen* (2012) 245 CLR 355, 366 [9] (Joint Judgment).

> whether the appellant is correct in his contention that, as a matter of the common law, upon their marriage in 1962 his wife had given her consent to sexual intercourse and thereafter could not retract her consent, at least while they remained lawfully married, with the result that he could not be guilty of raping her as charged.[15]

The majority, consisting of French CJ, Gummow, Hayne, Crennan and Kiefel JJ found that what was deemed 'the marital exemption' had ceased to be law by 1963. Heydon J and Bell J delivered separate dissenting judgments, finding instead that the immunity persisted beyond 1963. The status of the alleged legal fiction as to spousal immunity to rape was at the centre of the reasoning for both the minority and majority. However, their reasoning and ultimate orders rested on divergent understandings of the source, scope and power of that fiction.

The majority decision

The majority's decision undermined Hale's legal authority and, in so doing, the legal status of the spousal exemption which has been said to stem from it. Whereas the minority invoked the notion of the spousal 'immunity' for rape, the majority preferred to frame it as an 'exemption'. This distinction in language is reflective of their different understandings of the legal principle (Larcombe and Heath 2012: 787). The notion that Hale's dictum was weak or not properly supported by case law at the time it was crafted informs much of their reasoning in finding that at least by 1935 what they term the 'exemption' was no longer part of the common law. Their Honours did note that Hale's statement continued to be repeated in a range of works such as East's *A Treatise of the Pleas of the Crown* (1803); Chitty's *A Practical Treatise on the Criminal Law* (1819) and Russell's *A Treatise on Crimes and Misdemeanors* (1819). Yet they contended that what was lacking in all these standard texts was any statement and analysis of reasoning which might have supported the statement by Hale and its continued acceptance.[16] For the majority then, reliance on Hale's legal authority and the principle said to flow from it was problematic as it was 'a principle of the common law based upon a statement in a text published in 1736, many years after the death of the author, without citation of prior authority and lacking subsequent exposition in cases where it has been repeated'.[17]

The majority stressed the moveable and changing nature of the common law, and specifically that the 'common law with respect to the crime of rape did not remain static,' which was key to their determination.[18] Central to the

15 Ibid, 364–365 [3] (Joint Judgment).
16 Ibid, 365 [4].
17 Ibid, 371 [22].
18 Ibid, 364 [3] (Joint Judgment).

majority's reasoning was the presumption that wives' irrevocable consent had fallen away as a result of legislative reforms affording married women rights in matters of property and divorce. In the majority's view women's legal status had been altered by statutory reforms in a manner which rebutted the notion of wives' irrevocable consent presumed upon marriage. The legislation referenced in support of this proposition was: *Married Women's Property Act (1882)* (SA) and the *Commonwealth Franchise Act 1902* (Cth). Therefore, the foundation for the rule had fallen away.[19] Further because the foundation for the 'marital exemption' had dissolved, it was therefore 'no more than a legal fiction and is not to be maintained'.[20]

In coming to that conclusion, the majority relied upon the earlier statement by Dawson J in *R v L* that:

> [W]hatever may have been the position in the past, the institution of marriage in its present form provides no foundation for a presumption which has the effect of denying that consent to intercourse in marriage can, expressly or impliedly, be withdrawn. There being no longer any foundation for the presumption, it becomes nothing more than a fiction which forms no part of the common law.[21]

Crucially, the majority doubted that the 'marital exemption' ever was part of the common law of Australia but reasoned that in any case 'it had ceased to be so by the time of the enactment in 1935 of s 48 of the *CLC Act* and thus before the date of the commission of the alleged offences charged as count 3 and count 5'.[22] In finding that the appeal must be dismissed, the majority reasoned that the case did not give rise to 'any retrospective variation or modification' of the common law quite simply because 'the alleged offence the common law rule for which the appellant contends did not exist' at the relevant time.[23]

Heydon J

Whereas the majority's judgment sought to cast doubt on Hale's legal authority, Heydon J set about rescuing Hale's reputation as a jurist, at least insofar as the status of the immunity was concerned. Heydon J accepted neither the denigration of Hale's legal authority, nor the proposition that Mr P would have been prosecuted in 1963. He began his judgment with a powerful statement about the way in which the law was understood, reasoning that 'at the time it

19 Ibid, 373 [30].
20 Ibid, 373 [30].
21 *R v L* (1991) 174 379, 405 (Dawson J); *PGA v The Queen* (2012) 245 CLR 355, 374 (Joint Judgment).
22 *PGA v The Queen* (2012) 245 CLR 355, 369 [18] (Joint Judgment).
23 Ibid, 369 [18].

was universally thought in Australia that a husband could not be convicted of having sexual intercourse with his wife without her consent save where a court order operated or where there were other exceptional circumstances'.[24]

Heydon J was unable to accept either of South Australia's submissions, namely that either the immunity never existed, or in the alternative, if it did exist at some time, it had ceased to exist by 1963. Although his Honour was unconvinced by either submission, it is clear that he found the first submission especially exasperating. Heydon J did not think that the legislative amendments 'which [have] altered the status of wives over the last 150 years' were 'necessarily inconsistent with the immunity'.[25] For Heydon J to describe Hale's proposition as creating a 'presumption which no longer has any foundation, and as a fiction not forming part of the common law' was to misunderstand the role of legal fictions because it 'overlooks the fact that a common law rule can rest on a fiction, particularly when the rule in question develops a new and non-fictitious basis'.[26] Moreover, for Heydon J the fact that a rule is no longer liked or anachronistic does not mean that the rule simply dissolves or the courts (rather than the legislature) should abolish it.[27] For Heydon J one of the more concerning features of the majority's reasoning was that it would, in his Honour's view, effect a retrospective change in the criminal law. Heydon J describes as captious the argument that subsequent criminal liability could be made out 'because an historical investigation in 2010–2012 is said to reveal that changes in legal and social conditions at some unspecified time before 1963 caused the conduct to become criminal'.[28]

Conducting a survey of the actual judicial identities sitting on the benches of the Supreme Court of South Australia and the High Court of Australia at the relevant time in the 1960s, Heydon J reasoned that it is 'hard to see where a majority of three or four in favour of that view was to be found in this Court. Indeed, it is hard to find even one vote for that proposition'.[29] For Heydon J this finding was not simply 'a crass piece of legal "realism"', as he contended that it 'does not rest on the personal idiosyncrasies of the individual judges'.[30] Rather it rested on the ideas of the time, which Heydon J described as 'universal ideas among the Australian judiciary'.[31] Therefore, overturning Hale's proposition, 'or to deny that it ever had been the law, or to hold that it had earlier dissolved into nothingness' would 'widen the criminal law'.[32] He emphatically rejected the notion that 'history can be rewritten in complete

24 *PGA v The Queen* (2012) 245 CLR 355, 384–385 [67] (Heydon J).
25 Ibid, 399 [122].
26 Ibid, 399 [122].
27 Ibid, 400 [123]; 402 [126].
28 Ibid, 402 [128].
29 Ibid, 407 [140–141].
30 Ibid, 407 [141].
31 Ibid, 407 [141] (Heydon J).
32 Ibid, 407 [141].

defiance of all contemporary evidence' and in upholding the appeal reasoned that 'neither the Australian nor the English courts wavered, until 1991, from the view asserted and assumed until then that Hale's proposition was substantially correct'.[33]

Bell J

Bell J too evidenced a realist's skepticism commencing her judgment with a statement about the likelihood of prosecution within marriage for rape at the time the relevant offences were said to have taken place, reasoning 'it cannot be sensibly suggested that the appellant would have been prosecuted for those offences, had the allegations come to the attention of the authorities in 1963'.[34] In foreshadowing her own conclusion, Bell J explained that this 'is because at that time it was understood that the crime of rape could not be committed by a husband against his wife with whom he was living (the immunity)'.[35] Although Bell J did not go into much detail in the body of her judgment about the influence of feminist agitations for law reform regarding rape, feminist texts are to be found cited amongst her Honour's footnotes.[36]

In explaining this great social and political shift she wrote '[by] the 1970s, the idea that there could be any justification for conferring immunity on a husband for the rape of his wife was the subject of critical academic attention and pressure for reform of the law'.[37] Bell J cited a range of different sources in accounting for shifts in social and legal understandings of rape with some explicitly informed by feminist arguments such as Brownmiller's (1975) *Against Our Will* and Scutt's (1977) 'Consent in Rape'. Bell J acknowledged the common law as 'demeaning to women in its provision of the immunity,' but it was not the issue of demeaning treatment which was at the core of her Honour's reasoning.[38]

Perhaps the most significant component of Bell J's reasoning was her view of the majority's contention that a rule dissolves when its foundation no longer applies. For Bell J, it did not matter that the initial foundation for the rule had shifted or was flawed—rather the proper issue was the existence of the immunity. Her Honour reasoned that by 1963 'the justification for the immunity may have come to rest more on the notion that the criminal law ought not to intrude into the marital bedroom, than upon the fiction of the wife's irrevocable consent'.[39] Although Bell J was of the view that the foundation for the rule may have shifted, she nonetheless did not accept the majority's reasoning

33 *PGA v The Queen* (2012) 245 CLR 355, 414 [157] (Bell J).
34 Ibid, 415 [164–165].
35 Ibid, 416 [164].
36 Ibid, 417–418 [173].
37 Ibid, 417 [173].
38 Ibid, 445 [247].
39 *PGA v The Queen* (2012) 245 CLR 355, 417 [173] (Bell J).

that legislation had produced a state of affairs that was inconsistent with the immunity. Drawing on the interaction between legislative instruments dealing with property, adultery and rape in another Australian jurisdiction, Bell J found that the interaction between the legal status of married women and maintenance of the immunity did 'not appear to have been viewed at the time as inconsistent'.[40] Bell J cited the interaction between *Matrimonial Causes Amendment Act 1919* (Tas) (Royal Assent proclaimed on 17 May 1920) and the *Criminal Code* (Tas), s 185 to emphasise that the enactment of the former had not changed understandings of martial rape as the definition adopted nonetheless defined rape as 'involving "carnal knowledge of a female not his wife"'. She also conducted a survey of cases about marital rape and found that the existence of the immunity continued to be affirmed well into the latter part of last century.[41] Finally, Bell J was concerned about finding criminal liability retrospectively, and reasoned that it would be 'abhorrent' to do so in the present case.[42]

Responding in kind: the fiction of a (mere) fiction

Scholarly responses to the decision in *PGA* have been preoccupied, in one way or another, with legal fictions. This is the case irrespective of whether the response is critical or supportive of the majority's reasoning with regard to Hale's fiction. Although the majority's reasoning has been subject to fairly vociferous scrutiny, the minority's reasoning has not entirely escaped critique on this front. Criticisms of the decision have queried the way in which it recasts the history of marital rape in Australia in light of the lived experiences of women (Larcombe and Heath 2012; Naffine 2014), and the manner in which it subverts common law method and understandings of the proper role of legal fictions and myths in the process (Naffine and Neoh 2013; Sletvold 2012).

The tension which played out in the decision itself concerning the proper role and scope of legal fictions is mirrored in scholarly responses to the decision. Perhaps the most supportive response to the majority's decision is the case note authored by Lesses (2014: 833)[43] who argued that the decision was 'praiseworthy' because while 'there may have been a time and place when such treatment was considered acceptable and hence the possibility of a positive public policy for the marital immunity', 'that time had well and truly passed in Australia as at 1963'. He regarded the legal unity of husband and wife as a fiction which constituted 'the legal device that saw married women treated unfairly in the event of non-consensual sexual relations with their husbands' (Lesses 2014: 833). Conversely, Sletvold (2012: 579) argued that laws do not

40 Ibid, 438 [277].
41 Ibid, 433–437.
42 Ibid, 444 [245].
43 Lesses appeared as junior counsel for the prosecution in the High Court in *PGA*.

just 'vanish' and argued instead that 'something more than a mere change in the basis of a settled rule of the common law should be required before it can be overruled'. Sletvold (2012: 578) favoured Heydon J's conceptualisation of the proper role and function of legal fictions which stressed that 'a common law rule can rest on a fiction'. He additionally saw merit in the notion proposed by Bell J that the foundation for a law can shift without resulting in the evaporation of the rule itself.

Larcombe and Heath's (2012: 798) case note similarly took issue with the majority's reasoning insofar as legal fictions were concerned.[44] Although pointing to the ultimate wrong that had been done to women in the 'blunt denial of their experiences', they argued that the majority's reasoning (and not just the outcome) was deficient and a subversion of common law method. They argued that the majority, in deriding the old fiction propagated by Hale, invoked a more insidious fiction. This new fiction 'that the common law recognised rape in marriage throughout the 20th century', in their view was a fiction layered on the fictional 'legal condonation of marital rape' which 'similarly obviates women's experiences of gendered violence' (Larcombe and Heath 2012: 806).

Naffine and Neoh's (2013) critique was explicitly an exploration of fictions and myths in *PGA*, rather than a case note, so it is not surprising that this aspect of the decision received special and nuanced attention in their analysis. Although they acknowledged the utility of fictions and myths, they countered that they, like Bentham, accepted that legal fictions could be 'pestilential' when 'the creative work that they are doing is denied' (Naffine and Neoh 2013: 33). In their view this gets to the nub of the issue, namely that the majority's treatment of fictions and myths lacked candour. They took issue with the way in which legal fiction was invoked by the majority in *PGA*, arguing that the term legal fiction was misused and misappropriated as they used it to mean 'falsehood' rather than 'true legal fiction' (Naffine and Neoh 2013: 40).

Of course, the feminist judgment drafted in response to the original decision also made claims about the role and status of legal fictions, and in so doing, interacted within the original judgment in order to make claims about what ought to have been found. That it did so in a fictional space is perhaps all the more significant. Although the fiction of judgment writing is not the same as the kind of legal fictions understood in the Fullerian sense, imagination nonetheless punctuates the common law. The notion that common law rules develop within an imaginative framework further exposes the 'fictional and textual nature of all judgment writing and points to the intimate connection between politics and aesthetics in the judicial text' in ways that are of

44 Many of their arguments, particularly in relation to the majority's partial treatment of the case law in denying the existence of the immunity are reproduced, at least in part, in their alternative feminist judgment and I will examine those dimensions of their reasoning below.

immediate relevance in examining feminist judgment writing (Moran 2012: 289). While all judgment writing might well be fictional, the fictive feminist judge has more heavy lifting to do in having their claims taken seriously, perhaps because their reasons are not imbued with the trappings of judicial authority. We now turn to the fictive feminist judges' truth about law's fictions.

In what follows and in the spirit of the feminist judgment project I will 'suspend disbelief' and treat the alternative feminist judgment as though it forms part of the actual judgment. I will refer to the authors of that judgment as Larcombe and Heath JJ and include the paragraph numbers in reference to the fact that their judgment literally begins where the published judgment finished.

The feminist judgment

The re-imagined feminist judgment of Larcombe and Heath JJ ultimately agreed with the orders proposed by Bell and Heydon JJ. Indeed, much of their reasoning accords with that of the minority judgments in finding that the common law spousal immunity for rape was an offence known to the law of South Australia as at 1963. Larcombe and Heath JJ were however more explicit in their criticism of the immunity and its devastating effects and in accounting for the role of feminist agitation in its undoing. The key distinguishing feature then in their approach was to account for the lived experience of women in acknowledging explicitly that 'for generations, criminal courts failed to offer women redress for rape within marriage' (Larcombe and Heath 2014: 263).

Although Bell J had made reference to the fact that 'the common law was demeaning to women in its provision of the immunity',[45] Larcombe and Heath JJ went beyond this in offering an explicit apology. They took advantage of their status as 'judges of the final Court of appeal in Australia' and extended their 'sincere apologies to women injured as a result of the common law rule that afforded husbands immunity for marital rape' (Larcombe and Heath 2014: 263 [254]). In addition to offering an apology, Larcombe and Heath JJ's judgment can be distinguished in terms of the way in which they framed the implications and impact of feminist agitations for law reform in informing their reasoning. For example, in the introductory passage they referenced the role of these feminist agitations in explaining '[t]he immunity was assumed to be a common law rule into the 1970s, when it became one focus of feminist pressure for rape law reform' (Larcombe and Heath 2014: 263 [251]). Later in their judgment they, in concurrence with Heydon J, found 'that rejection of the immunity was the result of social and legal developments in the 1970s, in conjunction with the sustained feminist activism of the period' (Larcombe and Heath 2014: 270 [288]).

45 *PGA v The Queen* (2012) 245 CLR 355, 445 [247] (Bell J).

Larcombe and Heath JJ did not accept submissions questioning Hale's legal authority as part of a wider argument positing that the spousal immunity had never been law in Australia. Like their fellow minority judges, insofar as the status of Hale's proposition was concerned, they found 'Sir Matthew Hale's eminence as a jurist cannot be doubted' (Larcombe and Heath 2014: 264 [265]). While arguments from eminence are in themselves of dubious value, their point was not that their interpretation was proven because Hale's authority could be proven. Rather their aim was to establish that Hale's authority found expression as 'a rule of common law' across over two hundred years was demonstrated by 'the evidence from case law, legislation, commentaries and parliamentary sources' (Larcombe and Heath 2014: 264 [265]). Nonetheless, they acknowledged that 'textbooks, legislative and popular assumptions, and a lack of prosecutions cannot authoratively state the common law' (Larcombe and Heath 2014: 265 [266]). Their finding that the immunity formed part of the common law of Australia in historical terms drew on an examination of a line of cases which pointed to the existence of the immunity.[46] They argued that these cases 'indicated that Hale's proposition stated a common law rule, even when the inappropriateness and offensiveness of that rule is condemned' (Larcombe and Heath 2014: 266 [270]). In this respect their Honours' reasoning accords most closely with that of Bell J's 'observation that for much of the 20th century the immunity may have operated independently of the fiction of wives' consent' (Larcombe and Heath 2014: 267–268 [279]). In their view then 'criminal liability remains in force unless and until it is modified or overruled by judicial authority or expressly abolished by statute' (Larcombe and Heath 2014: 267 [276]). Further, Larcombe and Heath JJ were unconvinced by submissions which referenced statutory reform regarding property and voting rights as having the effect of undermining the presumption of marital consent, simply because there remained in the statute books many provisions which were 'consistent with the maintenance of the immunity' (Larcombe and Heath 2014: 267 [278]).

Their Honours posed the probing question 'is it better to rewrite or recognise the history of the common law?' Their answer recognised the history of the common law insofar as they argued that 'the common law's copybook should not be cleaned by erasing the role it has played in condoning sexual violence that many married women experienced during the life of the husband's legal immunity for rape' (Larcombe and Heath 2014: 271 [292]). In this important respect, the feminist judges can be distinguished from the majority and minority in their acknowledgment of the role of the law in effecting great harm to women:

> It is important to acknowledge the law's historic failure to recognize married women's dignity and rights. There is ample evidence that, prior to the

46 See: *R v Clarence (*1888) 22 QBD 23; *R v Clarke* [1949] 2 ALL ER 448; *Director of Public Prosecutions v Morgan* [1975] 2 ALL ER 347; *R v Cogan* [1976] QB 217.

> statutory abolition of the immunity, married women and their husbands ordered their affairs based on a belief that the immunity formed part of the common law
>
> (Larcombe and Heath 2014: 271 [294]).

For Larcombe and Heath JJ it was important to account not only for the reality of women's lived experiences, but also to make reference to the way in which the law was complicit in informing legal as well as social and cultural understandings of rape. They reasoned that a finding in 2012 that the immunity had lapsed sometime in the 1930s:

> would not only be contrary to legal and social evidence; it would make it appear that the law offered justice to women subject to spousal rape over a 50 year period in which policing, prosecution and judicial practices offered neither protection nor succour.
>
> (Larcombe and Heath 2014: 271 [295])

Conscious of notions of justice in arriving at their decision, they reasoned that 'history' and 'women's experiences, must serve as a form of justice in this instance' (Larcombe and Heath 2014: 272 [300]). In their view then '[i]t would be a cruel irony for this Court to rewrite the history of the common law so as to make it appear in 2012 that married women had the protection of the common law throughout the 20th century when this is manifestly not the case' (Larcombe and Heath 2014: 272 [300]).

The fairest fiction of them all? A conversation between judgments

With an understanding of each of these judgments, real and imagined, it is now necessary to explore how they speak to each other. This conversation is implicit in the very method of feminist judging, as feminist judges 'have taken on the law—dressing up as judges they have also dressed themselves in law, in order to expose or reveal it' (Davies 2012: 172). What does the imaginary feminist judgment tell us about the actual judgment? And what does the collision of the real, the fictional and the imaginary tell us about the prevailing gender regime within the High Court, judicial method and feminist judging?

As noted earlier in the book, the notion that women jurists will (or should) make a difference has in many key respects been subsumed by the notion that feminist judges 'are more likely (and indeed ought) to make a difference' (Hunter 2008: 7). Alternative feminist judgments are crafted for the very purpose of trying to redress some failing or lack in the original decision and to demonstrative the transformative potential (and plausibility) of feminist judging perspectives. But, as the editors of the Australian project make clear in their introductory remarks, 'what counts as feminist judging' is one of the problematised issues at the core of their enterprise (Douglas et al. 2014: 1). Hunter notes that 'there may be a diversity of possible feminist judgments that could be written in any given case' (Hunter 2012: 138). In the *English Feminist Judgments Project* 'five of the feminist judgments "rewrote" decisions of Baroness Brenda Hale, a self-declared feminist judge' (Hunter 2012: 138). It is clear then that the existence of an alternative feminist judgment does not discount the possibility that other feminist judicial voices might be heard in the text of the judgment being responded to. But, in enacting a conversation between real and imagined judgments, I want now to consider whether real life feminist judgments are more significant or powerful than strident but imaginative ones?

It is uncontroversial to assert that the imagined judgment of the feminist judges, given its central focus, accords with these feminist judging practices more overtly than the majority and minority judgments of the High Court. The majority judgment might immediately be discounted on the basis that its conceptualisation of the role and status of legal fictions failed to consider adequately women's lived experience. In the minority, Heydon J did acknowledge the great social changes of the last century and the role of feminist agitations in law reform campaigns regarding rape. That being said, his Honour's reasoning was not centred on addressing the wrong done to married women. Rather, his reasoning was concerned with rescuing Hale's reputation and defending the common law method and the place of fictions therein. Heydon J's judgment therefore reveals the way in which decisions might achieve results sought by feminist judges but for different reasons.

That leaves Bell J's judgment. While her Honour made neither apology nor overt statement as to the great wrong enacted by the immunity, she did describe the common law 'as demeaning in its treatment of women'.[47] Her Honour clearly recognised changing social attitudes to rape and drew on a range of sources that documented these shifts.[48] The real issue for her, however, was the abrogation of legal principle which would arise in finding retrospective liability in criminal law. Hence the primary concern for Bell J was not that the law was historically demeaning to women, but rather was to avoid any retrospective application of criminal law.

Each of the feminist judgments included in *Australian Feminist Judgments* is introduced by a critical commentary which provides background to the original judgment and context to the reimagined judgment. The conversation between judgments is therefore further brokered by the critical commentary, which 'plays an important role in knitting the new judgments into the old' (Moran 2012: 289). Naffine's commentary emphasises the gaps between the feminist judgment and the published reasons. She was especially critical of the approach adopted by the majority judgment:

47 *PGA v The Queen* (2012) 245 CLR 355, 445 [247] (Bell J).
48 Ibid, 417–418 [173] (Bell J).

> [T]here was preservation of the morality and principle of the past and loyalty displayed to past Australian law-makers. And this was achieved with minimal agonising and soul searching: almost in a perfunctory manner—only 10 pages to change centuries of thought. And hence no deep wrong was recognised, analysed or condemned. There was no critical reflection on past law and practice … . Moral outrage at the treatment of women is missing because the mistreatment is denied.
>
> (Naffine 2014: 259)

The light shed by the alternative feminist judgment implies that neither Bell J's nor Heydon J's judgment passed muster as a feminist judgment, despite the fact that the real and imagined judges are in agreement. Although Heydon and Bell JJ 'tell a less heroic tale of Australian law and its treatment of married women' they were seen as being 'more concerned to defend the great jurists of the past and to insure against the more abhorrent departure from principle which is retrospectivity' (Naffine 2014: 259). Naffine's observations therefore made a statement about what should count as feminist judging through the prism of Heath and Larcombe's contribution. Here we see that what counts as feminist judging is a question of substance rather than form. What rendered Heath and Larcombe's judgment more overtly feminist was their effort to write women's lived experiences into the legal history for the purpose of ensuring substantive equality.

There are some similarities between the minority judges and the feminist judges in their acknowledging, albeit to varying degrees, the place of creativity in their own and other's judicial performances. By taking judgment writing out of the hands of those imbued with legal authority, the broader critique offered by feminist judging as feminist method reveals the importance of judicial acknowledgment of imagination. Naffine's (2014: 261) appeal to truth in introducing the feminist judgment reminded us 'that judges are bound to state the legal truth, even if it is harsh'. Although writing only about the published judgments, Naffine and Neoh's points about judicial awareness of the role of creativity in judicial method were instructive in coming to an understanding about the role of 'truth' in judgment writing and law. This awareness is 'pivotal' because with it comes 'the acceptance of responsibility for the rules whose construction relies on fictions and myths' (Naffine and Neoh 2013: 33). Therefore, we know that the truth to which Naffine and Neoh alluded was not in deriding legal fictions as 'untrue'. Notwithstanding the contested nature of truth generally, legal truth for the feminist judges might be understood as recognition of the role of legal fiction and the place of judges within it. Legal truth from the vantage point of the feminist judges involves the explicit recognition of the enterprise of judging and the concomitant roles of imagination, fiction and performance in it.

The feminist judging response to *PGA* was not only faithful to legal formalism; the judgments were by and large faithful to the reasoning adopted by the minority. In effect, the judgments layered women's experiences over the reasoning adopted by the minority. They acknowledged the deep wrong effected by the spousal immunity, and in recognition of the complicity of the common law in this wrong, they proffered an apology in their capacity as judges of the highest court of appeal. The disruptive power of the feminist judgment was not to be found in their treatment of the law, but rather in the story about women's lived experiences woven around it.

It is the apology which really distinguishes the fictional feminist judgment from the published reasons. It is also the most overtly feminist aspect of the judgment insofar as feminist judging might be understood as revealing the gendered nature of the law and judges' complicity in it. Apologies are 'uncommon, unorthodox and in the eyes of many, unsuitable as a legal remedy' (Carroll 2013: 317). This is at least in part because of what it might mean about liability and the role of the law in redressing wrongs. The notion of a judicial apology is even more disruptive because it imports a sense of ownership and responsibility to courts and judges for the development of the common law.

When interviewed, Heath and Larcombe reflected on the importance of the apology to their judgment. Although an interview of this nature would not be available in the case of real judges, it further assists the enjoining of a conversation between the real and imagined in this context. For Larcombe (cited in Douglas et al. 2014b: 32), the apology recognised a deficiency in the common law's capacity to review its own rules:

> So the apology was on behalf of the Court, recognising that it, as the custodian if you like of the common law in Australia, had not been able to deliver justice to married women because its processes were flawed.

Similarly, Heath (cited in Douglas et al. 2014b: 32) saw the importance of any apology as 'recognition, of recompense, of social acknowledgement' and as such reflected the need for 'some other form of therapeutic or corrective justice beyond the decision'.

The feminist judgment shows up the majority and the minority judgments as lacking insofar as feminist reasoning is concerned. At first glance any of the published judgments might be seen as feminist-friendly: the majority for affording legal redress to the complainant, Heydon J for recognising the shifts in social understandings of rape at the instigation of feminist theorists, and Bell J for observing the demeaning treatment of women. However, the feminist judges, by framing their reasons around women's experiences, illuminated the absence of that story from any of the published judgments. In so doing they made clear the central role of those stories in feminist legal imaginations.

The lack of feminist reasoning in the published reasons in *PGA* means that we are not called upon to make any claims about which feminist voice is more significant or powerful. Comparing the real and imagined decisions raises important and contentious issues about the very meaning and purpose of feminist judging. Nonetheless, the interaction between the actual and the imagined in this instance demonstrates the power of feminist judgment as feminist method. While it remains quite possible that multiple feminist voices might be heard in the one case, the significance of the fictive feminist response in this instance is in revealing the lack of feminist reasoning in those imaginations which are afforded the status of law. Moreover, and this gets to the nub of the very purpose of feminist judgment writing, Heath and Larcombe JJ therefore 'expose the contingency and biases of existing decisions and disrupt the unique authority of the Courts and legal decision-making' (Hunter 2012: 137).

We know that the craft of judgment writing—whether real or fictive—is informed by certain contingencies on behalf of the judge in terms of the way in which legal concepts are understood. Featherstone and Winn acknowledge the impact of and literature around the judicial development of the law, which has been 'warped by implicit social and judicial acceptance of masculinist rape myths, with a fundamental distinction existing between the law as passed and the law as applied' (2019: 59). For Naffine and Neoh, the contingencies in the majority judgment in *PGA* posed a puzzle for both legal historians and legal theorists. In their view the 'puzzle for legal historians is, to put it simply, what happened between the time when Hale issued his now infamous statement about the common law of rape, and 1963 when the alleged offences occurred?' The puzzle is 'slightly, but crucially, different' for the legal theorist who is instead concerned 'with the judicial portrayal of history: with the creative legal means by which historical propositions are employed and manipulated to arrive at desired legal propositions' (Naffine and Neoh 2013: 35). Naffine and Neoh explained the 'imaginative aspect of law', drawing on White's argument in *The Legal Imagination* that law is 'not merely a system of rules or reducible to policy choices or class interests but' rather a language involving 'habits of mind and expectations—what might also be called a culture' (White 1973 cited in Naffine and Neoh 2013: 45). For Naffine and Neoh (2013: 45), White's argument in *The Legal Imagination* that 'the law makes a world' was recognised by the majority in *PGA* when they stated that, 'in addition to the substantive rules of the common law, what was received included the method of the common law' (Naffine and Neoh 2013: 45).[49] We see then, in the way in which (gendered and gendering) legal fictions are made, re-told and re-imagined and how feminist judging can intervene in those processes by presenting an alternative (but nonetheless infinitely possible and plausible) history, and therefore, future.

Fuller (1967: 10) provides that a 'fiction is either (1) a statement propounded with a complete or partial consciousness of its falsity, or (2) a false statement recognized as having utility'. So long as those invoking legal fictions recognise their falsity or utility then such fictions have a place in legal reasoning. However, legal fictions are at their most dangerous once they are believed.

49 See also *PGA v The Queen* (2012) 245 CLR 355, 371 [25].

Conversely, the more believable the feminist fiction is, the more likely it is 'that the imaginative gap between the legal establishment and feminist legal theory is at last being reduced' (Davies 2012: 168).

One does not need to search too far to find a legal fiction rendered dangerous over time. Hale's dictum, although now dismissed as a fiction without proper foundation, was no doubt rendered dangerous over the past several hundred years perhaps because it *was* sufficiently believed and accepted. The High Court majority in *PGA*, rather than declaring that Hale's statement had no utility, instead indulged in its own legal fiction and pretended that the fiction had not been believed and, as a corollary, enabled the majority to ignore the devastating effects of Hale's fiction on legal understandings of sexual autonomy for women. The conversation between the actual and imagined judgment in *PGA* reveals that the gap—that is the gap between feminist theory (or a judgment properly informed by feminist reasoning) and the actual judgment—is perhaps not requiring the leaps of imagination which might have once been needed. In fact, the similarities in reasoning adopted by the minority and the feminist judgments underscored the plausibility of feminist approaches to judicial reasoning.

The strength of feminist judgment writing as feminist critique has been its insistence on plausibility. That is, legally plausible within the constraints of legal formalism. In this respect feminist judgment writing is at once *more than* and *less than* critique. As Genovese (2014: 378) explained '[b]y taking law's doctrines and techniques seriously, feminist jurists have shown many times that to change law — to reform its practices or alter its perceptions — does not necessarily involve a polemical position that would force feminists to sit outside the door of the court'. Rather, 'the task has been to master law, to understand its rehearsed movements and its rules of interpretation, as well as to monitor its lived effects' (Genovese 2014: 378). But the trade-off for getting inside the law ('plausibility') is operating within the constraints of a masculinist legal system. Fitz-Gibbon and Maher's (2015) analysis of feminist judgment writing, informed by their experiences in writing an alternative feminist judgment,[50] is therefore illuminating. In approaching their task, they were cognisant of the difficulties in balancing the demands and conventions of legal method yet staying faithful to their responsibilities as feminist scholars:

> How did we reconcile our responsibilities to act as feminist scholars in the context of a troubling, male centric criminal justice system, a system Carol Smart (1989) has urged feminists to avoid? How could we effectively and responsibly animate feminist reasoning within discourses that so often

50 Together with Danielle Tyson and Jude McCulloch, Fitz-Gibbon and Maher were responsible for drafting the alternative sentencing feminist judgment in the case of *R v Middendorp* in which Luke Middendorp fatally stabbed his estranged partner, Jade Bownds, and was found guilty of the lesser charge of defensive homicide.

silence, victimise or vilify women while creating a judgment that was persuasive and authoritative in that context? (Fitz-Gibbon and Maher 2015: 254).

The notion of authority and judicial voice are important in the production of juridical texts, no less so in dressing up in judicial robes as feminist critique. For Fitz-Gibbon and Maher (2015: 255), the pressure to sound authoritative (the pressure to speak like a judge) 'in a system that continues to regulate and produce male privilege generated some uncomfortable strictures as legitimate feminist anger and critique had to be muted and rephrased'. For instance, they pondered 'How many times could we say "chilling" and still seem "judicial"'? (Fitz-Gibbon and Maher 2015: 265). The process of writing the feminist judgment thus made visible the 'relational and contingent nature of law and its operations' but also revealed "forcible citation of [norms]" (Butler 1993, 232; cited in Lloyd 2007, 64) 'that constitute gender, and the extent of the fictions of precedent that underpin the operation of the legal system' (Fitz-Gibbon and Maher 2015: 255 citations in original). Hence Fitz-Gibbon and Maher (2015: 268–269) argued that donning judicial robes is uncomfortable ('whether feminist or not') and queried whether it compromised 'aspirations for an equitable and adequate accounting for gendered violence and biases'. Hence another, perhaps more uncomfortable notion of plausibility comes to the fore. Given the extent to which Fitz-Gibbon and Maher felt straightjacketed by the confines of masculinist legal method—as feminist legal scholars producing judgment for an explicitly feminist purpose—it is perhaps not so difficult to imagine the institutional pressures which might militate against real life feminist[51] interventions.

Gender and judgment: legal fictions real and imagined

The common law is law's history insofar as it can be understood as the collected wisdom of judges and therefore depicts social, political and legal matters of the day. Part of the broad enterprise of feminist legal theory has been in uncovering the gendered nature of these ruminations of the legal imagination through piercing law's claim to universal truth. Feminist demands about the

51 This is not to deny the contributions of feminist judges who have made important contributions, nor is it to act as an apologist for judges who eschew feminist approaches. Rather, the point is that the masculinism embedded in law's approaches, systems and institutions problematises feminist interventions. It is certainly arguable that Bell J's approach is an example of a 'muted' feminist critique, consciously rephrased around legalistic notions such as retrospective laws and the doctrine of precedent so as to better fit within the strictures of judicial voice. We cannot know this as all we have to work with is the text of written judgment, which as contrasted with an explicitly feminist approach, certainly does not read as a feminist judgment.

need to overhaul the law's overarching story about rape also sought to make it easier for individual women to recount their stories. The tensions between these stories, at an individual and institutional level, came to the fore in *PGA*. In order to grant Mrs GP individual legal redress for alleged wrongs, the entire script about the legal conceptualisation of rape within marriage had to be reimagined. Unfortunately, the death of the accused, Mr PG, in 2012 means that the matter was never remitted for trial and therefore, despite the Court's finding of the legal existence of rape within marriage in 1963, we will never know whether he was, as a matter of law, guilty of it.

It is certainly not surprising that the women judges took divergent views. It is therefore not difficult to see why the decision in *PGA* has attracted criticism, especially from those informed by feminist understandings of the operation of the law with regard to rape. The feminist judges, and to a lesser degree, the minority judges in *PGA*, exhibited self-awareness in recognising the role of fiction and imagination in all legal judgments (including their own). The majority's treatment of legal fictions showed a disregard for the purpose, scope and implications of these fictions. The acceptance of judgment writing as a form of imagination might be averred by legal positivism, but the effectiveness with which feminist judgment writing separated judgment writing from official judicial authority demonstrated explicitly that it is an imaginative enterprise. To deny the role of imagination does not dull the danger, significance, or the power of it. Rather, feminist judging reveals in practice what feminist legal theory more broadly has sought to do. By revealing the imaginative and therefore human nature of the law, feminist judgments point to our complicity in it.

Legal fictions were deployed in the various judgments in *PGA* to construct both real and imagined understandings of the intersections of law and marital rape. By holding a mirror to the real and the imagined in this specific case the imaginative and contingent nature of judicial method was made apparent. The fictions about marital rape and the fictive feminist judgment revealed that the danger and power of legal imaginations rest on belief and plausibility. Fictions understood in the Fullerian sense are rendered more dangerous and therefore less useful the more they are believed, whereas feminist fictions are arguably more useful the more plausible or believable they are. The feminist response to *PGA* nonetheless provided that legal plausibility does not necessarily erode the disruptive or powerful nature of feminist reasoning. Stripped of the trappings of judicial authority, dressed up in judicial robes but just for show, we see that disrupting the gender regime in overt and explicit ways remains possible. That this is possible within the bounds of legal formalism is all the more significant as feminist judgment writing nominally disproves what once was understood as the antithetical interrelationship between feminism and judging. But, and this gets to the nub of the issue, the deviant challenge to the gender regime appears easier or more possible in dress up. Or it might be that the fictive feminists who get to do the dressing up (as judges) have far more affinity with the contextual approaches to legal reasoning which are able to take into account women's lived experience than those who are given their judicial robes by the executive.

In this respect, by reading the various judgments in the real decision together with the feminist judgment, we see—perhaps with renewed intensity—the gender regime in which judges operate on an institutional level on the High Court, and on a wider socio-political level too. When women judges are appointed, the gender slate is not wiped clean but rather they are required to navigate legal rules and processes (such as *stare decisis*) which might dull difference and disruption even *if* (and this, of course, is an important hurdle) the judge *wants* to do so. The gendered processes which have informed historical legal constructs about women's legal status and relationship are left deeply embedded in the law. By the same token the ways in which judging and legal reasoning are shaped, the way things are done on the High Court, cannot easily shake off longstanding gendered processes. These notions can be disrupted but usually only *consciously and deliberately* so.

Chapter 6

Gendered harms in *Monis v The Queen*[1]

In an historic first in *Monis v The Queen; Droudis v The Queen*[2] ('*Monis*'), the High Court of Australia split along gender lines. Mr Man Haron Monis (aided and abetted by his partner Ms Amirah Droudis) had been found guilty of using the postal service to transmit offensive material. Monis sent letters to the family members of soldiers killed in Afghanistan, as well as to elected officials. The letters criticised the Australian military presence in Afghanistan and contained personally 'denigrating and derogatory' comments about the dead soldiers. This was deemed offensive within the terms of s. 471.12 of the *Criminal Code 1995* (Cth) and hence Monis and Droudis were prosecuted by the NSW authorities. Monis and Droudis challenged the validity of the relevant provision as it applied to them, arguing their conviction should be quashed because s 471.12 infringed the implied freedom of political communication—the closest thing to freedom of speech in Australia. In a joint judgment, Crennan, Kiefel and Bell JJ found the provision to be valid, whereas in separate judgments French CJ, Heydon and Hayne JJ would have held that in the circumstances, the provision amounted to an impermissible burden on the implied freedom. A split decision such as this is a rarity because normally the Court's full complement of seven judges would prevent such an occurrence. However, at the time *Monis* was heard there were only six judges available, as Justice Gummow was due to retire and Justice Gageler had not yet been sworn in. The Court's tied decision meant that the decision of the Supreme Court of New South Wales (Court of Criminal Appeal) was affirmed.[3]

1 Parts of this chapter draw on and develop material and arguments previously published in McLoughlin. K. and Jose, J. 2017. 'The politics of the public and private spheres: the High Court's decision in Monis and the gendered privileging of free speech.' *Australian Journal of Political Science* 52.4: 565–579, copyright ©Australian Political Studies Association, reprinted by permission of Informa UK Limited, trading as Taylor & Francis Group, www.tandfonline.com on behalf of Australian Political Studies Association.

2 *Monis v The Queen; Droudis v The Queen* (2013) 249 CLR 92.

3 *Judiciary* Act 1903 (Cth) s 23. This meant that Monis and Droudis' convictions stood. The *Monis* decision subsequently became famous for a particularly tragic

DOI: 10.4324/9780429288531-7

The divergent opinions adopted by the men and women judges in *Monis* reflect some of the tensions feminist theorists have exposed in the law's dichotomous conceptions of its own reach in public and private spheres. Understood in this way, in *Monis* we see two views about the appropriate reach of the freedom of political communication when it intrudes into the home, or the very private sphere which law has sometimes feigned disinterest in. On one view, the view taken by the men judges, offensive communication is seen as the necessary byproduct of robust political debate. On the other, in the view taken by the women judges, the law should reasonably be able to prohibit the harm caused by seriously offensive communications in the context of an intrusion into the private sphere. These divergent opinions rest on different conceptions of the law's relationship with the political system and illustrate the way in which gendered rationalities can inform legal understandings.

These divergent understandings reflect liberalism's dichotomous conception of the public and private sphere, which situates the individual (man) of law. Further, the values entrenched in the constitutional framework are thereby exposed. But in order for the women judges to recognise (in substance) the dichotomous conception of the public/private spheres and the particularity of individuals within the institutional context, they adopted (in form) an approach akin to the benchmark 'man of law's' purported neutral rationality. Hence the *substance* of Crennan, Kiefel and Bell JJ's decision presented a disruption to the masculinist conception of the public/private sphere, but in *form* their judgment was very restrained and almost muted in terms of language, structure and narrative. Conversely, the men judges not only understood the political system in gladiatorial terms where there are winners and losers, their masculinist understanding of the polity was further reinforced in their emotive and persuasive approach to judgment writing.

A three–three decision itself conveys the imagery of balance. Moreover, free speech, even in the guise of implied freedom of communication, involves a balancing act, as freedoms by their very nature are never absolute.[4] In Australia, courts are therefore required to determine whether the law is reasonably appropriate and adapted to serve a legitimate end in a manner which is compatible with 'the system of government prescribed by the Constitution'.[5]

reason in December 2014. Man Haron Monis held 17 people hostage in Sydney at the Lindt Café where two hostages and Monis were killed.

4 For example, the prohibition of hate speech is seen as an appropriate limit on free speech although the balance between free speech and freedom from the harm hate speech engenders is contentious. It is beyond the scope of this chapter to examine this example of the balancing exercise; however, this issue has received considerable scholarly attention. In the Australian context see Gelber and Stone (eds) (2007) *Hate Speech and Freedom of Speech in Australia*. For a specific discussion of gender and hate speech in Australia see Weston-Scheuber (2012: 133–134).

5 See *Lange v Australian Broadcasting Corporation* (1997) 189 CLR 520, 567. The relevant legal test will be discussed more fully below.

Hence, the implied freedom does not create an individual 'right' to free speech, but rather, acts as a fetter on legislative power; it 'provides *freedom from* interference'.[6] That the women and men judges in *Monis* conceptualised the contours of freedom of political communication and notions of offence and harm in markedly different ways gives further pause to think about what is valued in and thus protected by the constitutional framework. The subject matter of the decision—military service and sacrifice, notions of harm as understood in public and private contexts, parental and spousal grief—meant that in considering whether the law was reasonably appropriate and adapted, the judges were called upon to balance competing individual and institutional values. The *Monis* judgment is therefore especially interesting as part of this book's examination of the gender balance on the High Court.

Feminist legal scholars have pointed out that the arrival of women judges 'puts us on notice' because 'it encourages us to both look for—and more importantly—find difference' (Rackley 2009: 16). This observation has a certain resonance in light of the decision in *Monis*. The way gender infuses the decision is more nuanced than simply suggesting that the decision is representative of feminine or masculine modes of reasoning solely contingent upon the gender of the judge. However, there are obvious dimensions to the decision which suggest that Crennan, Kiefel and Bell JJ's reasoning manifested at least a version of difference hypothesised by feminist theorists. This is most evident in the ways in which notions of 'harm' and 'home' infuse the Court's reasoning. This raises issues of significance for feminist legal scholars: the peculiarly gendered implications around free speech, citizenship, and representative democracy (see e.g. Pateman 1983; Phillips 1991; Irving 1996). For example, in the context of reviewing the decision in *Monis*, Irving (2013) noted that men and women have sometimes not been beneficiaries of free speech in equal measure and that 'women have long been sensitive to the down-side of free speech'.[7] Similarly, Appleby and Naffine (2015) drew attention to the role

6 See Stone (2001: 376), who has explained that the High Court's approach to the implied freedom means that it 'is a "negative" rather than a 'positive' right which means that it provides *freedom from* interference, rather than the *right to* engage in certain activities'. In this respect the freedom is understood as an immunity from laws which burden the implied freedom. Despite this, the language of 'validity' and 'invalidity' nonetheless infuses the judgments in *Monis*.

7 One of the more obvious examples of the gendered downside to free speech can be seen in the feminist debates about the regulation and prohibition of pornography. In the United States, Catherine MacKinnon and Andrea Dworkin argued that pornography was harmful to women (see e.g. MacKinnon and Dworkin 1998) and drafted an Anti-Pornography Ordinance which, although passed into law in two states, was ultimately struck down on the basis that it violated the First Amendment of the United States Constitution. This is not to say that MacKinnon and Dworkin's conceptualisation of pornography as harmful to women, necessarily represents *the* feminist perspective on the issue (for a contrary view see e.g. Strossen 1995). MacKinnon's (1984: 336) critique of the way in which a free speech justification

of gender in shaping the judges' understandings of the nature and limitations of free speech with respect to what was deemed acceptable or necessary for democratic political discourse in Australia. Notwithstanding the fact that Justices Crennan, Kiefel and Bell have eschewed (to varying degrees) specifically feminist identities,[8] there is scope to consider whether their approach in this decision evidenced the sensitivity to which Irving alludes. In any case, their contribution to this decision gives further insight into the gender regime all judges navigate.

This chapter therefore explores questions of gender, difference and judicial reasoning as they converge and bear on the constitutional issue before the Court of the state's legitimate scope for regulating political communication. The gender split in *Monis* is perhaps all the more interesting in that it is the exception which proves the rule. It was a decision in which the women judges not only wrote together but also adopted an approach which at least on the surface seems to challenge or disrupt masculinist legal understandings. Part of the analysis in this chapter considers the gendered notions of 'harm' and 'home' that infuse the Court's reasoning about the limits of the implied freedom of political communication. Significantly, the chapter is not concerned with the precedential value of *Monis*, nor does it aim to provide a comprehensive overview of the body of case law in this area.

In the context of the book's examination of the gender balance and the institutional gender regime of the High Court, the chapter is more broadly concerned with how the masculinism embedded in the very text and structure of the Constitution is part and parcel of the gender regime within which all the members of the High Court operate. Given that the very source of the implied freedom is a system of representative government crafted by men to the exclusion of women over one hundred years ago it is also necessary remind ourselves of the entrenched masculinism embedded in Australia's Constitution as outlined in Chapter 1. Although the source and limitations of this freedom have remained contentious, the constitutionally prescribed system of representative government is the pillar upon which the constitutional implication rests. The peculiar legal magic which is drawn from the representative system of government in Australia gives further impetus to unpacking the (gendered) values embedded in the Constitution itself, especially as this magic also appears to have been influential in framing how the men judges in the *Monis* case regarded the workings of Australia's democratic system. While arriving at their decision might have been business as usual for the men (though that remains to be seen), for the women judges the situation was much more complicated. The

'like virtually all liberal theory, presumes the validity of the distinction between the public and private' nonetheless revealed the gendered presumptions underpinning justifications for free speech.

8 Noting that Bell has not eschewed a feminist identity, but rather has denied that such an identity has any bearing on her approach to the judicial role.

aim of this chapter is thus to explore how these complications played out over an issue that at first blush seems a good distance from typical gender concerns. The discussion provides an analysis of the divergent reasoning adopted by the men and women judges in *Monis* and what it tells us about the gender balance of the decision, but more importantly what it might tell us about the dynamics of the Court's gender order. In so doing it will also enable more light to be shed on the overarching question about the difference that women judges might make.

Implied freedoms, representative government, and democracy

Neither representative democracy nor representative government appear in the actual text of the Constitution. Whatever rights are determined by the High Court are derived from the interaction between the common law, individual statutes and the Constitution (Galligan and Morton 2006: 17). Yet the juridical process has invested particular significance in these notions, most notably in the articulation in 1992 of an implied freedom of political communication because this involved claims about what representative government requires. This was determined in the 'twin cases' *Australian Capital Television Pty Ltd v Commonwealth* [9] and *Nationwide News Pty Ltd v Wills.* [10] Although this was not the first instance in which rights or freedoms were drawn by implication from the Constitution,[11] the authoritative recognition of such a freedom was constitutionally and politically significant. However, the recognition was complicated by divergent views as to the precise source and scope of the freedom. Competing 'wide' and 'narrow' views manifested most clearly in the ways in which the judgments conceived of the relationship between representative democracy and the text and structure of the Constitution. The precise source and scope of this freedom remained contentious for some years.[12]

The Court's unanimous decision in *Lange v Australian Broadcasting Corporation* (1997) 189 CLR 520 settled this uncertainty, anchoring the implied freedom of

9 *Australian Capital Television Pty Ltd v Commonwealth* (No 2) (1992) 177 CLR 106 concerned the validity of Part IIID of the *Broadcasting* Act 1942 (Cth).

10 *Nationwide News Pty Ltd v Wills* (1992) 177 CLR 1 concerned the validity of s 299 (1)(d)(ii) *Industrial Relations Act 1988* (Cth).

11 See Blackshield and Williams (2010: 1257) for a comprehensive survey of the earlier instances in which the High Court had been willing to recognise individual rights from the Constitution. They note early decisions (such as *R v Smithers; Ex parte Benson* (1912) 16 CLR 99). Significantly, in addition to pointing to these early origins, Blackshield and Williams further credit Justice Lionel Murphy as the catalyst for the implied right jurisprudence.

12 See for example the Court's decisions in *Theophanous v Herald Weekly Times Ltd* (1994) 182 CLR 104 and *Stephens v West Australian Newspapers* (1994) 182 CLR 211 which considered the relationship between the implied freedom and the common law of defamation.

political communication to the text and structure of the Constitution.[13] The Court made explicit the relationship between representative government and the text of the Constitution itself: 'to say that the Constitution gives effect to representative government is a shorthand way of saying that the Constitution provides for that form of representative government which is to be found in the relevant sections'.[14]

The Court specified that two questions needed to be answered in determining whether a 'law of a State or federal Parliament or a Territory legislature is alleged to infringe the requirement of freedom of communication imposed by ss 7, 24, 64 or 128 of the Constitution':

> First, does the law effectively burden freedom of communication about government or political matters either in its terms, operation or effect?
>
> Second, if the law effectively burdens that freedom, is the law reasonably appropriate and adapted to serve a legitimate end the fulfilment of which is compatible with the maintenance of the constitutionally prescribed system of representative and responsible government and the procedure prescribed by s 128 for submitting a proposed amendment of the Constitution to the informed decision of the people.[15]

Importantly, especially given the weight and clarity afforded by a unanimous decision, this remained the test for validity for almost two decades.[16] More recently, in *McCloy v New South Wales*, the High Court revised the second limb of the *Lange* test so as to provide "proportionality testing" in order to 'determine whether the restriction which the provision imposes on the freedom is justified'.[17]

13 *Lange v Australian Broadcasting Corporation* (1997) 189 CLR 520, 567: to the extent that the requirement of freedom of communication is an implication drawn from ss 7, 24, 64, 128 and related sections of the Constitution, the implication can validly extend only so far as is necessary to give effect to these sections. Although some statements in the earlier cases might be thought to suggest otherwise, when they are properly understood, they should be seen as purporting to give effect only to what is inherent in the text and structure of the Constitution.

14 *Lange v Australian Broadcasting Corporation* (1997) 189 CLR 520, 567.

15 Ibid.

16 A slight change to the wording was proposed by McHugh J in *Coleman v Power* so that it was expressed as 'in a manner consistent' rather than 'the fulfillment of which'. See *Coleman v Power* (2004) 220 CLR 1, 50 (McHugh J). This approach was subsequently affirmed by the Court in *Wotton v State of Queensland* (2012) 285 ALR 1, 25, 40–41, 77 and 82.

17 See *McCloy v New South Wales* (2015) 257 CLR, 193-194 [2] (French CJ, Kiefel, Bell and Keane JJ) where their Honours set out the revised proportionality test in full. *McCloy* concerned a challenge to sections of the *Election Funding, Expenditure and Disclosures Act* 1981 (NSW) which capped (and in some instances, banned) political donations in relation to New South Wales elections. The Court upheld the validity of the legislation, holding that it did not breach the implied freedom of

The explicit reference to sections understood collectively as 'the system of government prescribed by the Constitution' was significant in firmly grounding the freedom to the text and structure of the Constitution rather than to the more nebulous (and potentially wide-reaching) notion such as the fabric of the Constitution which had been crafted by Deane and Toohey JJ (Joseph and Castan 2006: 399). Significantly, the relevant sections of the Constitution relate to voting, an obvious component of democracy, but do not include s 41 where women's contributions to the Constitution's creation are arguably most visible. The very text and structure of the Constitution bears the hallmarks of its masculinist creation.

The implied freedom of political communication cases have called upon judges to consider what demands the Constitution itself makes as to representative government. Hence, even leaving to one side for the moment the specific textual issues which arise as to women's status within the constitutional framework, the Court's understanding of the meaning of political communication and its role in representative government is nonetheless imbued with certain masculinist conceptions of the relationship between the state and the individual. For example, Stone (2001: 375–376) considered that the Court's adamancy that the freedom does not confer personal rights could be understood as 'institutional' rather than 'personal'.

Understood in this way, the freedom is seen to privilege the institution of government as opposed to the individuals within it.[18] For the most part it can be argued that 'a recurring theme in the cases from 1992 onwards has been that the Court sees freedom of speech as a means to an end' where that end is logically understood to be a political end which in *Lange* turned on enabling the people of Australia 'to exercise a free and informed choice of electors' (Chesterman 2000: 21). In this respect the High Court's conception of democracy or self-government has also varied. By the end of the twentieth

political communication, because although the law amounted to a burden, it was held that it was for a legitimate end. Although Gageler and Gordon JJ (in separate judgments) agreed with the majority's conclusions regarding validity, their Honours did not regard the *Lange* test as requiring revision. In dissent, Nettle J similarly held that the impugned provisions were valid with the exception of Div 4A to the extent that it applied to property developers. This case is beyond the scope of the analysis undertaken in this chapter but it is certainly noteworthy that the Court revised the *Lange* test in the aftermath of the divided *Monis* decision. The composition of the Court had changed by the time *McCloy* was heard but it is nonetheless interesting that the judges still remaining on the Court (French CJ, Kiefel and Bell JJ) were joined by Keane J in writing the joint judgment which recast the proportionality test.

18 In *McCloy v New South Wales* (2015) 257 CLR the High Court reaffirmed its continued insistence that the freedom is not a personal right. Gageler J (at [119]), for example, emphasised that the purpose of the freedom is preserving the system of representative government and it therefore exists 'to protect: systemic integrity, not personal liberty; communication, not expression; and political communication, not communication in general'.

century it had shifted from a 'participatory' towards an 'institutional' version, with the balance of opinion moving

> away from individual citizen participation in political discussion and towards the requirement, as articulated by McHugh J in *ACTV*, that electors must have the freedom to receive information about government and political matters, in order that they may make informed political choices.
>
> (Chesterman 2000: 34)

Even though the Court's conceptualisation of the implied freedom necessarily makes claims as to what constitutes political communication, it has not evinced much interest in defining the parameters of political communication (Meagher 2004).[19] The Court has also eschewed exploring more conceptual or theoretical notions of representative government in accounting for the proper source and rationale for the freedom (Patmore 1998). *Lange* confirmed the textual foundation of the implied freedom, but an inquiry into what the Constitution 'prohibits, authorises and requires' is nonetheless capable of divergent interpretations as judges are left to insert their own understanding.

These considerations are significant—practically, theoretically and jurisprudentially. Remembering that the representation envisaged by the Constitution's framers was not absolute, it is a marvel of contemporary jurisprudence that notions of representative democracy have been put to work in the ways they have. In balancing the requirements of representative government and notions of free speech, judges necessarily make decisions about the value of both. These decisions are not always overtly gendered. However, decisions about what representative government looks like and what is required of it cannot be understood in a political, historical or social vacuum. It is for these reasons that the decision in *Monis* is particularly illuminating—because of the gendered identities of those sitting on the bench and the potential for gendered values to shape and inform the balancing. It is to that decision we now turn.

Decision in *Monis*

In April 2011 Man Haron Monis was charged with 12 counts of using a postal service in a way that a reasonable person would regard as being, in all the circumstances, offensive, contrary to s 471.12 of the *Criminal Code 1995* (Cth)

19 See Meagher (2004) for a critique of the Court's approach to defining the scope of political communication. Meagher (2004: 471) pointed to the nexus between the way in which the political communication is defined and the rationale for the freedom in acknowledging that *Lange* established 'that the implied freedom must be a home-grown, text-based project and that a nexus must exist between the communication and federal voting choices before it can attract constitutional protection'. As Meagher argues, notwithstanding the recognition of this nexus, this alone does not determine what may be considered political communication.

('the Act'). Amirah Droudis was indicted on eight counts of aiding and abetting Monis in the commission of a number of those offences. Section 471.12 of the Act provides that:

> A person is guilty of an offence if:
>
> a the person uses a postal or similar service; and
> b the person does so in a way (whether by the method of use or the content of a communication, or both) that reasonable persons would regard as being, in all the circumstances, menacing, harassing or offensive.

PENALTY: Imprisonment for 2 years.

The charges were in respect of a series of letters (and one audio recording) sent between 2007 and 2009. The letters were to the relatives of Australian soldiers killed while serving in Afghanistan and to the family of an AusAid official killed in one of the terrorist bombings in Indonesia. In those letters, Monis was not only critical of Australia's military involvement overseas, but also of the soldiers themselves, describing them as 'murderers' among other things.[20]

The issue for the High Court, however, was not whether Monis' conduct was offensive within the meaning of s 471.12, but whether the section impermissibly burdened the implied freedom of political communication. The judges agreed as to the construction of the term offensive,[21] that the letters constituted political communication in the relevant sense, and further, that the provision operated to burden the political communication, in satisfaction of the first *Lange* limb. The divergence was in the Court's application of second limb of *Lange*. Stellios (2015: 571) described *Monis* as a decision largely turning on 'differing views taken on the purpose of the provision'. Certainly, the Court disagreed as to the purpose and breadth of the provision, but underlying that disagreement was a bigger conflict of views about the law's reach in prohibiting certain forms of speech. In weighing up whether the legislation infringed the implied freedom, the judgments tell stories about the appropriate reach of the law into the public and private realms and therefore make important claims about what constitutes representative democracy and what should properly be protected within it. The judgments are now dealt with in turn.

An impermissible burden on the implied freedom

In separate but concurring judgments French CJ, and Hayne and Heydon JJ found for the appellants essentially on the basis that the impugned section

20 *Monis v The Queen; Droudis v The Queen* (2013) 249 CLR 92, 185 [255] (Crennan, Kiefel and Bell JJ).
21 *Monis v The Queen; Droudis v The Queen* (2013) 249 CLR 92; 128 [59] (French CJ); 138 [91] (Hayne J), 202 [310] (Crennan, Kiefel and Bell JJ).

infringed the second limb of the *Lange* test. For French CJ and Hayne JJ the breadth and purpose of the section meant that it went too far and therefore impermissibly burdened the implied freedom. Although there were some divergences in their reasons, the implication drawn from their reasons is the same—'robust political debate' which might cause harm is a necessary requirement of representative government. Heydon J saw the issue a little differently in that he questioned whether the seriousness of that harm and legislature's inability to prohibit it made a compelling case against the implied freedom, but nonetheless concurred with French CJ. Heydon J's judgment therefore warrants specific attention after canvassing French CJ and Hayne J's reasons.

Neither French CJ nor Hayne J was especially concerned with the facts which had given rise to the appeal and hence they were given fleeting reference.[22] For the Chief Justice the conclusions as to validity rested on the legislation rather than the facts in question.[23] Also, that the relevant section amounted to a burden on freedom of political communication was not especially controversial.[24]

Thus the determinative issue centred on the second limb of the *Lange* test, namely in determining whether the law was reasonably appropriate and adapted to serve a legitimate end. This obviously requires an examination of the purpose of the impugned provision, but also the substance and meaning of the constitutionally prescribed system of representative and responsible government. For Hayne J the purpose of the section was to secure civility of discourse and 'ensuring civility of discourse is not an end compatible with the constitutionally prescribed system of government'.[25] For French CJ, on the other hand, the purpose of the provision was to prevent the conduct it prohibits.[26]

Despite these different interpretations of purpose, French CJ and Hayne J nonetheless agreed that the breadth of the section's application meant it amounted to an impermissible burden in accordance with the second limb of *Lange*. This breadth meant that the purpose could not be regarded as consistent with the maintenance of the constitutionally prescribed system of government and involved the rejection of a range of submissions as to possible legitimate ends, for example:

22 *Monis v The Queen; Droudis v The Queen* (2013) 249 CLR 92, [3] French CJ; 135 [78] (Hayne J).
23 Ibid, 105 [3] (French CJ).
24 See French CJ at [71] where he noted that the section must be taken to effectively burden freedom of communication about government or political matters in its operation or effect. Hayne J at [93] was of the view that nothing turned on the comparative size of the burden. Hence even if the burden could be described as a 'little burden', the Court was nonetheless required to move to the second limb of *Lange*.
25 *Monis v The Queen; Droudis v The Queen* (2013) 249 CLR 92, 168 [199] (Hayne J).
26 Ibid, 108, [11] (French CJ).

> the protection of persons from being subjected to offensive material, the promotion and protection of postal and similar services that bring material into homes and offices, the regulation of postal services, the protection of the integrity of such services and the protection of those who participate in the constitutionally mandated system of government.[27]

French CJ and Hayne J thus dismissed any significance attaching to the protection of individuals from being subjected to offensive materials in their homes, unconvinced as their Honours were by the 'intrusion in private spaces' submissions.[28] Hayne J reasoned that the delivery of mail whether (at home or work) was an unremarkable feature of everyday life.[29] Hayne J further emphasised the point by stating that while ensuring civility itself might not be a legitimate object, 'ensuring civility of *private* discourse is even further removed from a legitimate object or end'.[30] It follows that in Hayne J's view, whatever takes place in the private sphere is not the concern of matters of representative government.[31] For Hayne J the kind of protection which might be afforded by the impugned section was not legally cognisable.[32]

What took precedence was the importance of robust political debate. French CJ noted that 'freedom of speech is a common law freedom' and that 'the common law and the freedoms it encompasses have a constitutional dimension', hence it forms part of 'the ultimate constitutional foundation in Australia'.[33] For the Chief Justice, 'reasonable persons would accept that unreasonable, strident, hurtful and highly offensive communications fall within the range of what occurs in what is sometimes euphemistically termed "robust" debate'.[34]

Similarly, for Hayne J, 'robustness' of political discourse was part and parcel of a healthy democracy. Causing offence 'is part of political discourse'—which can never be 'free from passion'[35]—and is thus a necessary byproduct of representative government. For Hayne J the 'very purpose of the freedom is to permit the expression of unpopular or minority points of view'; free speech itself is about the protection of unpopular opinion and therefore cannot be

27 Ibid, 133 [72] (French CJ).
28 Ibid, 124 [48] (French CJ).
29 Ibid, 170 [206] (Hayne J).
30 Ibid, 168 [199].
31 Ibid, 169 [200]. In delineating between public and private conduct, his Honour distinguished s 471.12 from the legislation in *Coleman v Power*, noting that 's 471.12 has no connection with any conduct in a public place, no matter whose conduct is considered: the sender of the communication, the carrier of the relevant postal article, or the recipient of what is communicated'.
32 Ibid, 170 [204].
33 *Monis v The Queen; Droudis v The Queen* (2013) 249 CLR 92, 128 [60] (French CJ) (Citations omitted).
34 Ibid, 131[67].
35 Ibid.

restricted to what '"right-thinking" members of society would consider appropriate'.[36] Thus, the legislation does not serve a legitimate end.

But for all their championing of the place of 'robust' discourse in a democracy, French CJ and Hayne J's line of reasoning still made value-laden claims not only about the quality and content of political discourse in Australia (Appleby and Naffine 2015), but also about the what constitutes a valid concern of the institutions of representative government and what does not. For French CJ and Hayne J the matter was resolved first by an interpretation of the impugned section which denied its protective purpose and, second, by the characterisation in particularly wide and trenchant terms of the kind of free speech necessary to underpin a healthy representative democracy.

Heydon J's judgment—his last before his retirement from the High Court—was both succinct and acerbic in its critique of the implied freedom of political communication. Although Heydon J agreed broadly with French CJ's reasons to find in the appellant's favour, much of his judgment was devoted to justifying why that very conclusion was in itself evidence of the deficiency of the law. This textual portrait deployed emotive narrative and even poetry as a foil for his position that the outcome in the case was 'an outcome so extraordinary as to cast doubt, and perhaps more than doubt, on the fundamental assumption and the chain of reasoning which led to it'.[37]

Of all the judgments in *Monis*, Heydon J's was most concerned with recounting the facts in all of their specificity. His Honour acknowledged that there were 'various ways of describing the communications which found the alleged offences in this case' and decided to 'concentrate on the actual language of the communications, unmediated by bland summary':

> One of the communications, for example, is couched in unctuous expressions of regret for the "difficult time" through which the parents are passing, "condolences for the loss of your son" and statements like "May God grant you patience and guide us all to the right path." But it calls the son a murderer of civilians. It expresses sympathy to his parents, but not to him. It compares the son to a pig and to a dirty animal. It calls the son's body "contaminated". It refers to it as "the dirty body of a pig". It describes Hitler as not inferior to the son in moral merit.[38]

Having set up the obviously upsetting content, Heydon J invoked notions of parental, which segued into paternal grief. His Honour explained that although the death of a parent is a sad event, the death of a child is especially sad for a parent:

36 Ibid, 146 [122] (Hayne J).
37 Ibid, 179 [237] (Heydon J).
38 *Monis v The Queen; Droudis v The Queen* (2013) 249 CLR 92, 179 [238] (Heydon J).

> But it is different when children die in their parents' lifetime. The natural order of events is reversed. The children have not fought their fight to finality. They have not run their full race.[39]

Emphasising the point, Heydon J—departing from traditional judgment writing techniques— shared the full text of Rudyard Kipling's poem, *My Boy Jack*. The poem explores a father's grief about the loss of his son.[40] In the poem, the father waits for news about his missing son, but none comes. The father asks 'Oh, dear, what comfort can I find!', and receives the reply:

> None this tide,
> Nor any tide,
> Except he did not shame his kind—
> Not even with that wind blowing, and that tide.
> Then hold your head up all the more,
> This tide,
> And every tide;
> Because he was the son you bore,
> And gave to that wind blowing and that tide[41]

Invoking images of rallying troops and comfort for those left with grief, the poem valorizes the sacrificial aspect of war, which appeals to a certain form of masculinity. Heydon J suggested that 'those killed in war are likely to experience a similar mingling of sadness and pride'.[42] Having conjured the imagery of profound grief (tempered by notions of militarism and nationalism), Heydon J considered the way in which recipients of Monis' communications might experience letters critical of their children. Some might simply ignore the letters, other 'recipients may have almost saintly capacities for forbearance and forgiveness', but '[m]any would regard the communications as sadistic, wantonly cruel and deeply wounding blows during the most painful days of their lives,' his Honour observed.[43]

Having described in particular terms the context and consequences of the communication, Heydon J reasoned that '[l]egislators, the members of the Executive who are responsible to the legislators, and the people who elect the legislators, can claim a legitimate interest in procuring legislation which seeks to punish and prevent conduct of that kind'.[44] Here Heydon J distinguished

39 Ibid, 179 [239].
40 See Tonie and Valmai Holt's (2008) *My Boy Jack? The Search for Kipling's Only Son* for an examination of the autobiographical features in Kipling's poem.
41 *Monis v The Queen; Droudis v The Queen* (2013) 249 CLR 92, 180 [240] (Heydon J).
42 Ibid, 180 [241] (Heydon J).
43 Ibid.
44 Ibid, 180 [242].

between matters which should be protected by notions of free speech and matters which should not:

> The offensiveness of remarks to and about political opponents, or politicians, may be a price to be paid for or an incidental side-effect of free speech. But offensive remarks of the kind alleged here are not within those categories.[45]

For Heydon J then (although he did not express it in this language), there were doubts about the communication in question constituting political communication.

Heydon J then turned to broad critique of the implied freedom and implied rights generally.[46] One aspect of critique was the origins of the implied freedom, wherein Heydon J emphasised its status as a judicial invention and an unnecessary one at that. Noting that it has sometimes been suggested that 'it was necessary to invent it [the freedom] in order to ensure that representative democracy operated properly', Heydon J made a sweeping counter-claim about the historical operation of representative and responsible government:

> It is hard to agree in view of the more than satisfactory operation of representative and responsible democracy in Australia for fifty years before Federation, and then for the period, more than ninety years long, between Federation and the invention of the implied freedom. Indeed, it is questionable whether the implied freedom does foster representative democracy.[47]

Although Heydon J's point about the extent to which the implied freedom fosters representative democracy may well be a valid one, the logic behind it rests on a particular understanding of what representative democracy entails. Here we see the assumption that representative government operated 'satisfactorily' prior to the discovery of the freedom in the 1990s, but also prior to Federation—an assumption which belies the exclusion of those who were not adequately represented. In addition to expressing concerns about the origin of the law, Heydon J also critiqued its substance. His Honour described the reasonably appropriate and adapted test as 'mysterious' and 'self contradictory',

45 Ibid.

46 Although Heydon J at [245] took issue with implied rights ('the unclarity of the implied freedom gives the Courts virtually untrammelled power to make of it what each judge wills'), he nonetheless expressed approval for more express rights and also invoked the notion of the right to dignity—a right he regarded as 'central to all other rights'.

47 *Monis v The Queen; Droudis v The Queen* (2013) 249 CLR 92, 183 [248] (Heydon J).

leading to the question, '[h]ow does the application of so amorphous a test avoid the dangers of judicial legislation?'[48]

The facts served as a powerful rhetorical device in Heydon J's judgment in demonstrating his view about the deficiencies of the freedom. Hence, Heydon J queried why such a freedom should be applied 'when it permits persons like the appellants to disregard the relatives of soldiers as ends, and treat the infliction of pain on them only as a means of achieving their own ends?'[49] Crucially for Heydon J, the fact that the legislature cannot protect the family members from harm was especially incongruous given the breadth of the law's protection against bodily harm or emotional harm caused by a prank.[50] Having canvassed the deficiencies in the process and reasoning by which the implied freedom was found—and the very test upon which it is based—Heydon J nonetheless found in favour of the appellant. He reasoned that the result was the only one available on the existing law and was therefore a result 'which, some may think, demonstrates how flawed that law is'.[51]

A permissible burden on the implied freedom

In a joint judgment the women judges, Crennan, Kiefel and Bell JJ, found against the appellants in holding that the impugned provision went no further than was reasonably necessary to achieve its purpose of preventing the misuse of postal services to effect an intrusion of seriously offensive material into a person's home or workplace.[52] Their conclusion was based on what they regarded as the protective purpose of the section. The kind of conduct captured by the word 'offensive' was 'at the higher end of the spectrum'.[53] In their view, the content of the letters met that level of offensiveness: recipients of the letters were confronted with accusations that the dead soldier was a murderer, and, in some cases, was likened to Hitler.[54]

A significant point of departure for their Honours was their view of the purpose of the section. They rejected the submission that the purpose of the provision was 'merely to ensure civility of discourse between users of the postal service'.[55] The joint judgment instead conceived as real the risk of physical harm but also fear which might arise from objects and substances sent by the post. Crennan, Kiefel and Bell JJ's understanding of the purpose of the section (and ultimately its validity) rests on the importance afforded to privacy in the home. In this regard, they acknowledged 'it may immediately be observed that

48 Ibid, 182 [246].
49 Ibid, 182–183.
50 Ibid, 181 [242].
51 Ibid, 184 [251] (Heydon J).
52 Ibid, 214–215 (Crennan, Kiefel and Bell JJ).
53 Ibid, 210–211 [336].
54 *Monis v The Queen; Droudis v The Queen* (2013) 249 CLR 92, 185 [255].
55 Ibid, 205 [318].

offensive, menacing or harassing communications will almost certainly be unsolicited'.[56] The section is, therefore, not concerned with mutual discourse. The section does not qualify an offensive communication as unsolicited, but the circumstance that it was sent unsolicited will be a circumstance relevant to the method of use to which the section refers.[57]

Significantly, the joint judgment considered the importance of freedom from intrusion in their interpretation of the impugned section. The personal domain was therefore afforded a particular importance in their reasons. For example, Crennan, Kiefel and Bell JJ made reference to the conceptions in English law which observed that "[e]very man's house is his castle" as justifying the conditions placed on search warrants (conditions that remain commonplace in contemporary Australia).[58] Their Honours further reflected on the concept of the home as castle and sanctuary in the jurisprudence from the United States:

> In *Rowan v United States Post Office Department* Burger CJ referred to the continuing "vitality" of the concept of the home as castle when considering whether there was a "right to communicate offensively with another". In that case, it was observed that people are often "captives" outside the sanctuary of the home, but that this does not mean that they must be captives everywhere.[59]

The joint judgment's conceptualisation of the importance of being free from intrusion further noted how this issue had been framed in English case law, specifically referencing cases where the broadcast of images of aborted foetuses into homes led the Court to determine that a person 'has a right not to be shocked or affronted by inappropriate material transmitted into the privacy of his home'.[60]

Crennan, Kiefel and Bell JJ's construction of s 471.12 therefore took seriously the notion that home could be construed as a sanctuary from intrusion:

> The Code, by s 471.12, seeks to protect people from the intrusion of offensive material into their personal domain. It does not create a right but may serve to deter persons from such misconduct. It may do so according to *Lange*, and relevantly, so long as it does not go too far.[61]

56 Ibid, 205 [318].
57 Ibid.
58 Ibid, 205–206 [321].
59 Ibid, 206 [322] (citations omitted).
60 Ibid, 206 [323] citing *(ProLife Alliance) v British Broadcasting Corporation* [2004] 1 AC 185. French CJ also cited this material at 112 [19] but distinguished it on the basis that the legal concept of 'rights of others' had no foundation at common law and was specific to the European context. Reference was also made to *Connolly v Director of Public Prosecutions* to make the point that the right also exists in relation to the workplace.
61 Ibid, 205 [320].

Construing a protective purpose was not especially controversial. Importantly, juxtaposing that purpose with the constitutionally prescribed system of government involved somewhat cautious and restrained reasoning. Hence, their Honours did not disrupt the orthodoxy that the implied freedom operates in an institutional rather than individual sense but rather emphasised that the freedom itself was not absolute:

> The Australian Constitution does not afford a person a right of protection against unwarranted intrusions of a seriously offensive kind. Nor does it provide a personal right of freedom to communicate regarding matters relating to politics and government. It implies a freedom of political communication which operates to restrict the exercise of legislative power in a manner that is incompatible with, or is likely to unduly restrict, that freedom. But the freedom is not absolute.[62]

Thus, for Crennan, Kiefel and Bell JJ the protective purpose of the impugned law and its restriction to preventing 'seriously offensive material' meant that they could by and large frame their case that the legislation was compatible with a constitutionally prescribed system of government without making claims about the appropriate nature of political discourse. In applying the first limb of the *Lange* test, the joint judgment acknowledged that the operation of s 471.12 amounted to a burden on political communication, but in their view 'it only incidentally burdens them in its operation'.[63] Nonetheless, the satisfaction of the first limb test requires examination of the second and it was here that the joint judgment's interpretation of the purpose and operation of s 471.12 was determinative.

Their Honours noted that the 'restriction of the offence to higher levels of offensiveness will limit the number of political communications which are caught by it' and the requirement of proof of fault would 'exclude from the scope of the offence those cases where the conduct could not be said to be intentional or reckless'.[64] Hence the joint judgment further pointed out that 'a distinction has been drawn between laws of this kind and laws which prohibit or restrict communications that are inherently political'.[65] Their Honours further outlined why it was not possible to 'read down' 'the degree of offensiveness of a communication which is to be the subject of the offence and retain a field of operation for the section consistent with its purpose'.[66] Significantly

62 Ibid, 206–207 [324].
63 Ibid, 212 [342].
64 Ibid, 212 [340]–[341].
65 Ibid. 212 [342].
66 Ibid, 214 [348]. Crennan, Kiefel and Bell JJ reasoned at [335] that reading down the section in this manner was not possible in light of the legislative history of the section which supported 'a construction which applies a degree of offensiveness to the quality of the communication which is intended to be prohibited; they do not support the creation of an exception by reference to its subject matter'.

then, for the joint judgment '[a] purpose of protecting citizens from such intrusion is not incompatible with the maintenance of the constitutionally prescribed system of government or the implied freedom which supports it'.[67] Hence Crennan, Kiefel and Bell JJ came to their ultimate conclusion that the provision was valid because the burden was proportionate to the ends sought.[68]

Gender: visible and invisible?

Gender is at once visible and invisible in the High Court's decision in *Monis*. It is of course most visible in the demarcation between the men and women judges. Perhaps unsurprisingly given the politically charged subject matter, there was considerable media interest in the decision, and at least some of the focus was on the gender split. An article published in *The Australian* ran with the headline, 'Justices split on gender lines over tenor of cleric's letters'.[69] In that article, Zifcak (2013) pointed to 'persuasive work in the psychological sphere which suggests that male and female conceptions of justice may differ'. He noted that whereas men 'tend to define justice in formal and contractual terms', 'women are inclined to see it in contextual and relational ones in which the private sphere assumes greater significance' and queried whether the split in *Monis* represented 'an intriguing example of that distinction at work'. The notion that *Monis* represents an example of the difference gender might make, even couched in understandings of difference which are deeply problematised, warrants some comment.

Gender is sometimes rendered visible because it has been made invisible. The absence of women from the creation and interpretation of the Constitution makes their arrival and contribution all the more striking. This explains the specific interest in women judges. In relation to *Monis*, various questions arise like what the decision can tell us about the masculinism entrenched in the

67 Ibid, 215 [349].
68 Ibid, 215 [350]–[351].
69 It is noteworthy but not unsurprising that the judges in question have rejected the notion that the judgment in *Monis* should be read as having any bearing on the gendered identities of those sitting on the Court, or the gender split in terms of authorship. Citing Zifcak's article, Bell J (2017: 13) rejected any notion that the decision reflected the fact that women are inclined to define justice in 'contextual and relational terms in which the private sphere assumes greater significance.' Rejecting this characterisation, Bell J (2017: 13) pointed out the joint judgment in *Monis* upheld the earlier decision of the New South Wales Court of Criminal Appeal, and therefore argued 'I can only marvel at the serendipity of three of the most senior male judges in New South Wales having been gifted with a female sense of justice.' Notwithstanding this position, my concern in this chapter is to examine the complex ways in which gendered meanings and hierarchies are reflected in legal judgment. Such an analysis need not rest on the notion that there are distinctly masculine or feminine approaches to justice or judgment, or that such approaches are necessarily congruent to the gender of the judge.

Constitution, particularly with regard to evolving notions of citizenship and representative democracy. What do the divergent views about the importance of representative democracy and protection from intrusion in the private sphere tell us about gendered understandings of public and private spheres? Given the way in which feminist theorists have conceived of this divide, are any of the decisions in *Monis* feminist decisions? Finally, what do the decisions in *Monis* reveal about gender, judgment writing, legal method and the judicial enterprise? In exploring these issues we see that gender is at once more nuanced and complicated than simply ascribing the approaches to men or women.

The divergent conceptions of the purpose of s 471.12, and by extension its validity, rested on markedly different approaches to the law's reach. Notably, the way in which the women judges conceived of the protective purpose of the impugned section and by extension, the reasonableness of protecting individuals from intrusions into their private domain, is the most obvious evidence of the distinct contribution of women judges. Certainly, the fact that the women judges acknowledged this aspect is reminiscent of some iterations of feminist thought. Here we get to nub of the issue. There is a tension here about matters which are 'not the law's business'. Yet feminist theorists have been mindful of the dangers of the epithet 'the personal is political' in terms of possible implications for intrusions into the private space (Thornton 1995a: 16). Nonetheless feminist critiques of this dichotomy have 'claimed that what occurred in the so-called private sphere should be the legitimate concern of the polity' (Thornton1995a: 9). However, despite the fears about collapsing the public and private spheres into each other, the fact remains that the 'public and private cannot be dealt with in separate worlds, as if one exists in a rhythm separate from the other' (Phillips 1991: 95).

This uncertainty around the public and private spheres, according to Pateman (1983: 285), developed for good reason—the conflation of the masculine and the individual. In this traditional conflation, the masculine individual is treated as universal, so that 'the apparently universal criteria governing civil society are actually those associated with the liberal conception of the male individual, a conception which is presented as that of *the* individual' (Pateman 1983: 285, original emphasis). In further unpacking the consequences which flow from the dominance of individualism within liberal theory, Pateman (1983: 285) argues that 'it is not surprising either that the private and the public appear as the "obvious" pair of liberal categories, or that the public gets stripped of its trousers and civil society is seen, above all else, as the sphere of private interest, private enterprise, and private individuals':

> The individual is the owner of the property in the person, that is to say, he is seen in abstraction from his ascribed familial relations and those with his fellow men. He is a "private" individual, but he needs a sphere in which he can exercise his rights and opportunities, pursue his (private) interests and protect and increase his (private) property. If all men ("individuals")

> are so to act in an orderly fashion, then, as Locke is aware, a public "umpire" (rather than a hidden—private?—hand), or a representative, liberal state, is required to make and enforce publicly known, equitable laws. (Pateman 1983: 285)

When those public umpires are also men, it is perhaps also not surprising that what is known about the public and private (and the manner in which the individual is situated within it) reproduces the universalism of a masculine individualism. Women as umpires then have the capacity to disrupt this universalism—yet as is obvious in the context of this thesis, such disruption has not always been a consequence of women's 'umpiring' role. Crennan, Kiefel and Bell JJ's construction of the purpose of the impugned section nonetheless represents the most obvious manifestation of a disruption of masculinist understandings of the law's reach. Say we accept the premise that their decision brings to bear a more contextual approach informed by their lived experience as women, or even by feminist concerns, would this mean that the judgments written by the men judges were therefore an expression of masculinism? Or phrased another way, what does it tell us that the divergence in opinion is more readily ascribed to the presence of women and to their difference? This is a telling example of the way in which gender is rendered invisible when we talk about men, but also about the ways that men as legal knowers are more readily and easily seen as disembodied rational knowers. In this regard the notion that certain understandings of representative government have been constructed for and about men is cast to the benefit of men as Appleby and Naffine (2015) so ably demonstrated in their discussion of the implications of *Monis* for the limits of civility of, and the role of gender in setting standards for, political discourse.

The rationale for the implied freedom of political communication as protecting the institutions of government (rather than individuals) revisits a familiar liberal sleight of hand that feigns disinterest in what happens in the private sphere while conceiving of a universal individual as a constitutive member of the liberal state. Crennan, Kiefel and Bell JJ did not subvert this understanding of the institutional basis of the implied freedom. Nonetheless they saw another freedom situated within the private sphere that for them reflected an individual's *desire* to be free from intrusion. Although this freedom was not to be confused with the far loftier freedom of political communication and its associated role in facilitating representative government, it is nonetheless significant that the joint judgment afforded value and weight to these matters. Crennan, Kiefel and Bell JJ's understanding of notions of harm and home refuted the liberal masculinist delineation between the public and private spheres. Their recognition that the separation of public and private was an artificial construct, one that was often arbitrarily demarcated and legitimised judicial judgments and arguments, set them apart from the men judges. But this is not to say that this much was made explicit in any overt sense in their judgment. Rather, their judgment set out the protective purpose of the relevant legislation, and its appropriate space within the constitutional framework, in a very restrained fashion.

This is where examining the gender regime becomes particularly significant. There is obvious slippage here between the wider gender regime and the one operating on the Court itself. This is not especially surprising because as Connell (2006: 839) acknowledged, a 'local gender regime may reproduce, but in specific ways may also depart from, the wider gender order (i.e., the whole societal pattern of gender relations)'. Relevantly, Appleby and Naffine (2015) situated their analysis about the silencing of women in public discourse within recent political events. Citing the example of Prime Minister Gillard's decision to ignore sexist political discourse (publicly), at least until the day of the Misogyny Speech, Appleby and Naffine (2015: 20) note that 'the incivility of political discourse in Australia' is gendered. Appleby and Naffine (2015) were not so much concerned with the gender dynamics of the Court as with the gendered logic of the men judges vis-à-vis their own focal point about civility. Hence the capacity for women's marginalisation from public debate about civility meant 'women may speak as women alongside women about women and about men and about civility, but choose not to present it as such'—which is what Appleby and Naffine (2015: 4) suggested occurred in *Monis*. What they touched upon here was the fact that *Monis* coincided with especially fraught times in Australia political discourse. This was seen not only in the gender politics of the time and the concomitant punitive consequences for speaking out against gendered incivility[70] but also in the broader masculinist claims about robust realities of political life involving offence and insult.

In her famous Misogyny Speech Prime Minister Gillard responded to a particularly sexist discourse by calling on the Leader of the Opposition to 'think seriously about the role of women in public life and in Australian society.'[71] That speech was delivered in October 2012, one month prior to oral arguments in *Monis*. In August of the same year, the then Federal Opposition Leader Tony Abbott (his conduct the subject of much of Gillard's speech) at an address to the Institute of Public Affairs attempted to rally political support

70 See Johnson (2015) for a discussion of the (gendered) invocation of the 'gender card' when women acknowledge publicly the sexist treatment they encounter.

71 Prime Minister Gillard's (*Hansard* 2012: 11581) 'Misogyny Speech' was immediately prompted by criticisms about her handling of allegations of sexual harassment against the then Speaker of the House, Peter Slipper. However, the unscripted response to the Opposition's motion drew upon a wide range of examples of what the Prime Minister regarded as sexist comments and conduct on behalf of the Leader of the Opposition and others. For example, in pointing out the hypocrisy of Mr Abbott's suggestion that her response to the allegations made against Slipper was sexist, Gillard argued that if Mr Abbott wanted to deal with sexism in parliament 'he could apologise for all his past statements and he could apologise for standing next to signs describing me as a witch and a bitch—terminology now objected to by the frontbench of the opposition'.

around the notion that freedom of speech in Australia was in jeopardy. The speech, entitled 'Freedom Wars', devoted particular attention to freedom of speech, which he characterised as 'essential to human integrity' and 'an essential foundation of democracy' (Abbott 2012). At least part of the impetus for this fear was the decision in *Eatock v Bolt* [2011][72] concerning a complaint of unlawful racial vilification by a prominent newspaper journalist, Andrew Bolt who was found to have contravened s 18C of the *Racial Discrimination Act* in publishing a number of factually incorrect articles which suggested that 'fair-skinned' Aboriginal Australians had embraced their indigeneity for some perceived political advantage.[73] Erroneously casting *Eatock v Bolt* as a prohibition of 'hurt feelings', Abbott promised to repeal 18C if elected, arguing that the section's prohibition of conduct amounted to an unacceptable limit on free speech. Hence for Abbott (2012: 4) 'expression or advocacy should never be unlawful merely because it is offensive'. Although Abbott acknowledged that Bolt's article might not have been 'his finest' and 'there may have been some factual errors', these were but necessary consequences of freedom of speech:

> Still, if free speech is to mean anything, it's others' right to say what you don't like, not just what you do. It's the freedom to write badly and rudely. It's the freedom to be obnoxious and objectionable. Free speech is not bland speech. Often, it's pretty rough speech because people are entitled to be passionate when they are arguing for what they believe to be important and necessary. Speech that has to be inoffensive would be unerringly politically correct but it would not be free.
>
> (Abbott 2012: 4)

Abbott's characterisation of the kind of speech necessary to uphold the tenets of democracy has a familiar ring to it. The characterisation of the kind of passionate, rough and robust speech was echoed in the men's judgments in *Monis*. In pointing to the similarity (especially in the language adopted by Justice Hayne), I do not suggest any impropriety. Rather, I would suggest that this is reflective of a certain masculinist justification for freedom of speech which fails to acknowledge that the experience of public and private spheres is not universal but instead shaped by the manner in which the public and the private as

72 See *Eatock v Bolt* [2011] FCA 1103.

73 Bolt's articles, published by the *Herald and Weekly Times* included provocative titles such as "It's so hip to be black" and "White fellas in the black" and asserted that a number of prominent Indigenous Australians were not genuinely Indigenous people. In finding that Bolt had contravened s 18C (the section makes it unlawful to publicly 'offend, insult, humiliate or intimidate' on the grounds of race, colour, or national or ethnic origin) Bromberg J placed particular emphasis on the manner in which Bolt made his points about race in Australia. For a discussion of the role of the Bolt case in mobilizing public discourse around libertarian notions of freedom of speech see Gelber and McNamara (2013).

spheres of social power are reflective of racial and gendered hierarchies (MacKinnon 1984: 336–337).

Feminist legal theorists have done much to expose the masculinism embedded in legal method in both *substance* and *form*. To that end, and in light of the characterisations of free speech noted above, it is not insignificant that there are some parallels between the different constructions of the free speech in the judgments and the methods, language and tone used to justify them. That is, the kind of passionate construction of free speech is mirrored in the textual approaches adopted in those judgments that espouse that very sentiment. In contrast, it might be argued that the joint judgment is bland or orthodox at least insofar as it includes none of the rhetorical colour or emotion of the other judgments. For example, Appleby and Naffine (2015: 11) noted that 'one of the striking features of the judgment of Crennan, Kiefel and Bell JJ is how devoid it is of emotion and passion. When compared with the other judgments, particularly those of Hayne and Heydon JJ, it is emotionally flat and even dry'. Knowing what we know about the approaches to judgment writing which might encourage others to join (see Kiefel 2017b), the style of the joint judgment is entirely unsurprising.

This issue is especially interesting in light of the persuasive devices employed by the various judgments in *Monis*, especially regarding the role of narrative/facts and the taken for granted assumptions deployed about political discourse. Against this backdrop, Heydon J's judgment stands as the most radically partial and emotive. It was an oddly non-masculinist rhetoric though couched in decidedly masculinist self-righteous legal bravado. As noted above, Heydon J invoked military mythologies involving notions of sacrifice and juxtaposed these against a trenchant critique of the implied freedom. Interestingly, his Honour construed the judicial enterprise in such a way as to sever his own complicity in it. Heydon J acknowledged the harm potentially wrought by offensive communications in the home, but in finding that the impugned section went beyond that which was permissible, he blamed 'the law' for the problematic result at hand. All of the aspects which disrupted traditional judgment writing conventions (most notably the emotive crafting of the facts and the recitation of poetry) served as a foil for Heydon J's ultimate (incongruous) conclusion. Here Berns' (1999: 205) theorisation of the conventions of judgment is especially apt:

> One consequence of these conventions is that judgment becomes most successful (and most completely lawlike) when particularity is completely eradicated. To the extent that particularity cannot be expunged, the authority of the judgment is open to question and to compromise. Doubt emerges as to whether it is the law that has spoken or the individual judge.

In that context, Berns (1999: 205; 231) has argued that judges who come to occupy an iconic status (she cited Justices Murphy and Barwick as Australian examples and Lord Denning in UK, but Justice Kirby comes to mind as a more contemporary example too) are examples where the public persona of the judge overshadowed their role and diminished rather than reinforced the weight of their judgments and associated legal authority. Berns (1999: 205) argues that 'for the written judgment to persuade, to fulfill the purpose for which it was written, it must be consonant with the conventions of legality. Particularity must be vanquished, the judge must speak simply as a judge'. It is tempting to conclude that Heydon J's concern for vanquishing particularity might have evaporated given his proximity to retirement, but it is perhaps equally arguable (especially given his proclivity to dissent and public comments about it) that he might be a judge for whom the public persona overshadowed his role. Could women judges adopt an approach akin to Heydon J's emotive, colourful approach and retain their authority as legal knowers? Notwithstanding Berns' point about the potential for men judges to become so iconic as to disrupt the disembodied legal persona of the judge, women's corporeality as legal knowers means that the stakes are even higher in securing their authority as legal knowers.

Another dimension to the Court's decision in *Monis* is the fact that the gender split makes it plain that each of the judgments must have been drafted by a person (or in the case of the women, persons) of one gender. The judgment of the women was not authored by one of the men on Court (*pace* Waterford 2012). Ordinary judgment writing in collegiate Courts, especially in the form of majority judgments, is one of the ways 'the conventions of judgment obliterate difference, submerge it beneath predetermined forms', especially by concealing the author to further reinforce the distinction between the individual and the law:

> If the majority delivers a joint judgment, even the identity of its principal author is obliterated by these conventions. What is important is not who the author is, but that the judgment speaks for the majority of the Court. All of this is in keeping with the ways the law wishes to be understood. It wishes to have an independent existence, wishes to insist that individuality and identity are unjudicial, too easily mistaken for bias, for a decision reflecting the personal whim of the judge and not the law.
>
> (Berns 1999: 207)

Yet the *Monis* judgments, like the 'first judgments' discussed in Chapter 4, leave no doubt about the gender of the writers. In *Monis* the individuality of each of the men judges was brought to life (obviously made easier by their separate decisions) yet the women judges' joint judgment means that their separate identities are obscured even if their combined 'womanhood' itself becomes mistaken for bias. Indeed part of the process of examining the way that gender informs the judgment reflects the very process to which Berns (1999) alludes. Although the law (traditionally framed) wishes to conceal or disguise the authors of juridical texts, that concealment is rendered more difficult by the arrival of women judges. But for women, perhaps conscious of claims (positively and negatively cast) that they are uniquely bringing their individuality to bear, there is much at stake. In the context of discussing the judicial style adopted by the women judges, Appleby and Naffine (2015: 12) queried whether it was in fact an attempt to not be seen as speaking in a woman's voice: '[p]erhaps the regimented legality of the judgment is an attempt to fend off such observations: not to be seen as women feeling and acting as women may be said to do'. Conversely, for French CJ and Hayne and Heydon JJ, to be seen to speak as men is no intrusion upon their judicial persona because to speak as the man of law is not to be seen to speak at all.

The men judges engaged in a distinctly masculinist style of analysis. They conceived of the political system in gladiatorial terms in which there are winners and losers, where engaging in political contests entails that words are weapons. Political communication will cause offence, but that was incidental to the legal facts in question. Hence Australia's representative system of government required that there be some sort of constitutional support for free political communication, even though Heydon J personally objected to the idea that this should take the form of a constitutionally derived implied right. In taking up this view of democracy in such a strident form, the men reasserted the masculinism of both the Court and the public sphere by maintaining the gendered vision of the latter as separate from the so-called private.

For the women, matters were more complicated. Their judgment differed from those of the men both in style and reasoning. Their style was almost deadpan insofar as it did not exhibit either the passion or emotion to be found particularly in the judgments of Hayne J and Heydon J. Discussing this case in terms of what it means for the regulation of civility in a democracy, Appleby and Naffine (2015: 12) canvas a number of reasons for this but conclude that perhaps the women did not want to 'be seen as … as speaking in a "woman's voice"'. Ironically, this then set them apart from the men while at the same time rendering them as proper legal knowers —that is, as more like legal men are assumed to be. Moreover, the men's judgments also conveyed another message, albeit implicit and cloaked in legal mystique, that the High Court too was an arena for debate and as such they should not be shy about taking their stand. In this respect the response of the women judges is not surprising. Finding themselves in more or less agreement, and separately from the men, they retreated to a more 'traditional' style of analysis. Perhaps the trade-off for writing together and challenging liberalism's dichotomous construction of the public/private divide meant that the women judges were thus compelled to act as 'men in skirts' or put another way, to don the trousers of the idealised supposedly neutral and rational liberal man of law.

As this chapter has shown, gender is ever present on the High Court—from the drafting of the Constitution, to the way women are situated within the constitutional framework and the broader conceptions of liberal democracy which are embodied within it, to the ways in which women must negotiate the still novel features of their status as public legal knowers. Despite the ever present nature of gender, the aspect which made *Monis* stand out is the corporeality of women as legal knowers reflected in the gender split, and especially manifest as the women joined together to mark out a space in opposition to that of the men. The decision gives imprimatur to examine the requirements of representative government within a wider gender regime but it is the gender regime on the Court itself as reflected in the split decision which arouses our attention. The imagery of the women judges grouped together was repeated very publicly at the occasion of Justice Crennan's judicial farewell in 2014 where the women judges comprised a bench of three. At the time it was already known that Justice Crennan was to be replaced by a man judge, and the announcement of the Court's fifth woman judge, Michelle Gordon, was still some months away. Hence, as the imagery of an almost equal gender balance potentially faded into oblivion, that imagery of Justices Crennan, Kiefel and Bell alone on the bench as part of the ceremonial farewell takes on a particular resonance regarding the legacy of the gender balance. It is to Crennan J's ceremonial farewell and the way in which it framed not only her Honour's individual legacy, but also that of the gender balance, that we now turn.

Chapter 7

The art of looking back

The farewell ritual and the construction of judicial legacies[1]

As Justice Susan Crennan delivered her ceremonial words of farewell from the High Court of Australia in late 2014, she was flanked on either side of the bench by the two women appointed during her tenure, Justice Susan Kiefel and Justice Virginia Bell. Justice Crennan's first ceremonial farewell was held in Sydney in November, and the second, in Melbourne, a month later in December 2014.[2] For a time, it looked as though her Honour's retirement marked the end of an era as the imagery of the gender balance on the bench faded from public view. Certainly, her replacement with Justice Geoffrey Nettle generated criticism at the time about what that meant for the politics of gender inclusion (Hobbs 2015; Rubenstein 2014a). The subsequent announcement of Justice Michelle Gordon's appointment to replace Justice Kenneth Hayne in 2015 did not prevent questions from arising about the need to ensure diversity in judicial appointments (McLoughlin 2015c). Although Justice Crennan herself (mostly) eschewed an identity as a woman judge during her tenure, questions inevitably remain about whether gender has had any bearing on her individual jurisprudential legacy.

This chapter examines critically the legacy Justice Crennan and others sought to craft about her upon her retirement from the Court. The idea of 'farewell'

1 Parts of this chapter draw on material and arguments previously published in K McLoughlin. 2016. '"Collegiality is not compromise": Farewell Justice Crennan, the Consensus Woman.' *The Australian Feminist Law Journal* 42: 241–271 copyright ©Australian Feminist Law Journal Inc., reprinted by permission of Informa UK Limited, trading as Taylor & Francis Group, www.tandfonline.com on behalf of Australian Feminist Law Journal Inc.

2 The transcripts of the special sittings to farewell Justice Crennan are available at http://www.austlii.edu.au/. The transcripts are not paginated. In this chapter Crennan J's contribution to these ceremonies are cited in text as Crennan (2014b) (the Sydney ceremony) and Crennan (2014c) (the Melbourne ceremony). Each of the speechmakers are simply cited in text by reference to their own name as it is clear in each instance that Justice Crennan was the judicial subject (as distinguished from Chapter 3 where the inclusion of a range of speeches complicated matters somewhat). For the sake of clarity Crennan (2014a) refers to the speech made in April 2014 titled 'Celebrating Women in the Law'.

DOI: 10.4324/9780429288531-8

serves as the central metaphor of this chapter, and as such I examine the formal farewell speeches made in recognition of Justice Crennan's contribution to the High Court, in addition to other public comments which give meaning to her 'publicly constructed'[3] judicial legacy. The judicial farewell is an overlooked site of analysis in this respect. Recent scholarship has paid increasing attention to swearing-in speeches because these social scripts provide revealing insights about the interaction between individual and institutional values in public legal discourse. As this chapter will demonstrate, farewell speeches are similarly revealing, with the additional advantage of offering reflection on the retiring judge's legacy.

Two motifs punctuate the farewell speeches in ways that speak to the gendered dimensions of Crennan J's legacy and, by extension, the legacy of the first gender balance on the High Court. First, her Honour's humanity was invoked in various ways by those who spoke in celebration of her contributions to the High Court. Second, there was a defence of, or valorisation even, of collegiality. Crennan (2014b) paid particular emphasis to notions of collegiality at her Sydney farewell, even literally demonstrating it by concluding her farewell speech with the words:

> Justice Kiefel on my right remarked of judgment writing, "Collegiality is not compromise". In that spirit, may I take the goodwill expressed toward me this morning as an appreciation of the work of the Court as a whole.[4]

These remarks, although seemingly innocuous in so far as gender is concerned, take on a particularly gendered significance when read in conjunction with her Honour's (2014a) criticism of journalistic assumptions 'that the women justices of the High Court make neither a significant contribution to the Court, nor write any of the judgments published jointly'. This critique, delivered as part of a speech titled, 'Celebrating Women in the Law' earlier in the same year, gives pause to consider the potential shifts in Crennan J's impression of (or even willingness to speak publicly about) the interaction between gender and judicial identity.

Drawing on these motifs of humanity and collegiality, this chapter revisits debates around authorship, collegiality and difference in the book's exploration of the gender regime. It does so by examining critically the public commemoration

3 The idea of judicial legacy is a 'public' concept in the sense that it draws upon the judge's status as a public legal knower. Judicial legacies are constructed in particular ways in the public imagination that often transcend what is recorded in the Commonwealth Law Reports as the official legal record. The persona of the judge and what we understand about her invariably draws on extra-legal material such as might be delivered at 'farewell functions.'

4 Justice Kiefel (2014) made these comments during the Richard Blackburn lecture in Canberra. Her Honour's lecture was titled 'The Individual Judge'. Kiefel J's (2014) comments about collegiality were also discussed in Chapter 4.

of not only Crennan J's time on the High Court but by extension the end of the first period where women had constituted a near majority on the High Court. The legacy that Crennan J and others crafted in the speeches commemorating the end of her judicial career has resonance regarding the gendered ways in which judicial authority and identity are constructed and understood. Judges might not be the most reliable historians but the ways in which they conceive their own judicial legacies are important, especially in terms of the intersections between gender, difference and judging. Although Crennan J's farewell and the concomitant valorisation of consensus serve as the focus for this chapter, the more thought-provoking concern is what this legacy might tell us about the impact of the near-equal gender balance on the workings of the Court's gender regime.

The chapter begins by providing some background to these speeches which mark the end of a judicial career. I then turn to an examination of the substance of those speeches made at Crennan J's judicial farewells. The aim is to identify how the speeches reveal the gendered ways in which her Honour's legacy was being crafted. This is followed by an examination of the speeches Crennan J made in response, which reveals her Honour's continued disinclination to identify as a woman judge and a defence of judicial collegiality. The chapter then considers some of the debates around collegiality and dissent before examining briefly the extent of the Court and Crennan J's collegiality during her tenure. This part affirms that the Court has been more 'collegial' in recent years and examines what this might tell us about changing gender practices within the gender regime. The chapter concludes by examining possible tensions between the gendered legacies crafted *by* and *about* the judicial subject.

Judicial farewell speeches: eulogising the judicial subject?

As discussed in Chapter 3 there has been burgeoning scholarly interest in judicial swearing-in speeches in recent times (see e.g. Moran 2006, 2011; Roberts 2012a, 2012b, 2014). In contrast, there has been far less interest in the end of the line equivalent, the farewell speech. Perhaps this is because unlike those social scripts attending the swearing-in, judicial farewells perform no particular legal magic or political purpose. There is no judicial oath to transform the individual into a judge, no need to begin projecting a judicial identity, and in many cases the judge continues to sit on the Court at least for a limited time after the farewell. As a marker of time, the farewell is literally yesterday's news as it shows the passing of the baton and the focus is reflective rather than predictive or pre-emptive. Supreme Court Justice Elizabeth Fullerton (2007: [55]) compared the process of preparing her swearing-out speech to preparing her own eulogy, 'with the singular advantage of being alive to deliver it'. Indeed, as with eulogies, the stories told at judicial farewells are markers of commemoration. Fullerton's caveat about 'being alive to deliver it' also emphasises an important aspect of judicial farewell speeches, as they provide judges with a unique opportunity to reflect publicly on their time on the Court while still sitting on it.

Traditionally, there have been ceremonial sittings of the full High Court attended by invited political leaders and legal luminaries for retiring Chief Justices[5] or memorial speeches upon a judge's death.[6] For retiring Justices, there has been institutional recognition in the form of remarks by the Chief Justice, sometimes speaking at another ceremonial occasion. For example, Chief Justice French (2015a) acknowledged Justice Crennan's retirement and contribution to the Court at a ceremony announcing the newly appointed Senior Counsels.[7] Chief Justice French (2015a) remarked that Justice Crennan was a 'valued colleague and friend to all of us' and 'we will miss her greatly'. As for Justice Crennan's intellectual contribution, the Chief Justice noted that her Honour's 'knowledge of the law, and particularly in the field of intellectual property, her legal historical perspectives and her impeccable command of the written word have enhanced the work and reputation of this Court' (French 2015a). On these occasions, however, the retiring judge does not have a speaking part.

More recently,[8] semi-formal farewell ceremonies not presided over by the Chief Justice have emerged, usually held at the Court registries outside of

5 See for example the speeches made at the farewell of Chief Justice Gleeson where the then Attorney General Robert McClelland (2008e) gave the lead speech, followed by speakers from leaders at the Bar and, finally, the retiring Chief Justice himself. A similar ritual was observed marking the retirement of Chief Justice Mason in 1995. Attorney General Michael Lavarch (1995) gave the lead speech, followed by leaders from the Bar, including one Mrs Susan Crennan, QC (President of the Australian Bar Association).

6 Chief Justice Gleeson (2005a, 2005b) presided over special memorial sittings for the late Sir Ronald Wilson and Sir Harry Gibbs. More recently, in 2015, Chief Justice French (2015c, 2015d) presided over special sittings in memory of the late the Hon. John Toohey and Sir Kenneth Jacobs.

7 However, in the case of Hayne J, French CJ (2015b) made approbatory remarks at a special sitting in honour of Hayne J's contribution to the Court. Although any commentary about the reasons for this would be purely speculative, it might have been that there were no other ceremonial sittings scheduled, or it could have been that French CJ wanted to afford special recognition to Hayne J on the occasion of the publishing of His Honour's last Full Court judgment. In any case, no provision was made for reply as part of this sitting but Hayne J did note how touched he was by this acknowledgment of his contribution at one of the later farewells.

8 The earliest transcript of such a ceremony on the Austlii database (the digital repository includes some material back to 1983 but full online records have only been kept since 1996) is 1997 where Justice Dawson's contribution to the Court was specifically acknowledged during his Honour's last sitting at the Melbourne registry. Of course, it might be the case that there are other examples, particularly earlier in the Court's history, but Justice Dawson's (1997) comments suggest that the practice might have been out of fashion for a time. His Honour said 'In recent years it has not been the custom in this Court to farewell departing Judges, at all events puisne judges. But the Chie f Justice who, at my request, is presiding over this my last sitting, said that if the profession wanted to say something he was not going to stop them and would overrule all objections'.

Canberra and framed around remarks from leaders at the Bar. These have afforded retiring judges an opportunity to speak to their judicial experiences and offer thanks and reflections. The context of these farewells directs the style and format of the speeches, with attention generally given to the experiences in the jurisdiction in question and at least some of the retiring Justice's response framed around thanking the Bar for their contribution to the development of the law. Speakers might provide a short biography, a career appraisal, and a summary of noteworthy achievements. Perhaps more obviously, with the judge's retirement from the Court imminent, there is also scope to reflect on their actual jurisprudential contributions.

The only woman judge to serve on the High Court (and therefore to retire) prior to Justice Crennan was Justice Gaudron. At Justice Gaudron's farewell, the only speaker, Mr Hughes (2002), described her Honour's 'distinguished career as a Justice' on the High Court and, arguably alluding to the criticisms her appointment had generated, said she had 'justified in the fullest possible measure sanguine expectations that people of sound judgment entertained about you when you were appointed'. Justice Gaudron's (2002) response was exceedingly brief. Her Honour simply thanked Mr Hughes for his 'very kind words' and asked that he convey her gratitude to the Bar for the 'assistance they have given me through their argument and through their research in the work that has had to be done'. We cannot know the reasons for her Honour's restraint. It might have been that she thought the time and place for public reflection were elsewhere, or it might simply have been that Hughes' remarks were unexpected, and she had not crafted a reply. Although Hughes (2002) made what might be construed as the most veiled of references to the gendered criticisms at the time of Gaudron J's appointment, he did not make explicit reference to her status as the first woman Justice of the High Court. Further, Gaudron J herself did not reflect on her status, perhaps instead preferring to be seen as simply 'one of seven'. As we will see, at Justice Crennan's farewell(s), gender features in far more visible ways. It is to those speeches we now turn.

Speeches made in Justice Crennan's honour

In all, four people spoke in recognition of Crennan J's retirement across two ceremonies. In Sydney, Ms Needham, then President of the New South Wales Bar Association, and Mr Gleeson, then Solicitor-General of the Commonwealth, spoke in farewell. In Melbourne, speeches were given by the then President of the Victorian Bar Association, Mr Peters QC, and by Mr Bowyer, then President of the Law Institute of Victoria. The farewells were decidedly shorter than the introductory equivalents in 2005 but they covered remarkably similar ground.

Examining the farewell speeches allows consideration of how gender was framed almost a decade on from Crennan's appointment. In light of the subsequent appointment of two women judges during her tenure, her farewell also provided something of a curtain call on the first gender balance on the High Court bench. When Crennan was sworn-in as the 45th judge of the High Court of Australia, her status as the second woman appointed to the Court punctuated the speeches made in welcoming her (see the discussion in Chapter 3). For her part, Crennan did not embrace an identity as a woman judge, a stance which she maintained across her career. Rather she echoed Justice Gaudron's sentiments of wanting to be seen as just 'one of seven',[9] and importantly, as an accepted member of that small group. It is clear from the sentiments expressed at her farewells, both by her Honour and those speaking about her, that she saw this as an important part of her legacy.

Thus it was that references to Justice Crennan's gender were present but muted, especially given how prominently it had featured in her swearing-in (and in the media commentary associated with her appointment) (see Chapter 3). Each speaker reflected broadly on her career. Mr Peters praised her as an 'outstanding advocate' and, pointing to the breadth of her legal knowledge and experience, noted that 'this wide scope of disciplines is unusual in this era of specialization today' (2014). Mr Bowyer similarly described Crennan as 'the most consummate barrister' and highlighted that her 'active commitment to the whole of the profession is legendary' (2014). Bowyer pointed specifically to Justice Crennan's efforts in 'building understanding and good relationships' between solicitors and the Bar. Mr Gleeson also commented on her overall achievements by drawing attention to the fact that she had 'contributed richly to our jurisprudence across many areas' and singled out constitutional law, public law, and intellectual property (2014).

In making these general comments (and others like them) the speakers also highlighted Crennan J's jurisprudential legacy. Of course, at such an occasion, not every case could be mentioned. As such, given that the speechmakers were leaders in the profession, it is fair to conclude that the particular cases were consciously chosen. Jane Needham singled out two constitutional cases: *Rowe v Electoral Commissioner* and *Williams v Commonwealth of Australia* (2014). Peters too made reference to those cases, as well as highlighting Justice Crennan's excellent expertise in intellectual property law, singling out *Lockwood (No 2), IceTV, iiNet, Apotex* and *Alphapharm* as examples (2014). And of course, Justice Crennan's first case, *Harriton v Stephens*, was also commented on, being referenced by both Peters and Gleeson.

Emerging from the various speeches was a curious but recurring theme. This was the idea of Crennan J's humanity. Peters (2014) referenced her understanding of and commitment to humanity four times in what was a relatively short speech. The first reference to humanity or the 'human condition' was annexed to her Honour's life and educational attainments:

9 Here I am referring to Gaudron's (1987) remarks at her swearing-in about wanting to be seen as 'one of seven'. As noted above she made no reference to these notions at her farewell.

> This, and your Honour's academic interest in English literature, are examples of the breadth of your Honour's achievements in education and also they exemplify your Honour's understanding of the human condition. These qualities well prepared your Honour for your role on this Court.

It is noteworthy that the focus here was about the qualities she brought to the Court, rather than what she actually did on the Court. Similarly, with his second referencing of her humanity, Peters (2014) suggested that she 'brought to this Court a foundation of a sound understanding of the law, the perspective of history, and the human qualities needed for the impartial dispensation of justice according to law'. He further noted her courtesy, which was not merely indicative of 'do[ing] right to all manner of people according to law, without fear or favour, affection or ill will', but more than that, she was 'considerate of the human condition of those who came before [her]'. Thus in Peters' view Crennan J performed on the bench with a clear sense of humanity.

Similarly, Gleeson (2014) drew attention to Crennan's humanity:

> whether sitting alone, or on a diverse and ever so occasionally querulous appellate bench, [she] showed a genuine respect for the parties, for their human condition and for the arguments, strong or not so strong, carefully crafted or unpolished, which their counsel sought to make.

Here Gleeson not only casts respect for the parties involved and the human condition as a judicial virtue, but he also situates Crennan as part of a 'diverse and ever so occasionally querulous appellate bench'. The phrase 'ever so occasionally' emphasised the infrequency of disagreements amongst the justices during her time on the bench. It is likely that Gleeson was referring to her Honour's contribution in the physical confines of the actual Court-room (where Justices question advocates in sometimes robust exchanges, particularly if the full bench is sitting), although the comments might also refer to the behind the scenes work done by the bench. While it would appear that he was not attributing that to Justice Crennan as such, it is reasonable to suggest that the implication was that diversity was a good thing and that any judicial disharmony was not its doing.

Both Peters and Gleeson drew on Crennan J's first lead judgment, *Harriton*, to make their points about her humanity. Peters (2014) described Justice Crennan's decision in *Harriton* as 'an analysis of the content of human existence'. Gleeson (2014) described the 'harrowing circumstances' of *Harriton* and quoted Justice Crennan's judgment which held that in 'the eyes of the common law of Australia all human beings are valuable in, and to, our community, irrespective of any disability or perceived imperfection'. Gleeson (2014) therefore argued that Crennan J's 'statement reflects perhaps more generally the regard which your Honour has shown for the humanity of all those whose fortunes have come before this Court'.

What is curious is why the rhetoric around both *Harriton* specifically and Crennan J's contributions more broadly saw a heavy focus on the idea of her humanity. Although no explicit link is made between her status as a woman judge and the socially constructed traits associated with womanhood, the use of 'humanity' in this context appears to be a veiled gender reference in the sense that it invokes the more gender-familiar idea that being a woman means that she is more closely connected to humanity and the human condition.[10] Clearly the comments are approbatory, but they might also be a means of accentuating or recognising Justice Crennan's womanhood, or a version of judicial womanhood, without saying as much.

The only woman speaker at either of the farewells (other than Justice Crennan herself), Jane Needham, was most explicit about her Honour's status as a trailblazing woman in the law. Needham (2014) was the only speaker to specifically mention Crennan J's status as the second woman appointed to the Court, noting that her Honour was 'the 45th person to be appointed, the 13th Victorian and the second woman'. Though she acknowledged Crennan J's hesitancy around her identity as a woman lawyer, Needham nonetheless emphasised her status as a trailblazer in the law:

> Perhaps your Honour might eschew the metaphor, but you have been a trailblazer for women at the Bar. In 1993 you were elected Chair of the Victorian Bar, and in doing so became the first woman to lead any bar council in Australia. In 1994 you became the first woman President of the Australian Bar Association. You were described as a "courageous and effective leader", who introduced significant reforms.
>
> (Needham 2014)

References to Justice Crennan's gender were made in less explicit terms by the men speakers. The only explicit reference made by Bowyer (2014) was recognition that Justice Crennan had, along 'with other recent women, Chairs of the Victorian Bar, Justice Melanie Sloss and Fiona McLeod, SC,' done much to bring the Law Institute and Bar 'relationships so much closer together'. Peters (2014) noted that on Crennan J's appointment to the High Court 'Chris Merritt of *The Australian* wrote that your Honour was "a Renaissance woman."' As outlined above, Peters (2014) linked these educational attainments to her Honour's 'understanding of the human condition'.

10 See, for example Pateman (1983) and Thornton (1995a) for examinations of the way in which liberalism constructed women as closer to nature (evidenced by nurturing and other roles associated with the feminine) in ways that rendered the masculine synonymous with disembodied reason and saw women's corporeality deployed as evidence of their lack of rationality and hence, suitability for public life and authority. There are also echoes here of Gilligan's *In a Different Voice* and the particular politics of difference that her work inspired within feminist thought.

In her own words: Justice Crennan's response to the speeches

Notions of collegiality informed Crennan J's short responses across both jurisdictions. The speech delivered in Melbourne, Crennan's home for much of her professional life, was more personal in focusing on the familial. Although Crennan had been disinclined to reflect critically on her status as a woman judge at her swearing-in, she hinted at the social and cultural changes which made her appointment possible: 'developments have occurred against a background of significant social change and major shifts in public and private values' (Crennan 2005). Almost a decade after her appointment, Crennan alluded to these changes in a more substantial way at her farewell:

> Manifold changes both to the law and to legal practice since I was first admitted reflect complex social changes, at least in part. It would be impossible to expatiate on such changes meaningfully in a speech as short as this must be. It can be remarked, however, that the Commonwealth Law Reports are perhaps the greatest natural archive of Australia's social, political and economic history. This reflects the firm tethering of the law in the spirit of every age.
>
> (Crennan 2014c)

Justice Crennan therefore gave away slightly more at her farewell—adverting to the challenges accompanying her entry to the profession and reflecting on her good fortune in being mentored by Dr Bennett (later, Solicitor General for the Commonwealth):

> For a person fresh from law school, unknown in legal circles, *and a woman*, I do not doubt there was an element of distributive justice in such generous mentoring arrangements, at least as carried out by David Bennett.
>
> (Crennan 2014b, my emphasis)

While it appears she was aware of the challenges facing a woman lawyer, and later, judge, she was not prepared to address these directly.

At her Sydney speech she also made reference to her to her time at the Bar in Sydney. She acknowledged her colleagues, noting that it had been her 'good fortune to serve on this Court with colleagues from New South Wales: former Chief Justice Gleeson, former Justices Gummow, Kirby and Heydon, and now Justice Bell on my left, and Justice Gageler'. Finally, Crennan (2014b) concluded her speech with a robust defence of collegiality, as noted in the introductory part of this chapter:

> From time to time, there is speculation about the authorship of joint judgments from this Court. Naturally, it is not always accurate. Earlier this

> year, Justice Kiefel on my right remarked of judgment writing, "Collegiality is not compromise". In that spirit, may I take the goodwill expressed toward me this morning as an appreciation of the work of the Court as a whole. We thank you for it.

In her Melbourne speech, Crennan J (2014c) similarly thanked the Victorian profession, including many individuals in Court and many now-judges, who had inspired her when they 'were all in active practice at the Victorian Bar'. Notably Crennan J also acknowledged the benefits of collegiality but in perhaps less pronounced terms than she had in her earlier speech:

> It has been my good fortune to be in chambers in Melbourne with Justice Hayne since 2005. The day-to-day work of the Court is made so much easier by collegiality, and the shared concern of all members of the Court for its institutional wellbeing.

Justice Crennan therefore linked notions of collegiality with the institutional wellbeing of the Court itself, a telling reminder of how she conceived the judicial role.

As noted above, the Melbourne speech was also more personal, arguably because Justice Crennan had spent much of her professional life in Melbourne:

> I am particularly glad my husband, Michael, is present in Court this morning, together with our children, Daniel and his wife Laura, Bridget with her husband Paul, and Kathleen, and our grandchildren, Hannah, Tomas and Lillian. Their unstinting patience and support has been crucial to me during the course of my time as a Justice of this Court. I am glad to have the opportunity to thank them.

I do not suggest that Justice Crennan's acknowledgment of her family is reflective of her status as a woman. Men also thank their families on such occasions although Moran (2011: 278) has noted (albeit in the context of swearing-in speeches) that 'when women do appear in the texts of male appointees', their role is 'confined to that other realm: domestic/biological reproduction'. No doubt, as more women occupy senior roles within the legal profession this is likely to change. For example, Hayne J (2015) acknowledged the support of his family in fulsome terms, saying that his wife and family 'have been and they remain the compass by which I steer', 'the light which permits me to see where I am going and what I am doing' and 'they remain the love which lifts my heart constantly'.

Curiously, the notion that the profession had been changed by the presence of women was not referenced in Justice Crennan's farewell, but it did feature at Justice Hayne's farewell a few months later. Mr Eades (2015), then President of Law Society of New South Wales, described the significant changes which had taken place since Hayne J's admission, including 'the feminisation of the profession, the emergence of new business models and areas of practice, globalisation' and major technological advances.

Mr Eades' (2015) reference to the 'feminisation' of the profession raises a number of salient points about gender and judicial identity. Responses to his characterisation were mixed. Ms Challans, Australian Women Lawyers President at the time, criticised the use of the 'archaic and outdated description', which emphasised 'traditional notions of femininity rather than the actual skills [brought] to the profession' (quoted in Walsh and Papadakis 2015). Conversely, Queensland Supreme Court Judge Margaret McMurdo saw no problem with the comment, arguing instead that it was a shorthand way of saying there are now more women lawyers: 'In 1969 the profession was male dominated but today it now offers both men and women excellent career opportunities' (McMurdo quoted in Walsh and Papadakis 2015). Yet the phrase 'feminisation of the profession' carries some freight beyond that of merely denoting an increased presence of women in the legal profession. The use of this phrase raises questions about what is valued within the legal profession and how women's contributions might be received from a masculinist viewpoint. This point was made by Ms Painter, SC who said, '[w]hile the High Court now has three women out of seven, women judges in superior courts are in every instance in the minority, and in courts other than the Family Court of Australia, in a significant minority' and this state of affairs could hardly be seen as the 'feminisation of the legal profession' (Painter quoted in Walsh and Papadakis 2015).

Moreover, what was not acknowledged in the responses to Eades' remarks was that the idea of 'feminisation' is less positively charged than 'masculinisation'. Within the dynamics of the dominant gender regime hegemonic masculinity exercises considerable sway such that, intended or not, the subtext of Eades' point concerned the diminishing of what men had previously thought was valuable within the profession. Although there was no such reference to feminisation in the speeches commemorating Justice Crennan—herself one of the first 'three of seven'—these tensions about what the arrival of women meant for the profession were nonetheless reflected in the ways her legacy was received and constructed. Central to the creation of that legacy are the issues of collegiality and authority and the ways that each contribute to the judicial identity that a judge might wish to have remembered.

In the balance? (Institutional) collegiality and (individual) authority

Collegiality does not have a technical legal meaning but in the context of this book it is understood as the writing of joint, rather than separate, judgments.[11]

11 This understanding is derived from the specific debates around authorship and judicial independence (see e.g. Heydon 2013; Kiefel 2014; Gageler 2014) canvassed in Chapter 4.

It can therefore indicate consensus (agreement) on the Court. In this context, Edwards (2003: 1645), an American circuit court judge and law professor, defined collegiality as:

> a common interest, as members of the judiciary, in getting the law right, and that, as a result, we are willing to listen, persuade, and be persuaded, all in an atmosphere of civility and respect. Collegiality is a process that helps to create the conditions for principled agreement, by allowing all points of view to be debated and considered.

One manifestation of this 'common interest' in getting the law right is joint judgments. Speaking in defence of collegiality, Justice Kiefel (2014: 4) thought that the purported 'risk' presented by the practice of joint judgments was not a lack of independence borne from the pressure of colleagues to join in (as her former colleague Justice Heydon had suggested), but rather one that 'may arise … from a personal desire to stand out, to have one's own voice and develop one's own reputation'. It follows that the cases selected by the speakers at Crennan J's farewells point to how this tension might play out, as they were almost all cases where Crennan J wrote alone or where the speaker appeared to assume that her Honour exercised a leadership role.

While there were various cases highlighted by the speakers, *Harriton* is a good case example to address here for various reasons. *Harriton* received the most fulsome attention from the speakers. It was the only decision where the speakers elaborated about judicial qualities in any detail. Specifically, the speakers used the decision as a means of establishing Justice Crennan's humanity, cast as a judicial virtue. Given that *Harriton* was her first judgment (see Chapter 4), it is noteworthy that it has been so significant insofar as judicial legacy is concerned. The authorship practices around first judgments mean that her contribution is discernible but it is also a rare example of the first judgment ritual being intruded upon by the inclusion of additional and even dissenting reasons. However, most interesting here is the way in which this case was invoked as evidence of her humanity, given the problematic features of this decision in relation to acknowledging women's lived experiences. This case involved a wrongful life claim where a child was born with serious congenital defects as a consequence of being infected with rubella *in utero*. Crennan J had to decide whether the child's claim (by her tutor) that her life with profound disabilities represented legally cognisable damages. Crennan J held that it did not, reasoning that 'it is odious and repugnant to devalue the life of a disabled person by suggesting that such a person would have been better off not to have been born.'[12] The decision—which ultimately found against the child but emphasised in principle the notion that a life with disabilities was better than no

12 *Harriton v Stephens* (2006) 226 CLR 52, 129 (Crennan J).

life at all—was invoked as evidence of her Honour's humanity by the speakers at her farewell. Consequently, humanity was constructed as a judicial virtue.

As we can see, even the mere snippets of a judicial career that feature in a short farewell speech evince connections between judicial authority, authorship and legacy. And it is easy to celebrate an individual judge's jurisprudential contributions if her authorship is readily discernible. Yet a feature of Crennan's career on the High Court is that the judgments were, for the most part, collaboratively written. Collaborative or joint judgments have become increasingly popular on the High Court, although they have also generated criticism. As these criticisms were examined in Chapter 4, it is not necessary here to rehash in detail Dyson Heydon's (2013: 212) warning about 'judicial herd behavior' and the potential institutional harm caused by 'excessively dominant personalities'. Important to note, however, is the way in which Justice Crennan at her farewell linked a positive appraisal of collegiality to the challenges facing women as legal knowers. Her decision to defend collegiality openly at her farewell adds a dimension to understanding the framing of her judicial legacy.

As noted previously, the connections between the appointment of women judges and the 'difference' (however construed) they might make is difficult to establish in any direct manner. However, it is at least possible to assert that the near gender balance on the High Court bench coincided with increased levels of consensus in decision-making. This did not preclude dissenting judgments but certainly none of the women judges took up the mantle of the 'great dissenter.'[13] Of course, dissent and consensus gain meaning when situated within the institutional gender regime in which they occur (Belleau and Johnson 2008). Lynch and Williams' annual tabulations[14] of judicial authorship practices on the High Court confirm that Justice Crennan's consensus-driven approach to judgment writing was certainly a feature of her time of the Court.[15] Reflecting on 2014, Crennan J's last year on the Court, Lynch and Williams (2015: 1092) surmised that the French Court was 'on track to be remembered as achieving a surprising degree of unanimity among its members, running at a combined rate of about 75 per cent of all matters'. As for Justice Crennan's individual contribution in 2014, Lynch and Williams (2015: 1088) emphasised her preference for majority judgments,[16] one which she shared with Justices Kiefel and Bell:

13 Lynch and Williams (2014: 545) observed that a consistent feature of their surveys of the Court's decision-making (undertaken since 1998) was 'the presence of one member (having been first Kirby J and then Heydon J) with an especially high rate of minority opinions relative to his colleagues'.

14 Here I am merely canvassing observations gleaned from Lynch and Williams' (2009, 2010, 2011, 2012, 2013, 2014, 2015) detailed individual and institutional profiles of the High Court, but space does not permit full exploration.

15 See Chapter 4 for further examination of the high levels of unanimity on the High Court identified by Lynch and Williams in 2009, 2010 and 2013.

16 Lynch and Williams were referring explicitly to Justice Crennan's approach to Constitutional matters but her involvement in majority decisions was high across the board in any case.

> Justices Crennan, Kiefel and Bell did not deliver a minority opinion. Even allowing for the low number of constitutional matters in 2014 as providing fewer opportunities for constitutional disagreement, it can hardly be said that these three members of the Court regularly deliver even a single minority judgment in such cases in any given year. Justices Crennan and Bell have each dissented just twice in a constitutional matter since being appointed to the Court. In the case of Crennan J, who retired after 10 years' service in early March 2015, that is a notable record—especially since, in respect of one of the two occasions on which she was tallied in dissent, the constitutional issue was, as we said at the time, peripheral to the case.

Debates about institutional collegiality and individual judicial legacy are not unique to Australia. A rich body of scholarship now exists, much of it from the United States (see e.g. Sunstein et al. 2006; Hettinger, Lindquist and Martinek 2006), which explores the conditions that foster and discourage collaborative judgment writing. It is fair to suggest that in the interaction between the institution and the individual, 'appellate Court judges are behaviorally interdependent by definition' (Martinek 2010: 75). This is because the decisions arrived at are the result of collective choices of judges made within the traditions of a Court in question. Bader Ginsburg (1990: 134), for example, explained:

> [There are] three patterns of appellate judgments by collegial Courts: seriatim opinions by each member of the bench, which is the British tradition; a single anonymous judgment with no dissent made public, which is the civil law prototype; and the middle way familiar in the United States—generally an opinion for the Court, from which individual judges sometimes disassociate themselves in varying degrees.

For Bader Ginsburg (1990: 142) '[c]oncern for the well-being of the Court on which one serves, for the authority and respect its pronouncements command, may be the most powerful deterrent to writing separately'. The 'middle way' appears to be the direction in which the High Court has been heading for some years, a broadly based consensus approach with occasional dissenting voices.

Sir Anthony Mason (2013: 109), retired Chief Justice of the High Court, similarly emphasised the importance of collegial relationships, reasoning that 'every Justice has a responsibility to endeavor to establish a working relationship with colleagues'. Some of the individual pressures which counter adopting collegial approaches to judgment writing have been recognised by Justice Kiefel (2014: 7), drawing upon comments of Lord Neuberger, President of the Supreme Court of the United Kingdom. Lord Neuberger has said:

> The desire to write your own judgment, particularly in an interesting and important case, can be quite considerable. The wish is reinforced where, as often happens, you think you can write an even better judgment than the

> one your colleague has produced. Virtually every appellate judge has been guilty of what might be called a vanity judgment.

Justice Kiefel (2014: 7) noted that Lord Neuberger 'admitted to having been guilty of this' and also confessed 'most of us would have to make the same admission'.[17]

Thus, collegiality is valorised as acting for the greater good, or even as nurturing the institutional wellbeing of the Court. Viewed in such a way, collegiality might accord with Elliott's (2001: 47) hypothesis that 'women may be drawn to the work required to come to consensus, thus ensuring continued collegialiy' and hence women's 'response to their position on the bench and the need to forge relationships with their male colleagues'. Despite the fact that such a view risks a problematic construction of the nature of women, such a position might then be further undermined by the willingness of men of law to expound the virtues of collaborative judgment writing. What then do these debates about collegiality and its manifestation on the High Court of Australia tell us about the gender balance or how women are situated as legal knowers?

The point here is not to suggest that collegiality is the preserve of women. It might be the case that Justice Crennan had a hand in fostering collegiality on the court, but the role of individuals in fostering such a culture is much more complex.[18] Rather, the point I wish to make is in drawing out the consequences collegiate judgment writing practices might have for how women's legal authority is received. There are clear justifications for writing joint judgments (clarity in the law, precedential value) but as Lynch and Williams (2011) pointed out it is exceptionally difficult to critique the contributions of individual judges when we cannot be sure of the way in which their jurisprudential contributions come to be written into the collaborative practices with their fellow judges. This has consequences for the construction of judicial legacy. Being perceived as the ultimate 'team player' (Pelly 2015) necessarily meant Justice Crennan 'never got the respect afforded to Murray Gleeson and Bill Gummow as leaders on the Court' (Pelly 2015).

Perhaps this mattered not to Justice Crennan, preferring instead to preference the development of law rather than individual legacy. Nonetheless, Pelly's points about judicial recognition, albeit couched in journalistic terms, reveal

17 In light of the examination undertaken in the previous chapter, one wonders if the desire to avoid a 'vanity judgment' in *Monis* might have underscored the decision of the three women judges to write together so as to reinforce and strengthen the precedential value of their decision. A similar point was made by Appleby and Naffine (2015: 12).

18 See for example Pierce's examination of the variables affecting 'institutional cohesion' on the High Court, which concluded that the Chief Justice being perceived 'as an intellectual leader does more to promote cohesion than any other factor' (Pierce 2008: 333).

two possible ways in which judges might stand out in the history books; leadership and difference.

What was also a feature of Crennan J's approach was that she was rarely a dissenting voice. The preference for unanimity and only mild levels of dissent would suggest that this was not a Court in which marked signs of difference (gendered or otherwise) might easily manifest itself. This is not to say that dissent has been absent from the Court, or indeed that the women judges never dissented. Significantly, dissent may well take place in the context of joint judgments so consent and collegiality are not *necessarily* at odds. But, Justice Crennan did not just evidence a tendency to write with her judicial colleagues, as we have seen she was also more likely to be in concurrence with the majority decision.

In their analysis of dissent on Canadian Supreme Court Belleau and Johnson (2008: 60) noted that they had

> wondered how, if at all, the gender of the judge might be visible in either "voting practices" (how often a judge was with the majority on result and reasons) or practices of "authorship" (how often the judge was the author of an opinion, majority or otherwise).

In their study, women's contributions were especially visible in view of the higher than usual levels of dissent produced by the first three 'trailblazer' women to sit on the Canadian Supreme Court (Justices Wilson, McLaughlin and L'Heureux-Dube). Belleau and Johnson (2008: 68) emphasised the relational nature of dissent but nonetheless suggested that their results showed that dissent pointed 'in the direction of identity' which might 'serve as a disruption to our traditional ways of theorising judicial judgment'. These findings serve to reinforce a potential relationship between women's appointment and the disruptive and transformative potential of dissent—one which has not been replicated on the High Court of Australia. Being collegial (manifest in the authoring of the joint judgments) might then jar against two disparate sets of gendered expectations around women judges, with one conceiving of women judges as disruptive and transformative dissenters, and the other regarding women as more conciliatory consensus builders. At the same time, an abiding issue is that collegiate practices obscure the contributions of the individual judge. Although collegial approaches to authorship might be a consequence of the influence of women as consensus builders, and the resulting decisions might be imbued with an 'openness to viewpoints previously marginalised' (Rackley 2013: 177), women's voices are nonetheless difficult to discern. It is not just that it makes it hard to discern a judge's influence on the Court, but more problematically it might undermine a judge's authority when queries are raised about individual contributions. The obscuring of her individual contribution does not seem to have been much of a disincentive for Justice Crennan in how she approached her role on the Court, but it does seem to have become a subsequent concern in her comments about how the legacy and contributions of women judges had been received. It is to that concern and her Honour's explicit response to it we now turn.

Justice Crennan's defence of her judicial legacy

Women judges are obviously not a singular category. The differences each brings to their role, in terms of individual personal and professional trajectories, will also contribute to their judicial reasoning and decisions. Even so, the notion of the disruptive woman judge looms large in the popular imagination, as does the figure of Rousseau's 'disorderly woman' (Rousseau 1759: 109), not to mention how Hegel's admonishment about women leaders and the state (Hegel 1820: §166), figures prominently within the philosophical imagination on which much jurisprudential thought draws. Women judges have stood out and made their presence felt. Yet in so doing they have tended to reinforce these popular stereotypes of disruption. Is there something about not standing out, or seeking a legacy framed around collegiality, that points to a different form of disruption, either to pre-existing expectations or to altering the dynamics of the prevailing the gender regime, even if ever so slightly?

This was perhaps the implicit message to be teased out of Justice Crennan's farewell speeches. It was clear from her comments that she was valorising consensus, and also that she wanted this to be seen as part of the institutional legacy of the High Court. In that way she positioned herself through those farewell speeches as someone who contributed to a consensus based, collegially focused High Court. While she clearly eschewed naming herself as a feminist judge (or even as a woman judge save for one reference to her status as a woman early in her career trajectory), she nevertheless acted in ways that suggested she was someone very much aware of the legacy, if not the ongoing impact, of the hegemonic masculinity embedded within the Court's institutional history. In a speech given in April 2014, a Foley's List event, 'Celebration of Women in the Law', Crennan (2014a: 9–10) revealed a keen awareness of the gendered ways in which women's legal authority is received:

> A theme of resentment, which some might think marred public discourse about women and the law in the 1980s and 1990s, is well illustrated by a joke told in the Victorian Supreme Court by a Canadian visitor, Professor Kathleen Mahoney. To appreciate the punch line you need to take your mind back before the proclamation in 1989 of the second Czech Republic.
>
> A male lawyer goes to heaven. St Peter explains that to enter he will need to pass a spelling test. He agrees. 'Spell 'God' says St Peter. 'G-O-D'. 'Okay, enter'. A second male lawyer arrives at the Pearly Gates—same story. 'Spell Man', commands St Peter. 'M-A-N'. 'Okay, you're in'. Then a female lawyer arrives at the Pearly Gates. St Peter explains the spelling test to her. When she agrees to take it, St Peter says 'Spell Czechoslovakia'.

> Although the joke certainly raised a smile, I thought at the time it worked as many jokes do, by exaggerating something recognisable. You can imagine some surprise years later to find journalists assuming occasionally, and no doubt inadvertently, that the women justices of the High Court make neither a significant contribution to the Court, nor write any of the judgments published jointly. Like any fallacy in human affairs, the sooner these assumptions peter out, the better. They are all the more startling since it is now commonplace to see accomplished women with successful practices as solicitors and barristers, partners, consultants and advisors in a great range of law firms and in the corporate domain. Women have chaired Bar Councils and other professional bodies and many women, including Victoria's Chief Justice, are part of the administration of justice at all levels of the judicial hierarchy throughout Australia.

Several things are revealed in this anecdote. First, she had clearly been stung by Waterford's (2012) journalistic comments a couple of years earlier in which he asserted that not only might the women judges be seen as 'a particular disappointment,' an outside observer might well conclude that all they did was to add their signatures to the judgments of the two senior men judges. Hence she dismissed the view as 'a fallacy' and pointed to the fact that women were now present 'at all levels of the judicial hierarchy throughout Australia'. Second, she exhibited a conciliatory approach to Waterford's opinion by suggesting that it was an 'inadvertent' observation. What we see here is not so much an appeal to reason such that Waterford would now correct his ill-judged opinion, but rather offering another interpretation of it that pointed in a different, and preferred, direction. She adopted a different form of reasoning that perhaps reveals a little of how she approached the construction of her judicial tasks when serving on the Court. And third, there was some ambiguity as to who or what constituted the 'resentment' that she thought 'marred the public discourse about women and the law in the 1980s and 1990s.' There are number of possibilities: Professor Mahoney (the reported teller of the joke); feminist critics of the way women were treated by and within the legal fraternity; men within the legal profession disturbed by the growing numbers of women in their ranks and the increased competition for senior positions such as a place on the High Court. While any or all of these might have been part of Justice Crennan's thinking at the time, the message appears to be more one of putting paid to such ways of thinking. Her point seemed to be more concerned with the way forward. In the retelling of the joke she juxtaposed the confrontational denial of women's right to be part of the profession and its rewards with a mode of reasoning that embraced collegiality.

In so doing, Justice Crennan's remarks were on a par with those she subsequently made at her farewell speech when she quoted her colleague, Justice Kiefel, to the effect that 'collegiality is not compromise'. But Crennan J's remarks about women lawyers arguably represented a shift in her thinking, or at least a shift in her willingness to express it. Women's historical exclusion from public life and authority, the achievements of women, and her own experiences as a woman were all present in the speech. For example, Crennan J (2014a: 3) noted that John Stuart Mill's argument about the construction of the nature of women as 'an eminently artificial thing', was prescient as it came to be an idea 'of leading feminists in the last quarter of the 20th century,' and she cited Butler's (1990) *Gender Trouble* and Rubin's (1975) *The Traffic in Women: Notes on the Political Economy of Sex*. Crennan J (2014a: 3) evidenced a keen awareness of women's struggles to dislodge liberal constructions of public rationality and reason when she observed that 'much more was required for the liberation and advancement of women than liberal support in the 19th century world of ideas'. Hence, Crennan J (2014a: 3) further remarked on the absence of women from public life at the beginning of the twentieth century, acknowledging that when 'the High Court was formally and ceremoniously opened in the Victorian Supreme Court building on 6 October 1903':

> Women were not much in evidence in public life, at least not in any professional capacity, as shown in Tom Robert's famous painting of 1903 depicting the Opening of Parliament in 1901, and in Marcus Beilby's later painting of the High Court's first sitting.

Although Justice Crennan painted a 'bleak account of the position of women in the law' she preferred to leave this in more distant past, emphasising that such matters began to 'improve discernibly in the 1970s'. Justice Crennan (2014a: 5), perhaps suggesting that her experience had not been marked by discrimination, said '[p]ersonal reminiscence is not a genre I have favoured over the years for myself, but luck and happenstance can play a remarkable role in life and perhaps should be acknowledged, if only to encourage others'. In this respect, Justice Crennan (2014a: 9) acknowledged that when asked to speak to the issue of women and the law, she had 'echoed Joan Rosanove, and said that balancing the demands of motherhood and a busy practice was not for the fainthearted,' she had sometimes been chided by 'women barristers who regarded that point of view as somewhat unimaginative.' Here Justice Crennan (2014a: 9) suggested that efforts of feminist scholars 'deserve to be applauded' and pointed to law reform work in areas of 'rape and sexual assault, domestic violence and sexual harassment' in addition to their efforts 'campaigning for social as well as political equality for women'. Significantly Justice Crennan (2014a: 9) acknowledged the role of feminists in agitating for the appointment of women judges:

> Women barristers of my generation were exposed to what were then novel arguments, namely that confidence in the public administration of justice would be enhanced by the appointment of women judges, a proposition now established as both verity and reality.

Although her remarks did not go as far as to suggest that women judges effect a transformation of the law, she nonetheless emphasised the *importance of* women judges.

In this speech, Justice Crennan engaged in reflection, informed by historical references and her own experiences, about how women have been situated as legal knowers. This kind of experiential reflection was absent from her formal farewell. Perhaps this is unsurprising. It is one thing to reflect on being a woman judge at an event celebrating women and law during the final year of your judicial career, but another entirely to do so in the institutional setting where you, for almost the last time, are literally dressed as the judge. But this speech is significant for two reasons. First, the speech evinces a willingness to speak to her experiences as a woman judge. This is certainly a shift from the attempts to distance herself from such an identity or feminist concerns in the period before her appointment (e.g. cited in Akerman 2005). Perhaps her experiences on the Court revealed a sexism (namely around the questioning of her judicial contributions and authority) which she had not previously encountered. It might be that her time on the Court, particularly shared with other women judges, reinforced the importance of women's access to positions of legal authority. In any case, and this points to the second issue to arise from this speech, it casts her Honour's subsequent very public defence of collegiality in a whole other light.

Viewed in light of her speech at the Foley's List *Celebration of Women in the Law*, Justice Crennan's defence of collegiality at her judicial farewell takes on an obviously gendered dimension and therefore forms a significant part in the public extra-curial crafting of her own judicial legacy. At the formal farewell, surrounded by the accoutrements of legal authority, Justice Crennan retreated from situating herself as a woman judge in any explicit way. She gave no reasons for her defence of collegiality, nor did she refer to being a member of the High Court, which for the first time in the nation's history had a membership comprising an almost equal gender balance. Without being said, awareness of this historical first was nonetheless there not least conjured by the presence of the women themselves on the bench. The retirement of Justice Crennan and remarks made in recognition of it were obviously centred specifically around her own individual legacy. An individual legacy is also institutional, particularly when framed around her contribution to the High Court (its 'institutional wellbeing') and for that reason is clearly relevant for any analysis of the Court's gender regime. That the law was described as 'feminised' only a few months after her Honour's retirement points to the tensions which still existed—and continue to exist today—in situating women as legal knowers and in the expectations which ensue from their appointment. Indeed, the recent events involving allegations of sexual harassment perpetrated by former High Court Justice Heydon during his time on the bench reveal just how far from a feminised profession we find ourselves. It is to these events, and to Chief Justice Kiefel's potentially disruptive and transformative response, that we now turn.

Chapter 8

The High Court today

Negotiating progress, privilege and hegemonic masculinity

Much has happened in the five years since Susan Crennan's retirement and her comments about the gendered ways in which her jurisprudential contributions had been received. It is almost 20 years since Mary Gaudron's retirement—and her subsequent replacement with Dyson Heydon, an appointment that restored the court to its traditional all-male composition, albeit relatively briefly. It is more than 30 years since Gaudron's appointment and at least 40 years since women began to study law in greater numbers—prompting suggestions that women's access to legal authority would be a forgone conclusion as a critical mass entered the profession. Although we know that progress has been much more meandering than that, Susan Kiefel's elevation to Chief Justice of the High Court of Australia shattered an especially resilient glass ceiling.

Susan Kiefel's elevation to Chief Justice of the High Court of Australia in 2017 marked an important symbolic milestone for women's access to legal authority in Australia. No doubt there will be considerable scope to examine Kiefel's legacy as a jurist and her leadership on the High Court. But that is not my specific interest in this chapter. Rather, I want to think about how the presence of a woman Chief Justice might change or disrupt the dynamics of the gender regime in terms by interrogating key moments where gender was really front and centre. How does the presence of a woman Chief Justice impact on the gender relations of the High Court? What does this reveal about the court's contemporary gender regime more broadly? Of course, the question is not simply about *a* woman in some abstract sense, it is about a particular woman. This chapter then, is about how Kiefel has navigated the still novel state of being a woman and Chief Justice and what this in turn reveals about the High Court as an institution a little over a century after its formation.

Some insight into the gender dynamics which have shaped the court came when news broke in June 2020 that the High Court had commissioned an independent investigation following allegations that former Justice Dyson Heydon had sexually harassed six staff members (five of whom were judges' associates) during his time on the Court (2003–2013). Chief Justice Kiefel made a public statement apologising to the women, acknowledging how difficult it must have been to come forward. Writing on behalf of the Court she

DOI: 10.4324/9780429288531-9

emphasized that she was ashamed that this could happen in the High Court of Australia and, importantly, that they had been believed. It must be stressed that through his lawyers Heydon denied any wrongdoing although he 'apologized for any offence that was caused' (cited in Maley and McClymont 2020). These revelations were explosive—although they recounted experiences that are all too common given how pervasive sexual harassment is in the legal profession and beyond (see for e.g. International Bar Association Report 2019[1]; Respect@Work: Sexual Harassment National Inquiry Report 2020)[2] the high-profile individual and institutional dimension heightened interest in the story and the allegations. Would a man Chief Justice have responded in the same way? Although there is no way to answer this question definitively, the fact that the complaints were raised under the leadership of a woman and Kiefel's gender certainly featured in the commentary at the time. For example, the Sex Discrimination Commissioner, Kate Jenkins (cited in Kelly 2020a) suggested that a woman Chief Justice and the gender balance on the High Court 'probably makes the most difference'. What then does it tell us about the High Court as an institution and the extent to which women's entry into the legal profession has made actual inroads into the culture and values of the dominant regime?

The High Court, of course, exists within the context of the wider society in which it is situated. To say this much is not only to express a jurisprudential view about the extent to which judging is shaped by context (although this is clearly my view), but it is also an observation about how institutions and the wider politics shape and are shaped by prevailing gender politics. Kiefel's tenure as Chief Justice has coincided with complex and evolving gender politics nationally and internationally. On the one hand women's capacity to exercise

1 *The International Bar Association's Us Too: Bullying and Sexual Harassment in the Legal Profession Report* was published in 2019. It was the largest ever global survey on bullying and harassment in the legal profession with nearly 7,000 respondents from 135 countries. The report found that sexual harassment was endemic across the globe. One in three female respondents had been sexually harassed in a workplace context, as had one in 14 male respondents. The report (2019: 23–24) further found that sexual harassment was particularly prevalent in Australia (even accounting for potential bias in reporting in a country where there was perhaps more widespread knowledge about what constitutes sexual harassment).

2 The Sex Discrimination Commissioner's forward to *Respect@Work* Report (2020: 10) noted the prevalence of sexual harassment generally, citing the 2018 National Survey which had found that "almost two in five women (39%) and just over one in four men (26%) have experienced sexual harassment in the workplace in the past five years. Aboriginal and Torres Strait Islander people were more likely to have experienced workplace sexual harassment than people who are non-Indigenous (53% and 32% respectively)." The *Respect@Work* Report made 55 recommendations for improving existing mechanisms to combat sexual harassment. It was provided to the Attorney-General, Christian Porter and tabled in Parliament on 5 March 2020 but at the time of writing only three recommendations from that report have been actioned.

legal and political power has been well demonstrated in terms of diminishing barriers to women's access to the very peak of political and legal institutions, both in Australia and elsewhere in the world. At the time of Kiefel's ascension Sian Elias was Chief Justice of New Zealand, Beverly McLachlin served as Chief Justice on the Canadian Supreme Court, and Georgina Wood served as Chief Justice of Ghana (each having been in those roles for some time).[3] In the United Kingdom, Brenda Hale's elevation to President of the UK Supreme Court would take place the same year as Kiefel's swearing-in as Chief Justice. These events situated Kiefel within a particular (albeit, discrete) international gender order too as she became part of an elite group of women judges.

Yet, for all of these markers of women's progress within the legal profession and beyond, one did not need to look too far to find reminders about the entrenched masculinist or patriarchal gender order the world over. Following the experiences of Australia's first woman Prime Minister, Julia Gillard, which demonstrated the gendered ways in which women's power and authority were received, Australia had returned to men Prime Ministers. There were concerns about Parliament not being a welcome place of work for women and the Liberal Party's dogged commitment to a masculinist meritocracy in the wake of its 2018 leadership spill had led to furore about its so called 'woman problem.'[4] On the international stage Donald Trump's election as United States President in late 2016 generated concerns about losing hard won gains in the pursuit of gender equality and inspired women's protest marches all over the world. Trump's (*New York Times* 2016) sense of entitlement to women's bodies was perhaps encapsulated by his claim (made in 2005) that as a star you can 'grab 'em by the pussy'. You can do anything'. Of course, as Cynthia Enloe (2018) put it 'the patriarchy is bigger than Donald Trump' but nonetheless his election in many ways came to be emblematic of the wider political context and the seemingly entrenched masculinist gender order. During this period, concerns about violence against women and children and the paucity of law's response to it, women's access to power (economic, social, political and legal) amplified rather than receded. One particular expression of this concern was the

3 This list is not intended to be exhaustive. These women judges are noted because of their joint role in the 2018 "First Women of the Supreme Courts in Conversation" discussed in this chapter.

4 As Wallace (2018) observed in the aftermath of the Liberal Party's 2018 leadership spill, the Liberal Party doesn't so much have a woman problem, but rather a man problem. She argued 'The Liberal Party room is dominated—and increasingly so over the past generation—by male MPs who anoint leaders in their own image.' The context here was the Party's decision to overlook then Foreign Minister Julie Bishop in favour of Scott Morrison in the leadership ballot, despite the widely held view that Bishop was more qualified and would be 'most likely to maximise the Liberal vote at the next election.' Beyond partisan politics there is a concern that parliament itself is not a welcome place of work for women generally, but these critiques certainly reflect the Liberal party's particularly dogged commitment to a masculinist meritocracy (see Chapter 2).

#MeToo movement—a concept developed by Tarana Burke but popularised in October 2017 by celebrity Alyssa Milano. The movement and its celebrity connections seem a long way from the High Court of Australia but by June 2020 it seemed that #MeToo had arrived at the very peak of the Australian legal profession. Kiefel's response[5] to the allegations about former High Court Justice Dyson Heydon's conduct attracted support and the allegations themselves reignited concerns about judicial appointment processes and the lack of accountability mechanisms for judges more broadly.

The chapter begins with an examination of Kiefel's elevation to Chief Justice and how gender was framed by those making this historic appointment and by the new Chief Justice herself. I consider Kiefel's increasing willingness to reflect on matters of gender and judging and women's place in the legal profession since her elevation to Chief Justice. The point to be made here is that although the appointment of Australia's first woman Chief Justice was heralded as an inspirational moment for women in law, gendered discourses of merit and 'the exceptional woman syndrome' meant that the appointment was framed in such a way as to not disrupt the prevailing gender order. That is, her appointment seemed to reinforce the notion that women's access to legal authority remains contingent and conditional. The same might be said of Kiefel's subsequent commentary about women in the profession. While acknowledging women's historic exclusion from the legal profession, she nonetheless remained faithful to the notion that the individual will be able to triumph and flourish through dint of hard work and determination—largely seeking to diminish or under-emphasise gender. Yet, her handling of the sexual harassment allegations against her former colleague Dyson Heydon, and the wider implications of these allegations, created the impression that something had shifted in terms of the Court's gender dynamics. Was it that a woman Chief Justice had 'made all the difference', as the Sex Discrimination Commissioner had argued? The third and final part of this chapter considers the implications of the High Court's #MeToo moment of reckoning not simply in terms of the ways in which it will inevitably shape the legacy of the individuals concerned, but more broadly in seeking to understand the institutional implications for the court's gender regime.

Elevation to Chief Justice: an exceptional woman

Kiefel's elevation to Chief Justice was certainly not unexpected.[6] In the lead up to Chief Justice French's retirement speculation was rife that Kiefel would be

5 I note that nothing about Kiefel's response specifically linked the allegations about Heydon to the #MeToo movement.

6 I examined the gendered implications of Chief Justice Kiefel's elevation in McLoughlin, K. 2017. Feminism, Women Judges, Judicial Diversity and the High Court of Australia. *feminists@law,* 7(2): 1–14. Some of the ideas and arguments presented in that article are reproduced in my discussion of the gendered politics of her appointment in this chapter.

appointed from within the court (see e.g. Walsh 2016; Whitbourn and McIlroy 2016). There are no special provisions regarding the appointment of the Chief Justice, but elevation from within the court has not been uncommon—of the thirteen Chief Justices (including Kiefel) appointed in the Court's history, roughly half have been elevated from within the Court, and half 'parachuted'. That being said, that Kiefel was named as the favourite says something about women's access to legal authority insofar as it meant that the idea of a woman sitting at the peak of Australia's judiciary was no longer as inconceivable as it might once have been.

Kiefel's elevation was framed in celebratory terms. It was presented as a sign that (individual) women can achieve anything. The then Prime Minister, Malcolm Turnbull (2016), emphasised the inspirational nature of Kiefel's story—pointing out that she had left school at 15 and gone from legal secretary to the High Court of Australia. He listed her catalogue of 'firsts' and described the achievement as one that 'crowns a great career with even greater judicial service yet to come.' Following a now familiar pattern in announcing the appointment of a woman judge, Attorney-General George Brandis (2016) was insistent every step Kiefel had taken in her career was 'a step that she took on merit.' Underscoring Kiefel's suitability for the role, Brandis (2016) emphasised that she had emerged as favourite in the process of consultation, noting that he had consulted with state Attorneys-General (as required by law) and the legal profession more broadly.

It is perhaps useful to note by way of comparison, that Brandis made no such appeal to merit in announcing Federal Court judge James Edelman's appointment to the High Court at the same time. Granted, there were comments about the precocious nature of his achievements in recognition of his age (he was 43 at the time he was sworn-in), making him one of the youngest judges in the Court's history but, it seemed that from the Attorney's perspective, there was no need to provide any reassurance about those steps being taken on merit.

The Prime Minister did not invoke the language of merit in the prepared portion of his remarks but when asked by a journalist about not appointing a South Australian (no person from that state has ever been appointed to the High Court of Australia) he asserted that 'judicial appointments are made entirely on merit' (Turnbull 2016). He also emphasised that there was a wealth of talent (e.g. people who would be eminently suitable to sit on the High Court) and limited opportunities to appoint. Although Turnbull's deployment of merit in this context was not gendered in the sense of singling out an appointee on the basis of their gender (indeed, in a broad sense, it is probably more likely the journalist was querying the decision to appoint Edelman, a Western Australian), it underscored some of the ongoing tensions in the politics of judicial appointment (whereby those making the decisions stress that decisions are made exclusively on merit as though this phrasing gives any insight into the decision-making process).

Beyond the explicit merit discourse there was an unspoken and gendered dimension to the narrative presented about Kiefel's trajectory 'from legal secretary to Chief Justice.' By framing her story in such a way, those appointing her underscored the inspirational (and aspirational) nature of her story. Unsurprisingly this particular dimension was prominent in the reporting of Kiefel's ascension (see for e.g. Coade 2016). The focus on her 'school dropout' status (she continued studying part-time) and her administrative career prior to legal admission mark her as an outsider (in terms of both gender and class) and without saying as much, spoke to the gendered division of labour not just within the legal profession, but in society more broadly. Although the gendered nature of administrative work is now arguably less pronounced than it was in the 1970s, it is no accident that we would struggle to find examples of men judges' elevation from the typist pool to the powerful echelons of the profession (McLoughlin 2017). In this way class punctuated the story but in a more muted way. Referencing Kiefel's aspirational ascent through the legal hierarchy the Prime Minister underscored the exceptionality of her achievement by acknowledging that she did so despite not having the benefit of the cultural capital of class ties and familial connections. He concluded his announcement by quoting the words of journalist Alan Reid who had expressed the sentiment that 'I'm always very polite to cadet reporters in the lift. Over the years I have found a lot of them end up being my Editors' (Turnbull 2016). Turnbull linked these sentiments to Kiefel's elevation, saying 'perhaps there are a lot of lawyers that will remember the paralegal and secretaries that they are working with perhaps may follow now in Susan Kiefel's footsteps and get admitted and become the Chief Justice of Australia.'

We saw a particular framing from those responsible for her Honour's elevation where they were able to lay claim to appointing the first women Chief Justice (and indeed the appointment of more women justices to the High Court than Labor) and their purported commitment to gender equality without making any explicit commitment to it or explicitly acknowledging the importance of judicial diversity. Thus, we saw in her ascension the repetition of a familiar political discourse whereby women's access to legal authority was conditional and contingent. That she had never embraced an identity as a woman judge or explicitly aligned herself with feminist causes or concerns (Roberts 2012b) meant that her elevation could be framed as an important milestone for Australian women but in a way that did not fundamentally disrupt the notion of the default Chief Justice (who, of course, up until this point had been a man). After almost a decade on the High Court, she was the second-most-senior judge after the then Chief Justice Robert French. It is certainly arguable that her appointment was politically astute irrespective of whether her eschewal of a feminist identity[7] had enhanced her suitability or the perception of such.

7 See my comments in the Introduction where I note that the fact that her Honour allegedly did not like 'lipstick feminists' featured in the discourse around her appointment. As I have argued elsewhere (see McLoughlin 2017) irrespective of the

Kiefel's swearing-in was, as far as these things go in a nation not renowned for making celebrities out of its judges, of considerable national interest. The ceremony, broadcast on ABC24 (the national public broadcaster), provided a glimpse into the traditions of an institution where television cameras have been a rarity. For Kiefel, it was not the first of such ceremonies —earlier appointments to the Queensland Supreme Court, the Federal Court, and indeed, the High Court meant that she had some depth of experience engaging with this particular ritual. But no doubt, this ceremony was of particular significance insofar as it represents the absolute pinnacle of legal authority and a significant personal achievement. The imagery was powerful —Kiefel sitting at the centre of the bench with Bell to the left of her. As one of the speakers commemorating Kiefel's swearing-in, Fiona McLeod, the then President of the Law Council of Australia, remarked, the fact that Justice Bell had administered Kiefel's judicial oath was 'a powerful and enduring image of equality and an inspiration to many.'[8] The focus was on one woman but she was not the sole woman in Court that day. In this ceremony women were represented in various roles—as judges (both sitting and retired), as associates and indeed as speakers in the ceremony itself. For the casual observer it might seem, visually at least, as though this was a place where women belonged, perhaps where they had always been. Yet the visibility of women at this ceremony (albeit still in disproportionate numbers to men) belies the reality of their exclusion. In the words spoken we get more insight into the story of women's exclusion from legal authority. Thus, perhaps unsurprisingly, although the extent of the resistance to women's inclusion is somewhat obscured by the speakers, we nonetheless see the masculinist foundations of this institution.

As we might expect, Kiefel's status as the *first* woman Chief Justice featured prominently in the speeches made in her honour at her swearing-in ceremony. Fiona McLeod described the occasion as 'a landmark moment for women in the history of this nation.'[9] Christopher Hughes, President of the Bar Association of Queensland, celebrated Kiefel's many firsts as 'the first woman to be made Queen's Counsel in Queensland, the first woman barrister to become a Supreme Court judge and the first woman from Queensland to sit on this Court'.[10] In the longest of the speeches, Attorney General Brandis emphasised

truth of such accounts (see Patrick 2017), they are significant insofar as they reveal an attempt to distinguish her Honour from feminists (or 'lipstick feminists') and by extension served as reassurance about her suitability for the role.

8 All speeches from Kiefel CJ's swearing-in are drawn from the following transcript http://www6.austlii.edu.au/cgi-bin/viewdoc/au/cases/cth/HCATrans/2017/7.html. As with previous chapters, reference to the transcript is set out in footnote to distinguish between speakers. See Transcript Ceremonial Sitting on the Occasion of the *Swearing-in of the Chief Justice the Honourable Susan Mary Kiefel [2017] HCATrans 7 AC* (McLeod).

9 *Swearing-in Ceremony, Kiefel CJ* (McLeod).

10 *Swearing-in Ceremony, Kiefel CJ* (Hughes).

the significance of the occasion in the history of the High Court as 'truly a great Australian story—a story to inspire women and men alike':

> In the more than 113 years that have passed since Sir Samuel Griffith was sworn in as the first Chief Justice of this Court on 6 October 1903, only 12 people have occupied that highest of judicial offices. Your Honour will be the 13th Chief Justice of this Court, the fourth from Queensland and the first woman.[11]

Brandis again revisited a familiar trope about merit that he had invoked in announcing her appointment a few months earlier, although he did not explicitly use those words at the swearing-in ceremony:

> It has been a feature of your Honour's story—as it is of today's ceremony—that you have, at several crucial steps in your career, been the first woman to occupy a particular office. But your professional advancement and success has had nothing to do with your gender and everything to do with your intelligence, diligence and skill.[12]

A similar sentiment was expressed by Hughes QC, (who as President of the Queensland Bar Association had a particular interest in the fact that Kiefel was a Queenslander) and emphasised that the appointment was based on her Honour's attributes and not her state of origin.[13] Indeed, although this point expressed a similar sentiment—the notion that her appointment was not about state of origin—in the politics of judicial appointment the notion that an appointee's state had some bearing on the decision-making process has never been as politically charged as the notion that gender might have been taken into account.

Another aspect of Kiefel's outsider status, that of class, was also touched upon by the Attorney who described her decision to go to the Bar at the age of 21 as an act of bravery 'with no family or other connections in the law but, of course, in those days, there were hardly any women in practice at the Bar in Brisbane.'[14] Linking the personal to the professional—indeed underscoring the extent to which Kiefel had managed to slough off her 'outsider status'—Brandis referenced his own ongoing professional relationship with the new Chief Justice, reminiscing about appearing as her junior. He cited as an example *Dowling v Dalgety* (1991), a case about the Goondiwindi saleyards, giving some indication of his own awareness of the challenges for women operating in masculine domains:

11 *Swearing-in Ceremony, Kiefel CJ* (Brandis).
12 *Swearing-in Ceremony, Kiefel CJ* (Brandis).
13 *Swearing-in Ceremony, Kiefel CJ* (Hughes).
14 *Swearing-in Ceremony, Kiefel CJ* (Brandis).

> Those were different times, and I recall that our rather blokey clients, representatives of the three great pastoral houses—Dalgety's, Elders and Primac—were a little hesitant about retaining a woman silk, but yielded to my assurance that you were one of the best in the business. Needless to say, by the end of the case, you had them eating out of your hand.[15]

This anecdote gives some insight into how women have been received as legal knowers and the ways in which their authority and competence has been met with suspicion. The underlying assumption here is that to be a woman afforded legal authority apparently raises questions about their suitability for the role. On the surface Brandis, while also trying to signal his own virtue vis-à-vis women's equality in the legal profession, appears sympathetic to the challenges women have faced in being accepted on equal terms within that profession. However, at a deeper level we can detect the contours of masculinism as normal. What does it mean when a junior colleague feels quite comfortable offering reassurances to a client that the more senior (and experienced) colleague, a woman, is up to the task?

This admission from the Attorney, juxtaposed with his insistence that Kiefel's elevation had 'nothing to do with gender' presents something of a conundrum. 'Nothing to do with gender' is meant as a compliment or reassurance that Kiefel was not the beneficiary of any particular affirmative action—that despite her gender she has succeeded. We see an attempt at reinforcing gender neutrality—the idea that gender does not matter—that it is not taken into account and women certainly have not been (and should not be) given a leg up. But the fiction of this neutrality is of course undermined by Kiefel's trailblazer status as a woman succeeding in her chosen profession, a success recounted by Brandis himself, albeit noting the 'blokey culture' she had to contend with. Although Brandis sought to emphasise the historic significance of Kiefel's elevation as the first woman Chief Justice he did so in such a way as to stress that being a woman was no advantage. Brandis aimed to reassure that the prevailing gender order did not have to be manipulated in her favour. Her appointment was not about shoring up some gender quota. In this context, Brandis' insistence that Kiefel's success has nothing to do with her gender reads as benevolent sexism, but also on a wider level it speaks to grappling with the complex re-negotiations at play when women begin to occupy spaces previously dominated by men. The very fact of her gender-neutral, meritorious elevation was emphasised to reinforce the unspoken reality; namely, that her elevation was not a threat to the prevailing gender order. After all, her elevation to the High Court ten years earlier was evidence that she had the personal qualities for such august legal authority. She was a safe pair of hands with whom the leadership of the

15 *Swearing-in Ceremony, Kiefel CJ* (Brandis). Although the transcript records the Attorney as citing the decision as being handed down in 1991, the citation for this decision is *Dowling v Dalgety* [1992] FCA 35

High Court could be entrusted. The conundrum of Brandis' comments reveals itself as another way of underscoring the fact that the exception proves the rule.

It is important here to emphasise that these references to Kiefel's historic elevation and status as first woman were certainly not the only focus of the speeches made that day. Her expertise in comparative law (and the important intellectual influence her time at Cambridge had on this front) and her collegiality were referenced as positive attributes by all of the speakers. For example, Brandis emphasised her collegiality—certainly not as evidence of not doing her part, but rather as an important and praiseworthy sign of leadership or influence that she was already exhibiting on the Court:

> Indeed, I am sure that it was at least partly due to your influence that the French Court was notable for its collegiality. No doubt you will continue to foster that ethic of collegiality as the leader of the Court.[16]

Similarly, her legal skills and expertise both at the Bar and at the bench were roundly praised by all of the speakers. Her skills in cross-examination were singled out by both McLeod who noted that she was 'sought after for [her] devastating cross-examination, never cross, but intimidating nonetheless'[17] and O'Sullivan who said she was 'known as an excellent cross-examiner and for [her] preparation and planning.'[18] Her intellect and leadership were acknowledged with McLeod describing her as 'an intellectual leader of this Court and one of its most popular and collegiate members' and Hughes recalled her 'acuity of mind', 'identification of the real issues' and 'fearlessness of accounts as a counsel.'[19]

For her own part, the new Chief Justice acknowledged the significance of the occasion as a milestone for women 'on two counts'—referencing of course her own history making elevation and that she was 'pleased to have been sworn in as Chief Justice by [her] dear colleague, Justice Virginia Bell.' Giving context to the historical significance, Kiefel gave some background to women's place in Australia's constitutional history:

> In the year preceding the opening of this Court, Australian women were given the right to vote at federal elections. It was then that they truly became part of "the people" to whom our Constitution refers. That year also saw the first woman graduate in law from an Australian university.[20]

Continuing this theme, she also referenced women's (historic) exclusion from the legal profession, acknowledging that 'it would not be until 1987 that a

16 *Swearing-in Ceremony, Kiefel CJ* (Brandis).
17 *Swearing-in Ceremony, Kiefel CJ* (McLeod).
18 *Swearing-in Ceremony, Kiefel CJ* (O'Sullivan).
19 *Swearing-in Ceremony, Kiefel CJ* (Hughes).
20 *Swearing-in Ceremony, Kiefel CJ* (Kiefel).

woman, the Honourable Mary Gaudron, was appointed to this Court.'[21] She acknowledged that her own entry to the profession (she came to Bar in 1975) occurred at a time when there 'were very few women members of the profession', but did not comment any further on the legal culture she encountered or the context of the dominance of men in the profession:

> This is not the occasion to consider why this was so. The point presently to be made is that this has changed and so has the composition of this Court.[22]

The reference to women's exclusion is fairly muted, both in its insistence that now is not the time to talk about it, and in what is left unsaid, particularly about the depth of resistance to women becoming part of 'the people' to whom our constitution refers. Of course, suffrage is especially significant in how we understand citizenship, but this was partial (see Chapter 1). 'People' has been an exclusionary concept in Australia's constitutional framework (not only on the basis of sex but race too) and inclusion within that category has been hard won (see Chapter 1).

Although Kiefel acknowledged recent improvements in the gender composition of the Court, this was framed more around women *now* possessing the necessary attributes to qualify them for appointment rather than about the ways in which the institution had excluded them:

> In more recent times the appointment of more women to this Court recognises that *there are now* women who have the necessary legal ability and experience, as well as the personal qualities, to be a Justice of this Court. There seems no reason to think that that situation will not be maintained in the future. It may well improve.[23]

Kiefel's reference to 'personal qualities' is significant here in terms of how we understand the (gendered) conditions which are attached to access to legal authority. What might Kiefel have meant by this reference to personal qualities? Is it a specifically oblique reference to gender? Do 'personal qualities' mean made of the right stuff, being a chap, or at the very least not disrupting the masculine status quo?

Nonetheless, the message here is measured optimism about her hopes for women's future in the legal profession. This is a marked departure from her 2007 swearing-in speech where she had avoided any reflection on women's place within the profession whatsoever (see Chapter 3). Perhaps being the first woman Chief Justice shifted something—either in terms of her own sense that

21 *Swearing-in Ceremony, Kiefel CJ* (Kiefel).
22 *Swearing-in Ceremony, Kiefel CJ* (Kiefel) (my emphasis).
23 *Swearing-in Ceremony, Kiefel CJ* (Kiefel).

the occasion merited some reference to her place in history (although she seemed to consciously avoid emphasising her own role in the story), or perhaps, even, that some of the need to be the sexless judge had gone. Reflecting on the extent to which Kiefel engaged these issues at her swearing-in as Chief Justice, Roberts (2017: unpaginated) acknowledged the reality that had 'Kiefel devoted significant attention in her speech to her identity as a woman lawyer, or the history of women in the law in Australia, press coverage of the event would inevitability have (over)emphasised that theme', but nonetheless countered that given the precarious nature of these gains, it was not a time for complacency.

Certainly, Kiefel's remarks about personal qualities and women's place in the legal profession (and her own place within that history) take on a particular significance when understood in the context of her prior remarks (or indeed relative silence) on this matter. While she had avoided references to gender in her High Court swearing-in remarks in 2007, she has been more willing to reflect on these matters at an earlier swearing-in ceremony on her appointment to the Supreme Court of Queensland. On that occasion she reflected on her own puzzlement and sadness about women not coming the Bar:

> I have for the most part enjoyed my time at the Bar. It has both puzzled and saddened me to observe that the rate of women law graduates coming to the Bar has not grown. I could not pretend to them that their day-to-day practice is likely to be as readily facilitated as some, but I hasten to add not all, men. Society has yet to deal with the more deeply entrenched and subtle institutionalized discrimination, but women will find that the Bar and the judiciary will treat them simply as a professional person and on merit. I encourage them to consider the benefits of the career which offers extraordinary variety and richness of experience.
>
> (Kiefel cited in Roberts 2012b: 126)

These earlier comments acknowledged the existence of sex discrimination, but it was framed in such a way that assumed that the legal profession was above or immune from it. The Bar and the judiciary will treat a woman as a professional person and on merit; gender is no longer relevant—that the legal profession will look beyond gender; that barristers and judges are not men and women but rather professional persons. Of course, the lynchpin here was Kiefel's concern that women were not coming to Bar (widely understood as also representing the traditional path to judicial appointment). She invoked the language of merit to reassure that women will be treated on their merits—as professional persons first and foremost. As we know, women's inclusion in the category of 'persons' has had a contentious past.

Looking back on Kiefel's public remarks, a few matters bear emphasising. Her emphasis on merit is significant. She seems concerned that there will be a perception that as a woman she has been appointed otherwise than on merit.

This insistence suggests that she would not have bristled at Brandis' remarks (and those reflecting a similar sentiment) about merit as she appeared to share the values implicit in Brandis' world view that there are now women who possess the personal qualities to work at the highest judicial levels.

Kiefel's elevation to Chief Justice was crafted by those who appointed her in such a way that celebrated her success as a milestone for women in the law, while leaving undisturbed the notion of the default judge. This is evidence of what Thornton (1996: 203) termed the 'exceptional women syndrome'. This syndrome allows women judges (and women in other positions of power or authority) 'to be distinguished from other women, so that the masculinist character of the office is not diminished' (Thornton 1996: 203). Granted, much was made of the exceptional woman aspect of Kiefel's story, of the woman who had succeeded beyond all obstacles, while simultaneously diminishing the significance of those obstacles and presenting the exceptional woman 'as *exactly the same* as their male counterparts: a lawyer first *and* second, neither man nor woman' (Rackley 2013: 137, original emphasis). The existence of such a syndrome is supported by former Australian High Court Justice Mary Gaudron's (1997: 123) view that many trailblazing women in the law became 'honorary men' and as such they 'neither questioned the way in which legal practice was organised nor articulated the possibility of the law's bias'. We see in Kiefel's elevation the deployment of 'the guise of the default judge' by those who appointed her and by Kiefel herself. Given what we know about the masculinist nature of legal institutions, this emphasis is not surprising since the desire is to fit in, to be worthy of the honour of appointment, to be 'one of seven', or indeed 'chief of seven'.

Yet Kiefel's comments at her own swearing-in are noteworthy in that they signal a willingness or perhaps at best an acknowledgement that her role would put the spotlight on her as a woman judge (a Chief Justice no less) and she would need to respond in some way to her new status. Certainly, Kiefel has been a little more willing to speak to women's place within the legal profession since becoming Chief Justice. She has been drawn on these matters since her swearing-in through speeches and her entry into an international 'club' (of sorts) of women judges. We now turn to her public comments about women in the legal profession in the time since her elevation.

A public voice: reflections on women in the legal profession

The Chief Justice is not so much the public face of the legal profession but the public voice. The role itself is fluid, shaped by the individual themselves and the prevailing institutional conventions. As former High Court Chief Justice Anthony Mason explained, the role is not fixed but rather 'varies with time, circumstance and personality' (Mason 2001: 91). As Mason (2001: 91) explained, the Chief Justice offers intellectual leadership, shapes the direction of the court, and, increasingly, communicates with the legal profession, and indeed the wider society, 'to explain the function of the courts and express views on matters of interest to the judiciary, the legal profession and the public' through speeches, papers or even giving interviews, which have become more important in recent years. The Chief Justice also represents the Court by making official visits to foreign courts and jurisdictions.

In keeping with accepted conventions about the role, Chief Justice Kiefel has made a number of extra-curial speeches both in Australia and abroad since her elevation, of which only one considered women's place in the legal profession in any detail. She also gave a welcome speech at the International Association of Women Judges Conference (held in Sydney in April 2017), but the subject matter was "The Community of Courts in the Asia Pacific Region" rather than women's relationship with the law as judges. Between 2009–2016 (before her elevation to Chief Justice) twenty-four speeches are credited to her Honour, none of which was about women and the law.[24] Nonetheless, in 2018, Kiefel made public remarks at two separate events that provide some insights into her conceptualisation of gender and the judicial role. This was something of a significant year for women in law in Australia as it marked the centenary of women's admission to practice in New South Wales. The centenary of women's admission in the United Kingdom was approaching, and events celebrating that milestone were also in the works. The first of Kiefel's remarks was a speech titled "*Women in the Australian Legal Profession: progress and a public voice*" delivered in Malaysia and coinciding with International Women's Day. The second was her participation at a panel event billed as "First Women of the Supreme Courts in Conversation" jointly hosted by Grays Inn London and the First 100 Years Project. Kiefel's comments at these events are suggestive of an increased willingness to reflect on women's place in the legal profession but framed in such a way that seemed to underscore a commitment to the prevailing gender order.

Kiefel's nod to women's historic exclusion from the legal profession at her swearing-in was fleshed out in more detail at the International Women's Day speech made in Malaysia at the High Commission. Opening with a more historical story of exclusion, Kiefel (2018: 1) drew on Professor Mary Beard's 2017 book *Women & Power* and its use of Homer's *The Odyssey* to frame her own discussion about women's voices in the public sphere. On Beard's account, Queen Penelope is at home waiting for the return of King Odysseus from his ten-year absence. Tired of the subject matter of the songs being performed in her court, she asks the bard to play something with a happier theme. But her son, Telemachus, is having none of it. He directs his Mother back to her quarters with the admonition for his mother to tend to her own work, women's work as 'speech will be the business of men, all men, and of me most of all'. For Beard this was a demonstration that women's voices were not just excluded from the public sphere, they were excluded from 'authoritative public speech, not the kind of chatting, prattling or gossip that anyone—women

24 For a list of Her Honour's selected speeches see: https://www.hcourt.gov.au/publications/speeches/current/speeches-by-justice-kiefel.

included, or especially women—could do' (Beard 2017: 11). Reflecting on Penelope's fate, Kiefel (2018: 2) acknowledged women's exclusion from the status as pubic knowers—not as something confined to antiquity—noting that 'with some exceptions, such as queens and saints, it would be a very long time before women would be accepted as having a public voice at all.'

In the legal profession, as we know, women were explicitly denied a public voice through their exclusion from the profession itself as well as through the various means by which the law has obscured women's perspectives. Kiefel (2018: 3) acknowledged that the first statute 'which expressly enabled women in Australia to practise law was passed in 1903'. She reflects on this in the following way:

> I say "expressly" because arguably the state legal practitioners Acts which preceded it already allowed that to occur. Those statutes provided that any "person" with the appropriate qualifications could practise and a "person" was defined by interpretation statutes to include women. The courts did not see the matter in this way and so legislation was necessary. … It would not be until the 1970s that more than a few individual women would practise at the Bars in Australia. There are a number of reasons why it took so long. Included amongst them are stereotypes about professional persons and perceptions of the role of women. This, sadly, has not entirely abated.

Kiefel (2018: 2) by her own admission has 'been more fortunate than Penelope'. Her good fortune is not only that she speaks for a living, but that her words carry authority. She explained:

> The advantage of speaking as a barrister or as a judge is that you have a captive audience. People have to listen to what you say and they have to take it seriously, or at least give the appearance of doing so.
>
> (2018: 2)

Although Kiefel emphasised that the nature of her position means people have to take her words seriously, she pointed out the ways in which women's contributions might be ignored or diminished. Interestingly, rather than drawing on her experience on the High Court (or other courts where she has sat), she turned to the political sphere to draw on remarks made by the then Australian Foreign Minister Julie Bishop (the first woman to occupy this role in Australia), about how her voice was heard.

> She explained that when she was the only woman in Cabinet she would often make a contribution to the debate, but it went un-remarked by her male colleagues. It sometimes happened that one of her male colleagues would subsequently make the same point. It would be immediately acknowledged by the other men as important.
>
> (2018: 2)

This example, and Julie Bishop's subsequent approach, give some insight into the strategies that might be deployed by women upon their entry into masculine domains. The point here is that Kiefel cited Bishop's approach in her speech—the idea being that if there are multiple women you back each other up. Citing Bishop's experience, Kiefel (2018: 2) noted that when 'more women came to be appointed to Cabinet they all agreed to make a great fuss if one of them made a comment about just about anything'. Perhaps the most noteworthy aspect here is that Kiefel chose this example to demonstrate her awareness of the way in which women's contributions are received (even if she was disinclined to reflect on her own personal experiences on this front), and the potential for multiple women to disrupt the status quo.

Despite an awareness of the past exclusion of women within the legal profession, Kiefel emphasised her own positive experiences at the Queensland Bar. She noted that by the time she was called to the Bar in 1975 'excluding women was largely a thing of the past':

> The Bar could not have been more accepting and supportive of me. Most of the work I received in my early days at the Bar was as a result of recommendations from barristers. I was given a chance to prove myself and that was all I asked for.
>
> (2018: 4)

This segued into acknowledging women's progress in the legal profession more broadly, which aligned her remarks with the "press for progress" theme for International Women's Day that year. She cited Australian examples showing numerical progress in women's entry into the legal profession. She further acknowledged her hosts and pointed to the inroads that have been made in Malaysia especially in terms of the appointment of women to the judiciary in Malaysia including to the highest court, the Federal Court. Here Kiefel (2018: 6) inserted a merit discourse into her speech, not through her own words but by citing the Chief Justice of the Federal Court of Malaysia who had 'made the point that their elevation was based upon merit, not to fulfil some quota.'

Kiefel (2018: 6) returned to the Australian example and what she regarded as the 'downside to the initiative taken by governments in Australia, in the last 20 years or so, to increase the number of women judges in the superior courts'. As Kiefel (2018: 6) explained 'it is usual to make appointments to those courts from the senior ranks of the Bar' but this approach had consequences in terms of the composition of the Bar:

> And so, it came about that almost as soon as a woman achieved this status she was appointed as a judge and most felt duty bound to take the appointment. This denied them the opportunity to be leaders of the Bar and it denied many junior female barristers women mentors. That situation

> is gradually being addressed by the increasing numbers of female barristers now taking silk who are able to resist a premature call to the Bench.

Kiefel's (2018: 6) critique was not levelled at the women accepting the appointment because it 'is difficult to decline such an appointment'. Rather, the issue, from Kiefel's perspective was that those 'appointing do not, however, have the welfare of the Bar in mind' and the result has been to deprive 'younger women and men at the Bar the benefit of the presence and models of senior women barristers'.

Given the regularity (relatively speaking) that Kiefel has spoken about this issue it is reasonable to infer that it is one to which she attaches some degree of significance. The idea that women were appointed too early to the bench and thus deprived the Bar of women leaders is a reasonable enough point, but failing to appoint women as judges deprives the judiciary of women leaders too. Although Kiefel does not suggest that women have been appointed without merit, her own concern with emphasising the importance of merit suggests at least a concern about the perception of such. Yet nowhere in this speech does she acknowledge the historical practices which have treated men's experiences (and preferences for men) as the norm, practices that effectively created affirmative action for men such that changing them to bring women into the mix comes to be seen as an unfair leg up for women in the sense that their appointment is not just seen as 'having jumped the queue' but that such women are not entitled to authoritative public speech and hence lack 'legitimate entitlement to exercise judicial authority, even among their own colleagues' (Mack and Roach Anleu 2012: 326). The concluding part of the International Women's Day speech was cautiously optimistic. In emphasising the progress that has been made in the legal profession, Kiefel acknowledged that these experiences are 'not reflective of the progress being made by women more generally in our society and in the world' (2018: 8). As a woman who has, by her own admission 'found her voice', or been afforded particular authority, Kiefel acknowledged that 'once found it can be used for the advancement of others.'

Kiefel reprised some of these themes at "First Women of the Supreme Courts in Conversation" panel event held at Grays Inn London. At this event she shared the stage with 'sister' judges, then President of the Supreme Court of the United Kingdom (2017–2020), Baroness Brenda Hale, former Chief Justice of Ghana (2007–2017), Georgina Wood, and former Chief Justice of Canada (2000–2017), Beverley McLachlin at an event billed as "First Women of the Supreme Courts in Conversation."[25] United State Supreme Court

25 A full recording of the 2018 "First Women the Supreme Courts in Conversation" is available online at: https://www.youtube.com/watch?v=FjFIb7-SD3M. The references which follow are attributed the relevant speaker based on my own transcription of the event.

Justice, Sonia Sotomayor had originally been billed to attend but was unable to do so. Kiefel's participation at this event is noteworthy in terms of her willingness to speak about being a 'first woman' in a more off the cuff panel style event. Perhaps her willingness to participate should be afforded another layer of significance given she would be in the company of women judges who have been much more willing to reflect on the relationship between gender and judging and have advocated for judicial diversity. For example, Justice Hale and Justice McLachlin have often commented throughout their careers on the relationship between gender and judging (see for e.g. Hale 2001, 2003, 2008; McLachlin cited in Hale 2003; McLachlin 2016) whereas Wood has been less inclined to offer commentary on these matters.[26]

The questions asked of these trailblazing women lawyers were perhaps what one might expect of an event framed in more celebratory than critical or analytical terms. What had prompted each of the women to enter the legal profession? What were the most challenging times in their careers? What would they like their legacy to be? And, finally, how had their experiences in life influenced their judgments? Their answers reflect the differences among and between women, and, some of the similarities in terms of the hurdles or difficulties they faced in navigating their way in the profession. That they would have different experiences and perspectives as women, and as lawyers and judges should come as no surprise at all. But in their answers to the question 'how have your experiences influenced your judgments' we see the expression of arguments that have plagued feminist accounts of gender and judging. The point of raising these differences in perspective is not to suggest that there is one correct or ideal way to be a woman and a judge. Nor is it to suggest that there is a feminist sensibility lying dormant in all women. Rather, the point is to gain insight into how they as individuals interpreted their experiences of the respective institutional gender regimes they have inhabited. And more specifically, my point is in drawing out the significance of Kiefel's remarks.

Hale and McLachlin (reflecting their widely publicised views[27] on these matters) were emphatic that being a woman *does* make a difference. However,

26 But see Josephine Dawuni and Alice Kang (2015) 'Her Ladyship Chief Justice: The Rise of Female Leaders in the Judiciary in Africa' 62:2 *Africa Today:* 45–69, 64 for an analysis of Chief Justice Wood's contributions. They argue, 'One unanswered question concerns the effects, if any, of having a woman chief justice or president of the constitutional court. Anecdotes suggest that some women leaders are making an impact in the judiciary, not just for women, but for the delivery of justice. Since taking office in 2007, Chief Justice Wood has openly advocated for the rights of women in the country. One of many programs undertaken under her administration has been the creation of gender-based violence courts to address issues of violence against women.'

27 It is important here to emphasise that while neither Hale or McLachlin has necessarily argued that there is a distinctly feminine judicial voice, both have recognised the significance of judicial diversity and suggested that women's lived experience might in turn shape their approach to the judicial role. A good summary of views

for Kiefel gender was not a determinative factor in her approach to judging. Rather, she saw judging a being connected in some way to a particular value system:

> a value system is common to all judges I don't think male or female there is a differentiation. I was brought up Christian values—that kind of morphed into ethical, moral values—they're an important part of who I am. Values, whatever they might be, imbue so much of what you do as a judge.

While acknowledging that class and gender were relevant aspects of her life experience, she did not see these markers of 'otherness' as having any particular bearing on her approach to judgment writing:

> I was not brought up with a privileged background. I had no introduction into anywhere. I left school at fifteen and have been working since I was fifteen. I think those kinds of things shape how you view the world and how you see people in it. But I think you could have a long debate about how much of an experience of being a woman affects judgment—it might affect our view of the world of world when you get annoyed. But when you actually come to write a judgment how much of that and in what areas it truly seeps through? I'm not sure we're in the best position to determine our own insights. I mean the areas where it's obvious crime and family law. I will leave it to academics to debate these things.

We see here Kiefel's deft handling of the questions about diversity. She effectively rejected the suggestion that gender informs or shapes her legal judgments but, perhaps conscious of her audience or the context, begs off a definitive conclusion by suggesting that this is not so much a concern for her but more so for those with an academic interest in such things.

attributed to Hale and McLachlin can be found in an extract from a speech given by Hale (where she cites McLachlin extensively) to Plymouth Law Society in 2003 and subsequently published as an opinion piece. See Hale, B. (2003) 'Welcome to white men's club'. *The Guardian*, 30 October. Hale cites (with approval) the four arguments McLachlin made in favour of increasing the representation of women on the bench ([namely that (1) representation is important for public confidence in the judicial system, (2) that such representation is symbolically important and that (3) utilitarianism demands that we use the intellectual resources of half the population]. The fourth and final reason is, according to Hale, the most important and the most controversial 'because we need the perspectives that women can bring to judging.' As Hale explained, 'We should not expect women judges to "make a difference" in the sense that they are likely to make different decisions from men. […] The difference is more subtle. As Chief Justice McLachlin put it: "jurists are human beings, and, as such, are informed and influenced by their backgrounds, communities, and experiences. For cultural, biological, social and historic reasons, women do have different experiences than men."'

Of interest here is Kiefel's response to the question about legacy. Whereas Wood wanted to be remembered as the Chief Justice who was fiercely protective of judicial independence, and Hale for changing the law and perhaps making it kinder, Kiefel emphasised collegiality and mentoring (younger women specifically) as part of her legacy.

> I would like to be remembered as someone who promoted a style of judgment writing and collegiate judgment making which allowed for the development of concise, clear judgments that make it easier for people to understand the judgment.

An important aspect of her 'style of judgment' was her emphasis on an institutional approach to judgment writing as distinct from an individual approach. This meant a form of collective writing in which collegiality was the key.

Kiefel's extra-curial remarks both before and after becoming Chief Justice repeatedly invoked her commitment to collegiality. Her work in consensus building has been a prominent feature of her chief justiceship. Certainly, the Kiefel Court, like the French Court before it, is a court marked by consensus, although this receded somewhat in 2019 (see Lynch 2020: 1228).[28] She has lifted the veil so to speak about the process of judgment writing and has given significant insight into the process of entrenching collegiality, and in so doing, given weight to the notion that high levels collegiality on the Court reflected, at least in part, her leadership.[29] This promised to be a significant judicial legacy. But now that legacy will surely be overtaken in importance by her decisive response to the sexual harassment allegations against Dyson Heydon. In this she has had to deal with gender in an entirely unexpected way. Indeed, her response to these allegations is perhaps all the more significant given what we know about her crafting of an identity as a judge (and later Chief Justice) in ways which have sought to diminish the significance of gender. It is to the implications of those allegations that I now turn.

28 Noting that the percentage of matters decided unanimously 'was the lowest since 2012 and dramatically lower than in the two preceding years of the Court under Chief Justice Kiefel', Lynch (2020: 1228–1229) observed 'the very low incidence of unanimity in 2019 and the commensurate rise of cases decided by multiple concurring opinions, points to a change that goes against, rather than with, the grain of the Chief Justice's remarks about how the Court's decisions are best made and presented to the community'. However, they did recognise that the 'the shift may prove fleeting, reflecting the particular features of the matters that arose over this period, but it is nonetheless discernible'.

29 See Chapters 4 and 7 for examination of Kiefel's comments about joint judgment writing prior to her elevation to Chief Justice. See the Hon Susan Kiefel AC (2017b) *Judicial Methods in the 21st Century*. Supreme Court Oration, Banco Court 16 March for a detailed account of approaches to judgment writing on the Kiefel Court.

'The enemy within': a hostile environment?

As has already been noted, in June 2020 it came to light that former Justice Dyson Heydon was alleged to have sexually harassed judicial associates. These allegations concerned Heydon's time on the High Court (2002–2013) (although there were also suggestions of a pattern of behaviour that extended much further back than that). An investigation by *Sydney Morning Herald* journalists Jaqueline Maley and Kate McClymont (2020) uncovered further allegations of Heydon's predatory behaviour, including an allegation from a judge who claims that he indecently assaulted her. A statement from the Chief Justice published on the High Court's website confirmed the findings of the inquiry commissioned by the Court in response to the allegations. Although the Chief Justice did not name any of the complainants in her public statement, they were named in the media reports. The fact that the High Court inquiry had confirmed the allegations to be true added significant weight to their story. This meant that the focus was less about whether the conduct had taken place, and more about what this meant for the legal profession. It also meant the story was more about Heydon (and indeed the legal and political institutions that had seemingly allowed this conduct to go unchecked), than about the young women or any of the usual questions about their motivations or credibility which all too frequently attend complaints such as these.

That some of young women had missed out on a career in the law was part of the story (one complainant had left the law altogether and another had abandoned plans of going to the Bar). Josh Bornstein (2020), lawyer for several of the complainants pointed out 'at the time that this sexual harassment occurred, Dyson Heydon was in his 60s, a conservative judge, a prominent Christian and a married man', whereas 'the women he employed were in their early 20s and often straight out of university'. Speaking to the particularly pronounced asymmetric power relationship between judge and associate, Bornstein explained that Heydon 'was one of the most powerful men in the country, who could make or break their future careers in the law.' Speaking of the delay in bringing these complaints forward, Bornstein explained that there was 'an extreme power imbalance between Mr Heydon and the young women he preyed on' and the 'fear of his power and influence meant that the women did not feel able to come forward until recently.' Would this be the moment of reckoning for the legal profession and its masculinist culture of silence?

In a strongly worded statement Kiefel said that the findings of the investigation were of extreme concern to her and other members of the Court. They were 'ashamed that this could have happened at the High Court of Australia'. She set out the details of the investigation as follows:

> The High Court was advised last year of allegations of sexual harassment against a former Justice and we immediately acted to commission an independent investigation. The investigation, conducted by Dr Vivienne

> Thorn AM, took some months to complete. We received Dr Thorn's report and have provided it to the six complainants and to the Justice in question. The investigation found that six former Court staff members who were Judges' Associates were harassed by the former Justice. The findings are of extreme concern to me, my fellow Justices, our Chief Executive and the staff of the Court.
>
> (Kiefel 2020)

Importantly, Kiefel offered a personal apology to the young women and stated in clear terms that the women had been believed. She further acknowledged the difficulties the women would have had in coming forward:

> We have made a sincere apology to the six women whose complaints were borne out. We know it would have been difficult to come forward. Their accounts of their experiences at the time have been believed. I have appreciated the opportunity to talk with a number of the women about their experiences and to apologise to them in person. I have also valued their insights and suggestions for change that they have shared with the Court.
>
> (Kiefel 2020)

Kiefel confirmed that the former Justice in question was the Hon Dyson Heydon AC QC. She noted that a number of the women had requested confidentiality and asked 'that the media respect the privacy of the complainants'. She further outlined the recommendations[30] made by the independent investigation and advised that the Court had acted upon each of these recommendations. Heydon, for his part, denied any allegations of predatory behaviour or breaches of the law. In a statement through his lawyers to the *Sydney Morning Herald*, it was noted that 'our client says that if any conduct of his has caused offence, that result was inadvertent and unintended, and he apologises for any offence caused' (cited in Maley and McClymont 2020). In response to the inquiry commissioned by the High Court, his lawyers have emphasised this process 'was an internal administrative inquiry conducted by a public servant rather than by a Court or Tribunal' (cited in Maley and McClymont 2020). I will return to the various ways in which questions of evidence and legal formalism came to punctuate the ensuing public debate, but for now it is

30 These recommendations included developing a supplementary HR policy relevant to the particular employment circumstances of the personal staff of Justices including associates; reviewing induction provided to associates; identifying an appropriate person to form a closer working relationship with associates; clarifying that the confidentiality requirements for associates relate only to the work of the Court; making clear to associates that their duties do not extend to an obligation to attend social functions; and finally, consider canvassing current associates to find out more about their experiences while working at the Court.

sufficient to note that this was the key emphasis from Heydon's legal team. Three of the complainants are pursuing civil claims for compensation and further allegations have since been made by other women—including by other former associates and outside of the High Court, by lawyer and former ACT Law Society President Noor Blumer as well as the Canberra Liberal Party leader Elizabeth Lee (reported in Foden 2020). At the time of writing, however, no women have yet come forward to lodge a complaint with police, which is a required step for any criminal investigation to commence.

There was widespread support for the Chief Justice's response. For example, a letter signed by over 500 legal women praised her Honour's response[31]:

> We thank you and the Court's Principal Registrar, Ms Philippa Lynch, in particular for the decisive action taken to ensure the complaints were thoroughly investigated by an independent process. We are grateful that you took this matter so seriously and treated the complainants with dignity, compassion and respect. We welcome your response to the inquiry's recommendations as to how to provide better protections to associates during their time employed at the Court, recognising their particularly vulnerable professional position.
>
> (Appleby et al. 2020)

As for Heydon's legacy, his conduct has been widely condemned by those who have been willing to be drawn on it, but it remains to be seen how this reputational damage will inform his jurisprudential legacy. One high profile exception to the condemnation was former Prime Minister John Howard who commented in an interview for SBS television news that he stood by his judicial appointments, and that 'Dyson Heydon was an excellent Judge of the High Court of Australia' (Howard cited in Maley and McClymont 2020).

An anonymous piece published in the *Spectator* criticised Kiefel's handling of the complaint 'as a capitulation to the fashionable and illiberal #MeToo movement, which has been able to extract rules seemingly designed just for Mr Heydon' (Anon 2020: unpaginated). This critique—anonymous as it might be—speaks to a wider critique of the #MeToo movement insofar as its critics have claimed that Kiefel's handling of the allegations represented a problematic departure from procedural fairness.[32] Indeed, Heydon's legal team invoked a similar narrative—criticising the process for a lack of procedural fairness because

31 As noted in Chapter 2 this correspondence also set out proposals for the creation of an independent complaints body and reforms to judicial appointment processes.

32 Although the particular strengths and weaknesses of the #MeToo movement are beyond the scope of this chapter, I note that the movement has been criticised for its effectiveness more broadly for co-opting a black woman's movement and for its Hollywood focus (or focus on otherwise privileged women) and effectiveness in translating awareness to more broadly scale structural reforms (see for e.g. Fileborn and Loney-Howes 2019).

it was 'conducted without having statutory powers of investigation and of administering affirmations or oaths' (cited in Maley and McClymont 2020).[33] Importantly, the *Spectator*'s account did not really attack the credibility of the complainants; rather it trivialized their complaints and thereby sought to minimise the former Judge's conduct. For the anonymous writer, the real issue was Kiefel's leadership and judgment. It is certainly never suggested that this alleged misstep is because she is a woman, but rather, was framed as a 'lack of judgment' and bias. The author argued that any announcement of this kind should have been made by the Court's manager rather than the Chief Justice herself. The result, in their view, was that 'the Chief has waded in personally, poured fuel on an intense fire and given tacit approval to a diabolical media witch-hunt.' For the most part the author accepted the veracity of the complaints against Heydon, but conceptualised the problem as one of sexual deviance of a minor variety:

> The allegations are what lawyers describe as low-level sexual harassment. The pattern of conduct is that a proposition generally occurs at or after an event where alcohol has been consumed. An inappropriate touch might occur. The advance is refused, and Mr Heydon retreats, apparently for good. There is no real suggestion of sexual assault. So we are not dealing with an alleged crime. We are dealing with inappropriate conduct that causes offence to the woman involved.

In the anonymous author's opinion, 'the Chief Justice's words and deeds left the Court exposed to the rare charge that it has undermined its own integrity.' The emphasis then was on the historic nature of the complaints and the fact that they were being raised beyond time (the time limit to bring a complaint under the *Sex Discrimination Act* 1984 (Cth) is 6 months although there is scope to extend it). The writer did not grapple with the potential deficiencies in the very laws they reference. Indeed, the anonymous author described the six-month window as based on sound policy reasoning. While not really specifying what this policy reason might be, they reverted to describing it as 'a breach of civil law which regulates conduct that merely causes offence, hurt or upset feelings.'[34] That a number of the complainants ended up losing their chosen

33 As barrister Kate Eastman SC (2020) observed at the time, 'the alleged perpetrator has no right to confront or cross-examine the complainant in person. This is not the purpose of a workplace investigation into sexual harassment. Cross-examination is for a court room under the supervision of a judge.'

34 Indeed, such a conceptualisation of 'mere' hurt feelings is somewhat reminiscent of the decision in *Monis* (see Chapter 6) insofar as the writer is seeking to minimise the harms of sexual harassment. Hurt feelings is simply a means of trivialising and minimising. We see here that the law (which could be improved to better reflect these harms in any case) references 'offence, humiliation and intimidation' as potential harms.

career paths was not something acknowledged by the anonymous author. Nor was there any understanding of the ways in which significant power imbalances make contemporaneous complaints very difficult.

Yet for many of the Chief Justice's supporters, it did not go unnoticed that it was under the leadership of a woman Chief Justice that these (historic) complaints came to be ventilated. Her handling of the complaints was framed as a positive consequence of having a woman Chief Justice. In an interview about the sexual harassment allegations, Commonwealth Sex Discrimination Commissioner, Kate Jenkins (cited in Kelly 2020a) was asked about the importance of having women serve in the highest ranks of the profession, and whether that makes a difference:

> It probably makes the most difference. I think it is absolutely no coincidence that this is a High Court which for the first time has gender balance, has three women, the Chief Justice is a woman.

This perspective is revelatory insofar as it assumes that the presence of women (and indeed a woman in a leadership position) will make a difference. What the Commissioner was referencing here is not necessarily that there's an inherent woman's voice, but rather that the presence of women changes the internal dynamics of the institution, or at least has the potential to do so (and that this in turns creates the necessary environment where complaints of sexual harassment can be appropriately ventilated and addressed). It was a sentiment shared by other senior women in the Australian legal profession. Senior barrister, Fiona McLeod (cited in Pelly 2020) said of the timing, that although it might be simply a coincidence, perhaps it might be

> the case that the Chief Justice is fully aware of the experience of women over decades and decided to send a very clear message that it's inappropriate in her court.

Former Chief Justice of the Family Court of Australia, Diana Bryant expressed similar sentiments—indeed, emphasising her own experience of sexual harassment as a more junior lawyer and how that had shaped her approach once she had the authority to implement changes. Recounting her experience of sexual harassment as a more junior lawyer, she told ABC radio 'this isn't about me complaining about a specific judge, this is about a systemic issue' (Bryant cited in Kelly 2020b). In that same interview she explained that she agitated for reform once she was on a position of power—making clear that associates are not personal employees of judges they work with. This account speaks to the benefit of diversity in public institutions insofar as it demonstrates how our lived experiences shape our understanding of the world with the *potential* for those experiences to challenge the taken for granted gendered rules and conventions.

We see in these events, of course, how the wider gender order shapes the institutional gender order. Sexual harassment is at once an individual and institutional problem and concern (Bacchi and Jose 1994; Bacchi 1998). Rejecting the argument that sees sexual harassment as a problem *for* institutions to manage 'as something exogenous to them in a sense', Bacchi (1998: 76) instead saw the institution itself as *the* problem 'because sexual harassment is seen as an institutional by-product of a setting unwelcoming or even hostile to women.' Importantly, this is not to discount the role of the individual within that institutional framework. All too often the structural and the individual are set up as polar opposites. A focus just on the individual only yields a partial picture, and a focus on only the structural approach 'depends on abstracting from manifold individualities to identify patterns or regularities' (Bacchi and Jose 1994: 5). As Bacchi and Jose explain, 'a way to break down this dichotomy is to focus upon the way in which individual behaviours reinforce oppressive structures'. The consequence of conceptualising sexual harassment this was is that we can acknowledge *both* the individual and institutional in the allegations about Dyson Heydon—this story is neither wholly about his predatory behaviour nor is it wholly about the High Court (and the wider legal profession) as an institution.

What then do the Heydon allegations and the Chief Justice's response tell us about the gender dynamics on the High Court? Gendered power structures have shaped (and continue to shape) the legal profession and the evolution of the legal profession enabled sexual misconduct to become an open secret. In fact, the arguments used to deny women's entry into the profession give us some insights into the present: women's supposed intellectual inferiority, the notion that women's sexuality might exercise a subversive effect on men and disrupt the separate spheres (an ordering of men and women which had women confined to private family life and men in public life) (Thornton 1996: 43). The allegations themselves speak to the masculinism of the institution and the way in which it has reproduced masculine power and privilege. If as reported, it is true that Heydon's conduct was an open secret, that tells us much about the extent to which a masculinist gender order has protected its own, ensuring that powerful men are protected to enjoy the fruits of their power. As has elsewhere been examined in this book, in a provocatively named speech, Heydon (2013) described more collaborative and collegiate approaches to judgment writing on the High Court as 'the enemy within' and as a threat to judicial independence. Yet for women, 'the enemy within' has been hegemonic masculinity and its masculine norms of behaviour which have allowed men to act with impunity—and therefore excluded women (both expressly and impliedly).

Indeed, it is certainly not difficult to imagine circumstances where the politically powerful knew about allegations of sexual assault or harassment and were not deterred in their attempts to appoint the judge in question. For a recent high-profile example from the United States, consider the experience around Brett Kavanagh's 2018 nomination and subsequent confirmation to the United States Supreme Court. As Fileborn and Phillips (2019: 110) argued, 'despite claims that #Metoo is a witch hunt', goes 'too far', and 'runs the risk of destroying the careers of (supposedly) innocent or otherwise undeserving men, it would seem such fears have not borne out in practice.' Reflecting specifically on Dr Christine Blaisey Ford's testimony under oath before the Senate Judiciary Committee (noting there was also a refusal to allow others who might offer corroboration to testify) where she accused Kavanaugh of attempted rape, they noted that 'Senator Mitch McConnell dismissed the allegations and declared to supporters that Kavanaugh will nonetheless be confirmed to the position. He stated, "… don't get rattled by all of this. We're going to plough right through it."' McConnell's declaration proved to be accurate, with Kavanaugh successfully appointed to the United States Supreme Court. That McConnell's position which was effectively to dismiss/ignore the testimony and protect the (alleged) perpetrator not only rebuts the notion that these kinds of allegations destroy men's careers. Indeed, the effectiveness of McConnell's response further underscores how power is protected in and by the patriarchy—through its legal systems and processes and through the trivialisation of complaints.[35]

Kiefel's response to the sexual harassment allegations against Heydon will likely form a major (if not defining) feature of her legacy. Of course, it might be argued that defining her legacy by reference to the misdeeds of a man is potentially problematic. Indeed, this emphasis potentially obscures the jurisprudential contributions of the Kiefel Court, and it remains to be seen how these will be received over time. But her handling of the allegations was much more significant than the misdeeds of one man. It was about making a statement about what is acceptable and what would be tolerated, not just on the High Court of the Australia, but by extension, the legal profession, and indeed, all workplaces. If this issue defines her legacy, then what is actually the defining dynamic is taking seriously the vows of office and in seeking to restore confidence in the High Court (and wider legal system). The timing is also relevant as at least some of the instances of harassment took place in the period where women judges also sat on the Court, when the Chief Justices were men. It is not possible to establish in any causal way that Kiefel the individual was the

35 Ensuring that powerful men are protected to enjoy the fruits of their power has been a critique of legal response to sexual harassment, and indeed gender-based violence more broadly. Indeed, one of the purported benefits of the #Metoo movement has been in its capacity to overcome at least some of the hurdles sexual harassment law has traditionally posed for complainants. As MacKinnon (2018) put it: 'This mass mobilization against sexual abuse, through an unprecedented wave of speaking out in conventional and social media, is eroding the two biggest barriers to ending sexual harassment in law and in life: the disbelief and trivializing dehumanization of its victims.'

decisive factor in terms of the complaints coming to light. But what we do know is that it has been alleged that the actions giving rise to these allegations were an open secret within the Court (McClymont and Maley 2020). They remained secret until someone decided to act on them and decided to make the outcome of those actions public. We know that when asked about the allegations after they came to light, former Chief Justice Murray Gleeson (1998–2008) declined to comment (McClymont and Maley 2020).[36] Kiefel could have done much the same. She might have reported the complaints but eschewed responsibility, instead suggesting that such complaints would need to be pursued through formal legal mechanisms. Or she might have issued a statement about the Inquiry, but without centring the victims or stating that they had been believed. But by stating that she believed them, that she understood how hard it was to come forward, Kiefel made an enormously significant statement about what would be tolerated in her Court. By her own admission her words carry a particular weight. Even when those words do not carry the authority of judgment, her voice is nonetheless elevated.

Allegations about sexual harassment at the very peak of Australia's legal profession demonstrated the unedifying consequences when privilege and power are permitted to run unchecked. They literally showed the most base way that a masculinist legal system has been maintained—sexual abuse, harassment and bullying (or indeed even the threat of the same) serves as a powerful disincentive for women to remain in the profession.[37] Perhaps a more sanguine observation though is that these events also demonstrated the potential to disrupt that gender order. A Chief Justice who had maintained that women, notably (junior) women, would find themselves treated simply as persons saw, perhaps not for the first time, that this did not hold true. That she wielded her power as Chief Justice in such a way, not just in terms of her

36 McClymont and Maley (2020) reported that according to the confidential report (of which their newspaper obtained) 'Justice Michael McHugh, who served on the court from 1989 until 2005, and the then Chief Justice Murray Gleeson, who headed the court for a decade until 2008, were told of their colleague's alleged behaviour. It is not known what steps were taken by then Chief Justice Murray Gleeson about Justice Heydon's behaviour.' They further noted that former Justice Mr McHugh declined to participate in the investigation. When contacted by the *Herald* and *The Age*, Mr Gleeson, now retired from the bench, said: "I am unwilling to comment". Mr McHugh, also retired from the bench, did not respond to emails and phone messages.

37 This was seen at the individual level in this case as a number of the complainants decided to leave the law or did not pursue careers at the Bar as they had intended. However, it is also seen at the wider institutional level with the prevalence of sexual harassment and bullying cited as a rationale for the women leaving the profession. See for e.g. *Law Council of Australia, Submission to Australian Human Rights Commission National Inquiry into Sexual Harassment in Australian Workplaces*, February 2019 URL: https://www.lawcouncil.asn.au/publicassets/1bde0b80-d23e-e911-93fc-005056be13b5/3587%20-%20AHRC%20NISHAW%20Submission.pdf.

decision and action, but in expressing her sympathy with the complainants, acknowledging the difficulties they would have had in coming forward, and emphasising that they had been believed and naming Dyson Heydon, she demonstrated the potential to disrupt the prevailing gender regime. In short, her voice provided a salutary reminder that who our judges are matters.

Conclusion

From non-persons to almost-parity: a masculinist gender order disrupted?

It has been a long journey for women to achieve recognition as judicial voices of legal authority at the peak tier of Australia's legal system. Women's 'letting in' to the legal profession—the necessary precursor to women being appointed as judges—was premised on women's (legal) status as 'persons'. But this formal recognition obscured the extent to which the masculine foundations of Australia's constitutional framework, of its High Court, and the wider legal profession continued to exclude women. At first glance the 'persons' cases which explicitly excluded women from the legal profession around the turn of the last century seem a long way from the here and now. A century on we might ask how much has changed and how much has stayed the same—to what extent does the High Court still reflect the masculinist origins of its creation? Have women been fully accepted as citizens of the jurisprudential community, or does their access to legal authority remain contingent and conditional?

Justice Mary Gaudron keenly perceived the weight of expectations generated by her appointment to the High Court of Australia in 1987. As the first woman to sit at the apex of Australia's judicial hierarchy she well understood the historical significance of her appointment. This is partly reflected in her insistence at the time that she wanted to be seen as just 'one of seven'. It is also reflected in comments she made ten years later that she did not want to be 'the first and last' or give occasion for people to say 'we tried a woman once and it did not work'.[1] Events suggest that it worked, particularly if the success of appointing a woman is measured by the subsequent appointment of more women judges. But has the success of appointing women to the most visible and powerful levels of judicial authority been sufficient to make redundant Thornton's (1996: 3–4) now more than two-decade old claim that women have 'not been fully accepted as citizens of the jurisprudential community'? Given that women have been appointed to the High Court to the point where there is now a near-equal gender balance, surely this signals their formal acceptance into or

1 These comments are cited in Burton's (2010: 269) biography of Mary Gaudron. Gaudron made the comments in the context of the interviews undertaken for the 1998 documentary *The Highest Court.*

DOI: 10.4324/9780429288531-10

membership of the jurisprudential community? But given Mary Gaudron's insistence that she was just 'one of seven', in spite of her understanding of the difference women might bring to bear as lawyers and judges, and that the other women justices similarly made light of being women judges, this raises questions about the conditions of that membership. Are women received as legal knowers on the condition that they are 'just men in skirts'?

To answer that question this book examined how the Court's gender regime operated once there was more than one woman on the bench. This involved exploring a number of questions: How have the Court's gender relations accommodated the presence of women judges? How did the women themselves accommodate those pre-existing gender relations? How might the legal judgments and reasoning have changed as a result of changing gender dynamics on the bench? Hence in addressing the question of whether women were 'just men in skirts' the book also explored how women were situated as legal knowers within the very specific jurisprudential community of the High Court of Australia. This is a community that remains marked by its masculinist history. Women's exclusion from the formation of and subsequent interpretation of law has had wide-reaching implications for the substance of law and for women's engagement with it. Because of law's power to define rights and relationships and to legitimise or delegitimise gendered experiences and understandings, women's relationship with the law as judges matters. For some feminist legal theorists, women judges would be the panacea to law's gender-blindness. It was anticipated by many (but not all) feminist theorists and activists that the transformative potential of women judges—their 'difference' variously construed—could and should change the substance, scope and effect of law. In more recent times, many feminist legal theorists, cognisant of the many problems with the idea of difference (especially the trap of essentialism), abandoned some of the more problematic assertions about the types of difference women judges would make. Perhaps the most significant shift has been a realisation that *feminist* judges rather than *women* judges are what might be required to make a feminist difference.

However, the question immediately arises as to the extent to which identifying and appointing feminist judges is possible within an existing gender regime where the purported neutrality of law (and by extension, judges) fixates on the fiction of the default genderless judge. As we have seen, women judges appointed to the High Court of Australia mostly do not embrace feminist identities, or at least emphatically reject the notion that a feminist sensibility might inform their judging. One example of this kind of thinking is in Bell's (2017: 9) rejection of the notion that her feminism informed her judging in any way. In her speech launching the *University of New South Wales Law Journal* thematic issue about 'The Individual Judge', Bell was generally critical about academic interest in the individual judges, and especially so of approaches which had examined the potential for feminist approaches to inform the judicial role (e.g. Hunter and Tyson 2017). Perhaps demonstrating the extent to which Bell wanted to distance herself from these arguments, she quipped, 'that school are apt to counter by saying that women who have been appointed to the judiciary are almost inevitably captives of the patriarchy' (Bell 2017: 9). In the video recording of the speech, the viewer sees that this line was delivered by a seemingly exasperated Bell—perhaps playing up her outrage for effect but nonetheless keen to dismiss out of hand this seemingly preposterous idea. Certainly, it was delivered to considerable laughter from those present. But, are we all not captives of the patriarchy?

Given what we know about the masculinist nature of legal institutions (and how difficult it is to disrupt these regimes), eschewing a feminist identity (or adopting such an identity but maintaining that it is nonetheless entirely separate to the judicial role), is not surprising since the desire is to fit in, to be worthy of the honour of appointment, to be 'one of seven'. This is not to suggest that there is feminist sensibility to be found dormant in women judges, or even that there should be. Rather, it is to emphasise that 'the judge is the paradigmatic figure of legal authority and has long remained resistant to the feminine' (Thornton 2020: 237). The very notion of feminist reasoning seems so disruptive because masculinist legal reasoning was simply legal reasoning. The fiction of the genderless judge is so deeply entrenched in law that to speak *as a man* judge is not to speak *as a* man at all; it is simply to speak as the judge. So much is evident in Justice Kirby's rallying justification for the appointment of women judges which ventured that women are important because they are not 'just men in skirts'. Although the word *just* implies that women might offer something more, the statement accepts the reality that men have historically done the judging.

Gendered difference is the issue, but it only becomes so when there is more than one woman on the bench, indeed even when it is only one woman on the bench. The arrival of women not only puts the pre-existing gender regime on notice, potentially at least, it also renders it visible. But, of course, gender was there all along. Both *PGA* and *Monis* exposed, albeit in different ways, how an ordinarily benign masculinism remains embedded in law, especially in terms of how the law conceives of the public and private spheres. If a reminder were needed about the contingency of legal reasoning, or the potential for values to shape legal reasoning, we saw it in these decisions. The potential for approaches to legal reasoning infused with a feminist perspective to transform law was explicit in the fictive feminist response to *PGA* but tellingly, it was also present in the joint judgment in *Monis*. What was so significant about the decision in *Monis* was that it demonstrated the potential for women to challenge gendered legal understandings. For whatever reason, the tradeoff for the substance of their decision (which acknowledged the dichotomous construction of the public/private) is a judgment that reads as restrained and emotionally muted in contrast to the flagrantly value-laden judgments produced by each of the men judges. The men reasserted the masculinism of both the Court and the public sphere by maintaining the gendered vision of the latter as separate from the so-called private. Against the backdrop of the High Court's decision in *Monis* we saw how women are situated in the polity, and the gendered conditions which attach to their public authority. Debates about gender and public authority are apposite insofar as how Prime Minister Gillard's criticism of the overtly sexist nature of much of the discourse around her Prime Ministership was received. Although Gillard's Prime Ministership was plagued by issues of legitimacy (at least in part informed by the method by which she had taken power), that she had publicly spoken out against the sexist commentary about her meant that she had 'played the gender card' and further compromised her authority. This revealed the ways in which women must negotiate the still novel features of their status as public legal knowers.

The joint judgment in *Monis* gave glimpses of a feminist viewpoint, demonstrating how legal decisions are imbued with understandings of gender and have gendered meanings and gendering effects. Crennan, Kiefel and Bell JJ's approach in this decision revealed the *potential* for women judges to draw upon their experiences within the wider gender regime. But the precondition of being 'more than just men in skirts' by way of substance, meant that in form, they adopted a very restrained approach and did their best impersonation of the rational man of law. The performative aspect of judging, the literal donning of the sartorial trappings of judicial authority, presupposed certain gendered conventions, understandings and approaches. Within these conventions, the women judges were able to challenge particular masculinist understandings of harm and the appropriate limits of freedom of expression. This not to say the decision was a feminist decision, or that the judges were feminist judges. It is obvious that explicitly feminist judges and judgments offer more in the way of a deliberate and conscious challenge to gendered legal concepts, understandings and narratives. Therefore, we might need to think about the strategies involved in securing their appointment.

The conditions necessary for the appointment of explicitly feminist judges who are liberated from the confines of liberal legalism may in turn require more seismic shifts in how women are received as public knowers. Indeed, the resistance to reforming judicial appointment practices in the wake of the Heydon revelations demonstrates the depth of commitment to the prevailing gender regime. There were calls for reforms to enhance the accountability and transparency of judicial appointment including the adoption of publicly available criteria (such as legal knowledge, skill and expertise in addition to essential personal qualities e.g. integrity and good character). It was further proposed that the value of diversity in judicial appointments should also be respected in formulating criteria. These were hardly radical calls for reforms—they were in step with reforms adopted elsewhere in the world and were framed around a broad commitment to diversity. There was no suggestion of quotas or initiatives to appoint judges with a feminist or gender-sensitive perspective. The commitment to the existing model (as examined in Chapter 2) whereby the executive has unfettered discretion in making these appointments underscores the ways in which the politically powerful dictate the conditions for joining the institution. The reluctance to adopt even modest reforms which would include greater transparency in the appointments demonstrates a particularly dogged commitment the gendered status quo.

The gender dynamics on the High Court have been carefully crafted. Up until 2020 no woman had ever replaced another woman—lest anyone get the idea that there are seats reserved for women. Moreover, decision-makers have usually been insistent that gender is not taken into account. In the lead up to most recent High Court appointments in late 2020, Kim Rubenstein (2020) implored the government to appoint two women, arguing that 'a High Court made up of four women and three men would signal equality coming of age'. She argued:

> It may also break the last vestiges of the High Court ever being considered again as a male stronghold and a place to affirm the job applications of good old boys who went to the "right" school, know the "right" people and can be relied upon to make the "right" decisions.

In appointing one man and one woman to replace Justice Geoffrey Nettle and Justice Virginia Bell, respectively, the Government went with the status quo. Although the implications of the appointment of Justice Jacqueline Gleeson and Justice Simon Steward are beyond the scope of this book, the assumption that Justice Bell would be replaced by a woman suggests that there had been a shift in terms of the importance of gender diversity at the peak of Australia's legal profession, even if this shift has largely been unsaid or unacknowledged by those making the appointments.[2] Certainly, Gleeson's appointment, and that of Justice Gordon in 2015 suggests that at least for now, the presence of women as members of the Court seems secure. Assuming that both Gordon and Gleeson are able to stay on the bench until they reach the constitutionally prescribed retirement age of 70, the High Court of Australia is guaranteed at least two women until 2034 (Gordon is expected to retire in 2034 and Gleeson in 2036). In 2024 Susan Kiefel is expected to retire and a new Chief Justice will be appointed. Will a woman be appointed as the new Chief Justice from within the Court or 'parachuted' in? Perhaps there might be a sense that women have had their turn? Will we see a High Court that is comprised of a majority of women?

On this point—the notion of an all-woman Court—United States Supreme Court Justice Ruth Bader Ginsburg's famed response to queries about when there will be 'enough' women judges is salutary:

2 In the lead up to the appointments of Gleeson and Steward most commentators assumed that a woman would need to be appointed to replace Bell—as though this was the taken for granted state of affairs, when in fact it was the first time a woman had been appointed to replace another woman. See McLoughlin (2020) for a brief examination of these matters.

> So now the perception is, yes, women are here to stay. And when I'm sometimes asked when will there be enough [women on the Supreme Court]? And I say when there are nine, people are shocked. But there'd been nine men, and nobody's ever raised a question about that.
>
> (Ginsberg quoted in Filipovic 2012)

The point is a powerful one insofar as it reveals how normalised an all-man bench is, especially when juxtaposed against the seemingly fantastical idea of an all-woman bench. Also referenced in Justice Bader Ginsburg's comment is the confident assertion that 'women are here to stay'. Given that women have been appointed to the High Court of Australia with similar regularity, it might be that the shift from one to three is of similar importance. But it still must be stressed (and indeed this is very point that Bader Ginsburg was pressing), whether we are talking about one woman out of seven, or three out of seven, or three out of nine—the starting point is the assumption that a male bench is the norm. Given what we know about the 'sticky' nature of gender regimes, what might the implications of an all-woman High Court be? Taking Ginsburg's provocative question seriously, Baines (2017: 290) interrogated the implications of an all-woman bench, arguing that 'obviously an entirety of women judges on a constitutional court could eliminate judicial patriarchy.'

Is it in fact a *fait accompli* that an all-woman bench could eliminate judicial patriarchy? Baines examined the various hurdles to achieving an all-woman court—pointing out that Ginsburg's proposal moves beyond prevailing proposals, those of parity and feminism (e.g. the appointment of feminist judges), in important ways, especially taking heed of the extent to which these efforts 'have plateaued or even regressed'. As Baines (2017: 312) notes, we do not have the tools to predict the effect of an all-woman constitutional court, but it raises a number of significant questions:

> Is it likely their decisions would be unanimous where unanimity is optional, or would there be dissents or concurrences? Would some subject matter be particularly contentious? If so, would controversies attach to conventional constitutional issues involving the rule of law, interpretive approaches, judicial review, federalism, civil rights, indigenous rights, pluralism and/or competing rights? Would intersectional claims focused on race, ethnicity, gender, sexuality, religion, disability, age, and others, unite or divide women-dominated constitutional courts? Would their constitutional decisions comport with and promote feminist conceptions of justice?

As Baines (2017: 312) acknowledged, these questions are largely unanswerable—as we 'have no hypotheses, let alone answers, for the foregoing questions about all-women constitutional courts.' Yet we might draw some insights from what has taken place not in the realm of the imaginary, but the real-life High Court of Australia, which as we have examined, has reflected something close to parity in its gender composition. We might dismiss out of hand the very premise that an all-woman bench would end judicial patriarchy because, as we know, an almost-equal composition of men and women itself has not eliminated judicial patriarchy. Perhaps there is some kind of magic to be found in an all-woman bench? It would depend, of course, on who those women might be. And under what circumstances might an all-woman bench come to be constituted? Is such a state of affairs possible within our current political landscape?

An all-woman bench itself seems fantastical but even if one was constituted there is every chance it would still bear the hallmarks of a masculinist institution. Why? Because we might assume it would still be working with a constitutional framework that is deeply gendered (and raced and classed) in what it has valued and thus protected. This very notion is reminiscent of the probing question posed by Menkel-Meadow (1985: 49): 'what would our legal system look like if women had not been excluded from its creation?' As we see, we can never know the answer to this question. Nor can these institutions necessarily be remade in a way that escapes their masculinist origins. Yet, the process of 'letting women in' might chip away at these foundations and open up possibilities for transformation.

Returning from the imaginary to the present day, the visibility of women on the High Court bench, literally and figuratively, cast by the almost-equal gender balance, made an important symbolic statement about women's admission to legal authority in Australia. In this very key respect, the gender balance has made a difference. But was that difference only one of symbolism and access to authority? There were instances which showed the difference gender diversity can bring to bear in judicial decision-making. As I have argued in this book, that is not to assert that there is an inherent woman's judicial voice, but rather to acknowledge that legal decisions are imbued with understandings of gender and have gendered and gendering effects. The High Court did not see the disruptive disorderly arrival of women as imagined by some constructions of difference but instead saw historically high levels of consensus. Indeed, the fact that some constructions of the difference women might bring to adjudication have imagined the disorderly dissenting woman judge, whereas others have cast women as consensus-builders speaks to the dilemmas and contradictions of difference (and of the dangers of justifying women's access to legal authority only on the basis this purported difference). But this is not to say that we should not continue to agitate for women judges (or, more diversity amongst the judiciary generally), or seek to illuminate possibilities for gender-sensitive approaches to reimagine the law.

The notion that legal authority is the preserve of men has been particularly hard to dislodge as was evidenced by the need for Justice Crennan to set the record straight publicly about the contributions of the women on the Court. Perhaps less overtly, Chief Justice Kiefel's extra-curial comments about the institutional benefits of more collegiate approaches to judgment writing have also rebutted the notion that women have not contributed to the Court. The suggestion that collegial authorship practices indicated that women 'weren't pulling their weight' or 'weren't quite up to it' gives us some insight into the gendered ways in which judicial authority is constructed, legitimated and understood. That the legal profession was described as 'feminised' (Eades 2015) in the period shortly after Justice Crennan's retirement is itself reflective of the prevailing masculinist regime insofar as the arrival of women into what was once an exclusively masculine domain is recast as 'feminisation'. Accounts that emphasise 'feminisation' greatly overstate the extent to which women's entry into this masculine domain have been able to reshape the institution. The premature assertion that the legal profession has been 'feminised' is something with which feminist legal theorists have grappled for as long as women began to enter the profession in significant numbers (Sommerlad 1994; Mossman 2006). In part, much of this depends on how we understand the very concept of 'feminised'. Although it has sometimes been understood in terms of numerical participation, it has also been understood in more complex terms about whether so-called feminine qualities have been recognised and appreciated or, conversely, not by reference to stereotypical attributes but by whether a feminist influence might be discerned (Menkel-Meadow 1987). As has been demonstrated in this book (and elsewhere) a preoccupation with numbers does not tell the whole story.

Yet by any measure (whether numerical or in terms of how women have been received as legal knowers or the extent to which they have been able to disrupt the masculine status quo), the legal profession and indeed the High Court have not been 'feminised'. Granted, in terms of the most measurable marker—numerosity—women have entered the profession in significant numbers. Far from 'feminised', the profession continues to reflect the masculinist ethos of its foundations. In a way, it is less about whether the profession has been feminised but more about how entrenched masculinism is. Are women, as Thornton (1996: 3–4) put it almost a quarter of a century ago, still 'fringe dwellers in the jurisprudential community'? Or put another way, are women *really* legal persons yet? In the text of the law, we know that (white) women have been afforded this status (in most jurisdictions) in Australia for more than a century. The conditional nature of women's access to authority in Australia's constitutional framework (as seen in the gendered preoccupation with 'merit', the way in which women's legal authority is received, the unspoken notion that women will be appointed only if the masculine character of the office is undisturbed) suggests that women remain 'fringe dwellers in the jurisprudential community.'

Of course, that powerful visual imagery (of women as fringe dwellers in the legal community) is disrupted by the powerful imagery of a woman Chief Justice literally sitting at the centre of the High Court bench. Indeed, the ascension of Susan Kiefel to Chief Justice made an important symbolic statement about women's admission to legal authority in Australia. But what difference did it make to the gender dynamics of the Court? These matters came to the fore in the Chief Justice's response to historic sexual harassment allegations. As I argued in the previous chapter, that she wielded her power as Chief Justice in such a way—expressing her sympathy with the complainants, acknowledging difficulties they would have had in coming forward, emphasising that they had been believed and naming Dyson Heydon—she demonstrated the potential to disrupt the prevailing gender regime. Importantly, sexual harassment allegations were a powerful reminder about the historic gender dynamics on the Court and about the ongoing difficulties in entering (and transforming) masculine domains. These events have served as a reminder that history shapes the present. First, we see that women's exclusion from the profession is ongoing, despite the publicly celebrated gains. Women's admission had been vigorously denied and then only grudgingly accepted. Although formal rules now accept women, the gendered division of labour and men's continued dominance explains the conduct and it explains the lack of consequences. The law remains a hostile place for women. Second, it speaks to the gap between law and experience and the deficiency in the law's response to sexual harassment.

As we have seen, when an institution once occupied only by men admits women into its space, the existing gender relations and gender norms cannot remain unaffected. What then might be the lessons from the High Court of Australia? Although this book's analysis was confined to the High Court of Australia as a case study, the wider implications (or the 'lessons' so to speak) provide a frame of reference for (re)conceptualising the relationship between gender and judging, both individually and institutionally. This is because women judges' relationship with the law is a relationship that is shaped as much by the individual judge as by the institutional context in which they operate. Conceptualising courts (especially constitutional courts) as reflecting a particular gender regime, and interrogating the gender dynamics crafted by the arrival of almost-parity, opens the space for examination of the importance of diversity and the extent to which law and its institutions remain steeped in the masculinism of the past (and the present). We see that simply appointing women will not necessarily reshape this masculinist gender order but that is not to discount the possibility that this regime might be disrupted—*perhaps* through approaches to judging which are more gender sensitive but also in terms of reshaping institutional norms about what is appropriate (e.g. in terms sexual harassment), or a combination of both.

In law, given the weight of history in upholding certain power arrangements, gender norms do appear to be especially sticky. By identifying 'the gender foundations of taken-for-granted rules and practices' (Chappell and Waylen 2013: 603) underpinning the High Court, this book examined whether women judges make a difference—not necessarily in the sense that women might have a distinctive judicial voice, but rather in terms of disrupting the masculinist gender regime. It did so by examining a number of discrete aspects of this gender regime in the inter-related practices/rituals and cases in which key elements of an ongoing, fluid gender regime were seen in operation. The production and reproduction of the Court's symbols, beliefs and patterns of behaviour inform its gender regime. Indeed, identifying these rules and practices is part of the process of disrupting or challenging their taken-for-grantedness. The near-majority of women judges has had an impact and so too has a woman Chief Justice. Even when they were doing their best to accommodate the already existing traditions, rituals and practices of the High Court, the women were not necessarily 'just men in skirts,' though the dynamics within which they performed their tasks encouraged them to be just that.

Bibliography

Primary sources

Cases

Alphapharm Pty Ltd v H Lundbeck A/S (2014) 254 CLR 247
Apotex Pty Ltd v Sanofi-Aventis Australia Pty Ltd (2013) 253 CLR 284
Attorney-General (Vic) (Ex rel Dale) v Commonwealth (Pharmaceutical Benefits Case) (1945) 71 CLR 237
Australian Capital Television Pty Ltd v Commonwealth (No 2) (1992) 177 CLR 106
Bebb v Law Society [1914] 1 CH 286
Coleman v Power (2004) 220 CLR 1
Commissioner of Taxation v ANZ Savings Bank (1998) 194 CLR 328
David Grant & Co Pty Ltd v Westpac Banking Corporation (1995) 184 CLR 265
Director of Public Prosecutions v Morgan [1975] 2 ALL ER 347
Dowling v Dalgety [1992] FCA 35
Eastman v Director of Public Prosecutions (ACT) (2003) 214 CLR 31
Eatock v Bolt [2011] FCA 1103
Harriton v Stephens (2006) 226 CLR 52.
Hickson v Goodman Fielder (2009) 237 CLR 130
IceTV Pty Ltd v Nine Network Australia Pty Ltd (2009) 239 CLR 458
In re Edith Haynes (1904) 6 WAR 209, 214
Kendirjian v Lepore [2017] HCA 13 (29 March 2017)
Keramianakis v Regional Publishers Pty Ltd (2009) 237 CLR 268
Lange v Australian Broadcasting Corporation (1997) 189 CLR 520
Lockwood Security Products Pty Ltd v Doric Products Pty Ltd (No 2) (2007) 235 CLR 173
McCloy v New South Wales (2015) 257 CLR
Mills v Commissioner of Taxation (2012) 293 ALR 43
Monis v The Queen (2011) 215 A Crim R 64; 256 FLR 28
Monis v The Queen; Droudis v The Queen (2011) 256 FLR 28; [2011] NSWCCA 231
Monis v The Queen; Droudis v The Queen (2013) 249 CLR 92
Nationwide News Pty Ltd v Wills (1992) 177 CLR 1
Penney v R (1998) 155 ALR 605
PGA v The Queen (2012) 245 CLR 355
Queensland Nickel Pty Limited v Commonwealth of Australia [2015] HCA 12 (8 April 2015)
Queensland Premier Mines Pty Ltd v French (2007) 235 CLR 81

Re Minister for Immigration and Multicultural Affairs; Ex parte Meng Kok Te (2002) 212 CLR 162
R v Clarence (1888) 22 QBD 23
R v Clarke [1949] 2 ALL ER 448
R v Cogan [1976] QB 217
R v Howard [1965] 3 All ER 684
R v Johns, Supreme Court, SA No. SCCRM/91/452, (26 August 1992) (Bollen J)
R v L (1991) 174 CLR 379
R v Middendorp [2010] VSC 202
R v Monis; R v Droudis (2011) 12 DCLR (NSW) 266; [2011] NSWDC 39
R v P, GA (2010) 109 SASR 1
R v Pearson; Ex parte Sipka (1983) 152 CLR 254
R v Smithers; Ex parte Benson (1912) 16 CLR 99
Roadshow Films Pty Ltd v iiNet Ltd (2012) 248 CLR 42
Rowe v Electoral Commissioner (2010) 243 CLR 1
Smith v The Queen [2015] HCA 27 (5 August 2015)
Stephens v Western Australian Newspapers Ltd (1994) 182 CLR 211
SZOQQ v Minister for Immigration and Citizenship [2013] HCA 12
Theophanous v Herald & Weekly Times Limited (1994) 182 CLR 104
Williams v Commonwealth of Australia (No 1) (2012) 248 CLR 156
Williams v Commonwealth of Australia (No 2) (2014) 252 CLR 416
Wotton v State of Queensland (2012) 285 ALR 1
Wynbergen v Hoyts Corporation (1997) 149 ALR 25

Speeches and transcripts

Abbott, T. 2012. "Freedom Wars" An Address to the Institute of Public Affairs. Speech, 6 August. Sydney: news.com.au. http://resources.news.com.au/files/2012/08/06/1226443/820701-aus-na-file-abbott-speech.pdf. Consulted 13 January 2016.
Bell, V. 2009. Swearing-in of Justice Bell, Canberra [2009] HCATrans 4 (3 February).
Bell, V. 2018. By the Skin of Our Teeth—The Passing of the Women's Legal Status Act 1918, Francis Forbes Lecture, 30 May. https://cdn.hcourt.gov.au/assets/publications/speeches/current-justices/bellj/bellj30May2018.pdf. Consulted 20 January 2021.
Beazley. M. 2018a. 100 Years of Women in Law in NSW, Carroll & O'Dea Lawyers Sydney, 18 October. https://www.supremecourt.justice.nsw.gov.au/Documents/Publications/Speeches/2018%20Speeches/Beazley_20181018.pdf. Consulted 12 August 2020.
Bowyer, G. 2014. Transcript of Proceedings, Ceremonial—Farewell to Crennan J—Melbourne [2014] HCATrans 287 (12 December).
Brandis, G. 2015b. Ceremonial—Swearing in of Gordon J—Canberra [2015] HCA-Trans (9 June).
Brandis, G. 2015c. Ceremonial—Swearing-in of Nettle J—Canberra [2015] HCATrans 5 (3 February).
Brandis, G. 2017a. Ceremonial Sitting on the Occasion of the Swearing-in of the Chief Justice the Honourable Susan Mary Kiefel AC [2017] HCATrans 7 (30 January).
Brandis, G. 2017b. Ceremonial Sitting on the Occasion of the Swearing in of Edelman J [2017] HCATrans (30 January).

Catanzariti, J. 2013. Transcript of Proceedings, Swearing-in of Keane J, Canberra [2013] HCATrans 40 (5 March).

Corcoran, J. 2009. Swearing-in of Justice Bell, Canberra [2009] HCATrans 4 (3 February).

Crennan, S. 2005. Transcript of Proceedings, Crennan J—Swearing-in, Canberra [2005] HCATrans 895 (8 November).

Crennan, S. 2014a. Foley's List Event: "Celebration of Women in the Law". Speech, 16 April. Melbourne: High Court of Australia. http://www.hcourt.gov.au/assets/publications/speeches/current-justices/crennanj/Celebration_of_Women_in_the_Law_-_16-04-2014.pdf. Consulted 4 December 2015.

Crennan, S. 2014b. Transcript of Proceedings, Ceremonial—Farewell to Crennan J—Sydney [2014] HCATrans 258 (14 November).

Crennan, S. 2014c. Transcript of Proceedings, Ceremonial—Farewell to Crennan J—Melbourne [2014] HCATrans 287 (12 December).

Bell, J. 2017. Examining the Judge: Launch of Issue 40(2) UNSW Law Journal, Sydney. University of New South Wales (29 May). https://cdn.hcourt.gov.au/assets/publications/speeches/current-justices/bellj/bellj29May2017.pdf. Consulted 9 September 2020.

Dawson, D. 1997. Ceremonial Sitting—Farewell to the Honourable Sir Daryl Dawson AC KBE, Sydney [1997] HCATrans 265 (25 August).

Dixon, O. 1952. Swearing In of Sir Owen Dixon as Chief Justice (1952) 85 CLR xi at xvi.

Dreyfus, M. 2013. Transcript of Proceedings, Swearing-in of Keane J—Canberra [2013] HCATrans 40 (5 March).

Eades, J. 2015. Transcript of Proceedings, Ceremonial—Farewell to Hayne J—Sydney [2015] HCATrans 90 (17 April).

Edelman, J. 2017. Ceremonial Sitting on the Occasion of the Swearing in of Edelman J [2017] HCATrans (30 January).

Fraser, H. 2007. *Transcript of Proceedings*, Swearing-in of Kiefel J Canberra [2007] HCATrans 493 (3 September).

French, R. 2008. *Transcript of Proceedings*, Swearing-In of Chief Justice, the Hon R.S. French, Canberra [2008] HCATrans 318 (1 September).

French, R. 2015a. Ceremonial—Announcement of Appointment of Senior Counsel [2015] HCATrans 4 (2 February).

French, R. 2015b. Ceremonial—Farewell to Hayne J—Canberra [2015] HCATrans 105 (13 May).

French, R. 2015c. Ceremonial—Sitting in Memory of the Late the Honourable John Leslie Toohey AC—Perth [2015] HCATrans 182 (10 August).

French, R. 2015d. Ceremonial Sitting in Memory of the Late the Honourable Sir Kenneth Jacobs KBE QC, Canberra [2015] HCATrans 258 (13 October).

Fullerton, E. 2007. Swearing in Ceremony of the Honourable Elizabeth Fullerton SC. Swearing-in speech, 19 February. Sydney: Supreme Court of New South Wales. http://www.supremecourt.justice.nsw.gov.au/Documents/fullerton_2007.02.19.pdf. Consulted 10 July 2015.

Gageler, S. 2012. Transcript of Proceedings, Swearing-in of Gageler J, Canberra [2012] HCATrans 258 (9 October).

Gaudron, M. 1997. Australian Women Lawyers. Speech, 19 September. Melbourne: High Court of Australia. http://www.hcourt.gov.au/assets/publications/speeches/former-justices/gaudronj/gaudronj_wlasp.htm. Consulted 14 January 2016.

Gaudron, M. 2000. Speech to Launch 'Corporate Women, Children, Careers and Workplace Culture: The Integration of Flexible Work Practices into the Legal and Finance Professions'. Speech, 14 July. Sydney: NSW Parliament House.

Gaudron, M. 2002. Ceremonial—Remarks of Final Sitting of Gaudron J—Sydney S00/2002 [2002] HCATrans 636 (13 December).

Gillard, J. 2003. Winning the Culture War. Speech to the Sydney Institute, 11 March. Sydney: Parlinfo. http://parlinfo.aph.gov.au/parlInfo/search/display/display.w3p;orderBy=customrank;page=0;query=winning the culture war;rec=0;resCount=Default. Consulted 12 December 2015.

Gleeson, M. 1998. Transcript of Proceedings, Swearing-In of the Chief Justice, The Honourable Anthony Murray Gleeson, AC C00/1998 [1998] HCATrans 192 (22 May).

Gleeson, M. 2005a. Ceremonial—Sitting in Memory of the Right Honourable Sir Harry Gibbs, Canberra [2005] HCATrans 475 (3 August).

Gleeson, M. 2005b. Ceremonial—Sitting in Memory of the Late Sir Ronald Wilson, Perth [2005] HCATrans 873 (25 October).

Gleeson, J. 2014. Transcript of Proceedings, Ceremonial—Farewell to Crennan J—Sydney [2014] HCATrans 258 (14 November).

Gordon, M. 2015. Ceremonial—Swearing in of Gordon J—Canberra [2015] HCA-Trans (9 June).

Hayne, K. 1997. Transcript of Proceedings, Swearing in Ceremony, Hayne J, Canberra [1997] HCATrans 294 (22 September).

Hayne, K. 2015. Ceremonial—Farewell to Hayne J—Melbourne [2015] HCATrans 115 (15 May).

Howard, M. 2017. Ceremonial Sitting on the Occasion of the Swearing in of Edelman J [2017] HCATrans (30 January).

Hughes, C. 2017. Ceremonial Sitting on the Occasion of the Swearing-in of the Chief Justice the Honourable Susan Mary Kiefel AC [2017] HCATrans 7 (30 January).

Hughes, T. 2002. Ceremonial—Remarks of Final Sitting of Gaudron J—Sydney S00/2002 [2002] HCATrans 636 (13 December).

Katzmann, A. 2009. Swearing-in of Justice Bell, Canberra [2009] HCATrans 4 (3 February).

Keane, P. 2013. Transcript of Proceedings, Swearing-in of Keane J, Canberra [2013] HCATrans 40 (5 March).

Keane. P. 2014. The Idea of the Professional Judge: The Challengers of Communication. Speech to the Judicial Conference of Australia Colloquium, Noosa, 11 October. https://cdn.hcourt.gov.au/assets/publications/speeches/current-justices/keanej/The_Idea_of_the_Professional_Judge_-_JCA_Colloquium_Noosa_October_2014_-_Justice_P_A_Keane.pdf. Consulted January 2020.

Kiefel, S. 2007. Transcript of Proceedings, Swearing-in of Kiefel J, Canberra [2007] HCATrans 493 (3 September).

Kiefel, S. 2014. The Individual Judge. Speech delivered at the 2014 Sir Richard Blackburn Lecture, 13 May. Canberra: ACT Law Society. https://www.actlawsociety.asn.au/documents/item/944. Consulted 26 August 2015.

Kiefel, S. 2017a. Ceremonial Sitting on the Occasion of the Swearing-in of the Chief Justice the Honourable Susan Mary Kiefel AC [2017] HCATrans 7 (30 January).

Kiefel, S. 2017b. "Judicial Methods in the 21st Century". Supreme Court Oration, Banco Court 16 March. https://cdn.hcourt.gov.au/assets/publications/speeches/current-justices/kiefelj/KiefelCJ16Mar2017.pdf. Consulted 20 January 2021.

Kiefel, S. 2018. "Women in the Australian Legal Profession: Progress and a Public Voice", International Women's Day, Kuala Lumpur, 8 March. https://cdn.hcourt.gov.au/assets/publications/speeches/current-justices/kiefelj/KiefelCJ8March2018.pdf. Consulted 15 August 2020.

Kiefel, S. 2020. Statement by the Hon Susan Kiefel, AC Chief Justice of Australia, Chambers of the Chief Justice, High Court of Australia. 22 June. https://cdn.hcourt.gov.au/assets/news/Statement%20by%20Chief%20Justice%20Susan%20Kiefel%20AC.pdf. Consulted 20 January 2021.

Kirby, M. 1996. Transcript of Proceedings, Swearing-in Ceremony, Kirby J, Canberra [1996] HCATrans 24 (6 February).

Kirby, M. 2003. "Women in Law—Doldrums or Progress?" Speech to Women Lawyers of Western Australia, 22 October. Perth: High Court of Australia. http://www.highcourt.gov.au/speeches/kirbyj/kirbyj_22oct.html. Consulted 18 April 2011.

Lavarch, M. 1995. Ceremonial Sitting—Retirement of Chief Justice Mason, C00/1995 [1995] HCATrans 110 (20 April).

McClelland, R. 2008c. Transcript of Proceedings, Swearing-in of Chief Justice, the Hon R.S. French, Canberra [2008] HCATrans 318 (1 September).

McClelland, R. 2008d. Judicial Appointments Forum. Speech delivered at the Bar Association Annual Conference, 17 February. Gold Coast: NSW Bar Association. http://www.nswbar.asn.au/circulars/agspeech_180208.pdf. Consulted 29 November 2015.

McClelland, R. 2008e. Ceremonial—Retirement of Chief Justice the Hon A.M. Gleeson, AC, Canberra [2008] HCATrans 317 (29 August).

McClelland, R. 2009. Swearing-in of Justice Bell, Canberra [2009] HCATrans 4 (3 February).

McHugh, M. 2005. "Working as a High Court Judge". Speech, 17 August. Newcastle: Women Lawyers Association of New South Wales and the Law Society of Newcastle. http://www.womenlawyersnsw.org.au/FileUpload/WORKING_AS_A_HIGH_COURT_JUSTICE.pdf. Consulted 11 June 2011.

McLachlin, B. 2016. "Canada's Legal System at 150: Democracy and the Judiciary". Speech 3 June, Empire Club of Canada Toronto Ontario. https://www.scc-csc.ca/judges-juges/spe-dis/bm-2016-06-03-eng.aspx. Consulted 9 December 2020.

McLeod, F. 2017. Ceremonial Sitting on the Occasion of the Swearing-in of the Chief Justice the Honourable Susan Mary Kiefel AC [2017] HCATrans 7 (30 January).

McMillan, K. 2005. Transcript of Proceedings, Crennan J—Swearing-in, Canberra [2005] HCATrans 895 (8 November).

Needham, J. 2014. Transcript of Proceedings, Ceremonial—Farewell to Crennan J—Sydney [2014] HCATrans 258 (14 November).

Peters, J. 2014. Transcript of Proceedings, Ceremonial—Farewell to Crennan J—Melbourne [2014] HCATrans 287 (12 December).

Peters, J. 2015. Ceremonial—Swearing in of Gordon J—Canberra [2015] HCATrans (9 June).

Roxon, N. 2012c. Transcript of Proceedings, Swearing-in of Gageler J, Canberra [2012] HCATrans 258 (9 October).

Ruddock, P. 2005b. Transcript of Proceedings, Crennan J—Swearing-in, Canberra [2005] HCATrans 895 (8 November).

Williams, D. 1997. Transcript of Proceedings, Swearing in Ceremony, Hayne J, Canberra [1997] HCATrans 294 (22 September).

Legislation

Broadcasting Act 1942 (Cth)
Commonwealth Constitution Act 1900 (Imp)
Commonwealth Franchise Act 1902 (Cth)
Criminal Code 1924 (Tas)
Criminal Code 1995 (Cth)
Criminal Law Consolidation Act 1935 (SA)
Criminal Law Consolidation (Abolition of Time Limit for Prosecution of Certain Sexual Offences) Amendment Act 2003 (SA)
Election Funding, Expenditure and Disclosures Act 1981 (NSW)
Female Law Practitioners Act 1911 (SA)
High Court of Australia Act 1979 (Cth)
Industrial Relations Act 1988 (Cth)
Judiciary Act 1903 (Cth)
Law Reform (Miscellaneous Provisions) Act 1965 (NSW)
Legal Practitioners Act 1893 (WA)
Legal Practitioners Act 1905 (Qld)
Married Women's Property Act 1882 (SA)
Matrimonial Causes Amendment Act 1919 (Tas)
Practitioners Act 1904 (Tas)
Racial Discrimination Act 1975 (Cth)
Sex Discrimination Act 1984 (Cth)
Sex Disqualification (Removal) Act 1919 (UK)
Women's Legal Status Act 1923 (WA)
Women's Legal Status Act 1918 (NSW)
Workers Compensation Act 1987 (NSW)

Newspapers and other media sources

ABC News Online. 2014. "Geoffrey Nettle appointed to replace Susan Crennan as justice of High Court". *ABC News Online*. 4 December. https://www.abc.net.au/news/2014-12-04/geoffrey-nettle-appointed-justice-of-high-court/5940408.

Anon. 2020. "The cancellation of Mr Heydon." *Spectator* 4 July. https://www.spectator.com.au/2020/07/the-cancellation-of-mr-heydon/.

Ackland, R. 2002. "Same gender, same city, same university, same club … now the same court". *Sydney Morning Herald* 20 December: 15.

Akerman, P. 2005. "Left alone: A woman who courted no one". *The Daily Telegraph* 22 September. http://newsgroups.derkeiler.com/Archive/Soc/soc.men/2005-09/msg01024.html. Consulted 14 June 2011.

Albrechtsen, J. 2007. "May the best person preside". *The Australian* 14 August: 14.

Albrechtsen, J. 2008. "The High Court is no place for gender politics". *The Australian* 1 December. http://www.theaustralian.com.au/news/opinion/no-place-for-gender-politics/story-e6frg7bo-1111118333562. Consulted 13 June 2011.

Appleby, G. et al. 2020. "Deep cultural shifts required: Open letter from 500 legal women calls for reform of way judges are appointed and disciplined". *The Conversation* 6 July. https://theconversation.com/deep-cultural-shifts-required-open-letter-from-500-legal-women-calls-for-reform-of-way-judges-are-appointed-and-disciplined-142042. Consulted 7 July 2020.

Baird, J. 2013. "In Australia, misogyny lives on". *New York Times*. 5 July. https://www.nytimes.com/2013/07/06/opinion/in-australia-misogyny-lives-on.html. Consulted 26 July 2020.

Bornstein, J. 2020. "Damning investigation upholds sexual harassment complaints against former High Court Judge Dyson Heydon". Maurice Blackburn Lawyers Media Statement 22 June. https://www.mauriceblackburn.com.au/about/media-centre/media-statements/2020/investigation-upholds-sexual-harassment-complaints-high-court-judge-dyson-heydon/. Consulted 30 June 2020.

Coade, M. 2016. "From Legal Secretary to Chief Justice". *Lawyers Weekly*. https://www.lawyersweekly.com.au/corporate-counsel/20124-from-legal-secretary-to-high-court-chief-justice.

Crabb, A. 2003. "Under horsehair, they lauded Heydon". *The Age* 12 February: 8.

Donald, P. 2002. "No gender considerations in High Court Appointment". PM ABC Radio Transcript 18 December. https://www.abc.net.au/pm/stories/s750021.htm.

Eastman, K. 2020. "Natural justice is a golden rule of investigations. Has it been followed in the Heydon case?" *The Guardian*. https://www.theguardian.com/commentisfree/2020/jun/24/natural-justice-is-a-golden-rule-of-investigations-has-it-been-followed-in-the-dyson-heydon-case. Consulted 25 July 2020.

Editorial. 2016. "Susan Kiefel is a worthy and inspirational Chief Justice". *Sydney Morning Herald*, 30 November 2016. http://www.smh.com.au/comment/smh-editorial/susan-kiefel-worthy-and-inspirational-chief-justice-20161128-gszn78.html. Consulted 5 December 2016.

Enloe, C. 2018. "Patriarchy is bigger than Donald Trump: International Political Studies Association Plenary". *Broad Agenda* 6 August 2018. https://www.broadagenda.com.au/2018/patriarchy-is-bigger-than-donald-trump-plenary-by-cynthia-enloe/. Consulted 5 December 2020.

Filipovic, J. 2012. "Justice Ginsburg's distant dream of an all-female supreme court". *The Guardian* 1 December 2012. http://www.theguardian.com/commentisfree/2012/nov/30/justice-ginsburg-all-female-supreme-court. Consulted 10 January 2016.

Foden, B. 2020. "Dyson Heydon sexual harassment: Women plan to sue for compensation after allegations upheld". *Canberra Times* 23 June. https://www.canberratimes.com.au/story/6802907/women-plan-to-sue-heydon-after-investigation-upholds-sexual-harassment-allegations/. Consulted 15 December 2020.

Gans, J. 2014. "News: 'Geoffrey Nettle's surprise appointment'". Opinions on High Melbourne Law School Blog. 4 December. https://blogs.unimelb.edu.au/opinionsonhigh/2014/12/04/news-justice-geoffrey-nettles-surprise-appointment/.

Gaze, B. 2002. "Letters to the Editor". *The Age* 19 December. http://www.theage.com.au/articles/2002/12/19/1040174343712.html. Consulted 1 September 2011.

Gronow, M. 2002. "Letters to the Editor". *The Age* 19 December. http://www.theage.com.au/articles/2002/12/19/1040174343712.html. Consulted 1 September 2011.

Hale, B. 2003. "Welcome to white men's club". *The Guardian* 30 October. https://www.theguardian.com/world/2003/oct/30/gender.uk. Consulted November 2020.

Irving, H. 2013. "Constitutional interpretation: A woman's voice?" A Woman's Constitution. Blog, 20 March. Sydney: University of Sydney. http://blogs.usyd.edu.au/womansconstitution/2013/03/constitutional_interpretation_1.html. Consulted 12 July 2014.

Kelly, F. 2020a. Sex Discrimination Commissioner on allegations in Australia's highest court. Radio National Breakfast with Fran Kelly, June 23. https://www.abc.net.au/radionational/programs/breakfast/sex-discrimination-commissioner-on-allegations-in/12383054. Consulted 9 August 2020.

Kelly, F. 2020b. Former Family Court Chief Justice reveals own experience of sexual harassment in workplace. Radio National Breakfast with Fran Kelly, 24 June. https://www.abc.net.au/radionational/programs/breakfast/former-family-court-chief-justice-reveals-own-experience/12386738. Consulted 9 August 2020.

Lee, J. 2014. "Court of Appeal Judge Geoffrey Nettle appointed to the High Court". *Sydney Morning Herald*. 4 December. https://www.smh.com.au/national/court-of-appeal-judge-geoffrey-nettle-appointed-to-the-high-court-20141204-120e65.html.

MacKinnon, C. 2018. "#MeToo has done what the law could not". *New York Times* 4 February. https://www.nytimes.com/2018/02/04/opinion/metoo-law-legal-system.html. Consulted 9 August 2020.

Maley, J., and McClymont, K. 2020. "Dyson's dirty deeds: The public v private face of 'sexual harrasser'". *Sydney Morning Herald* 27 June. https://www.smh.com.au/politics/federal/dyson-s-dirty-deeds-the-public-v-private-face-of-sexual-harasser-20200626-p556i9.html. Consulted 5 November 2020.

McClymont, K. and Maley, J. 2020. "Two High Court Judges 'knew of complaints against Heydon'". *Sydney Morning Herald* 25 June. https://www.smh.com.au/national/two-high-court-judges-knew-of-complaints-against-dyson-heydon-20200624-p555pd.html. Consulted 5 November 2020.

McLoughlin, K. 2015c. "Two-for-one: A good new High Judge and woman to boot". *The Conversation* 15 April. https://theconversation.com/two-for-one-a-good-new-high-court-judge-and-a-woman-to-boot-40217. Consulted 13 January 2016.

McLoughlin, K. 2020. "Meet Australia's new High Court judges: A legal scholar's take on the Morrison government's appointees". *The Conversation* 28 October. https://theconversation.com/meet-australias-new-high-court-judges-a-legal-scholars-take-on-the-morrison-governments-appointees-148982. Consulted 11 December 2020.

Merritt, C. 2013. "Roxon Appointments were her saving grace". *The Australian* 8 February. http://www.theaustralian.com.au/opinion/roxon-appointments-were-her-saving-grace/story-e6frg6zo-1226573041797. Consulted 8 December 2015.

Nelson, F. 2015. "Do we need quotas for female judges?" *Lawyers Weekly* 27 April. http://www.lawyersweekly.com.au/news/16435-do-we-need-quotas-for-female-judges. Consulted 12 January 2016.

New York Times. 2016. "Transcript Donald Trump's taped comments about women". *New York Times* 8 October. https://www.nytimes.com/2016/10/08/us/donald-trump-tape-transcript.html. Consulted 11 August 2020.

Patrick, A. 2017. "Conservatives look for free speech ally in new High Court chief Justice Susan Kiefel". *Australian Financial Review* 10 January. http://www.afr.com/business/legal/conservatives-look-for-free-speech-ally-in-new-high-court-chief-justice-susan-kiefel-20161213-gtafa9. Consulted 12 January 2017.

Pelly, M. 2005. "Ex-teacher, legal dynamo and, oh yes, a woman: Welcome to the High Court". *Sydney Morning Herald* 21 September. http://www.smh.com.au/news/national/exteacher-legal-dynamo-and-oh-yes-a-woman-welcome-to-the-highcourt/2005/09/20/1126982062304.html. Consulted 13 June 2011.

Pelly, M. 2007. "Third time's a charm". *The Australian* 14 August: 11.

Pelly, M. 2008. "High Court hopefuls led through judicial pageant". *The Australian* 17 June: 31–32.

Pelly, M. 2009. "Bell gets tick of approval". *The Australian* 20 March: 27.

Pelly, M. 2015. "Susan Crennan leaves the High Court with a team player reputation". *The Australian* 6 February. http://www.theaustralian.com.au/business/legal-affairs/susan-crennan-leaves-high-court-with-a-team-player-reputation/news-story/97b1fa773eadc839da8acda8054b0127. Consulted 8 December 2015.

Pelly. M. 2020. "Women at the bar are just exhausted dealing with this". *Australian Financial Review* 24 June. https://www.afr.com/politics/women-set-to-change-culture-of-sexual-harassment-in-legal-20200622-p5554p. Consulted 8 November 2020.

Roberts, H. 2017. "Ceremony matters: The lasting significance of the swearing-in ceremony of Chief Justice Susan Kiefel". AUSPUBLAW blog, 9 February. https://auspublaw.org/2017/02/ceremony-matters/. Consulted 4 August 2020.

Rubenstein, K. 2002. "In High Court selection, like promotes like". *Australian Politics* 20 December. http://www.australianpolitics.com/words/daily/archives/00000137.shtml. Consulted 1 September 2011.

Rubenstein, K. 2014a. "Rethink needed as new High Court Justice appointment seems to maintain gender imbalance". *Canberra Times* 12 December. <http://www.canberratimes.com.au/comment/rethink-needed-as-new-high-court-justice-appointment-seems-to-maintain-gender-imbalance-20141210-1243jo.html. Consulted 9 December 2015.

Rubenstein, K. 2020. "Time's up for old boys' club on the High Court". *Financial Review* 11 August. https://www.afr.com/policy/economy/time-s-up-for-old-boys-club-on-the-high-court-20200811-p55khh. Consulted 12 August 2020.

Saville, M. 2020. "Questions of probity: was 'Dirty' Dyson biased against women?" *Crikey*, June 23. https://www.crikey.com.au/2020/06/23/was-high-court-justice-dyson-heydon-biased/. Consulted 20 July 2020.

Shiel, F. 2005. "Bench pressure should suit court's new face". *The Age* 24 September. http://www.theage.com.au/news/general/bench-pressure-should-suit-courts-new-face/2005/09/23/1126982231914.html. Consulted 5 September 2011.

Spry, I.C.F. 2004. "Affirmative action for judges". *National Observer* 59. http://www.nationalobserver.net/2004_summer_legal1.htm. Consulted 30 May 2011.

Steketee, M. 1986. "Gaudron not a token, Hawke says". *Sydney Morning Herald* 10 December: 3.

Wallace. C. 2018. "'A woman problem'? No, the Liberals have a 'man problem' and they need to fix it". *The Conversation* 30 August. https://theconversation.com/a-woman-problem-no-the-liberals-have-a-man-problem-and-they-need-to-fix-it-102339. Consulted 1 November 2020.

Walsh, K. 2016. "High Court judge Susan Kiefel favourite to replace chief justice Robert French". *Australian Financial Review* 27 October 2016. https://www.afr.com/companies/professional-services/high-court-judge-susan-kiefel-favourite-to-replace-chief-justice-robert-french-20161027-gsbncs. Consulted 1 November 2016.

Walsh, K. and Papadakis, M. 2015. "The 'feminisation' of law up for debate". *Australian Financial Review* 21 May. http://www.afr.com/business/legal/the-feminisation-of-law-up-for-debate-20150423-1mrmmw. Consulted 12 January 2016.

Waterford, J. 2012. "Judges rest their writing hands". *Canberra Times* 7 April. http://www.canberratimes.com.au/federal-politics/judges-rest-their-writing-hands-20120406-1wgbl.html. Consulted 9 December 2015.

Whitbourn, M. and McIlroy, T. 2016. "High Court judge favourite to land chief justice role". *Sydney Morning Herald* 28 October. https://www.smh.com.au/politics/federal/high-court-judge-susan-kiefel-favourite-to-land-chief-justice-role-20161026-gsb3oy.html. Consulted 1 November 2016.

Zifcak, S. 2013. "Justices split on gender lines over tenor of cleric's letters". *The Australian* 15 March. http://www.theaustralian.com.au/business/legal-affairs/justices-split-on-gender-lines-over-tenor-of-clerics-letters/story-e6frg97x-1226597684532. Consulted 8 December 2015.

Parliamentary papers, debates and media releases

Barlin, L.M. ed. 1997. *House of Representatives Practice*, 3rd edition. Canberra: Australian Government Publishing Service.

Brandis, G. 2015a. "Appointment of the Hon Michelle Gordon to the High Court of Australia". Media release, 14 April. Attorney-General for Australia. http://www.attorneygeneral.gov.au/Mediareleases/Pages/2015/SecondQuarter/14-April-2015-Appointment-of-the-Honourable-Michelle-Gordon-to-the-High-Court-of-Australia.aspx. Consulted 26 August 2015.

Brandis. G. 2016. "Appointment of the Hon Susan Kiefel to Chief Justice of the High Court". Joint Press Conference with the Prime Minister, 29 November. https://pmtranscripts.pmc.gov.au/release/transcript-40621. Consulted 1 October 2020.

Commonwealth Parliament of Australia [Hansard]. 2012. *House of Representatives Parliamentary Debates*, official Hansard, 9 October, column 11581.

McCann, J. 2013. "Electoral quotas for women: An international overview". Research Paper. Canberra: Parliamentary Library. http://parlinfo.aph.gov.au/parlInfo/download/library/prspub/2840598/upload_binary/2840598.pdf;fileType=application/pdf. Consulted 12 January 2016.

McClelland, R. 2008a. Joint press conference with Attorney General, Robert McClelland, Prime Ministers Courtyard, Parliament House. Joint media release. 30 July. Parliament of Australia. http://parlinfo.aph.gov.au/parlInfo/download/media/pressrel/XL5R6/upload_binary/xl5r60.pdf;fileType=application%2Fpdf#search=%22Mcclelland%202008%20High%20court%20appointment%22. Consulted 17 June 2011.

McClelland, R. 2008b. "New Justice of the High Court (Justice Virginia Bell)". Statement, 15 December. Canberra: Parliament of Australia. http://parlinfo.aph.gov.au/parlInfo/download/media/pressrel/KNDS6/upload_binary/knds60.pdf;fileType=application%2Fpdf#search=%22Mcclelland%202008%20High%20court%20appointment%20media%202000s%202008%2012%2015%22. Consulted 17 June 2011.

New South Wales, Legislative Assembly, Parliamentary Debates (Hansard), 5 December 1918, at 3470 (The Hon J Lane Mullins).

New South Wales, Legislative Assembly, Parliamentary Debates (Hansard), 5 December 1918, at 3464 (the Hon Dr Nash).

Roxon, N. 2005. "Labor welcomes the appointment of Justice Crennan to the High Court". Media release, 20 September. Parliament of Australia. http://parlinfo.aph.gov.au/parlInfo/download/media/pressrel/AQCH6/upload_binary/aqch61.pdf;fileType=application%2Fpdf#search=%22roxon%20labor%20welcomes%20crennan%22. Consulted 15 June 2011.

Roxon, N. 2012a. "New Justice of the High Court of Australia (Justice Stephen Gageler)". Media release, 12 August. Parliament of Australia. http://parlinfo.aph.gov.

au/parlInfo/download/media/pressrel/1864976/upload_binary/1864976.pdf;fileType=application%2Fpdf#search=%22roxon%202012%20new%20justice%22. Consulted 12 July 2015.

Roxon, N. 2012b. "New High Court Justice and Federal Court Chief Justice (Justice Patrick Keane and Chief Justice James Allsop)". Media release, 20 November. Parliament of Australia. http://parlinfo.aph.gov.au/parlInfo/download/media/pressrel/2056989/upload_binary/2056989.pdf;fileType=application%2Fpdf#search=%22roxon%202012%20chief%20justice%22. Consulted 15 July 2015.

Ruddock, P. 2005a. "High Court Appointment; naming of Court building". Press conference transcript, 20 September. Melbourne: Commonwealth Parliamentary Offices. http://parlinfo.aph.gov.au/parlInfo/download/media/pressrel/TQCH6/upload_binary/tqch61.pdf;fileType=application%2Fpdf#search=%22ruddock%202005%20media%20pressrel%20court%20building%202000s%202005%2009%22. Consulted 17 June 2011.

Ruddock, P. 2007. "Justice Kiefel appointed to High Court". Media release, 13 August. Prime Minister's Office, Blue Room, Canberra. http://parlinfo.aph.gov.au/parlInfo/download/media/pressrel/1DYN6/upload_binary/1dyn61.pdf;fileType=application%2Fpdf#search=%22ruddock%202007%20media%20pressrel%202000s%202007%2008%2013%22. Consulted 10 May 2011.

SSCL&CA [Senate Standing Committee on Legal and Constitutional Affairs]. 1994. *Gender Bias and the Judiciary*. Canberra: Senate Printing Unit, Parliament House.

SSCL&CA [Senate Standing Committee on Legal and Constitutional Affairs]. 2009. *Australia's Judicial System and the Role of Judges*. Canberra: Senate Printing Unit, Parliament House.

Turnbull, M. 2016. Appointment of the Hon Susan Kiefel to Chief Justice of the High Court. Joint Press Conference with the Attorney-General, 29 November. https://pmtranscripts.pmc.gov.au/release/transcript-40621. Consulted 1 October 2020.

Other online resources

Australian Human Rights Commission. 2020. *Respect@Work: Sexual Harassment National Inquiry Report*, March 2020. https://humanrights.gov.au/our-work/sex-discrimination/publications/respectwork-sexual-harassment-national-inquiry-report-2020. Consulted 13 October 2020.

Australian Institute of Judicial Administration Statistics. http://www.aija.org.au/online/JudgesMagistrates.pdf. Consulted 5 December 2020.

Gooda, M. 2011. *Constitutional Reform: Creating a Nation for All of Us*. Aboriginal and Torres Strait Islander Social Justice Commissioner. Australian Human Rights Commission. https://humanrights.gov.au/sites/default/files/content/constitution/reform/constitutional_reform2011.pdf. Consulted 10 July 2020.

Law Council of Australia. 2019. Submission to Australian Human Rights Commission National Inquiry into Sexual Harassment in Australian Workplaces, February 2019. ttps://www.lawcouncil.asn.au/publicassets/1bde0b80-d23e-e911-93fc-005056be13b5/3587%20-%20AHRC%20NISHAW%20Submission.pdf. Consulted 18 December 2020.

OECD [Organisation for Economic Co-operation and Development]. 2015. *Government at a Glance 2015*. Paris: OECD Publishing. http://dx.doi.org/10.1787/gov_glance-2015-en. Consulted 8 January 2016.

OECD [Organisation for Economic Co-operation and Development]. 2019. *Government at a Glance 2019.* Paris: OECD Publishing. https://www.oecd.org/gov/gov-at-a-glance-2019-australia.pdf.

The International Bar Association. 2019. *Us Too: Bullying and Sexual Harassment in the Legal Profession.* Report, May 2019. https://www.ibanet.org/bullying-and-sexual-harassment.aspx. Consulted 13 October 2020.

The Trailblazing Women and the Law Project (ARC Linkage LP120200367). http://www.tbwl.esrc.unimelb.edu.au. Consulted 8 January 2016.

Secondary sources

Anderson, B. 1991. *Imagined Communities: Reflections on the Origins and Spread of Nationalism.* Revised edition. London: Verso.

Appleby, G. and Naffine, N. 2015. Civility, gender and the law: Critical reflections on the judgments in *Monis v the Queen. Griffith Law Review* 24(4): 616–639.

Auchmuty, R. 2011. Whatever happened to Miss Bebb? *Bebb v The Law Society* and women's legal history. *Legal Studies* 31(2): 199–230.

Augustine, R. 1990–1991. Marriage: The safe haven for rapists. *Journal of Family Law* 29: 559–590.

Ayres, P. 2003. *Owen Dixon.* Melbourne: Miegunyah Press.

Bacchi, C. 1998. "Changing the sexual harassment agenda". In M. Gatens and A. Mackinnon (eds), *Gender and Institutions: Welfare, Work and Citizenship.* Cambridge: Cambridge University Press, pp. 75–89.

Bacchi, C. and Jose, J. 1994. Dealing with sexual harassment: Persuade, discipline, or punish? *Australian Journal of Law and Society* 10: 1–14.

Backhouse, C. 2003. The chilly climate for women judges: Reflections on the backlash from the Ewanchuk case. *Canadian Journal of Women and the Law* 15(1): 167–193.

Bader Ginsburg, R. 1990. Remarks on writing separately. *Washington Law Review* 65: 133–150.

Baines, B. 2013. "Must feminist judges self-identify as feminists?" In U. Schultz and G. Shaw (eds), *Gender and Judging.* Oxford: Hart Publishing.

Baines, B. 2017. "Women judges on constitutional courts: Why not nine women". In H. Irving (ed.), *Constitutions and Gender.* Cheltenham: Edward Elgar Publishing.

Batrouney, J. 2004. The contribution that the Hon Mary Gaudron QC has made to women and the law. *Public Law Review* 15: 339–344.

Bauer, G. and Dawuni, J. (eds). 2018. *Gender and the Judiciary in Africa. From Obscurity to Parity?* New York: Routledge.

Beard, M. 2017. *Women and Power: A Manifesto.* London: Profile Books.

Beazley, M. 2018b. 100 years women in the law. *Judicial Officer's Bulletin* 30(11): 105–108.

Belleau, M. and Johnson, R. 2008. Judging gender: difference and dissent at the Supreme Court of Canada. *International Journal of the Legal Profession* 15(1–2): 57–71.

Berns, S. 1999. *To Speak as a Judge: Difference, Voice and Power.* Dartmouth: Ashgate.

Biegel, S. 2010. *The Right to Be Out: Sexual Orientation and Gender Identity in America's Public Schools.* Minneapolis, MN: University of Minnesota Press.

Blackshield, A. 2000. "The appointment and removal of Federal Judges". In B. Opeskin and F. Wheeler (eds), *The Australian Federal Judicial System.* Melbourne: Melbourne University Press.

Blackshield, A. and Williams, G. 2010. *Australian Constitutional Law and Theory*, 5th edition. Sydney: The Federation Press.
Bourdieu, P. [1972; 2002]. *Outline of a Theory of Practice*. R. Nice, trans. Cambridge: Cambridge University Press.
Brenner, H. and Knake, R. 2012. Rethinking gender equality in the legal profession's pipeline to power: A study on media coverage of Supreme Court nominees. *Temple Law Review* 84: 325–384.
Brown, W. 1988. *Manhood and Politics: A Feminist Reading in Political Theory*. Totowa, NJ: Rowman & Littlefield.
Brownmiller, S. 1975. *Against Our Will: Men Women and Rape*. New York: Simon & Schuster.
Burton, C. 1988. *Redefining Merit*, Affirmative Action Agency, Monograph No 2. Sydney: Ambassador Press.
Burton, P. 2010. *From Moree to Mabo: The Mary Gaudron Story*. Perth: UWA Publishing.
Butler, J. 1987. *Subjects of Desire: Hegelian Reflections in Twentieth-Century France*. New York: Columbia University Press.
Butler, J. 1990. *Gender Trouble: Feminism and the Subversion of Identity*. New York: Routledge.
Butler, J. 2004. *Undoing Gender*. New York: Routledge.
Campbell, E. 1961. Women and the exercise of public functions. *The Adelaide Law Review* 1(2): 190–204.
Campbell, E. and Lee, H.P. 2001. *The Australian Judiciary*. Melbourne: Cambridge University Press.
Carroll, R. 2013. Apologies as a legal remedy. *Sydney Law Review*35: 317–347.
Cass, D. and Rubenstein, K. 1995. Representation/s of women in the Australian constitutional system. *Adelaide Law Review* 17: 3–48.
Chappell, L. and Mackay, F. 2017. "What's in a name? Mapping the terrain of informal institutions and gender and politics". In G. Waylen (ed.), *Gender and Informal Institutions*. New York: Rowman & Littlefield, pp. 23–44.
Chappell, L. and Waylen, G. 2013. Gender and the hidden life of institutions. *Public Administration* 91(3): 599–615.
Chappell, L., Brennan, D. and Rubenstein, K. 2012. "A gender and change perspective on intergovernmental relations". In P. Kildea, A. Lynch, and G. Williams (eds), *Tomorrow's Federation: Reforming Australian Government*. Sydney: The Federation Press.
Chesterman, M. 2000. *Freedom of Speech in Australian Law: A Delicate Plant*. Dartmouth: Ashgate.
Conaghan, J. 2013. *Law and Gender*. Oxford: Oxford University Press.
Connell, R. 1987. *Gender and Power: Society, the Person and Sexual Politics*. Cambridge: Polity Press.
Connell, R. 2002. *Gender*. Cambridge: Polity Press.
Connell, R. 2006. Glass ceilings or gendered institutions? Mapping the gender regimes of public sector worksites. *Public Administration Review* 66: 837–849.
Cook, B.B. 1981. "Will women judges make a difference in women's legal rights? A prediction from attitudes and simulated behaviour". In M. Rendel (ed.), *Women, Power and Political Systems*. New York: St. Martin's Press.
Cooney, S. 1993. Gender and judicial selection: should there be more women on the courts. *Melbourne University Law Review* 19: 20–44.
Cornell, D. 1991. *Beyond Accommodation: Ethical Feminism, Deconstruction and the Law*. New York: Routledge.

Cox, E. 2000. "Feminism and citizenship". In W. Hudson and J. Kane (eds), *Rethinking Australian Citizenship*. Melbourne: Cambridge University Press.

Davidson, A. 1997. *From Subject to Citizen: Australian Citizenship in the Twentieth Century*. Melbourne: Cambridge University Press.

Davies, M. 1997. "Taking the inside out: Sex and gender in the legal subject". In N. Naffine and R.J. Owens (eds), *Sexing the Subject of Law*. Sydney: Sweet and Maxwell.

Davies, M. 2008. *Asking the Law Question*, 3rd edition. Sydney: Lawbook Company.

Davies, M. 2012. The law becomes us: Rediscovering judgment, review of Feminist Judgments: From Theory to Practice. *Feminist Legal Studies* 20(2): 167–181.

Davis, A. 1983. "Rape, racism and the myth of the black rapist". In *Women Race and Class*. New York: Vintage Books.

Davis, R. and Williams, G. 2003. Reform of the judicial appointments process: Gender and the bench of the High Court of Australia. *Melbourne University Law Review* 27: 819–863.

Davis, S. 1993. Do women judges speak "in a different voice?": Carol Gilligan, feminist legal theory, and the Ninth Circuit. *Wisconsin Women's Law Journal* 8: 134–139.

Dawuni, J. and Kang, A. 2015. 'Her Ladyship Chief Justice: The rise of female leaders in the judiciary in Africa. *Africa Today* 62(2): 45–69.

Day O'Connor, S. 1991. Madison Lecture: Portia's progress. *New York University Law Review* 66: 1546–1558.

de Beauvoir, S. [1949; 1997] *The Second Sex*. H.M. Parshley, trans. New York: Random House.

Delgado, R. 1989. Storytelling for oppositionists: A plea for narrative. *Michigan Law Review* 87: 2411–2441.

Di Stefano, C. 1983. Masculinity as ideology in political theory: Hobbesian man reconsidered. *Women's Studies International Forum*, 6: 633–644.

Di Stefano, C. 1991. *Configurations of Masculinity: A Feminist Perspective on Modern Political Theory*. Ithaca, NY: Cornell University Press.

Dixon, R. 2010. Female Justices, feminism, and the politics of judicial appointment: A re-examination. *Yale Journal of Law and Feminism* 21(2): 297–338.

Dominello, F. and Neuman, E. 2001. "Background of Justices". In T. Blackshield, M. Coper and G. Williams (eds), *The Oxford Companion to the High Court of Australia*. Melbourne: Oxford University Press.

Douglas, H., Bartlett, F., Luker, T. and Hunter, R. (eds). 2014a. *Australian Feminist Judgments: Righting and Rewriting Law*. Oxford: Hart Publishing.

Douglas, H., Bartlett, F., Luker, T. and Hunter, R. 2014b. "Reflections on rewriting the law". In H. Douglas, F. Bartlett, T. Luker and R. Hunter (eds), *Australian Feminist Judgments: Righting and Rewriting Law*. Oxford: Hart Publishing.

Duerst-Lahti, G. 2008. "Gender ideology: Masculinism and feminalism". In G. Goertz and A. Mazur (eds), *Politics, Gender and Concepts*. New York: Cambridge University Press, pp. 159–192.

Easteal, P. 1998. "Rape in marriage: Has the license lapsed?" In P. Easteal (ed.), *Balancing the Scales, Rape Law Reform and Australian Culture*. Sydney: The Federation Press.

Edwards, H. 2003. The effects of collegiality on judicial decision making. *University of Pennsylvania Law Review* 151(5): 1639–1690.

Ehrlich, S. 2001. *Representing Rape: Language and Sexual Consent*. London and New York: Routledge.

Eisenstein, H. 1996. *Inside Agitators: Australian Femocrats and the State*. Philadelphia, PA: Temple University Press.

Elliott, H. 2001. The difference women judges make: Stare decisis, norms of collegiality, and "feminine jurisprudence": A research proposal. *Wisconsin Women's Law Journal* 16: 41–51.

Farbert, D. and Sherry, S. 1995. Is the radical critique of merit anti-Semitic? *California Law Review* 83: 853–884.

Featherstone, L. and Winn, A. 2019. Marital rape and the marital rapist: The 1976 South Australian Law Reforms. *Feminist Legal Studies* 27(1): 57–78.

Fileborn, B. and Loney-Howes, R. 2019. "Introduction: Mapping the emergence of #MeToo". In B. Fileborn and R. Loney-Howes (eds), *#MeToo and the Politics of Social Change*. Palgrave Macmillan.

Fileborn, B and Phillips, N. 2019. "From 'me too' to 'too far'? Contesting the boundaries of sexual violence in contemporary activism". In B. Fileborn and R. Loney-Howes (eds), *#MeToo and the Politics of Social Change*. London: Palgrave Macmillan.

Fitz-Gibbon, K. and Maher, J.M. 2015. Feminist challenges to the constraints of law: Donning uncomfortable robes? *Feminist Legal Studies* 23(3): 253–271.

Fuller, L. 1967. *Legal Fictions*. Stanford, CA: Stanford University Press.

Gageler, S. 2014. Why write judgments? *Sydney Law Review* 36(2): 189–203.

Galea, N., Powell A., Loosemore, M. and Chappell, L. 2020. The gendered dimensions of informal institutions in the Australian construction industry. *Gender Work and Organisations* 27(3): 1–18.

Galligan, B. 1987. *Politics of the High Court*. St Lucia: University of Queensland Press.

Galligan, B. and Morton, F.L. 2006. "Australian exceptionalism: Rights protection without a Bill of Rights". In T. Campbell, J. Goldsworthy and A. Stone (eds), *Protecting Rights Without a Bill of Rights: Institutional Performance and Reform in Australia*. Aldershot: Ashgate Publishing.

Gatens, M. 1991. "A critique of the sex/gender distinction". In Sneja Gunew (ed.), *A Reader in Feminist Knowledge*. London: Routledge.

Gee, G. and Rackley, E. (eds). 2018. *Debating Judicial Appointments in an Age of Diversity*. Abingdon: Routledge.

Gelber, K. and McNamara, L.J. 2013. Freedom of speech and racial vilification in Australia: 'The Bolt case' in public discourse. *Australian Journal of Political Science* 48(4): 470–484.

Gelber, K. and Stone, A. (eds). 2007. *Hate Speech and Freedom of Speech in Australia*. Sydney: The Federation Press.

Genovese, A. 2014. "The practice of feminist judgment in family law". In H. Douglas, F. Bartlett, T. Luker and R. Hunter (eds), *Australian Feminist Judgments: Righting and Rewriting Law*. Oxford: Hart Publishing.

Gherardi, S. and Poggio, B. 2001. Creating and recreating gender order in organizations. *Journal of World Business* 36(3): 245–258.

Gilligan, C. 1982. *In a Different Voice: Psychological Theory and Women's Development*. Cambridge, MA: Harvard University Press.

Goodin, R.E. 2008. *Innovating Democracy: Democratic Theory and Practice After the Deliberative Turn*. Oxford: Oxford University Press.

Graycar, R. 1998. The gender of judgments: Some reflections on "bias". *University of British Columbia Law Review* 32: 1–30.

Graycar, R. and Morgan, J. 1990. *The Hidden Gender of Law*. Sydney: The Federation Press.

Graycar, R. and Morgan, J. 2015. On the hidden gender of law: A public talk. *Australian Feminist Law Journal* 41(1): 29–36.

Grey, A. 2006. Harriton v Stephens: Life, logic and legal fictions. *Sydney Law Review* 28: 545–560.

Grimshaw, P., Lake, M., McGrath, A. and Quartly, M. 1994. *Creating a Nation 1788–1990*. Melbourne: McPhee Gribble.

Groves, M. and Smyth, R. 2004. A century of judicial style: Changing patterns in judgment writing on the High Court 1903–2001. *Federal Law Review* 32: 255–280.

Guettel Cole, S. 1996. "Oath ritual and the male community at Athens". In J. Ober and C. Hedrick (eds), *Demokratia: A Conversation on Democracies, Ancient and Modern*. Princeton, NJ: Princeton University Press.

Hale, B. 2001. Equality and the judiciary: Why should we want more women judges? *Public Law*: 489–504.

Hale, B. 2008. Maccabean Lecture in Jurisprudence: A minority opinion? *Proceedings of the British Academy* 154: 319–336.

Hale, M. 1736. *History of the Pleas of the Crown*, Volume 1.

Hall, J.D. 1983. "'The mind that burns in each body': Women, rape and racial violence". In A. Snitow, C. Stansell and S. Thompson (eds), *Powers of Desire: The Politics of Sexuality*. New York: Monthly Review Press.

Hamilton, B. 1995. Criteria for judicial appointment and "merit". *Queensland University of Technology Law Journal* 15: 10–22.

Handsley, E. and Lynch, A. 2015. Facing up to diversity? Transparency and the reform of Commonwealth judicial appointments 2008–2013. *Sydney Law Review* 37(2): 187–215.

Harris, A.P. 1990. Race and essentialism in feminist legal theory. *Stanford Law Review* 42 (3): 581–616.

Hawkesworth. M. 1997. Confounding gender. *Signs* 22(3): 649–685.

Heath, M. 1998. "Disputed truths: Australian reform of the sexual conduct elements of common law rape". In P. Easteal (ed.), *Balancing the Scales, Rape Law Reform and Australian Culture*. Sydney: The Federation Press.

Heath, M. and Naffine, N. 1994. Men's needs and women's desires: Feminist dilemmas about rape law "reform". *The Australian Feminist Law Journal* 3: 30.

Hegel, G.W.F. [1807; 1977] *Phenomenology of Spirit*. A.V. Miller, trans. Oxford: Clarendon Press.

Hegel, G.W.F. [1820; 1967] *Philosophy of Right*. T.M. Knox, trans. Oxford: Clarendon Press.

Henning, T. and Bronitt, S. 1998. "Rape victims on trial: Regulating the use and abuse of sexual history evidence". In P. Easteal (ed.), *Balancing the Scales, Rape Law Reform and Australian Culture*. Sydney: The Federation Press.

Hettinger, V., Lindquist, S. and Martinek, W. 2006. *Judging on a Collegial Court*. Charlottesville, VI: University of Virginia Press.

Heydon, D. 2013. Threats to judicial independence: The enemy within. *Law Quarterly Review* 129: 205–225.

Hobbs, H. 2015. Finding a fair reflection on the High Court of Australia. *Alternative Law Journal* 40(1): 13–18.

Hobbs, H., Lynch, A. and Williams, G. 2017. The High Court under Chief Justice Robert French. *Australian Law Journal* 91: 53–71.

Hocking, J. 1997. *Lionel Murphy—A Political Biography*. Melbourne: Cambridge University Press.
Holt, T. and Holt, V. 2008. *'My Boy Jack?' The Search for Kipling's Only Son*. Yorkshire: Pen and Sword Books Ltd.
Horn, P., Leniston, M. and Lewis, P. 1983. The maiden speeches of New Zealand women members of parliament. *Political Science* 35: 229–266.
Htun, M. 2005. What it means to study gender and the state. *Politics & Gender* 1(1): 157–166.
Hunter, R. 2003. "Women barristers and gender difference". In U. Schultz and G. Shaw (eds), *Women in the World's Legal Professions*. Oxford: Hart Publishing.
Hunter, R. 2004. Fear and loathing in the Sunshine State. *Australian Feminist Studies* 19 (44): 145–157.
Hunter, R. 2008. Can feminist judges make a difference? *International Journal of the Legal Profession* 15(1–2): 7–36.
Hunter, R. 2010. "An account of feminist judging". In R. Hunter, C. McGlynn and E. Rackley (eds), *Feminist Judgments: From Theory to Practice*. Oxford: Hart Publishing.
Hunter, R. 2012. The power of feminist judgments? *Feminist Legal Studies* 20: 135–148.
Hunter, R. 2013. "Justice Marcia Neave: Case study of a feminist judge". In U. Schultz and G. Shaw (eds), *Gender and Judging*. Oxford: Hart Publishing.
Hunter, R. 2015. More than just a different face? Judicial Diversity and Decision-making. *Current Legal Problems* 68(1): 1–23.
Hunter, R., McGlynn, C. and Rackley, E. (eds). 2010. *Feminist Judgments—From Theory to Practice*. Oxford: Hart Publishing.
Hunter, R., McGlynn, C. and Rackley, E. 2010. 'Feminist Judgments: An introduction'. In R. Hunter, C. McGlynn and E. Rackley (eds), *Feminist Judgments—From Theory to Practice*. Oxford: Hart Publishing.
Hunter, R. and Tyson, D. 2017. Justice Betty King: A study of feminist judging in action. *UNSW Law Journal* 40(2): 778–805.
Irigaray, I. 1985. *The Sex Which is Not the One*, trans. Catherine Porter, with Carolyn Burke. Ithaca, NY: Cornell University Press (first published 1977).
Irving, H. 1996. "Fair federalists and founding mothers". In H. Irving (ed.), *A Woman's Constitution? Gender & History in the Australian Commonwealth*. Sydney: Hale & Iremonger.
Irving, H. 1997. *To Constitute a Nation: A Cultural History of Australia's Constitution*. Cambridge: Cambridge University Press.
Irving, H. 2007. Federalism is a feminist issue: What Australians can learn from the United States commerce clause. *Adelaide Law Review* 28: 159–176.
Jackson, V. 2016. "Feminisms and constitutions". In K. Rubenstein and K. Young (eds), *The Public Law of Gender: From the Local to the Global*. Cambridge: Cambridge University Press.
Jewel, L.A. 2012. Merit and mobility: A progressive view of class, culture and the law. *University of Memphis Law Review* 43: 239–318.
Johnson, C. 2015. Playing the gender card: The uses and abuses of gender in Australian Politics. *Politics & Gender* 11: 291–319.
Joseph, S. and Castan, M. 2006. *Federal Constitutional Law: A Contemporary View*, 2nd edition. Sydney: Lawbook Co.
Karpin, I. and O'Connell, K. 2005. "Speaking into a silence: Embedded constitutionalism and the rights of women in Australia". In B. Baines and R. Rubio-

Marin (eds), *The Gender of Constitutional Jurisprudence*. Cambridge: Cambridge University Press.

Kaspiew, R. 1995. Rape lore: Legal narrative and sexual violence. *Melbourne University Law Review* 20(2): 350–382.

Kennedy, D. 1990. A cultural pluralist case for affirmative action in legal academia. *Duke Law Journal* 39(4): 705–757.

Kenney, S. 1996. New research on gendered political institutions. *Political Research Quarterly* 49: 445–466.

Kenney, S.J. 2008. Thinking about gender and judging. *International Journal of the Legal Profession* 15(1): 87–110.

Kenney, S.J. 2013. *Gender and Justice: Why Women in the Judiciary Really Matter*. New York: Routledge.

Kenny, S. 2004. Concepts of judicial responsibility: The contribution of the "one of seven". *Public Law Review* 12: 283–288.

Kirby, M. 2002. Women in the law—what next? *The Australian Feminist Law Journal* 16(1): 148–156.

Krefting, L. 2003. Intertwined discourses of merit and gender: evidence from academic employment in the USA. *Gender, Work and Organization* 10: 260–278.

Lanham, D. 1983. Hale: Misogyny and rape. *Criminal Law Journal* 7: 148–166.

Larcombe, W. 2005. *Compelling Engagements: Feminism, Rape Law and Romance Fiction*. Sydney: The Federation Press.

Larcombe, W. and Heath, M. 2012. Developing the common law and rewriting the history of rape in marriage in Australia: PGA v The Queen. *Sydney Law Review* 34: 785–807.

Larcombe, W. and Heath, M. 2014. "PGA v R judgment". In H. Douglas, F. Bartlett, T. Luker and R. Hunter (eds), *Australian Feminist Judgments: Righting and Rewriting Law*. Oxford: Hart Publishing.

Laster, K. and Douglas, R. 1995. Feminized justice: The impact of women decision makers in the lower courts in Australia. *Justice Quarterly* 12(1): 177–205.

Lesses, K. 2014. PGA v The Queen—marital rape in Australia: The role of repetition, reputation and fiction in the common law. *Melbourne University Law Review* 37: 786–833.

L'Heureux-Dubé, C. 1997. Making a difference: The pursuit of a compassionate justice. *Canadian Journal of Family Law* 14: 103–127.

Lowndes, V. 2020. How are political institutions gendered? *Political Studies* 68 (3): 543–564.

Lowndes, V. and Roberts, M. 2013. *Why Institutions Matter: The New Institutionalism in Political Science*. Basingstoke: Palgrave Macmillan.

Lynch, A. 2020. The High Court on Constitutional Law: The 2019 statistics. *University of New South Wales Law Journal* 43(4): 1226–1243.

Lynch, A. and Williams, G. 2008. The High Court on Constitutional Law: The 2007 statistics. *University of New South Wales Law Journal* 31(1): 238–257.

Lynch, A. and Williams, G. 2010. The High Court on Constitutional Law: The 2009 statistics. *University of New South Wales Law Journal* 33(2): 267–285.

Lynch, A. and Williams, G. 2011. The High Court on Constitutional Law: The 2010 statistics. *University of New South Wales Law Journal* 34(3): 1030–1047.

Lynch, A. and Williams, G. 2012. The High Court on Constitutional Law: The 2011 statistics. *University of New South Wales Law Journal* 35(3): 846–865.

Lynch, A. and Williams, G. 2013. The High Court on Constitutional Law: The 2012 statistics. *University of New South Wales Law Journal* 36(2): 514–533.
Lynch, A. and Williams, G. 2014. The High Court on Constitutional Law: The 2013 statistics. *University of New South Wales Law Journal* 37(2): 544–564.
Lynch, A. and Williams, G. 2015. The High Court on Constitutional Law: The 2014 statistics. *University of New South Wales Law Journal* 38(3): 1078–1097.
Lynch, A. and Williams, G. 2017. The High Court on Constitutional Law: The 2016 and French Court statistics. *University of New South Wales Law Journal* 40(4): 1468–1491.
Lynch, A. and Williams, G. 2018. The High Court on Constitutional Law: The 2017 statistics. *University of New South Wales Law Journal* 41(4): 1134–1158.
Lynch, A. and Williams, G. 2019. The High Court on Constitutional Law: The 2018 statistics. *University of New South Wales Law Journal* 42(4): 1443–1458.
Mack, K. and Roach Anleu. S. 2010. "Women in the Australian judiciary". In P. Easteal (ed.), *Women and the Law in Australia.* Chatswood: LexisNexis Butterworths.
Mack, K. and Roach Anleu. S. 2012. Entering the Australian judiciary: Gender and court hierarchy. *Law and Policy* 34(3): 313–347.
MacKinnon, C.A. 1983. Feminism, Marxism, method, and the state: Toward feminist jurisprudence. *Signs* 8(4): 635–658.
MacKinnon, C.A. 1984. Not a moral issue. *Yale Law and Policy Review* 2(2): 321–345.
MacKinnon, C.A. 1987. *Feminism Unmodified: Discourses on Life and Law.* Cambridge, MA: Harvard University Press.
MacKinnon, C.A. 1989. *Towards a Feminist Theory of the State.* Cambridge, MA: Harvard University Press.
MacKinnon, C.A. and Dworkin, A. (eds). 1998. *In Harm's Way: The Pornography Civil Rights Hearings.* Cambridge, MA: Harvard University Press.
Majury, D. 2006. Introducing the Women's Court of Canada. *Canadian Journal of Women and the Law* 18(1): 1–12.
Malleson, K. 2003. Justifying gender equality on the bench: Why difference won't do. *Feminist Legal Studies* 11: 1–24.
Malleson, K. 2006. Rethinking the merit principle in judicial selection. *Journal of Law and Society* 33(1): 126–140.
Martin, E. 1982. Women on the federal bench: A comparative profile. *Judicature* 65(6): 307–313.
Martinek, W.L. 2010. "Judges as members of small groups". In D. Klein and G. Mitchell (eds), *The Psychology of Judicial Decision Making.* New York and Oxford: Oxford University Press.
Mason, A. 1986. The role of a constitutional court in a federation: A comparison of the Australian and the United States Experience. *Federal Law Review* 16(1): 1–28.
Mason, A. 2001. "Role of the Chief Justice". In T. Blackshield, M. Coper and G. Williams (eds), *The Oxford Companion to the High Court of Australia.* Melbourne: Oxford University Press.
Mason, A. 2013. Reflections on the High Court: Its judges and judgments. *Australian Bar Review* 37: 102–117.
Matthews, J.J. 1984. *Good and Mad Women: The Historical Construction of Femininity in Twentieth Century Australia.* Sydney: Allen & Unwin.
McLoughlin, K. 2015a. The politics of gender diversity on the High Court of Australia. *Alternative Law Journal* 40(3): 166–170.

McLoughlin, K. 2015b. A particular disappointment? Judging women and the High Court of Australia. *Feminist Legal Studies* 23(3): 273–294.

McLoughlin, K. 2016a. Judicial fictions and the fictive feminists: Re-imagination as feminist critique in PGA v The Queen . *Griffith Law Review* 24(4): 592–615.

McLoughlin, K. 2016b. 'Collegiality is not compromise': Farewell Justice Crennan, the consensus woman. *The Australian Feminist Law Journal* 42: 241–271.

McLoughlin, K. 2017. Feminism, women judges, judicial diversity and the High Court of Australia. *feminists@law* 7(2): 1–14.

McLoughlin, K. and Jose, J. 2017. The politics of the public and private spheres: The High Court's decision in Monis and the gendered privileging of free speech. *Australian Journal of Political Science* 52(4): 565–579.

McLoughlin, K and Williams, J. 2019. An age of diversity: Where to next for the judicial diversity project? Review of *Debating Judicial Appointments in an Age of Diversity* (Graham Gee and Erika Rackley (eds)). *UNSW Law Journal Forum* 9: 1–15.

McSherry, B. 1998. "Constructing lack of consent". In P. Easteal (ed.), *Balancing the Scales, Rape Law Reform and Australian Culture.* Sydney: The Federation Press.

Meagher, D. 2004. What is political communication? The rationale and scope of the implied freedom of political communication. *Melbourne University Law Review* 28: 438–473.

Medea, A. and Thompson, K. 1974. *Against Rape.* New York: Farrar, Straus and Giroux.

Menkel-Meadow, C. 1985. Portia in a different voice: Speculations on a women's lawyering process. *Berkeley Women's Law Journal* 1: 39–63.

Menkel-Meadow, C. 1987. The comparative sociology of women lawyers: The 'feminization' of the legal profession. *Osgoode Hall Law Journal* 24: 897–918.

Millett, K. 1970. *Sexual Politics.* London: Abacus.

Moran, L. 2006. Judicial diversity and the challenge of sexuality: Some preliminary findings. *Sydney Law Review* 28: 565–598.

Moran, L. 2011. Forming sexualities as judicial virtues. *Sexualities* 14: 273–289.

Moran, L. 2012. Review of feminist judgments. *Modern Law Review* 75(2): 287–290.

Moreton-Robinson, A. 2009. Imagining the good indigenous citizen: Race war and the pathology of patriarchal white sovereignty. *Cultural Studies Review* 5(2): 61–79.

Mossman, M.J. 2006. *The First Women Lawyers: A Comparative Study.* Portland, OR: Hart Publishing.

Mossman, M. 2009. 'The law as a profession for women': A century of progress. *Australian Feminist Law Journal* 30: 131–145.

Naffine, N. 1990. *Law & The Sexes: Explorations in Feminist Jurisprudence.* Sydney: Allen & Unwin.

Naffine, N. 2014. "Admitting legal wrongs: PGA v R (Commentary)". In H. Douglas, F. Bartlett, T. Luker and R. Hunter (eds), *Australian Feminist Judgments: Righting and Re-writing Law.* Oxford: Hart Publishing.

Naffine, N. and Neoh, J. 2013. Fictions and myths in PGA v The Queen. *Australian Journal of Legal Philosophy* 38: 32–51.

Neave, M. 1995. The gender of judging. *Psychiatry, Psychology and Law* 2(1): 3–23.

O'Brien, M. 1981. *The Politics of Reproduction.* London: Routledge & Kegan Paul.

O'Connor, D. 1977. Rape law reform—the Australian experience—Part 1. *Criminal Law Journal* 1: 305–319.

Oldfield, A. 1992. *Women's Suffrage in Australia: A Gift or a Struggle?* Melbourne: Cambridge University Press.

O'Rourke, C. 2014. Feminist legal method and the study of institutions. *Politics & Gender* 10(4): 691–697.

O'Sullivan, D. 1996. Gender and judicial appointment. *University of Queensland Law Journal* 19(1): 107–124.

Patapan, H. 1997. The dead hand of the founders? Original intent and the constitutional protection of rights and freedoms in Australia. *Federal Law Review* 25(2): 211–235.

Pateman, C. 1983. "Feminist critiques of the public/private dichotomy". In S.I. Benn and G.F. Gaus (eds), *Public and Private in Social Life*. New York: St Martin's Press.

Pateman, C. 1986. "Introduction". In C. Pateman and E. Gross (eds). *Feminist Challenges: Social and Political Theory*. Sydney: Allen & Unwin, pp. 1–12.

Pateman, C. 1988. *The Sexual Contract*. London: Polity Press.

Patmore, G. 1998. Making sense of representative democracy and the implied freedom of political communication in the High Court Australia: Three possible models. *Griffith Law Review* 7(1): 97–123.

Phillips, A. 1991. *Engendering Democracy*. Cambridge: Polity Press.

Pierce, J. 2008. Institutional cohesion in the High Court of Australia: Do American theories travel well down under. *Commonwealth & Comparative Politics* 46(3): 318–340.

Priest, S. and Williams, G. 2010. "Women in public law". In P. Easteal (ed.), *Women and the Law in Australia*. Chatswood: LexisNexis Butterworths.

Posner, R.A. 1990. Duncan Kennedy on affirmative action. *Duke Law Journal* 39(5): 1157–1162.

Power, M. and Berardone, M. 1998. Speaking in Parliament: First speeches of men and women. *Journal of Applied Social Behaviour* 4(2): 42–55.

Rackley, E. 2002. Representations of the (Woman) judge: Hercules, the Little Mermaid, and the vain and naked emperor. *Legal Studies* 22(4): 602–624.

Rackley, E. 2006. Difference in the House of Lords. *Social and Legal Studies* 15(2): 163–185.

Rackley, E. 2007. Judicial diversity, the woman judge and fairy tale endings. *Legal Studies* 27(1): 74–94.

Rackley, E. 2009. Detailing judicial difference. *Feminist Legal Studies* 17: 11–26.

Rackley, E. 2012. Why feminist legal scholars should write judgments: reflections on the feminist judgments project in England and Wales. *Canadian Journal of Women and Law* 24(2): 389–413.

Rackley, E. 2013. *Women, Judging and the Judiciary: From Difference to Diversity*. Oxford: Routledge.

Rackley, E. and Auchmuty, R. 2019. "Women's legal landmarks: An introduction". In E. Rackley and R. Auchmuty (eds), *Women's Legal Landmarks: Celebrating the History of Women and the Law in the UK and Ireland*. London: Hart.

Rhode, D. 1988. The "woman's point of view". *Journal of Legal Education* 38: 39–46.

Roberts. H. 2012a. "Swearing Mary": The significance of the speeches made at Mary Gaudron's swearing-in as a Justice of the High Court of Australia. *Sydney Law Review* 34(3): 493–510.

Roberts, H. 2012b. "Women judges "maiden speeches" and the High Court of Australia". In B. Baines, D. Barak-Erez and T. Kahana (eds), *Feminist Constitutionalism*. New York: Cambridge University Press.

Roberts, H. 2014. Telling a history of Australian women judges through courts' ceremonial archives. *Australian Feminist Law Journal* 40(1): 147–162.

Rousseau, J.-J. [1759; 1960]. *Politics and the Arts: Letter to D'Alembert*. A. Bloom, trans. Glencoe, IL: Free Press.

Rubenstein, K. 2004a. Introduction to the Public Law Review collection honouring Justice Mary Gaudron. *Public Law Review* 15: 281–282.

Rubenstein, K. 2004b. Meanings of membership: Mary Gaudron's contributions to Australian citizenship. *Public Law Review* 15: 305–313.

Rubenstein, K. 2006. "Feminism and federalism". Gilbert and Tobin Constitutional Law Conference: The Death of Federalism, 24 February. http://www.gtcentre.unsw.edu.au/sites/gtcentre.unsw.edu.au/files/mdocs/7_KimRubenstein.pdf. Accessed 7 January 2021.

Rubenstein, K. 2014b. "R v Pearson; Ex parte Sipka Judgment". In H. Douglas, F. Bartlett, T. Luker and R. Hunter (eds), *Australian Feminist Judgments: Righting and Rewriting Law*. Oxford: Hart Publishing.

Rubin, G. 1975. "The traffic in women: Notes on the 'political economy' of sex". In R.R. Reiter (ed.), *Toward an Anthropology of Women*. New York: Monthly Review Press. pp. 157–210.

Rush, P. 2010. "Criminal law and the reformation of rape in Australia". In C. McGlyn and V.E. Munro (eds), *Rethinking Rape Law: International and Comparative Perspectives*. London: Routledge.

Sackville, R. 2005. Judicial appointments: A discussion paper. *Journal of Judicial Administration* 14: 117–143.

Sawer, M. 1990. *Sisters in Suits: Women and Public Policy in Australia*. Sydney: Allen & Unwin.

Schultz, U. 2003. "Introduction: Women in the world's legal professions: Overview and synthesis". In U. Schultz and G. Shaw (eds), *Women in the World's Legal Professions*. Oxford: Hart Publishing.

Scutt, J. 1977. Consent in rape: The problem of the marriage contract. *Monash University Law Review* 3: 255–288.

Scutt, J. 1997. *The Incredible Woman*, Volume 1. Melbourne: Artemis Publishing.

Serisier, T. 2007. Speaking out against rape: Feminist (her) stories and anti-rape politics. *Lilith: A Feminist History Journal* 16: 84–95.

Sherry, S. 1986a. The gender of judges. *Law and Inequality* 4: 159–169.

Sherry, S. 1986b. Civic virtue and the feminine voice in constitutional adjudication. *Virginia Law Review* 72: 543–616.

Sletvold, R. 2012. PGA v The Queen: Do laws just disappear? *Adelaide Law Review* 33: 573–579.

Smart, C. 1989. *Feminism and the Power of Law*. New York: Routledge.

Smart, C. 1990. "Law's truth/women's experience". In R. Graycar (ed.), *Dissenting Opinions, Feminist Explorations in Law and Society*. Sydney: Allen & Unwin.

Sommerlad, H. 1994. The myth of feminisation: Women and cultural change in the legal profession. *International Journal of the Legal Profession* 1(1): 31–54.

Sommerlad, H. 2013. "Let history judge? Gender, race, class and performative identity: A study of women judges in England and Wales". In U. Schultz and G. Shaw (eds), *Gender and Judging*. Oxford: Hart Publishing.

Songer, D.R., Davis, S. and Haire, S. 1994. A reappraisal of diversification in the federal courts: Gender effects in the courts of appeals. *Journal of Politics* 56(2): 425–439.

Stellios, J. 2015. *Zines's The High Court and the Constitution*, 6th edition. Sydney: Federation Press.

Stone, A. 2001. Rights, personal rights and freedoms: The nature of the freedom of political communication. *Melbourne University Law Review* 25: 374–417.

Stretton, D. 2006. Harriton v Stephens; Waller v James: Wrongful life and the logic of non-existence. *Melbourne University Law Review* 30: 972–1001.

Strossen, N. 1995. *Defending Pornography: Free Speech, Sex and the Fight for Women's Rights*. New York: Scribner.

Summers, A. 2013. *The Misogyny Factor*. Sydney: NewSouth Publishing.

Sunstein, C., Schkade, D., Ellman, L. and Sawicki, A. 2006. *Are Judges Political? An Empirical Analysis of the Federal Judiciary*. Washington, DC: Brookings Institution Press.

Takayanagi. M. 2020. Sacred year or broken reed? The Sex Disqualification (Removal) Act 1919. *Women's History Review* 29(4): 563–582.

Thornton, M. 1995a. "The cartography of public and private". In M. Thornton (ed.), *Public and Private: Feminist Legal Debates*. Melbourne: Oxford University Press.

Thornton, M. 1995b. "Embodying the citizen". In M. Thornton (ed.), *Public and Private: Feminist Legal Debates*. Melbourne: Oxford University Press.

Thornton, M. 1996. *Dissonance and Distrust: Women in the Legal Profession*. Melbourne: Oxford University Press.

Thornton, M. 2000. "Legal citizenship". In W. Hudson and J. Kane (eds), *Rethinking Australian Citizenship*. Melbourne: Cambridge University Press.

Thornton, M. 2007. Otherness on the bench: How merit is gendered. *Sydney Law Review* 29(3): 391–413.

Thornton, M. 2018. Challenging the legal profession a century on: The case of Edith Haynes. *University of Western Australia Law Review* 44: 1–20.

Thornton, M. 2020. Trailblazing women still needed. *Alternative Law Journal* 45(4): 237.

Toohey, J. 1999. "Without fear or favour, affection or ill-will": The role of the courts. *University of Western Australia Law Review* 28(1): 1–12.

Toole, K. 2011. Marital rape in South Australia: R v P, *GA. Criminal Law Journal* 35(4): 237–251.

Ward, C. 1995. *Attitudes Towards Rape: Feminist and Social Psychological Perspectives*. London: Sage Publications.

West, C. and Zimmerman, D. 1987. Doing gender. *Gender and Society* 1(2): 125–151.

Weston-Scheuber, K. 2012. Gender and the prohibition of hate speech. *QUT Law & Justice Journal* 12(2): 132–150.

White, J. 1973. *The Legal Imagination*. Chicago, IL: University of Chicago Press.

Williams, G. 2008. High Court appointments: The need for reform. *Sydney Law Review* 30: 163–169.

Wilson, B. 1990. Will women judges really make a difference? *Osgoode Hall Law Journal*. 28: 507–522.

Winterton, G. 1987. Appointment of federal judges in Australia. *Melbourne University Law Review* 16(2): 185–212.

Young, S. 2007. Political and parliamentary speech in Australia. *Parliamentary Affairs* 60(2): 234–252.

Index

www.ingramcontent.com/pod-product-compliance
Ingram Content Group UK Ltd.
Pitfield, Milton Keynes, MK11 3LW, UK
UKHW020147200926
475702UK00016B/2595